The Concise Dictionary _of_ Religion

Concise Dictionary of Religion
Copyright ©1993 by Irving Hexham

Reproduced 1999 by Regent College Publishing, an imprint of the Regent
College Bookstore, 5800 University Boulevard, Vancouver, B.C. Canada V6T
2E4. The views expressed in works published by Regent College Publishing
are those of the author(s) and do not necessarily represent the official position
of Regent College.

Website: www.regent-bookstore.com
Orders toll-free: 1-800-334-3279

Cover illustration: Roberta Polfus

Printed in Canada

Library of Congress Cataloguing-in-Publication-Data has been requested.

ISBN 1-57383-120-4

The Concise Dictionary of Religion

Irving Hexham

REGENT COLLEGE PUBLISHING
VANCOUVER, BRITISH COLUMBIA

CONTENTS

Preface

Twenty years' experience of teaching introductory courses in religious studies to undergraduates convinced me of the need to write a short reference work to guide them through the confusion of names, technical terms and dates. The present work has grown directly out of class handouts I have distributed over the years and has benefitted from student comments and criticism.

My aim throughout has been to produce a book which would be of practical value to the struggling student. Therefore my selection of items and the amount of space given to each has been governed by a number of related considerations. First of all, I recognize that even today the vast majority of courses in religious studies departments in Britain and North America are essentially Christian in orientation. As a result there are relatively more entries dealing with the Western tradition than with other religions.

Second, information on some items can prove very difficult to obtain. Therefore I have addressed each item not according to an evaluation of its overall importance in religious studies generally, but in terms of the difficulty students are likely to encounter in gaining information. This means, for example, that I may spend more time discussing a relatively obscure figure like Abraham Kuyper than I do on Thomas Aquinas, or that the Plymouth Brethren may be given more space than certain other better-known churches.

Third, in addition to items related to major traditions and world religions I have included materials on African and other neglected religious traditions as well as new religious movements commonly known as cults. This is because I believe there is an overemphasis on certain narrowly defined academic traditions in religious studies to the neglect of studies dealing with religion as it actually occurs in the world. In other words, academics are happy to study other academics regardless of what is actually happening in everyday life. Thus, for example, although many of my colleagues would disagree, I believe that the founder of Mormonism, Joseph Smith, is a far more influential figure and deserves as much attention as the "father of modern theology," Friedrich Schleiermacher, yet current textbooks and course offerings invariably mention Schleiermacher but rarely pay any attention to Joseph Smith. By recognizing the importance of living religions, popular piety and sociological studies, I hope more balance will enter religious studies.

Fourth, some readers may be surprised that I have retained the essentially Christian system of dates B.C. and A.D. instead of the increasingly popular Common Era, or C.E., and B.C.E. This is because the Common Era is common to Jews and Christians but still excludes Buddhists, Hindus and Muslims. It is therefore a very misleading term. For this reason I prefer the traditional Western usage to a modern innovation which does not even have the saving grace that it developed in a homogeneous society.

I acknowledge my debt to my original teacher, Ninian Smart, whose professionalism and enthusiasm for religious studies kindled my own interest. From him I learned the value of empathy and philosophical analysis. Later, from Fred Welbourn, I realized the importance of "getting one's hands dirty" by studying living religions, not only texts abstracted from their social setting.

I must confess the use of many sources, the most important of which are P. A. Angeles, *Dictionary of Philosophy*; S. G. F. Brandon, *A Dictionary of Comparative Religion*; F. L. Cross, *The Oxford Dictionary of the Christian Church*; J. D. Douglas, *The New International Dictionary of the Christian Church* and *The New Bible Dictionary*; P. Edward, *The Encyclopedia of Philosophy*; W. A. Elwell, *Evangelical Dictionary of Theology*; S. B. Ferguson and D. F. Wright, *New Dictionary of Theology*; H. A. R. Gibb and J. H. Kramers, *Shorter Encyclopedia of Islam*; L. A. Loetscher, *Twentieth Century Encyclopedia of Religious Knowledge*; E. L. Lueker, *Lutheran Cyclopedia*; G. MacGregor, *Dictionary of Religion and Philosophy*; D. G. Reid, *Dictionary of Christianity in America*; B. Walker, *Hindu World*; P. P. Wiener, *Dictionary of the History of Ideas*; in addition to Gordon Melton's various reference works on new religions, Karl Rahner's works, and handouts provided by my various teachers, especially Colin Lyas, Edward Conze, Bob Morgan, David Catchpole and Jacob Zakkie (James Dickie).

Finally, I suspect that a careful analysis of my text might find passages which look like plagiarism. Three comments deserve attention. First, any dictionary of this sort is going to be somewhat similar to another. It is impossible not to repeat certain facts or definitions, which are in general usage, and not to write in much the same way, particularly when the form is abbreviated. Second, although I have consciously attempted to avoid plagiarism, many of my notes are now so old that I simply do not know where I obtained the original information. Therefore, some unintentional use of the words and phrases used by other people could have crept into the text. If this has happened, I can only admit my guilt and plead that writing a dictionary is quite different from writing a normal book because the nature of the enterprise demands certain minimum agreement with other people's works, shared definitions, and the common consensus of scholarly usage and opinion. Third, I hope that the text will be judged in terms of its attempt to meet the needs of students, the way items were selected, and its overall value as a research tool which brings together a vast amount of information in a highly condensed form. It is in this final area that I believe the originality of this work rests.

In conclusion I wish to express my thanks to Avril Dyson, who typed the final manuscript, the many earlier drafts, revisions and the class handouts which are incorporated into this book. Mrs. Dyson also proved to be an excellent proofreader and went to great lengths to check and recheck the accuracy of many of the entries. I must also thank my colleagues, professor Leslie Kawamura and Ms. Nusrat Mirza, who were invaluable in their help with checking a wide range of issues dealing with Eastern religions and Islam, and my colleagues, Professors Hugo Meynell, Alan Sell, Michael Hahn, Eliaizer Segal, G. C. "Pippin" Oosthuizen and Karla Poewe, for the many stimulating discussions I have had with them.

Note on cross-referencing: In each article, where the title of another article is mentioned for the first time, it is printed in small capitals (e.g., BUDDHISM; CALVIN). It should be noted that the form of the word in small capitals may differ from the form used in the actual title of the entry (e.g., ISLAMIC is a cross-reference to ISLAM).

A

A PRIORI: known by reason alone prior to sense experience; knowledge which depends on reasoning and intuition and is not dependent on empirical observation or fact.

AARON: the brother of MOSES in the HEBREW BIBLE and high PRIEST of the ancient ISRAELITES.

ABBÉ: originally an ABBOT. This French term has come to refer to any PRIEST.

ABBOT: the chief officer or PRIEST in charge of a monastery.

'ABD AL-BAHĀ, 'Abbas Effendi (1844-1921): the successor to Bahā'Ullāh as leader of the worldwide BAHĀ'Í faith.

ABEL: son of ADAM and EVE who was murdered by his brother Cain according to the HEBREW BIBLE.

ABELARD, Peter (1079-1142): medieval philosopher and theologian best known for his tragic love of Héloise. His philosophy, CONCEPTUALISM, rejected both REALISM and NOMINALISM by suggesting that UNIVERSALS require real things for their existence. His views generated both strong opposition and loyal support and were often condemned by the church as heretical.

ABHAYA-HASTA: a gesture of encouragement and blessing in HINDUISM and BUDDHISM.

ABHIDHARMA: an early BUDDHIST collection of literature which outlines the basic DOCTRINES of Buddhism. The most complete version of the Abhidharma is found in the third and most recently written collection of PALI manuscripts. In these works, which number seven books, the teachings of the BUDDHA concentrate on psychological and philosophical analysis arranged thematically using mnemonic devices to aid memorization by MONKS. The earliest extant documents of the Abhidharma date from around the sixth century A.D.

ABLUTION: the RITUAL practice of cleansing before PRAYER or any other religious act. Usually ablution takes the form of washing or some other means of PURIFICATION, including certain forms of FASTING. In certain religions, such as ISLAM, the performance of ablutions is far more important than in others, such as PROTESTANT CHRISTIANITY. Ablution marks an emphasis on a sharp distinction between the SACRED and PROFANE.

ABORTION: the termination of a pregnancy. Although not encouraged, abortion is generally allowed in most YOGIC RELIGIONS. In JUDAISM and ISLAM it is allowed for strong social or medical reasons. Traditionally, ROMAN CATHOLICS, ANGLICANS and other traditional PROTESTANTS have allowed abortion under special circumstances. Many FUNDAMENTALIST Christians totally reject abortion. Much of the contemporary debate focuses on whether the fetus is a human being.

ABRAHAM: the biblical patriarch and ANCESTOR of the Jews whose story is told in Genesis 11:26—25:8. He is represented as a man of FAITH who is the friend of God (Genesis 15:6; 2 Chronicles 20:7; Romans 4) with whom God establishes his COVENANT (Genesis 17). HEBREW RELIGION, CHRISTIANITY, JUDAISM and ISLAM all trace their origins to Abraham who is "the father of the faithful" (Romans 4:11). Although some scholars see the stories of Abraham as LEGENDARY, most believe that he lived sometime between 2100 and 1700 B.C. The three major religions which claim Abraham as their common ancestor are JUDAISM, CHRISTIANITY and ISLAM. They are often wrongly identified as "Western religions" and are better designated ABRAMIC RELIGIONS.

ABRAMIC RELIGIONS: those religions, sometimes called Western religions, which claim the patriarch ABRAHAM as their ANCESTOR and as a model of faith and practice. The major Abramic religions are CHRISTIANITY, ISLAM and JUDAISM, all of which accept a CREATOR GOD. Abramic religions stand in sharp contrast to the other major group of WORLD RELIGIONS found in the YOGIC TRADITION.

ABSOLUTE: a concept popularized by HEGEL and used by many philosophers in the nineteenth century to signify self-subsistence, unconditionedness, the ultimate, the first cause, or GOD. It is a term for DEITY which has been revived in the twentieth century by various thinkers promoting Eastern, or YOGIC, religious ideas.

ABSOLUTE IDEALISM: a philosophical

tradition usually associated with HEGEL which stresses that all REALITY is an idea of GOD or the ABSOLUTE.

ABSTINENCE: ritual self-denial. Voluntarily withdrawing from eating certain foods or enjoying physical pleasures.

ABSTRACT: (1) a quality or attribute considered in isolation from the subject in which it inheres; e.g., "blueness"; (2) a theory considered apart from any concrete application; e.g., "abstract" truth.

ABSTRACTION: the process by which abstract ideas are created by the mind from concrete sense impressions. Such things as FORMS and ARCHETYPES are abstractions.

ABSURD: logically contradictory; e.g., a triangle with two sides. This term is used in EXISTENTIALISM to speak about the human condition.

ABŪ BAKR (d. 634): strong friend and supporter of MUHAMMAD, he became the CALIPH, or spiritual leader, of ISLAM after Muhammad's death. Through his activities and success in warfare, Islam developed from a local, tribal RELIGION of the Arabs to a world FAITH.

ABŪ DAWUD, al-Sijistani (817-889): the author of the *Kitāb al-sunan*, a collection of MUSLIM TRADITIONS which are recognized as canonical by SUNNIS.

ABŪ HANĪFA (699-767): regarded by MUSLIMS as the founder of the Hanafi School of Muslim Law. He was a theologian and religious lawyer who insisted on the use of REASON and employed ANALOGY and personal judgment to great effect. Although he did not write any books, his opinions were preserved by students and discussed by later Islamic thinkers.

ABŪ HURAIRA (d. 678): the major source of recorded MUSLIM TRADITION about MUHAMMAD. Although he was actually only a believer for four years before his death, Huraira recorded a number of traditions which clearly come from many sources.

ACADEMY: a school. Originally it signified the park and gymnasium established as a school of philosophy by PLATO in 385 B.C. Plato's Academy was dissolved by JUSTINIAN in A.D. 529.

ĀCĀRYA: an honorific term for a HINDU teacher or theologian.

ACCIDENT: a philosophical term derived from ARISTOTLE which distinguishes between what is essential to an entity, its *substantia* or ESSENCE, and its accidents, or unessential ATTRIBUTES. The idea enters CHRISTIAN THEOLOGY with the ROMAN CATHOLIC DOCTRINE of TRANSUBSTANTIATION, which teaches that the essence of the bread and wine of the MASS actually become the body and blood of CHRIST, although outwardly remaining bread and wine.

ACQUISITION: an Islamic DOCTRINE intended to reconcile the idea of man's responsibility and the belief that GOD is the prime agent in all things.

ACTON, Lord [Dalberg-Acton, John] (1834-1902): famous British historian and ROMAN CATHOLIC LAYMAN noted for his saying "power corrupts; absolute power corrupts absolutely." He opposed the SYLLABUS OF ERRORS, published by the pope in 1864, the DOCTRINE of papal INFALLIBILITY and ULTRAMONTANISM.

ACUPUNCTURE: an ancient Chinese medical technique which involves placing needles into specific areas of the body. Some doctors believe that the procedure stimulates natural processes and releases body chemicals which speed recovery. In the East and in HOLISTIC MEDICINE, however, its effects are often given an OCCULT explanation.

AD HOC HYPOTHESIS: pertains to one case alone and cannot be tested by being placed in new situations; disconnected hypothesis which is unrelated to the other hypotheses in the system. Ad hoc hypotheses are considered a mark of weakness in a WORLDVIEW.

AD HOMINEM: "to the man"; an appeal to passions or prejudices rather than to the intellect. It refers to using a premise for which your opponent is responsible as an aid in refuting the opponent; e.g., "Smith says apples are good to eat. Don't believe him—he owns an orchard."

AD INFINITUM: without limit or end; something which will go on forever.

ADAM: the first human being, according to the HEBREW BIBLE, NEW TESTAMENT and QUR'ĀN. In CHRISTIAN THEOLOGY Adam acts as the representative of the human race before GOD and through the FALL allows SIN and EVIL to enter the world. In the NEW TESTAMENT, JESUS is called the "last Adam" because he also represented the human race and through his DEATH and RESURRECTION he restored the relationship between humans and God.

ADAMSKI, George (1891-1965): American OCCULTIST and promoter of PSEUDOSCIENCE who popularized the idea of UFOs, or Flying Saucers, through his claim to have been contacted by "space brothers." The author of one SCIENCE FICTION novel, *Pioneers in Space*, he became famous through his book *Flying Saucers Have Landed* (1953), which he wrote with Desmond Leslie. This book draws on theosophical (*see* THEOSOPHY) sources and propagates the basic ancient astronautics theory found in later writers such as Erich von Daniken and Shirley MACLAINE. Adamski's work is important in understanding the NEW AGE MOVEMENT.

ADHĀN: call to PRAYER in ISLAM.

ADHARMA: what is opposed to DHARMA; EVIL in HINDUISM.

ĀDI-BUDDHA: a term used in MAHĀYĀNA BUDDHISM, especially in Nepal and Tibet, to designate the primordial BUDDHA. The idea distinguishes secondary FORMS of the Buddha's manifestations on earth from the essential CONCEPT of Buddhahood itself.

ADLER, Alfred (1870-1937): Austrian psychiatrist whose passionate concern with social problems led him to embrace socialism. Many of his ideas, like the "inferiority complex," have been incorporated into popular speech. His books include *Understanding Human Nature* (1928) and *What Life Should Mean to You* (1932).

ADONAY: a Hebrew word meaning "LORD" used as a substitute for the divine name in the HEBREW BIBLE.

ADOPTION: in Roman law adoption meant that the adopted person was regarded as completely and utterly the son or daughter of their adopted parents. This idea is taken over by the APOSTLE PAUL in the NEW TESTAMENT to refer to the CHRISTIAN's relationship with GOD.

ADOPTIONISM: a CHRISTIAN HERESY which argued that the man JESUS became GOD by divine adoption. This is usually said to have taken place at the BAPTISM of Jesus, when God declared, "You are my Son, whom I love" (Mark 1:11). Although the view originated in the EARLY CHURCH, it took on particular importance in the seventh and eighth centuries, when it seems to have been advocated by Spanish theologians as a theological view acceptable to MUSLIMS.

ADVENT: the period prior to the celebration of the birth of CHRIST, CHRISTMAS, which marks the beginning of the church year. Traditionally CHRISTIANS fasted and prayed during Advent and celebrated it in a similar way to LENT.

ADVENTISM: the belief that CHRIST'S return is imminent and that he will inaugurate a millennial kingdom (*see* MILLENNIALISM). Throughout Christian history various adventist groups have arisen. In the nineteenth century, they flourished in America as a result of the teachings of a BAPTIST minister, William MILLER (1782-1849). Out of his "prophetic conferences" (*see* PROPHECY) various Adventist movements developed, the most famous being SEVENTH-DAY ADVENTISM.

AELFRIC (955-1020): English Benedictine PRIEST who sought to revive CHRISTIANITY by promoting the translation of texts into English for use by the CLERGY. His work also had an important SECULAR impact in promoting the English language.

AESTHETICS: the philosophy or SCIENCE of the beautiful which attempts to give reasons for judging one thing more beautiful than another. In THEOLOGY an argument for beauty is sometimes used as a means of proving the EXISTENCE of GOD.

AFRICAN INDEPENDENT CHURCHES: since the late nineteenth century thousands of new religious movements have developed in Africa. Most claim to be CHRISTIAN, yet they reject traditional MISSIONARY churches and attempt to incorporate many traditional African beliefs and practices into their WORSHIP and THEOLOGY. Many of these churches are thoroughly Christian, although some are clearly closer to AFRICAN TRADITIONAL RELIGIONS than to Christianity. Various scholars, including LUTHERAN BISHOP Bengt Sundkler in *Bantu Prophets in South Africa* (1948) and ANGLICAN THEOLOGIAN Fred Welbourn in *East African Rebels* (1961), have convincingly argued that many African Independent Churches originated as a result of highly paternalistic and sometimes outright racist attitudes on the part of white missionaries and colonial church leaders. Therefore, in assessing the ORTHODOXY of such groups the educational level, social experience, and intent of the leaders and followers are important, if neglected, factors.

AFRICAN ISRAEL CHURCH NINEVEH: an East AFRICAN INDEPENDENT CHURCH which grew out of a REVIVAL movement inspired by Canadian PENTECOSTAL MISSIONARIES in Tanzania in 1927. The church was founded, after a dispute over the paternalistic attitude of a white missionary, by Paul David Zakayo Kivuli (b. 1896) in Kenya in 1940, and it obtained its present name in 1956. In their classic study *A Place to Feel at Home* (1966) F. B. Wellbourn and B. A. Ogot argue that, *in intent* and the aims of its leaders, the church is an essentially orthodox Christian church (*see* ORTHODOXY) adapted to African society through an emphasis on HEALING, dreams and use of the HEBREW BIBLE.

AFRICAN RELIGIONS: although some

books speak about "African religion," it is clear that there are many religions in Africa. The main ones are AFRICAN TRADITIONAL RELIGIONS, CHRISTIANITY and ISLAM. The study of African religions is greatly neglected in RELIGIOUS STUDIES where a tendency exists to group many diverse TRADITIONS together as "African religion." In fact African traditions are highly complex and deserve much better treatment than they have received from Western scholars in the past.

AFRICAN THEOLOGY: often mistakenly identified with LIBERATION THEOLOGY or BLACK THEOLOGY, both of which share many of its concerns, African theology is a complex theological development among African pastors and theologians seeking to ground the gospel in the realities of African life. Although strongly critiqued and finally rejected by the Kenyan EVANGELICAL theologian the late Byang H. Kato in his book *Theological Pitfalls in Africa* (1975), it is a dynamic movement which at worst descends into a rejection of CHRISTIAN ORTHODOXY but at best is a genuine attempt to express traditional concepts in African terms. Gabriel M. Setloane's *African Theology* (1986), Kwesin A. Dickson's *Theology in Africa*, Luke Pato's *Towards an Authentic Christianity* (1989), and Gwinyai H. Muzorewa's *The Origins and Development of African Theology* (1985) represent attempts to find genuine expressions of Christianity in the context of African society.

AFRICAN TRADITIONAL RELIGIONS: the RELIGIONS of African peoples have developed within various African CULTURES without being influenced by major world religions such as CHRISTIANITY, HINDUISM or ISLAM. Although there is an infinite variety of traditional religions in Africa, beliefs such as WITCHCRAFT and the role of the ANCESTORS seem to be common themes in many societies. African traditional religions stress HEALING and the spiritual well-being of people and are usually expressed through dance and music. Healers, PROPHETS and other RITUAL specialists play an important role in these religions, although not all have people easily identified as PRIESTS. The main religious divisions in Africa follow geographic lines and are North Africa, West Africa, Central Africa, East Africa and South Africa. In many ways East and South African traditional religions, which lack professional priests, share common elements which make them quite distinct from West and North African religions, where professional priests play an important role in traditional religious practices.

AGA KHAN: this is the title of the IMĀMS of the Nizaris, first given to Hasan ʿAli Shah (d. 1881) in 1834 by the Shah of Persia. His descendants have assumed the title and are the spiritual leaders of the ISMĀʿĪLĪ SECT of ISLAM.

ĀGAMA: one of the three collections of MAHĀYĀNA BUDDHIST SCRIPTURES found in the TRIPIṬAKA.

AGAPĒ: Greek term for LOVE and friendship used in the NEW TESTAMENT to distinguish CHRISTIAN love from lust.

AGE OF AQUARIUS: astrological theory of "star ages" during which the earth and its inhabitants are subject to astral influences. Each star age lasts approximately 2,200 years. The last star age began shortly before the birth of CHRIST and is now believed to be coming to an end as the new OCCULT Age of Aquarius dawns. The term became popular in the 1960s through the musical stage play *Hair*.

AGNI: the fire god in HINDUISM and the most important DEITY after INDRA in the RG VEDA, which contains over two hundred hymns in his praise.

AGNOSTICISM: the DOCTRINE that all knowledge of such entities as a divine BEING, IMMORTALITY and a SUPERNATURAL world is impossible. The word is attributed to the nineteenth-century SKEPTIC T. H. HUXLEY and is used by people who wish to avoid professing dogmatic ATHEISM.

AHIMSĀ: nonviolence in HINDUISM.

AHMAD, al-Badawī (1199-1276): the

most popular of MUSLIM SAINTS in Egypt whose tomb is a major site of PILGRIMAGE. His work is the basis of a major Egyptian ṢŪFĪ order.

AHMAD, ibn Hanbal (780-855): Islamic theologian and traditionalist who taught that the QUR'ĀN is eternal and uncreated. His collection of TRADITIONS is the basis of the Hanbalī of Islamic Law which influenced the FUNDAMENTALIST Wahhābīs who are best represented by the present rulers of Saudi Arabia.

AHMADĪYA: an Islamic SECT found among non-Arab Muslims and considered HERETICAL by the orthodox. It was established in nineteenth-century India by Mirzā Ghulām AHMAD. It began as a REVITALIZATION MOVEMENT within ISLAM, but in 1889 Ahmad said he had received a REVELATION giving him the right to receive homage and claimed to be the MAHDI, or world teacher, expected by ZOROASTRIANS, HINDUS and BUDDHISTS. He said he was an AVATĀR of KRISHNA, who had come in the spirit of MUHAMMAD. Defending his beliefs against the orthodox, he held that Sūra LXI of the QUR'ĀN speaks of him. He claimed his personality had been merged with that of Muhammad, so to call him a PROPHET did not contradict Islamic belief. He is believed to have performed SIGNS and MIRACLES as proof of his AUTHORITY. After his death, his son Bashir al-Dīn Mahmūd Ahmad was appointed his successor. The movement's MISSIONS have spread to many parts of the world and its teachings can be found in *The Teachings of Islam* (Ahmad, 1963). Regarding CHRISTIANITY, Ghulām Ahmad taught that JESUS was crucified, but taken from the cross alive. Jesus then went to Kashmir where he preached, married and died at the age of 120.

AHMAD, Mirzā Ghulām (1855-1908): born in the Punjab, he claimed the dignity of a MAHDĪ and founded the AHMADĪYA SECT of ISLAM. His teachings are set out in *The Arguments of the Ahmadīya*, the first volume of which appeared in 1880. Or-

thodox MUSLIMS regard him and his writings as HERETICAL.

AHMED, Khan (1817-1898): Indian MUSLIM REFORMER who sought to modernize Islamic belief and practices in terms of Western ideas, which had greatly impressed him. He founded two universities and various educational and reform movements intended to bring ISLAM into line with modern thought.

AHRIMAN: principle of EVIL in ZOROASTRIANISM.

AHURA MAZDĀH: the wise principle or CREATOR GOD, the god of ZOROASTRIANISM.

AKHENATEN [Amenhotep IV] (1372-1354 B.C.): Egyptian king and earliest religious REFORMER known to HISTORY. He sought to weaken the power of the PRIESTHOOD and impose a form of MONOTHEISM on his people. After his death the priests regained power and almost completely destroyed his work.

AKIBA [AQIBA], ben Joseph (50-135): Jewish RABBI who played a crucial role in preserving JUDAISM after the destruction of the temple in A.D. 70. He is credited with many of the teachings later written down in the *Mishnah* and with laying the foundation for later rabbinic scholarship. He was executed for supporting a revolt against the Romans.

ALADURA, THE CHURCH OF THE LORD: also known as the Cherubim and Seraphim Churches. Growing out of several prophetic movements (*see* PROPHECY) in the Niger Delta during the 1890s, and strongly affected by the 1918 influenza epidemic, a number of AFRICAN INDEPENDENT CHURCHES came into existence which have since spread throughout West Africa with branches in Europe and North America. These churches combine an emphasis on prayer and HEALING with African custom and the acceptance of what is at times a somewhat confused, African, yet, in its intent, an essentially orthodox Christian theology (*see* ORTHODOXY).

ALBERTUS, Magnus (1200-1280): Dominican theologian who expounded the teachings of ARISTOTLE in terms of Christian thought. He is best remembered as the teacher of Thomas AQUINAS, who was to continue his work of creating a SYNTHESIS between Aristotelian and Christian thought.

ALBIGENSES: Christian HERETICAL SECT named after the city of Albi in the South of France. It arose in the eleventh century, and flourished in the twelfth and thirteenth centuries before being brutally suppressed by the INQUISITION. It professed a form of Manichaean DUALISM (*see* MANICHAEISM) which regarded CHRIST as an ANGEL with a phantom body, proclaimed that the ROMAN CATHOLIC CHURCH was corrupt, and taught a form of ESOTERIC and OCCULT knowledge as the means of SALVATION.

ALCHEMY: originally a form of early chemistry developed in Egypt. It led to attempts to transmute metals, i.e., turn lead into gold, and by the Greco-Roman period had acquired a mystical dimension (*see* MYSTICISM). Alchemy flourished as a bogus SCIENCE in medieval Christian and Islamic cultures. It fell out of favor with the coming of the REFORMATION and the rise of modern science.

ALCUIN (735-804): English MONK who directed the revival of learning during the reign of CHARLEMAGNE. He established schools where dialogue was the mode of instruction and knowledge of classical WISDOM was kept alive.

ALEXANDER TECHNIQUE: a method of developing good body posture and correct breathing which has had spectacular results with certain forms of illness and among the physically disabled. Although essentially a SECULAR therapy, it has sometimes been incorporated into some forms of HOLISTIC MEDICINE and given OCCULT significance.

ALEXANDRIAN THEOLOGY: distinctive CHRISTIAN teachings which developed in the Egyptian city of Alexandria from the late second to fifth century A.D. Its most famous representatives are ATHANASIUS, CLEMENT OF ALEXANDRIA, and ORIGEN. Alexandrian theology sought to interpret Christian FAITH in terms of PLATONIC PHILOSOPHY and laid great emphasis on the idea of the LOGOS, or eternal word of GOD.

'ALĪ, 'Abd al-Rāziq (1888-1935): Egyptian religious REFORMER and author of *Islam and the Principles of Government*. He argued that MUHAMMAD's teachings were purely religious and could find expression in a SECULAR State. His work was condemned by other MUSLIMS as heretical for its separation of religion and the state.

ALIENATION: an English word originating in the fourteenth century to describe an action of estranging or state of estrangement. In modern usage it means: (1) a cutting-off or being cut off from GOD; (2) a breakdown of relations between individuals or groups; (3) the action of transferring the ownership of anything to another; (4) loss of connection with one's own deepest feelings and needs. HEGEL and MARX argued that what is alienated is an essential part of human nature and that the process of alienation must be seen historically. FEUERBACH described God as the product of human alienation in the sense of his being a projection of the highest human ATTRIBUTES from people to a divine BEING. Marx said humans create themselves by creating their world, but in class-society they are alienated from their essential NATURE.

ALLAH: the Arabic name for God in ISLAM. Allahy yna is the one eternal God to whom humans are servants. He is the CREATOR God who reveals himself in his HOLY REVELATION, the QUR'ĀN.

ALLEGORICAL INTERPRETATION: a means of interpreting the BIBLE by means of ALLEGORIES which are said to reveal the spiritual meaning of the text. It was practiced by the Jewish philosopher PHILO, was very popular in the EARLY CHURCH and in the Middle Ages, and survives today in some conservative Christian circles. The method reads a text with the presupposition that its apparent meaning conceals another "deeper" or "true" meaning; e.g., instead of treating the story of King David in historical terms, allegorical interpretation reads the account of his life in terms of the PILGRIMAGE of the SOUL toward final SALVATION.

ALLEGORY: a sustained or prolonged metaphor; the use of language to convey a deeper and different MEANING from that which appears on the surface.

ALTAR: an elevated surface used for RITUAL SACRIFICE.

ALTRUISM: disinterested concern for the welfare of others. This SECULAR term coined by Auguste COMTE approximates the Christian VIRTUE of AGAPE.

AMA-NAZARETHA: known as "Nazarites." This is the largest Zulu AFRICAN INDEPENDENT CHURCH. The THEOLOGY of the Nazarites is a blend of Christian and Zulu beliefs. Their founder, Isaia SHEMBE, was a BAPTIST, but his followers have tended to deify him and to see him as a black MESSIAH. The group was founded in 1911 and split into two rival camps following the death of Isaia Shembe's son, Johannes Galilee SHEMBE, in 1976.

AMALEKITES: one of the peoples mentioned in the HEBREW BIBLE who were bitter enemies of the Israelites.

AMBROSE (A.D. 339-397): popular BISHOP of Milan. He was a humane theologian and teacher of ETHICS who opposed the execution of HERETICS and state brutality. He is best remembered for the role he played in the CONVERSION of Saint AUGUSTINE.

AMIDA: the BOHDISATTVA or SAVIOR figure in BUDDHISM who is represented as a being of infinite light. He is worshiped in central and east Asia and seems to have originated in Tibet, although today he is most popular in Japan. As Lord of the Western Paradise, or PURE LAND, Amida is able, as a result of his MERIT, to offer his devotees a resting place free from the cares of this world from which they may attain NIRVANA. The LOTUS SUTRA of the good law is devoted to the worship of Amida.

AMISH: ANABAPTIST group originating in the late seventeenth century and named after Jakob Ammann, a Swiss MENNONITE. The Amish are best known today for their rejection of modern technology and their simple lifestyle.

AMORC: the Ancient and Mystical Order of the Rosae Crucis which was founded in 1915 by the folklore specialist and OCCULT writer H. Spencer Lewis. It is now based in California and has scattered groups throughout the world. Through its correspondence courses and other propaganda it has tremendous influence in promoting NEW AGE-type ideas in places like Africa. Essentially the philosophy of the movement is a soft OCCULTISM that emphasizes spiritual EVOLUTION, REINCARNATION, health, wealth and happiness. (*See* also ROSICRUCIANS.)

AMULETS: magical objects used to give protection against EVIL forces. Amulets are often worn on clothing or as jewelry. Larger amulets may be used to protect buildings or special places.

ANABAPTISTS: a collective name for a number of sectarian PROTESTANT GROUPS originating in Germany in the early years of the sixteenth century. Their DOCTRINES varied, but the name stems from their common denial of the validity of INFANT BAPTISM and emphasis on the purity of the visible CHURCH. Historically, with some justification, they were viewed as fanatics who disturbed civil order, often resorting to violent means to attain their ends. Out of this movement the more moderate and pacifist MENNONITES and HUTTERITES emerged.

ANALOGY: similarity of two things in relation to each other; e.g., an ocean liner is like a floating city; or, GOD is like a loving father.

ANALYTIC PHILOSOPHY: characterizes a widespread conviction concerning the aims of PHILOSOPHY and the method to be used to attain those aims. It is currently the dominant philosophy in university Departments of Philosophy in Britain and America. Traditionally, the aim of philosophy was to construct a comprehensive account of human experience and REALITY: a WORLDVIEW or WELTANSCHAUUNG. The aim of analytic philosophy is to clarify the logical status of various kinds of utterances and to eliminate paradoxes and confusions arising when the limits and function of language are not observed; e.g., what does it mean to say "GOD is merciful"? Is this the same kind of statement as "The judge is merciful"?

ANALYTIC-SYNTHETIC DISTINCTION: a distinction made by KANT between different kinds of propositions. The statement "All unmarried women are spinsters" is true by definition, but the statement "My car is red" depends on factual information. The first proposition is said to be ANALYTIC, the second SYNTHETIC. Many modern logicians, such as QUINE, and philosophers, including DOOYEWEERD, deny that the distinction holds true.

ĀNANDA (?): perhaps the best known of the BUDDHA's disciples and a cousin of the Buddha. His name means "Joy." He lived with the Buddha for twenty-five years as his personal attendant and was entrusted by the Buddha with the task of teaching DOCTRINE. He is remembered as a champion of women and the person responsible for persuading the Buddha to allow women to enter the MONASTIC order. After the Buddha's death, a dispute broke out between Ānanda and the other MONKS who resented his support for women and charged him with not obtaining sufficient information from the Buddha to distinguish between minor precepts which could be changed and major ones which were unchangeable. He was also accused of not requesting the Buddha to live longer among his followers. Ānanda denied any wrongdoing but confessed his faults to pacify his fellow monks.

ĀNANDA COMMUNITY: founded in 1968 by an American, J. Donald Walters, who called himself SWAMI Kriyananda. This is one of the more successful NEW AGE types of communities to have developed out of the 1960s COUNTER-CULTURE. The community has around 300 members and finds its inspiration in the work of Swami Paramahansa YOGANANDA.

ANARCHISM: a political DOCTRINE propounded by Joseph Proudhon and Mikhail Bakunin which holds that all forms of AUTHORITY and civil government are bad. In its extreme form it supports violent REVOLUTION and terrorism to destroy all structures of authority.

ANATHEMA: a term used by the EARLY CHURCH in their CREEDS to signify the cutting off of those who reject the FAITH.

ANAXAGORAS (499-422 B.C.): Greek philosopher who promoted a type of atomic theory about the NATURE OF MATTER. He also taught that the sun and moon were not divine but rather made out of MATTER similar to the earth.

ANAXIMANDER (610-547 B.C.): one of the earliest Greek philosophers and mathematicians. His work is largely unknown. According to tradition he was a pupil of THALES of MILETUS. He is said to have produced the first map of the world and to have believed that the "boundless" was the starting point and origin of all things.

ANAXIMENES (588-524 B.C.): early Greek philosopher who taught that air is the divine principle and fundamental element in the UNIVERSE. He taught a cyclic view of HISTORY and believed that the world was flat.

ANCESTORS: in many RELIGIONS, especially PRIMAL RELIGIONS, the ancestors, or living dead, play a crucial role in maintaining the well-being or in bringing misfortune to the living. Many AFRICAN TRADITIONAL RELIGIONS largely center on ancestors, almost to the complete exclusion of GOD.

ANCHORITE: a solitary HERMIT, often living in a small cell or in the desert, who devotes time to prayer and the worship of God.

ANDERSON, Rufus (1796-1880): American MISSIONARY statesman and theorist who developed the concept of self-supporting indigenous CHURCHES. From 1832 to 1866 he was the general secretary of the American Board of Commissioners for Foreign Missions, the major American missionary organization in the nineteenth century. His major work is *Foreign Missions: Their Relations and Claims* (1869).

ANDROGYNY: a state where sexual differentiation has not arisen. This state was highly prized in some GNOSTIC systems as more perfect than that of male or female. Such systems disparaged human sexuality by emphasizing an unworldly SPIRITUALITY.

ANGELS: originally messengers of GOD in CHRISTIANITY, JUDAISM and ISLAM. Angels are believed to be divided between those who are GOOD and continue to serve God, and those who have rebelled against him and become EVIL. MUSLIMS believe that God dictated the QUR'ĀN to MUḤAMMAD through the agency of an angel. AMA-NAZARETHA believe that their HYMNS were first sung by the angels and then recited by Isaia SHEMBE. Angels are also found in ZOROASTRIANISM, MANICHAEISM and some forms of Chinese religion.

ANGLICAN: a member of the CHURCH OF ENGLAND; pertaining to the Church of England.

ANGLO-CATHOLICISM: the HIGH CHURCH movement within the CHURCH OF ENGLAND, sometimes known as the OXFORD MOVEMENT. Its adherents emphasize their CATHOLIC roots and adopt Roman Catholic practices and beliefs.

ANICCA: key BUDDHIST DOCTRINE regarding the impermanence of all things. It forms the first of the three characteristic marks of EXISTENCE. It is a feature of all existence which Buddhists claim can be observed empirically and supports their view of the UNIVERSE. Everything is in a state of FLUX but more importantly the mind, or consciousness, is essentially impermanent and consciousness arises or ceases from moment to moment. Recognition of the impermanence of physical things is easy, but to see that consciousness is similar is much more difficult and one of the tasks of Buddhism. Only when this is done can the INDIVIDUAL go on to recognize that there is no permanent SELF or that there is no such thing as a SOUL. Everything, including individual consciousness, is impermanent. This doctrine separates Buddhism from all other RELIGIONS in that it denies the essential spiritual nature of the person and sees such a belief as an illusion which binds sentient BEINGS to existence.

ANIMISM: a very misleading term often used to characterize African and other nonliterate religious systems. The term was first introduced by Sir Edward B. TYLOR as a "minimum definition" of RELIGION. He argued that from sleep experiences such as dreams "primitive man" developed the idea of anima, or the spiritual principle, which animates material objects. Thus rivers, trees, stones, the sun, moon and SACRED objects such as masks were said to possess spiritual power caused by the indwelling of SPIRIT BEINGS. These ideas, Tylor argued, produced fear which led to WORSHIP and the development of religion. Today the term animism has fallen into disuse among many scholars of religion although it is retained by some MISSIOLOGISTS. The reason most academics have rejected this term is because it fails to recognize the highly complex nature of many of these religions and assumes that non-literate peoples lack the INTELLECTUAL ability to develop complex religions and PHILOSOPHIES. It is therefore best abandoned to allow for the recognition of the complexity of religious systems. The British anthropologist E. E. EVANS-PRITCHARD did more than anyone else to dispel simplistic notions about "primitive religion" in books such as *Witchcraft, Oracles and Magic among the Azande* (1936) and *Nuer Religion* (1956).

ANKH: the Egyptian religious SYMBOL of life formed by a cross with two loops at the top. Today it is often seen in NEW AGE religious groups and is a popular form of jewelry.

ANSELM (1033-1109): ARCHBISHOP of CANTERBURY and an important figure in medieval church-STATE disputes. He is best remembered for his philosophical works, including his ONTOLOGICAL ARGUMENT for the EXISTENCE of GOD, and for his work on the ATONEMENT, *Cur Deus Homo?* where he argued that CHRIST died to satisfy the outraged majesty of God created by human SIN.

ANTECEDENT: going before, prior, preceding; e.g., the egg to the chicken.

ANTHONY (251?-356): Egyptian HERMIT and mystical theologian whose reputation for HOLINESS greatly influenced the development of MONASTICISM.

ANTHROPOCENTRISM: traditional HUMANISM has followed PROTAGORAS in proclaiming "man is the measure of all things." Recently some people in the ecology movement have expressed the view that an anthropocentric outlook is wrong because it is arrogant and self-defeating and leads to the wasteful exploitation of nature.

ANTHROPOLOGY: the SCIENCE of humanity, human biological origins, and social and cultural behavior. In THEOLOGY it denotes that section of systematic theology dealing with humanity as a creature of GOD. As an academic discipline, anthropology is generally divided between physical, social and cultural anthropology.

ANTHROPOMORPHISM: the attribution of human characteristics, activities, or emotions to GOD; e.g., "God the Father" attributes the qualities of a human father to God.

ANTHROPOPATHISM: the attribution of human emotions to inanimate objects, a specific environment, or the world in general. It is sometimes called the pantheistic fallacy.

ANTICHRIST: the word used by the author of the Johannine epistles for those who deny CHRIST (1 Jn 2:18-22; 2 Jn 7). The NEW TESTAMENT implies that at the end of human HISTORY the antichrist will appear to wage war on the CHURCH. This belief has fueled many MILLENARIAN MOVEMENTS.

ANTICULT MOVEMENT: a North American movement involving parents, friends and ex-members of NEW RELIGIOUS MOVEMENTS. The movement has spread worldwide and invokes the notion of BRAINWASHING to explain CONVERSION to new RELIGIONS. Through the skillful use of the media, especially television, it has become a powerful social force and is seen by many social scientists as an essentially antireligious movement with profound implications for all religious groups and a threat to religious FREEDOM. The anticult movement bases its theories about brainwashing on the work of British psychiatrist William SARGANT. His book *The Battle for the Mind* (1957) was a violent attack on EVANGELICAL CHRISTIANITY provoked by the success of the Billy GRAHAM crusades in England.

ANTIMODERNISM: a philosophical and social movement opposed to MODERNITY and all things MODERN which is associated with ROMANTICISM and the glorification of the Middle Ages or rural society.

ANTINOMIANISM: the claim that the CHRISTIAN is free from all moral obligations or principles. It is derived from two Greek words, *anti*, meaning against, and *nomos*, the law, and thus its meaning is "against the law."

ANTINOMY: the conflict of two contradictory conclusions. In KANT the term is used to designate such a situation where the conclusions are deducted from apparently VALID premises.

ANTIOCHENE THEOLOGY: a tradition

in the THEOLOGY of the EARLY CHURCH which developed in Antioch using Aristotelian philosophy (see ARISTOTLE). It placed an emphasis on historical events, as opposed to the ALLEGORICAL INTERPRETATIONS of ALEXANDRIAN THEOLOGY, which was based on the work of PLATO.

ANTI-SEMITISM: an attitude of hostility toward Jewish people and JUDAISM. It has been linked to the belief that "the Jews" as a race were responsible for the death of JESUS. This belief has been repudiated by most CHRISTIAN theologians and was rejected by the Second VATICAN COUNCIL (1965-1966).

ANTITHESIS: the opposite. The term was developed by KANT, FICHTE and HEGEL; MARX used it to develop a theory to replace the traditional logic of ARISTOTLE with a form of reasoning that denies ABSOLUTE TRUTH in favor of relative truths.

ANUSSATI: a PALI term for BUDDHIST teachings about recollection which form a basis for some types of MEDITATION.

APOCALYPSE: refers to the book of Revelation, the last book of the NEW TESTAMENT, which is attributed to the APOSTLE JOHN. More generally the term refers to ancient HEBREW and CHRISTIAN visionary PROPHETIC literature. These books are written in figurative language and are very difficult to interpret, although many writers try to see in them a PHILOSOPHY of HISTORY foretelling the end of the world.

APOCALYPTIC LITERATURE: a genre of literature frequently characterized by its mysterious allusions to the SIGNS preceding the events to occur in the last days of world HISTORY. The Society for Biblical Literature has defined apocalyptic literature as a genre of revelatory literature with a narrative framework where REVELATION is mediated by otherworldly BEINGS to human recipients disclosing a transcendental REALITY that is temporal (ESCHATOLOGICAL SALVATION) and spatial (involves another, supernatural world).

APOCALYPTISM: belief in the imminent end of the world or other impending disasters resulting from divine JUDGMENT.

APOCRYPHA: in Greek this means "hidden things" and is a term applied to the fourteen books of the SEPTUAGINT that are not a part of the HEBREW BIBLE. They are not accepted as part of the official CANON OF SCRIPTURE by Protestants or Jews, but some are accepted as deuterocanonical by the Roman Catholic, Russian and Greek Orthodox churches.

APOCRYPHAL NEW TESTAMENT: a collection of writings which the EARLY CHURCH deemed uncanonical (see CANON OF SCRIPTURE) and rejected because they did not teach orthodox DOCTRINES. In recent years apocryphal literature such as the *Gospel of Thomas* has become popular among alternative religious groups and has formed a basis for NEW AGE beliefs. Many wild claims have been made about apocryphal writings but the truth is that most were written well into the second century A.D. and lack all HISTORICAL connection with the man JESUS.

APOLLO: the Greek god associated with music, medicine, cattle and prophecy whose chief shrine was in Delphi. He was son of ZEUS.

APOLLONIAN: the RATIONAL, harmonious and orderly. A term used by NIETZSCHE to describe one tradition of Greek art. The other tradition he described as Dionysian (see DIONYSUS).

APOLOGETICS: the reasoned defense of the Christian RELIGION against INTELLECTUAL objections, and attempts to establish certain elements of CHRISTIANITY as true or, at least, as not demonstrably false. Christians appeal to such NEW TESTAMENT verses as 1 Peter 3:15, Luke 1:1-4, and 1 Corinthians 15:12-19 as a basis for apologetics.

APOSTASY: the abandonment or renunciation of a RELIGION, such as CHRISTIANITY or ISLAM, either voluntarily or by compulsion. There are frequent biblical allusions to the EVILS and the dangers of apostasy. It is described as departure from the FAITH (1 Timothy 4:1-3) and as being carried away by the error of lawless men (Hebrews 3:12). The great apostasy, "The Rebellion" (2 Thessalonians 2:3), is associated with the return of CHRIST and the end of the world or JUDGMENT Day.

APOSTLE: a term used in the NEW TESTAMENT for someone who saw the risen CHRIST and received a commission to preach the gospel. It is also used by ANALOGY to refer to pioneering MISSIONARIES and, occasionally, important leaders within the CHRISTIAN CHURCH. Today certain religious movements, such as the MORMONS and some CHARISMATIC Christian groups, claim to be led by apostles.

APOSTLES' CREED: one of the earliest statements of the CHRISTIAN FAITH, this creed dates from around the fourth century.

APOSTOLIC FATHERS: CHRISTIAN writers, such as CLEMENT OF ROME and IGNATIUS, who lived immediately after the time of the APOSTLES.

APOSTOLIC SUCCESSION: the theory developed by ROMAN CATHOLIC theologians that theological ORTHODOXY is preserved through an unbroken line of BISHOPS who derive their AUTHORITY from CHRIST.

APOTHEOSIS: the DEIFICATION of a person, such as a Roman emperor, after their DEATH.

APPEARANCE: that which stands in contrast to REALITY. A term similar to the HINDU concept of MĀYĀ.

AQUINAS, Thomas (1224/27-1274): known by his contemporaries as "Doctor Angelicus," he is the most important philosopher and theologian of the ROMAN CATHOLIC TRADITION. Educated by BENEDICTINES and DOMINICANS, he studied in Paris and Cologne. Later he taught in Paris (1252-59, 1269-72) and Italy (1259-69, 1272-74). He was responsible for "baptizing" the PHILOSOPHY of ARISTOTLE which he made the basis of Roman Catholic THEOLOGY and APOLOGETICS. His

Aristotelianism was opposed by the FRANCISCANS, but his teachings were made the official DOCTRINE of the Dominican Order. He was canonized in 1323 and made a Doctor of the Church in 1567. The study of Thomas Aquinas was made part of all theological training in 1366. Made patron of all Roman Catholic universities in 1880, his authority as teacher was reaffirmed in 1923. In his thought the relation of REASON to FAITH is one of subalternation, in which the lower (reason) accepts principles of the higher (faith). He rejected ANSELM'S ONTOLOGICAL ARGUMENT, preferring the COSMOLOGICAL and TELEOLOGICAL ARGUMENTS for the EXISTENCE of GOD. For Aquinas there is a level of knowledge attainable by reason alone; another attainable by reason for skilled thinkers and by faith for unskilled thinkers; the highest level, however, is attainable only by faith. The system Aquinas developed is called "Thomism" and his followers, "Thomists."

ARAHANT: a PALI term for a person who reaches the final stage of spiritual progress. The word literally means "the worthy" and was applied to the BUDDHA by his contemporaries. Previously it had been used of the founder of JAINISM, MAHĀVĪRA, but later it was applied to Buddhist SAINTS both in life and after their death.

ARCANE SCHOOL: the organization established in 1923 by Alice BAILEY to propagate a form of THEOSOPHY and the teachings of the GREAT WHITE BROTHERHOOD. Originally a member of the THEOSOPHICAL SOCIETY proper, Bailey clashed with Annie BESANT over Besant's belief that Jiddu KRISHNAMURTI was the expected world savior. Instead she received SPIRITUALIST communications promising the return of CHRIST in the form of the Buddhist BODHISATTVA Maitreya. In recent years Benjamin Creme has claimed that he is the fulfillment of this prophecy. Through its many books and writings the

Arcane School has been a major influence on the NEW AGE MOVEMENT.

ARCHBISHOP: a title originating in the CHRISTIAN CHURCH in the fourth century A.D. used to designate the head of an important DIOCESE. It was later applied to the head of all the BISHOPS in a province or country.

ARCHETYPE: a notion used by PLATO to signify the original FORM of things as contrasted with their APPEARANCE in the world. It was picked up by JUNG as a term for the collective representation of SYMBOLS found in art and dreams.

ARCHIMEDES (287-212 B.C.): probably the greatest Greek scientist, mathematician and engineer.

ARIANISM: CHRISTIANITY's most troublesome schism, Arianism was named after its principal exponent ARIUS, who was a thoroughgoing Greek RATIONALIST. He inherited the almost universally held LOGOS CHRISTOLOGY of the Eastern Roman Empire. He contended that GOD was immutable and unknowable, and therefore CHRIST had to be a created, being made by God as the first in the created order. The orthodox counter-attack on Arianism pointed out that Arian THEOLOGY reduced Christ to a demigod and in effect reintroduced POLYTHEISM into Christianity, because Christ was worshipped among Arians. Politically, Arianism has been accused of seeing the emperor as a semi-divine being and promoting the sacralization of the state. In February 325, Arius was condemned as a heretic at a Synod in Antioch. The Emperor Constantine, who was sympathetic to Arianism, then called the first ECUMENICAL council—known as the Council of Nicaea—which met in May 325 and also condemned Arius and his teachings. But instead of resolving the issues, the Council launched an empire-wide christological debate during which it often seemed that Arianism would triumph as the dominant form of Christianity. Only after a hundred years of heated debate did OR-

THODOXY emerge triumphant. Today, a form of Arianism has been revived among UNITARIANS and the JEHOVAH'S WITNESSES. Claims are also made by various OCCULT groups about Arianism as a persecuted source of occult knowledge.

ARISTOBULUS OF PANEAS (3rd-2nd centuries B.C.): Jewish Alexandrian philosopher who sought to reconcile JUDAISM with Greek PHILOSOPHY through the ALLEGORICAL INTERPRETATION of the HEBREW BIBLE. He argued that the Hebrew Bible was, in reality, the true source of many philosophical ideas among the Greeks. He is known to have written a commentary on the PENTATEUCH, but this has been lost and is only known through quotations in CHRISTIAN writings.

ARISTOTLE (384-322 B.C.): born in the Greek colony of Stagira, he was sent to Athens at the age of 18 where he remained in close association with the ACADEMY of PLATO for twenty years. The logic of Aristotle, called ANALYTIC, is, he argued, a discipline prior to all others because it sets forth the requirements of scientific inquiry and proof. Aristotelian logic depends on formal relations and the possibility of discovering principles, i.e., UNIVERSALS and CAUSES. Aristotle is fond of tracing the transition in knowledge from the particulars of sense experience—the things we can know—to the universals, which are grasped by INTUITIVE reason. For Aristotle every sensible object is a union of two principles, MATTER and FORM. Matter is regarded as potentiality and the form as that which actualizes it. The fact of motion or change is then accounted for as a process by which potential BEING passes over through form into actual being. Aristotle has had a long and profound influence on Western THEOLOGY, especially since his work was used as the basis of theological reflection by Thomas AQUINAS in the twelfth century. Aristotle's philosophy provides the basis for many classical APOLOGETIC arguments, including the COSMOLOGICAL and

TELEOLOGICAL ARGUMENTS for BELIEF in GOD, whom Aristotle called "the unmoved Mover." His ideas also lent LEGITIMATION to the ROMAN CATHOLIC doctrine of TRANSUBSTANTIATION and not surprisingly were strongly rejected by early PROTESTANT REFORMERS such as Martin LUTHER and John CALVIN. They were reinstated as the basis for CHRISTIAN scholarship by later reformers and are the official basis for Roman Catholic teachings.

ARIUS (250-336): regarded as the arch-heretic of the EARLY CHURCH, he seems to have been a highly successful preacher and was revered for his ASCETICISM. Arius appears to have written little, preferring instead to embody his teachings in popular songs. He rejected the orthodox definition of the DEITY of CHRIST, the TRINITY, and related doctrines, replacing them with a form of subordination which made Christ the first created BEING but not GOD (see ARIANISM).

ARJUN (?): the fifth SIKH GURU who was the Sikh leader from 1581 to 1606. He was responsible for the building of the Golden TEMPLE in Amritsar and for the compilation of the first authoritative version of the Sikh SCRIPTURES. He died after torture and imprisonment by the Muslim Mughal overlords. This act led to the militarization of the Sikh community.

ARMAGEDDON: the name used in the book of Revelation 16:16 for the site of the final battle between the forces of GOOD and EVIL.

ARMENIANS: the first nation to embrace CHRISTIANITY in a form similar to Greek Orthodoxy (see ORTHODOX CHURCH). They were slaughtered in an organized massacre in 1918 and driven from their traditional homeland in Eastern Turkey.

ARMINIANISM: a general term embracing the teachings of Jacobus ARMINIUS. The THEOLOGICAL views of Arminius and his followers were summed up in five points which were designed to counter the prevailing CALVINIST ORTHODOXY of his day. They are: (1) GOD from all ETER-NITY predestined to ETERNAL LIFE those whom he foresaw would remain steadfast in FAITH; (2) CHRIST died for all humanity, not only the elect; (3) through FREE WILL a person cooperates in his CONVERSION; (4) humans may resist divine GRACE; (5) humans may fall from grace. At the Synod of DORT the Arminian teachings were condemned by orthodox Calvinists as heretical. Today, Arminianism is the major theological force among North American EVANGELICAL CHRISTIANS.

ARMINIUS, Jacobus (1560-1609): Dutch theologian and critic of CALVINISM. His views were condemned by the Synod of DORT but spread rapidly in the Netherlands and France. They were introduced into the CHURCH OF ENGLAND by Archbishop LAUD where they degenerated into a form of PELAGIANISM. A modified form of ARMINIANISM characterized the METHODIST revival of the eighteenth century and dominates EVANGELICAL THEOLOGY in America today.

ARMSTRONG, Garner Ted (1930-): son of Herbert W. Armstrong and for many years heir apparent. In 1974 a series of allegations about his alleged sexual infidelities forced him to leave the WORLDWIDE CHURCH OF GOD to establish his own rival organization.

ARMSTRONG, Herbert W. (1909-): radio and television preacher who founded the WORLDWIDE CHURCH OF GOD College, and the well-known magazine *The Plain Truth*. He promoted a form of ARIANISM laced with an Americanized version of BRITISH ISRAELITISM and strengthened by a strong premillennial ESCHATOLOGY.

ARNOLD, Matthew (1822-1888): son of Thomas ARNOLD, he was an English poet, essayist, and critic who has been described as "the great English APOSTLE of CULTURE." Although he professed an INTELLECTUAL appreciation for the ideals of the FRENCH REVOLUTION, he was shocked by DEMOCRACY in America and propounded a sophisticated snobbery in the guise of an attack on the "philistinism" of the English middle classes. In fact, his ideals are a continuation of the social views of his father, Thomas Arnold. He dabbled in THEOLOGY, opposing traditional ORTHODOXY in a desire to dispense with the miraculous and SUPERNATURAL elements of religion which he believed conflicted with modern SCIENCE.

ARNOLD, Thomas (1795-1842): ANGLICAN CLERGYMAN and Headmaster of Rugby School. He is famous for his REFORMS of the English elite private school system and is unique among educational reformers in that his "reforms" limited social mobility and strengthened the English class system. Although hailed by many as a wise and brilliant CHRISTIAN educator who infused education with a moral purpose, his work is seen by others as having had a devastating effect by creating deep social divisions in British SOCIETY.

ARYANS: a SANSKRIT term meaning "the Noble Ones" which, in the nineteenth century, led to a great debate about Aryan RELIGION and languages. In the twentieth century the term was used by Nazi propagandists in their philosophy of racial purity.

ĀSANA: YOGA posture or mode of sitting.

ASAṄGA: BUDDHIST philosopher and founder of the YOGĀCĀRA school who lived in the fourth century A.D. His ideas are similar to both MANICHAEANISM and NEOPLATONISM.

ĀSAVA: a PALI term for the influences, influxes or taints which in BUDDHISM are regarded as intoxicating the mind and thus preventing spiritual progress. These influences are sensuality, lust for life, false views and ignorance.

ASBURY, Francis (1745-1816): a founder of METHODISM in America and one of the first Methodist BISHOPS in America, where Methodism is characterized by its recognition of bishops.

ASCENDED MASTERS: a term popularized by THEOSOPHY that refers to super-human BEINGS who are said to guide human destiny. They are often depicted as living in remote places like Tibet or, more recently, on other planets or in UFOs, from where they telepathically communicate with selected human beings.

ASCENSION OF CHRIST: the Christian belief that after his resurrection JESUS ascended to HEAVEN, from where he continues to rule over all creation.

ASCETICISM: religious practices which lead to the neglect of the body and SPIRITUAL EXERCISES which involve extreme FASTING, FLAGELLATION and other discomforts. Asceticism is characteristic of all forms of MONASTICISM.

ASH'ARĪ, al- (A.D. 873-935): a follower of AḤMAD ibn Ḥanbal, he taught that the QUR'ĀN is God's speech and therefore shares the eternal ATTRIBUTES OF GOD. He also believed that GOOD and EVIL were both created by God and that all, even MUSLIMS who sinned, may be tortured in HELL before eventually entering HEAVEN. He taught that although the Qur'ān refers to the hand, face, etc., of God, these expressions are to be understood as figurative. God is incorporeal, and therefore we do not fully understand language which speaks of God in human terms.

ĀSHRAM: a HINDU term for a retreat center or hermitage.

AŚOKA (3rd century B.C.): the ruler of the Mauryan Empire of Northern India who, after many bloody conquests, became a BUDDHIST in reaction to the violence of his own reign. He sought to promote Buddhism yet was tolerant of other RELIGIONS. He left behind a wealth of inscriptions mentioning the DHARMA (PALI term) as well as his own achievements.

ĀŚRAMAS: the four stages of life's journey in HINDUISM. They are: the student, the householder, the HERMIT and the wandering recluse.

ASSASSINS: the European name for members of a minor branch of the IS-MĀ'ĪLĪ SECT of ISLAM who smoked hemp (*canabis sativa*) to gain a foretaste of paradise. They were associated with Syria and religious fanaticism and were believed to specialize in the murder, or assassination, of religious opponents. As a movement they were suppressed by the Mongols between 1256 and 1272.

ASSUMPTION: a presupposition or POSTULATE. Something that is taken as a "given" in any argument.

ASSUMPTION OF MARY: a ROMAN CATHOLIC DOCTRINE promulgated in 1950 declared that MARY the Mother of JESUS was taken up into HEAVEN and thus avoided the pangs of death.

ASSYRIAN RELIGION: the ancient religion of Assyria which centered on the worship of Ashur who was a warrior king associated with a city of the same name. He is said to have formed the universe out of preexisting matter.

ĀSTIKA: a HINDU term for correct teachings or ORTHODOXY.

ASTROLOGY: the ancient BELIEF that both individual and national destinies are influenced by the stars. The role of the stars in the life of individuals is known as "natal" astrology while "mundane" astrology deals with the fate of nations and concepts like the AGE OF AQUARIUS. Although popular in many CULTURES in the past, astrology was discredited in the seventeenth century by a combination of the rise of modern SCIENCE and a series of well-publicized predictions by prominent astrologers which were completely wrong.

AŚVAGHOSA (1st or 2nd century A.D.): BUDDHIST writer—or possibly school of writers—who authored various works preserving Buddhist TRADITION and expounding Buddhist DOCTRINE. Various scholars dispute when, where, and how many Aśvaghosas actually lived.

ATHANASIAN CREED: a Christian CREED dating from the fifth century, attributed to ATHANASIUS, which concentrates on the DOCTRINES of the INCARNATION and the TRINITY.

ATHANASIUS (296-373): champion of ORTHODOXY against ARIANISM. He was Egyptian by birth but Greek by education. Athanasius took no official part in the proceedings of the Council of Nicaea but, as secretary to BISHOP Alexander, he wrote notes, circulars, and encyclicals that had an important effect on the outcome of the council. Because Arianism had a wide following in the empire and enjoyed the sympathies of Roman emperors, Athanasius was hounded through five exiles totalling seventeen years of flight and hiding. His later years were spent peacefully at Alexandria. Almost single-handedly Athanasius saved the CHRISTIAN CHURCH from the PAGAN intellectualism of Arianism. As a young man he was impressed by Christian MARTYRS and eventually had a great influence on the MONASTIC movement, especially in Egypt. He wrote *On the Incarnation, Against the Arians* and *Letters Concerning the Holy Spirit.*

ATHANASIUS (10th century): a Greek ORTHODOX MONK who established the monastery of Lavra on Mount ATHOS.

ATHEISM: the view that holds that God does not exist. The term was originally used in Greece of all those who disbelieved in the official state GODS. SOCRATES was the classic instance. In the Roman Empire the term was applied to CHRISTIANS but sometimes Christians, like POLYCARP, would turn the term against their persecutors. Until the expression "AGNOSTICISM" came into general use in the nineteenth century, the term "ATHEISM" was popularly used to describe those who thought the EXISTENCE of God an unprovable thesis.

ATHOS: mountain in Greece which became a site of PILGRIMAGE and the monastic life. Today it houses a number of monasteries and is a center of ORTHODOX SPIRITUALITY.

ATLANTIS: in his dialogue *Timaeus* PLATO mentions an EVIL people whose city was destroyed by an earthquake which submerged it under the sea. For at least four hundred years after he wrote *Timaeus* Plato's story was recognized as a PARABLE. Some Roman writers then began to take it literally, but it was not until the nineteenth century, with the work of Ignatius T. T. Donnelly, that the idea of such a "lost civilization" became widespread. From Donnelly it was adapted and given OCCULT significance by Helena BLAVATSKY, and has since become uncritically accepted and widely used by occult writers, who use it as an APOLOGETIC device to promote their claims.

ĀTMAN: a key HINDU term for the individualization of REALITY. It is often translated as SOUL but actually means something more like the ESSENCE of life or fundamental SELF. In some UPANISHADS and VEDĀNTA Ātman is identified with BRAHMAN.

ATOMISM: the ancient theory found in both India and Greece that sees the UNIVERSE as composed of building blocks known as atoms. Modern atomic theory takes its name from this PHILOSOPHY.

ATONEMENT: reconciliation or "at-onement." In CHRISTIAN THEOLOGY it refers to the restoration of the broken relationship between GOD and humans accomplished by the DEATH and RESURRECTION of JESUS CHRIST.

ATTRIBUTE: a term developed by ARISTOTLE who divided the world into SUBSTANCES and their attributes. Attributes describe substances; e.g., "hard" is an attribute of stone. In THEOLOGY attributes describe the NATURE and character of GOD.

ATTRIBUTES OF GOD: those characteristics applicable to the divine BEING. Two classical ways of arriving at the attributes of God have been: (1) the way of negation, which rather than saying what God is, says what he is not; e.g., "God is unlimited"; (2) the way of ANALOGY, which compares God to things known from human experience; e.g., "God the Father" likens God to a human father. Many theologians make a distinction between the communicable and incommunicable attributes of God. Communicable attributes are those which are reflected in the lives of human beings such as love, and incommunicable attributes are uniquely God's.

AUGSBURG CONFESSION: the great LUTHERAN statement of FAITH drawn up in 1530 to review the abuses of the ROMAN CATHOLIC CHURCH and set forth Lutheran DOCTRINE.

AUGUSTINE OF CANTERBURY (d. 604): a MISSIONARY to the English; made ARCHBISHOP of CANTERBURY in 596 by POPE GREGORY THE GREAT.

AUGUSTINE OF HIPPO (354-430): the greatest of the Latin CHRISTIAN Fathers and African theologians and one of the outstanding thinkers of all time. Augustine was of Berber descent and almost certainly black. His mother, Monica, was a Christian whose virtues he praised. But at Carthage he was drawn into sexual excesses; later, while studying RHETORIC and PHILOSOPHY, he came under the influence of MANICHAEISM followed by NEOPLATONISM. In the spring of 387, after many sessions with AMBROSE, BISHOP of Milan, and the study of the BIBLE, Augustine was BAPTIZED. These events are recorded in his *Confessions,* a spiritual classic and the first real work of Christian autobiography. His CHRISTIANITY remained strongly ASCETIC, and his writings display a remarkably African ethos. In 396 he was consecrated BISHOP of HIPPO and remained a PASTOR until his death. For more than thirty years Augustine was the leading theologian in African Christianity. In 410 the Goths sacked Rome, and the PAGANS blamed the Christians whose GOD they said caused the disaster. Augustine defended the Christians against this charge in his great work *The City of God.* Augustine's THEOLOGY helped bring about the PROTESTANT REFORMATION and deeply influenced early Protestant theologians such as Martin LUTHER and John CALVIN.

AUGUSTINE, RULE OF: an early MONASTIC rule attributed to AUGUSTINE OF

HIPPO outlining life in the monastery. It deeply influenced the Dominican Order.

AUROBINDO, Sri (1872-1950): the founder of a vigorous Hindu REFORM and MISSIONARY movement. He was educated in England and served the British in India until he was arrested for alleged support of rebels. In jail he had a MYSTICAL experience and devoted the rest of his life to RELIGION. In his book *The Life Divine* he seeks to interpret HINDUISM in terms of evolutionary theory in a manner similar to the Jesuit TEILHARD DE CHARDIN. He taught what he called "integral YOGA" which integrated spiritual and practical disciplines. In the 1920s he was joined by a French convert whom he eventually called "the Mother" and with whom he is said to have practiced various forms of TANTRA or SPIRITUAL EXERCISES of a sexual nature. After his death "the Mother" took over and ran his ĀSHRAM in Pondicherry which, unlike most ashrams, accommodated married as well as single people and made many concessions to modern technology.

AUROVILLE: a model community which has influenced NEW AGE thinkers. Founded in India as an international village based on the teachings of Sri AUROBINDO, it was designed and run by Mira Richards (1878-1973), who was known as "the Mother."

AUTHENTICITY: a term used by existentialist philosophers to designate true human existence freed from all forms of deception.

AUTHORITY: the true source of authority is one of the most crucial points of debate between different religious traditions. For some, authority is inherent in the CHURCH, or in a person who is especially HOLY or who represents GOD; for EVANGELICAL Christians, true authority rests with the BIBLE as the inspired and infallible word of God. Modern sociology sees religious authority as springing from the CHARISMA of a person, book or teaching and is transmitted through a recognized TRADITION.

AVATĀR: a HINDU term meaning "descent" which signifies the manifestation of a GOD on earth in human or animal form.

AVERROES (A.D. 1126-1198): one of the most influential MUSLIM philosophers and a native of Cordova, Spain. He was an important commentator on the works of ARISTOTLE and a strong defender of REASON against appeals to mystical illumination. He wrote many books on law, PHILOSOPHY and RELIGION and argued against the ALLEGORICAL INTERPRETATION of the QUR'ĀN. His views led to accusations of ATHEISM and exile but were very influential in CHRISTIAN Europe and helped spur Christian thinkers to "rediscover" Aristotle and develop a Christian Aristotelianism.

AVICENNA (930-1037): an Islamic philosopher who greatly influenced Christian thought in medieval Europe through his use of PLATO and ARISTOTLE.

AVIDYĀ: in Hindu thought, the ignorance which is the explanation for the endless cycle of birth and REBIRTH which binds humans to the WHEEL OF EXISTENCE.

AXIOM: a self-evident TRUTH used as the basis for an argument.

AYER, Sir Alfred Jules (1910-1989): English linguistic philosopher and humanist whose best work *Language, Truth and Logic* (1936) introduced LOGICAL POSITIVISM to the English-speaking world. The central demand of this work was the "elimination of METAPHYSICS" based on his interpretation of the VERIFICATION PRINCIPLE. His understanding of this was slightly modified and greatly clarified in the introduction to the second edition of the book published in 1946. In 1988, shortly before his death, he wrote an article describing a near-death experience which had forced him to question his earlier views.

ĀYUR-VEDA: a collection of medieval HINDU manuscripts containing medical knowledge and magical ideas (*see* MAGIC) which greatly influenced Oriental medical practices.

B

BA AND KA: two aspects of the SOUL in ancient EGYPTIAN RELIGION. Ba was conceived of as a bird with a human head which left the body at death, and Ka was the intellect.

BAAL: "possessor" or "LORD"; a term applied to the GODS in CANAANITE religions.

BABEL, TOWER OF: from the biblical story found in Genesis 11:1-9. It is symbolic of human arrogance and the desire to "be like God." According to the story the confusion of languages and human races began with the destruction of the tower which "reached to heaven."

BABYLON: one of the greatest cities of the ancient world. It was located on the left bank of the Euphrates near modern Baghdad. In the BIBLE it is symbolic of human pride and a world system opposed to GOD.

BABYLONIAN CAPTIVITY: the 70-year exile of the Jewish people from JERUSALEM which began in 597 B.C. In CHRISTIAN thought it became a symbol of corruption in the CHURCH and was applied to the removal of the papacy from Rome to Avignon between 1305 and 1378.

BACH, Johann Sebastian (1685-1750): one of the greatest composers of all time. His LUTHERAN FAITH inspired such masterpieces as the *Christmas Oratorio* and *St. Matthew's Passion.*

BACON, Francis (1561-1626): English jurist and philosopher who championed EMPIRICISM, the use of INDUCTION and experimental SCIENCE. He is the author of *The Advancement of Learning* (1605) and *The New Atlantis* (1624).

BACON, Roger (1214-1292): English FRANCISCAN philosopher who promoted ARISTOTLE and developed an interest in experimental SCIENCE. His major work is *Opus Maius* (1268).

BAHÁ'Í FAITH: a new religious movement originating from ISLAM and considered HERETICAL by the orthodox. It was founded in Persia by Baha'ullah (1817-1892), who suffered imprisonment and exile for his beliefs. Toward the end of his life he lived at Bahji near Acre where he wrote *Kitáb-i-Íqán* (Book of Certitude), the basic doctrinal work of his religion and numerous other works. GOD is held to be transcendent and unknowable, but he makes himself manifest through his creation and especially through prophets, who are mirrors in which God's will and attributes are reflected. The movement promotes (1) universal peace, (2) the unity of the human race, (3) removal of prejudices, (4) the essential unity of all religions and (5) PRAYER for the dead. After his death his son, 'Abbas Effendi ('ABD AL-BAHĀ), was recognized as the interpreter of his father's writings and undertook MISSIONARY work in Europe and America. The movement has spread widely in Europe, America, Africa and Eastern countries. The administrative center is at Haifa, Israel.

BAILEY, Alice (1880-1949): English OCCULTIST who at the age of fifteen had a VISION of a being she said was CHRIST but later, under theosophical influence, decided was a mystic teacher, Koot Hoomi. In later life she claimed to have contact with another "master," Djwhal Khul, a Tibetan, who dictated books through her by automatic writing. After a dispute with the THEOSOPHICAL SOCIETY in 1920, she founded the ARCANE SCHOOL. Her most important idea was the coming of a new world master who would unite East and West. Her books include *The Unfinished Autobiography* (1951), *Initiation: Human and Solar* (1922) and *A Treatise on White Magic* (1934).

BALA: BUDDHIST term for power. In the PALI CANON there are five powers, referred to as: (1) faith, (2) energy, (3) mindfulness, (4) concentration, (5) wisdom. Other powers, such as shame, are mentioned singularly, and others as members of groups. In the MAHĀYĀNA TRADITION there is a list of the ten powers which are the attributes of a BODHISATTVA: (1) a mind turned from worldliness, (2) ever stronger faith, (3) disciplined exercises, (4) intuitive reading of minds, (5) fulfilled PRAYER, (6) ability to work to the end of time, (7) ability to create the means of SALVATION, (8) PURIFICATION of the world, (9) the awakening of ENLIGHTENMENT, (10) the ability to utter a phrase with UNIVERSAL appeal.

BALANCE: Islamic term referring to the last JUDGMENT when human deeds will be weighed in the balance.

BALLARD, Edna Anne Wheeler (1886-1971): American OCCULTIST and cofounder, with her husband Guy BALLARD, of the Saint Germain Foundation. She became the leader of the "I-AM" MOVEMENT.

BALLARD, Guy (1878-1939): American OCCULTIST who in 1930, while hiking on Mount Shasta, California, had a MYSTICAL encounter with an entity he claimed was Saint Germain. During the remaining years of his life he and his wife promoted the teachings of Saint Germain and other ASCENDED MASTERS.

BALTHASAR, Hans Urs von (1905-): acclaimed ROMAN CATHOLIC theologian and philosopher whose multivolume work *The Glory of the Lord* has been described as the most important theological work since Karl BARTH'S *Church Dogmatics.*

BANARAS: considered as the most HOLY city in India. It is referred to as the "City of Light."

BAPTISM: RITUAL immersion or sprinkling with water; a symbol of REPENTANCE and NEW BIRTH. It developed in JUDAISM prior to the time of JESUS and became a central practice in the work of JOHN THE BAPTIST and later the Christian ritual of initiation. Within CHRISTIANITY strong doctrinal disputes exist as to both the mode and appropriate subjects of baptism. Until the REFORMATION most Christian groups baptized entire families, including children. Sectarian groups, later to be known as BAPTISTS, objected to this practice, claiming that FAITH was a necessary prerequisite for baptism. Defenders of infant baptism argue either that the act itself mystically REGENERATES the individual, or that the practice is justified in terms of God's COVENANT with the CHURCH. Advocates of infant baptism usually accept sprinkling as an acceptable mode of baptism on the grounds that this was common in Judaism. Baptists usually insist on adult baptism by total immersion, while ORTHODOX CHURCHES insist on the total immersion of infants.

BAPTISM OF THE HOLY SPIRIT: the CHRISTIAN DOCTRINE that at CONVERSION believers are indwelt by the HOLY SPIRIT. Among Pentecostal and Charismatic Christians the baptism of the Holy Spirit is often separated from the process of conversion and seen as a SECOND BLESSING which is associated with the CHARISMATIC GIFTS, including SPEAKING IN TONGUES.

BAPTISTS: Baptists claim to trace their origin to the NEW TESTAMENT, but acknowledge that as an identifiable movement they emerged in the seventeenth century, when they were known as "ANABAPTISTS." They believe that the BAPTISM of professed believers is a necessary condition of CHURCH membership. They strongly emphasize the independence of the local church, although individual churches may be linked to associations of various kinds. Early on they split into two groups: General Baptists, who are ARMINIAN in THEOLOGY, and Particular Baptists, who are CALVINIST. Today Baptists form a loose family of churches, with their main numerical base in the USA. Although there are international and national associations, many Baptist churches belong to neither, and hence there is a great diversity of belief and practice.

BARLAAM AND JOASAPH: medieval Byzantine legend believed to be a legend of the BUDDHA adopted for CHRISTIAN purposes by JOHN OF DAMASCUS.

BARMEN DECLARATION: a statement issued in 1934 by the German CONFESSING CHURCH. In opposition to Nazi attempts to manipulate the church it renounced all political allegiances and declared its dedication to GOD alone. It was strongly influenced by the theologian Karl BARTH.

BARTH, Karl (1886-1968): he began as a minister at Geneva (1909-1911) and was for ten years (1911-1921) pastor at Safenwil. It was here, under the shadow of the war of 1914-1918, that in direct relation to his pastoral responsibility he was led to

a radical questioning of current theological notions and wrote his *Commentary on Romans* (1919). In 1921 he became a professor at Göttingen. The BARMEN DECLARATION of 1934 was largely the work of Karl Barth. In 1935 he became professor of theology at Basle and retired in 1962. In 1927 he began publishing his massive and uncompleted *Church Dogmatics*, the last volume of which appeared in 1967.

BARTHOLOMEW'S DAY MASSACRE: on August 23, 1572, over 10,000 HUGUENOTS in Paris and other French cities were slaughtered on the orders of CATHERINE DE MEDICI. The event left a lasting impression on PROTESTANTS and greatly contributed to anti-ROMAN CATHOLIC feeling for several centuries.

BARZAKH: this term originates with Sūra XXIII.102 in the QUR'ĀN which speaks of the unrighteous dead seeking to return to earth to do some GOOD. It is taken to refer to either the period between DEATH and RESURRECTION or the place of the dead.

BASIL THE GREAT (A.D. 330-379): the brother of GREGORY OF NYSSA and one of the three CAPPADOCIAN FATHERS of the CHRISTIAN CHURCH who became BISHOP of Caesarea in A.D. 370. A staunch defender of ORTHODOXY, he opposed ARIANISM and defended the DIVINITY of the HOLY SPIRIT. An able administrator, he promoted hospitals and the care of the poor. His rule for monastic living is followed by the ORTHODOX CHURCH.

BASIL, RULE OF: the MONASTIC RULE followed by members of the Greek ORTHODOX CHURCH and named after Basil the Great who propagated it in the fourth century.

BASMALA: an abbreviation for the Arabic phrase which is translated "In the name of GOD, the Merciful, the Compassionate."

BASTIAN, Adolf (1826-1905): German physician and early anthropologist (*see* ANTHROPOLOGY) who pioneered the idea of fieldwork before MALINOWSKI and advocated the establishment of ethnographic museums. He was strongly opposed to DARWINISM and argued for the psychic unity of all people. His many books include *Die Vorgeshichte der Ethnologie* (1881) and *Der Mensch in der Geschichte* (1860).

BATHING: ritual bathing is found in many religions and appears to have been practiced in the INDUS VALLEY CIVILIZATION around 2500 B.C. Today it remains an important practice in HINDUISM and SHINTŌ.

BATSON, Gregory (1904-1980): British anthropologist (*see* ANTHROPOLOGY) and at one time the husband of Margaret MEAD. His work *Steps to an Ecology of Mind* (1972) played an important role in the development of many new religions in the 1970s as well as in the NEW AGE MOVEMENT of the 1980s.

BAUER, Bruno (1809-1882): German theologian and historian. Originally a conservative Hegelian (*see* HEGEL), in 1839 he adopted a position even more extreme than that of D. F. STRAUSS and attributed the gospel story to the imagination of the CHRISTIAN community. In 1842 he was deprived of his teaching post. The guiding principle of his many writings was a belief that the origins of Christianity were to be found in Greco-Roman PHILOSOPHY.

BAUR, Ferdinand Christian (1792-1860): German theologian and founder of the Tübingen School. He was a disciple of SCHLEIERMACHER and greatly influenced by HEGEL'S PHILOSOPHY of HISTORY. He caused great controversy by suggesting there was an essential conflict between the Saint PAUL and Hellenistic Christians, and the Jewish Christians represented by PETER. This interpretation came from his application of Hegel's theories to the NEW TESTAMENT.

BAVINCK, Herman (1854-1921): NEO-CALVINIST Dutch Reformed theologian and associate of Abraham KUYPER. His works include *The Doctrine of God* (1895), *The Philosophy of Revelation* (1908-1909) and *Our Reasonable Faith* (1909).

BAVINCK, J. H. (1895-1964): nephew of Herman BAVINCK. He was an outstanding Reformed Christian missiologist whose works include *An Introduction to the Science of Missions* (1960) and *The Church Between Temple and Mosque* (1961).

BAXTER, Richard (1615-1691): English PURITAN divine whose work *The Saints' Everlasting Rest* (1650) is considered a spiritual classic. His *Reformed Pastor* (1656) was taken as a model for the ministry in REFORMED churches while his *Christian Directory* (1673) gave practical instruction on a host of subjects including the economic life of the household.

BAYLE, Pierre (1647-1706): French RATIONALIST philosopher whose work inspired many ENLIGHTENMENT thinkers.

BEATIFIC VISION: a vision of GOD.

BEATIFICATION: the Roman Catholic practice of conferring the title "blessed" on a deceased person to permit VENERATION. Prior to the twelfth century any BISHOP could perform the rite, but it is now the exclusive right of the POPE.

BECKET, Thomas à (1118-1170): an English nobleman and friend of King Henry II. In 1162 he was appointed by the king to be ARCHBISHOP of CANTERBURY to help control the English church. To the surprise of his contemporaries, Becket took his responsibilities seriously and upheld the rights of the church. Disputes with the SECULAR authorities led to his murder on December 29, 1170. Soon after his death MIRACLES were reported from his tomb, and he was eventually elevated to sainthood (*see* SAINT). Becket's life has been the subject of many studies, the most notable being a play and film, *Murder in the Cathedral* (1935), by T. S. ELIOT.

BECOMING: any being whose characteristic is change and FLUX.

BEDE, the Venerable (673-735): called the "father of English history," he was a CHRISTIAN MONK who spent his life at the monasteries of Wearmouth and Jarrow and devoted himself to scholarship. He is best remembered for his classic work *The Ecclesiastical History of the English People*.

BEHAVIORISM: a materialistic (*see* MATERIALISM) school of PSYCHOLOGY associated with B. F. SKINNER which seeks to interpret human actions in terms of conditioned reflexes similar to the actions of a computer or mechanical device.

BEING: the existent. The Greek philosopher PARMENIDES believed that the real, as pure being, is not subject to change, FLUX or motion.

BELGIC CONFESSION: a statement of FAITH drawn up by Flemish and Walloon Churches in 1561 which became one of the basic documents of Dutch CALVINISM.

BELIEF: what is believed; trust, FAITH or intellectual assent; a form of knowledge which may or may not be based on FACTS. In religion belief is often a form of commitment to a way of life and involves the acceptance of the DOGMA of a religious community.

BELLARMINE, Robert (1542-1621): outstanding JESUIT theologian and Roman Catholic apologist (*see* APOLOGETICS) who was made a CARDINAL in 1599. He played an important role in the dispute between the CHURCH and GALILEO where he argued that all SCIENTIFIC THEORIES should be treated as tentative ideas subject to revision and not as ABSOLUTE TRUTH.

BENDA, Julien (1867-1956): French RATIONALIST philosopher and novelist who strongly opposed the system of Henri BERGSON. His work *The Treason of the Intellectuals* (1928) was a prophetic analysis of FASCISM and the dangers implicit in certain types of idealist PHILOSOPHY (*see* IDEALISM).

BENEDICT OF NURSIA (480-547): the founder of Western MONASTICISM and author of *The Rule of St. Benedict*. He was sent to Rome to study but, revolted by the degenerate life of the capital, fled to a cave near Subiaco where he became a HERMIT. Later he established the monastery of Monte Cassino and remained there until his death.

BENEDICT, RULE OF: the MONASTIC RULE based on the Rule of BASIL drawn up by BENEDICT at Monte Cristo. This became the basis of the BENEDICTINE ORDER.

BENEDICTINE ORDER: one of the great MONASTIC orders. It evolved out of the work of BENEDICT and was based on his MONASTIC RULE. The order has encouraged both learning and the practice of PIETY, and it has played an important role in the development of Western LITURGY. Its members are recognized by their black robes.

BENEDICTION: the pronouncement of a blessing in CHRISTIAN CHURCHES.

BENTHAM, Jeremy (1748-1832): English philosopher, political theorist and founder of UTILITARIANISM. His work *The Handbook of Political Fallacies* is a classic of common sense.

BERDYAEV, Nikolai (1874-1948): born in Kiev, Russia. He was attracted to MARXISM (*see* MARX), although he was a member of the Russian ORTHODOX CHURCH. He was brought to trial by the church in 1914 for his nonconformist religious views and was only saved from sentencing by the onset of the Russian REVOLUTION. He was expelled from his post as a professor of philosophy at Moscow University and from the USSR in 1922. A prolific writer, he emphasized freedom, creativity and the reality of the TRANSCENDENT. He is often referred to as a CHRISTIAN EXISTENTIALIST. His books include *The Destiny of Man* (1933), *Freedom and the Spirit* (1935) and *The Beginning and the End* (1952).

BERG, David "Moses" (1919): known as "Mo" to his followers, he was founder of the infamous CHILDREN OF GOD. Berg began as a PENTECOSTAL preacher, but his spiritual REVELATIONS and PROPHECIES led him further and further from ORTHODOXY. In his writings he claims to have received "revelations" from a host of spiritual BEINGS, including "The Abominable Snowman" and "The Pied Piper," which led him to advocate polygamy, sexual recruitment of new members—

known as "flirty fishing"—and various other questionable sexual practices.

BERGER, Peter L. (1934-): American-Austrian SOCIOLOGIST who is best known for his work on the social construction of reality. Many of his ideas have been misinterpreted to imply RELATIVISM, which Berger strongly denies. His best-known works are *Invitation to Sociology* (1963), *The Social Construction of Reality* (1966) with Thomas Luckmann, and *The Social Reality of Religion* (1967). More recently he has written *The War Against the Family* (1984), in collaboration with his wife, Brigitte Berger, and various books on RELIGION, economics and social theory such as *Pyramids of Sacrifice* (1974).

BERGSON, Henri Louis (1859-1941): French philosopher whose theories of COSMIC EVOLUTION have inspired various religious thinkers and contributed to the growth of PROCESS THEOLOGY. His best-known philosophical work is *Creative Evolution* (1907).

BERKELEY, George (1685-1753): Irish CLERGYMAN and philosopher of a theistic IDEALISM. He was the author of *A Treatise Concerning the Principles of Human Knowledge* (1710).

BERNARD OF CLAIRVAUX (1090-1153): French CISTERCIAN MONK and AB-BOT of Clairvaux. His book *Loving God* is regarded as a classic of medieval MYSTICISM. He praised knighthood and supported both the Order of Templars and the Second Crusade. In his time he was probably the most influential figure in Europe.

BERNADETTE OF LOURDES (1844-1879): a French peasant who at age fourteen claimed to have received many visions of the VIRGIN MARY. Her visions led to the establishment of a SHRINE at LOURDES where many people claim to have received miraculous HEALING.

BESANT, Annie (1847-1933): born in London of EVANGELICAL parents, she married a pious but dull CLERGYMAN whom she eventually divorced. Her religious PILGRIMAGE led from ANGLICANISM to ATHEISM, and from SPIRITUALISM to THEOSOPHISM. In England she was notorious for her affair with Charles BRADLAUGH and her promotion of radical causes, including birth control. After her CONVERSION to theosophy, in 1889 she moved to India where she established a number of educational institutions, including the Central Hindu College of Banaras (1898) and the University of India (1907). She played an important role in agitating for Indian independence from British rule and was active in the Indian National Congress and even elected its president. She proclaimed her adopted son Jiddu KRISHNAMURTI a new Messiah, but he later repudiated this view. After the death of Helena BLAVATSKY she became the president of the THEOSOPHICAL SOCIETY. Her works include *The Ancient Wisdom* (1897) and *The Religious Problems of India* (1902).

BETHEL: a town and center of worship in ancient Israel whose name comes from a Hebrew word meaning "the house of GOD."

BETHLEHEM: the city of the biblical figure King David and birthplace of JESUS.

BEZA, Theodore (1519-1605): author of the first critical edition of the text of the NEW TESTAMENT and an important CALVINIST theologian.

BHAGAVAD-GĪTA: literally translated "The Song of the Lord." Probably the most popular book of HINDU SCRIPTURE in the West. In context it forms part of the great Indian EPIC, the MAHĀBHĀRATA, which is usually dated somewhere between 200 B.C. and A.D. 200, although no manuscript copies exist from before the sixteenth century A.D. For many modern Hindus it represents the ESSENCE of their religion with its message that there are many ways to SALVATION. It consists of a long dialogue between the hero ARJUNA and his chariot driver who, unknown to Arjuna, is really the Lord KRISHNA in human form. On the eve of the battle of Kuruksetra, Arjuna has scruples about the prospect of killing his fellow humans, some of whom are his kinsmen, but he is told by Krishna that he must perform his duty in a disinterested way appropriate to his CASTE as a warrior. The BUDDHIST scholar Edward CONZE and others have argued that the DEVOTIONAL tone of the *Gīta* reflects the influence of CHRISTIANITY and that it was probably written to counter Christian teachings.

BHAKTI: this term means devotion; it denotes movements within Indian RELIGIONS, especially HINDUISM, which emphasize the love of GOD or the gods. Bhakti is the loving submission of the believer to the DEITY as a means of GRACE and SALVATION. The HARE KRISHNA MOVEMENT is probably the best-known Bhakti movement in the West.

BHATTA: a title of respect for a BRAHMIN.

BHUTAS: an EVIL spirit in HINDUISM.

BIBLE: the SACRED book of CHRISTIANS comprising the HEBREW BIBLE and NEW TESTAMENT.

BIBLICAL CRITICISM: a type of academic inquiry which arose in the nineteenth century through the application of eighteenth-century RATIONALIST assumptions to the study of the BIBLE. It originated with anti-CHRISTIAN writers who sought to discredit the biblical text by ridiculing it on the basis of arguments derived from a Newtonian WORLDVIEW and DEISTIC ETHICS. More sympathetic scholars developed biblical criticism to accommodate CHRISTIANITY to the Newtonian worldview by explaining away biblical references to PROPHECY, MIRACLES and the SUPERNATURAL on literary and textual grounds. Eventually even orthodox scholars accepted the validity of many critical methods for answering such questions as: "What are the most reliable and trustworthy texts of the HEBREW BIBLE and NEW TESTAMENT? What is the relationship between the various books? When and by whom were the texts written and for what purpose? What sources, if any, did the authors use? What is the relationship of these sources to other oral and written material of the time?" Biblical criticism today is understood as the application of general historical principles and RATIONALIST assumptions to the Bible and has evolved into various subdisciplines such as redaction criticism, source criticism, FORM CRITICISM and literary criticism. In recent years CONSERVATIVE scholars have increasingly made use of various forms of biblical criticism, although traditionally they have made a distinction between "higher criticism" which they see as essentially rationalistic and "lower criticism" which is understood as a legitimate quest for textual purity.

BIORHYTHMS: a fad of the 1970s which sought to find links between human emotional changes, physical well-being and a rhythmic cycle in nature. The idea goes back to a nineteenth-century physician Wilhelm Fliess whose work was popularized by George S. Thommen in the late 1960s and 1970s. There seems to be no scientific basis for this view, and it is rapidly losing popularity through its failure to actually help people cope with living.

BISHOP: literally an "overseer." From as early as the second century A.D. bishops formed part of an organizational hierarchy in CHRISTIANITY. IGNATIUS, one of the Church Fathers, speaks of bishops, PRESBYTERS and DEACONS as forming the structure of AUTHORITY in the CHURCH. Originally each church seems to have had its own bishop. Later on bishops came to control a specific territory or DIOCESE, and then ARCHBISHOPS and eventually the POPE were added by the Western Church. In the East, bishops retained much of their earlier status and powers. Bishops had the power to ordain PRIESTS and were the guardians of ORTHODOXY.

BLACK FRIARS: a common name for members of the Dominican Order derived from their black hood.

BLACK MASS: a blasphemous RITUAL enactment of the MASS used by SATANIC groups.

BLACK MUSLIMS: a remarkably successful new religious movement which began as a CULT and developed into an orthodox branch of ISLAM in North America. The group was founded by Wallace D. FARD (or Wali Farad Muhammad) around 1930 and originally preached a race war against whites in which blacks were to be aided by spacemen. Under the able leadership of Elijah Muhammad and his successors the group has become increasingly Islamic and has reached out to embrace the MUSLIM world. Today it is a fast-growing movement with an impressive record of social action among American blacks. The most famous member of the movement was Malcolm X, who was assassinated in 1965.

BLACK THEOLOGY: a form of LIBERATION THEOLOGY but grounded in the realities of black life rather than in Marxist analysis. It was popularized by James Cone in his book *Black Theology and Black Power* (1969), which sought to express CHRISTIAN THEOLOGY in terms of the experience of black Americans. The publication of Mokgethi Motlhabi, ed., *Essays on Black Theology* (1972), which includes an essay by Cone, marks the beginning of the black theology movement in Africa. Subsequently South Africa produced many of the best black theologians. Steve Biko's *I Write What I Like* (1978), Desmond Tutu's *Hope and Suffering* (1983) and Alan Boesak's *Black and Reformed* (1984) are well known. The works of some important lesser-known writers are found in Itumeleng J. Mosala and Buti Tlhagale, eds., *The Unquestionable Right to Be Free* (1986), which should be read alongside Simon Maimela, *Proclaim Freedom to My People* (1987).

BLAKE, William (1757-1827): English poet and MYSTIC whose writings were inspirational to the COUNTERCULTURE of the 1960s.

BLASPHEMY: action or speech which is derogatory to GOD, the SACRED or RELIGION. In the HEBREW BIBLE and in ISLAMIC lands blasphemy is a capital offense. Until the ENLIGHTENMENT it was severely punished in Europe and America.

BLAVATSKY, Helena Petrovna (1831-1891): born and educated in Russia, she appears to have led an adventurous life with numerous affairs. She became a SPIRITUALIST in New York in the 1870s. Claiming to have visited Tibet and India, she elaborated on the basic practices of spiritualism by adding a rich ECLECTIC mythology (*see* MYTH). Eventually she called her system THEOSOPHY and formed the THEOSOPHICAL SOCIETY in 1875. Her most important books are *Isis Unveiled* (1877) and *The Secret Doctrine* (1888).

BLIK: a term used by R. M. Hare, an English philosopher, to describe a religious stance, outlook or basic PRESUPPOSITION.

BLOCH, Ernst (1880-1959): German Marxist philosopher whose work strongly influenced theologians Jürgen Moltmann and Harvey Cox. His major works are *The Spirit of Utopia* (1918) and *Thomas Munzer as Theologian of Revolution* (1921).

BOAS, Franz (1858-1942): a German-American Jew who is considered one of the founders of ANTHROPOLOGY. He pioneered the techniques of fieldwork among the Kwakiutl of British Columbia. His works include *The Social Organization and Secret Societies of the Kwakiutl Indians* (1897), *The Mind of the Primitive* (1911) and *Kwakiutl Ethnography* (1966).

BODHI: Indian term for spiritual "ENLIGHTENMENT" or "awakening," which takes on particular meaning in BUDDHISM.

BODHI TREE: the traditional tree under which GAUTAMA—the BUDDHA—received ENLIGHTENMENT.

BODHISATTVA: SANSKRIT term used in BUDDHISM for one who aspires to BODHI or Buddhahood. In the MAHĀYĀNA TRADITION the idea is developed to replace the term ĀRHANT as the Buddhist ideal, and the Bodhisattva becomes a SAVIOR figure who forgoes ENLIGHTENMENT to bring SALVATION to all sentient beings.

BODIN, Jean (1530-1596): French ROMAN

CATHOLIC political philosopher and theorist whose work legitimating monarchy and political absolutism provided a basis for various DIVINE RIGHT theories. His main works are *Method for the Easy Comprehension of History* (1566) and *Six Books of the Republic* (1576).

BODYWORK: a popular NEW AGE expression referring to massage and various other techniques associated with holistic health.

BOEHME, Jacob (1575-1624): German LUTHERAN MYSTIC whose speculations about GOD and his relationship to CREATION drew upon NEOPLATONISM, the Jewish CABBALA and ALCHEMY and were expressed in his *The Way to Christ* (1624). He has been accused of being both a PANTHEIST and a DUALIST, but his work influenced PIETISM, ROMANTICISM and modern NEW AGE mystical movements, as well as the writings of William LAW and Isaac NEWTON.

BOETHIUS, Ancius Maniatus Severinus (A.D. 480-524): Roman CHRISTIAN philosopher executed by the ARIAN Emperor Theodoric. His most influential work, written while in prison awaiting execution, was a vindication of divine PROVIDENCE: *The Consolation of Philosophy*.

BONAVENTURE (1217-1274): ROMAN CATHOLIC mystical theologian whose childhood religious experience, associated with a VISION of FRANCIS OF ASSISI, led him to a religious life and a MYSTICISM founded on DOGMA, moral THEOLOGY and contemplative PRAYER. His works include *The Seven Journeys of Eternity* and *The Journey of the Mind to God*.

BONHOEFFER, Dietrich (1906-1946): German CONSERVATIVE LUTHERAN theologian whose opposition to the Nazi regime led to his brutal execution. He is the author of *The Cost of Discipleship* (1937) and *Letters and Papers from Prison* (1951).

BONIFACE (680-754): MISSIONARY to the Germans whose courage in felling the SACRED oak tree of Thor at Geismar won him a considerable following. After establishing a thriving CHURCH in Germany he was martyred in Friesland in what is now the northern part of the Netherlands.

BONNET, Charles (1720-1793): Swiss naturalist and philosopher who developed a theory of vitalism and an evolutionary philosophy (*see* EVOLUTION).

BOOK OF COMMON PRAYER: one of the classics of Christian LITURGY, originally written by Archbishop CRANMER to provide services in English for the CHURCH OF ENGLAND. It contains many memorable phrases such as "Dust to dust, ashes to ashes," and has had a profound influence on the development of the English language.

BOOK OF LIFE: an idea found in Egyptian, HEBREW, CHRISTIAN and ISLAMIC sources that GOD, or the gods, keeps a record of human activities which he will bring forth on the day of JUDGMENT.

BOOK OF THE DEAD: in Egyptian and Tibetan religious traditions, a book of MAGICAL texts which was placed in the grave alongside the corpse to secure blessing in the afterlife.

BOOTH, William (1829-1912): a native of Nottingham of Jewish parentage, he converted to METHODISM in 1844 to become a REVIVALIST preacher. In 1861 he left the Methodists and, with the help of his wife, Catherine Booth, who was also a powerful preacher, established his own Christian MISSION which became the SALVATION ARMY and was noted for its revivalist preaching and social concern. His book *In Darkest England and the Way Out* (1890) drew a vivid picture of social evil and decay.

BORN AGAIN: to become a CHRISTIAN; to be converted (see CONVERSION). The term is based on a dialogue of JESUS recorded in chapter three of the Gospel of John.

BOURGEOIS: the solid citizen whose mode of life is at once stable and solvent. The earliest adverse meanings show an aristocratic contempt for the middle class and a PHILOSOPHICAL and intellectual disdain for their ideas. MARX attacked what he called the "bourgeois political theory" which was based on CONCEPTS and institutions considered UNIVERSAL. He argued they were merely the concepts and institutions of a specifically bourgeois society.

BRACKETING: a term used in PHENOMENOLOGY to designate the practice of attempting to lay aside one's own presuppositions and experiences. In RELIGIOUS STUDIES it is common to ask students to "bracket," i.e., temporarily to lay aside their own BELIEFS while attempting to understand the beliefs of others.

BRADLAUGH, Charles (1833-1891): freethinker and follower of Thomas PAINE. He made a name for himself as a lecturer under the title of "iconoclast" and became president of the London SECULAR SOCIETY (1858-1890). From 1860 he ran the periodical *National Reformer* in defense of free thinking, and in 1880 he was elected a member of parliament for Northampton. In his last years he was actively interested in promoting social and political REFORM in India and attended the Indian National Congress of 1889. He disassociated himself from Annie BESANT after she became a theosophist. His works include *The Bible: What It Is* (1861).

BRADLEY, Francis Herbert (1846-1924): English philosopher and advocate of ABSOLUTE IDEALISM who opposed UTILITARIANISM. His book *Appearance and Reality* (1893) has been described as the most original English work on METAPHYSICS in the nineteenth century.

BRAHE, Tycho (1546-1601): Danish astronomer noted for his work in confirming the Copernican (*see* COPERNICUS) view of the UNIVERSE. He subsequently modified his early ideas.

BRAHMĀ: CREATOR GOD in HINDUISM often associated with VISHNU and Śiva. Brahmā is not mentioned in the VEDIC HYMNS where Prajāpati is the creator god. Brahmā is the masculine word for the neuter BRAHMAN or SACRED power which is ultimate REALITY. Although VISHNU and

Śiva are worshiped, there is no CULT of Brahmā as an object of BHAKTI or devotion.

BRAHMA SŪTRA: the basic texts of the VEDĀNTA tradition within HINDUISM. They were probably composed in the second or third century A.D. and are traditionally ascribed to Bādarāyaṇa. These texts expound the UPANISHADS. They were used extensively by ŚANKARA, RĀMĀNUJA and MĀDHAVA to develop their theologies, and they provide the basic non-DUALISM of modern Vedānta.

BRAHMACĀRIN: first of the four stages of life for an orthodox HINDU. It is the life of the young student who must remain celibate.

BRAHMAN: a neuter term which refers to the MAGICAL or SACRED power implicit in the RITUAL SACRIFICES of VEDIC RELIGION. It forms the basis of the word Brāhmana or BRAHMIN which refers to the PRIESTLY class that performed the sacred rituals. In some UPANISHADS Brahman is identified with the UNIVERSE, but in others he is regarded as a personal GOD, or identified with ĀTMAN or the eternal self within men. Within medieval Hindu theology there were various disputes about the true nature of Brahman. The most important were between ŚANKARA, who denied personal attributes, and RĀMĀNUJA, who treated Brahman in a highly personalized manner.

BRĀHMAṆAS: a collection of prose works giving instruction on sacrifice which were appended to the VEDIC HYMNS.

BRAHMINS: priestly caste within HINDUISM. This is the anglicized form of the SANSKRIT BRĀHMAṆA, meaning "one endowed with Brahman," that is, with sacred power derived from sacrificial ritual. They were the highest of the four varnas—or CASTES—of Vedic society and retain high status even today.

BRĀHMO SAMĀJ: a HINDU reform movement founded by RAM MOHAN RAY in 1828. It developed a unitarian theology (*see*

UNITARIANISM) influenced by British UTIL-ITARIANISM and was strongly opposed to such things as TEMPLE CULTS, suttee (or SATI) and the CASTE system. The movement fostered Western education and sought to renew Indian society using European principles.

BRAINWASHING: a term first used by an American journalist, Edward Hunter, in his book *Brain-washing in Red China* (1951) to describe techniques used by Chinese Communists to overcome the resistance of their ideological opponents. The term was also popularized by Robert J. Lifton in his book *Thought Reform and the Psychology of Totalism*, where he examined the application of psychological and physical pressure by Chinese Communists to American prisoners of war during the Korean War. It was applied to religion as a theory explaining CHRISTIAN CONVERSION by London University psychiatrist William SARGANT in his book *Battle for the Mind* (1957) in the wake of the Billy GRAHAM Crusade in London. Sargant concentrated on biblical accounts of conversion and the work of John WESLEY using the theories of PAVLOV to discredit religious experience. When the book first appeared it was attacked by such prominent Christians as the physician-preacher Martyn LLOYD-JONES in *Conversions: Psychological and Spiritual* (1958) as "extremely dangerous." But in the early 1970s Sargant's ideas were picked up by the American ANTI-CULT MOVEMENT and popularized in such books as *Snapping* by Flo Conway and Jim Seigelman.

BRANHAM, William Marion, "Bill" (1909-1966): REVIVALIST preacher who popularized PENTECOSTALISM and HEALING ministries in America. His crusades developed into "prophetic" events which led him in his later years to see himself as a PROPHET. His influence has been recognized as a factor in the emergence of the CHARISMATIC MOVEMENT.

BREATHING CONTROL: an essential aspect of YOGA and other meditation practices within YOGIC RELIGIONS.

BRETHREN OF THE COMMON LIFE: a ROMAN CATHOLIC association founded in the fourteenth century to promote SPIRITUALITY and education of LAYMEN.

BRIGHT, William Rohl, "Bill" (1921-): the founder and president of CAMPUS CRUSADE FOR CHRIST. He was strongly influenced by Henrietta MEARS and after studying at Princeton and Fuller Theological Seminaries became an EVANGELIST in 1947. His decision to found Campus Crusade followed a VISION of CHRIST. He is the author of numerous books and other publications, including *Come Help Change the World* (1979).

BRITISH ISRAELITISM: a form of FUNDAMENTALISM, originating in the eighteenth century, which claimed that the English people were the descendants of the ten "Lost Tribes" of ISRAEL and therefore heirs to all the biblical promises made in the BIBLE to the Jewish people. Today the most common form of this BELIEF is to be found in its Americanized version preached by Herbert W. ARMSTRONG and the WORLDWIDE CHURCH OF GOD.

BRUNNER, Emil (1889-1966): Swiss theologian and one of the most influential Christian scholars of the interwar years. He parted company with Karl BARTH in the 1930s over the issue of NATURAL THEOLOGY, which Barth repudiated and Brunner accepted. His early thought was influenced by CHRISTIAN SOCIALISM. His book *The Mediator* (1927) was the first presentation of the DOCTRINE of CHRIST in terms of dialectical theology (see NEO-ORTHODOXY). Brunner saw the gospel as an exposition of the first commandment and was deeply influenced by both KIERKEGAARD'S dialectic and Martin BUBER'S "I-THOU" CONCEPT. He regarded SCRIPTURE as somehow normative, though not above criticism, and REVELATION as always indirect. Unlike Barth, he believed in an already existing point of contact between the gospel and non-Christian people.

BRUNO (1032-1101): founder of the

ROMAN CATHOLIC Carthusian Order (1084).

BRUNO, Giordano (1548-1600): Italian Dominican PRIEST and theologian who developed a PANTHEISTIC view of the universe based on the Copernican theory (see COPERNICUS). He was burnt at the stake for HERESY.

BUBER, Martin (1878-1965): Jewish philosopher and theologian who did much to bring about a Jewish intellectual RENAISSANCE in Central Europe in the 1920s. Influenced by KANT, NIETZSCHE and KIERKEGAARD drew upon the Jewish HASIDIC TRADITION with its DOCTRINE that GOD is to be found in everything and everything in God and that the created world is to be redeemed rather than escaped. His most famous work is the poem-essay I and Thou (1923-1937), which influenced many Christian thinkers, including Paul TILLICH and Gabriel MARCEL.

BUCER, Martin (1491-1551): German Dominican who became a follower of LUTHER and a leader of the PROTESTANT REFORMATION in Switzerland. In 1549 he became professor of theology at Cambridge, England. His THEOLOGY of the EUCHARIST mediated between that of LUTHER and ZWINGLI.

BUCHMAN, Frank Nathan Daniel (1878-1961): American Lutheran minister, CHRISTIAN MYSTIC and EVANGELIST who was strongly influenced by the KESWICK CONVENTION and in 1938 founded Moral Re-Armament, a movement to promote moral awareness and world peace.

BUDDHA: a title in BUDDHISM which means an ENLIGHTENED being. Just as the title CHRIST has become a name for JESUS, so the title Buddha has become associated with GAUTAMA.

BUDDHAGHOSA (4th-5th century A.D.): THERAVĀDA BUDDHIST MONK and scholar who lived in Ceylon (modern Sri Lanka) and is famous for his commentaries on the PALI CANON of Buddhist SCRIPTURES and a compendium of Buddhist thought known as the *Visuddhimagga*, or "Path of Purification."

BUDDHISM: the Western name for the RELIGION of the BUDDHA, known in Asia as the Buddha-Śasana, or path of discipleship. Buddhism appears to have originated in modern Nepal in the sixth century B.C. and according to TRADITION was the result of the religious experience of a young prince and son of a ruler of the Śakya tribe, GAUTAMA (GOTAMA), whose personal name was SIDDHARTHA. His spiritual insight, or ENLIGHTENMENT, occurred at a place now known as Bodh-Gayā, on the banks of one of the southern tributaries of the Ganges. He began to preach the DHARMA, a set of DOCTRINES which analyzes the human condition. Concentrating on the human situation, personal existence and the nature of personality he argued that the basic characteristic of existence is radical suffering. Once the truth of existence is recognized, the Dharma provides a means whereby the radical suffering which characterizes mortal life may be transcended by breaking the bonds of KARMA to free the sufferer, or sentient being, from the WHEEL OF EXISTENCE, or SAMSARA.

The Buddha's example and preaching attracted disciples who were subsequently organized into MONASTIC communities known as the SAṄGHA. The Buddha taught that speculation about the gods or a CREATOR was worthless because even the gods were bound by the bonds of karma. A formal priesthood with sacrificial rituals and other functions was rejected in favor of the quest for enlightenment. At the time of its origin the movement was regarded by contemporary HINDU priests, or BRAHMINS, as HERETICAL, and in many discourses (Sutta) the Buddha is presented in controversy with BRAHMINS. The community founded by the Buddha appears to have had egalitarian tendencies which rejected the Indian CASTE system, although information about this is highly speculative.

Buddhism is distinguished from most

other religions in that it has no place for a god or gods and in its denial of the soul, or permanent aspect of human personality. The earliest Buddhist inscriptions date from the reign of Aśoka in the fourth century B.C. The earliest extant Buddhist documents date from the seventh century A.D.

BUDDHIST SCHOOLS OF THOUGHT: a large number of distinct Buddhist groups exist throughout the world. The first major split in the SANGHA is traditionally dated to the Council of Vaiśālī about 100 years after the death of the BUDDHA in 383 B.C. Disagreement arose concerning the way monastic discipline was to be observed. The dissenting movement, the Mahāsaṃghikas—the Great Saṅgha Party, claimed the most followers for its lenient interpretation of the monastic requirements. The Sthaviras, or Elders, took a more strict or CONSERVATIVE position. They later divided into eighteen different schools, the most important being THERAVĀDAN BUDDHISM. The Mahāsaṃghikas also fragmented and eventually evolved into MAHĀYĀNA BUDDHISM which developed out of the Mahāsaṃghikas tradition. The MĀDHYAMIKA and YOGĀCĀRAS were the two main Mahāyāna traditions in India. In China and Japan the Mahāyāna developed into further schools, the most important being the T'ien-t'ai or TENDAI, the CH'AN or ZEN, the Chên-yen or SHINGON, PURE LAND and NICHIREN Buddhism.

BULTMANN, Rudolf (1884-1976): from 1921 until 1951 professor of NEW TESTAMENT studies at Marburg. Bultmann further developed the method of FORM CRITICISM as a radical methodological SKEPTICISM. With this historical skepticism he combined dialectical theology (see NEO-ORTHODOXY) and the LUTHERAN DOCTRINE of *sola fide* (faith alone) to create an EPISTEMOLOGY that separated HISTORY and FAITH. In his later work he developed a program of DEMYTHOLOGIZING the New Testament in terms of the existentialist

PHILOSOPHY of Martin HEIDEGGER. His works were numerous and highly influential, including *The History of the Synoptic Tradition* (1921), *Jesus Christ and Mythology* (1960) and *Theology of the New Testament* (1952 and 1955 vols. 1 and 2).

BUNYAN, John (1628-1688): one of the greatest influences on popular CHRISTIAN PIETY of all time. A PURITAN preacher and writer, he was frequently imprisoned for his radical religious and political beliefs. While in prison he wrote *Grace Abounding* (1666), *The Pilgrim's Progress* (1678) and *The Holy War* (1682). These classic works have been translated into many languages and have had a significant effect on popular religious and political movements throughout the world.

BUREAUCRACY: derived from "bureaucratie," a French word meaning "bureau," "writing-desk" or "office." Max WEBER developed the term technically to refer to a system of managerial control. In the SOCIOLOGY OF RELIGION the role of bureaucracy is used to explain the process by which the original enthusiasm of a new religious movement, often based on a charismatic leader (see CHARISMA), is transformed into a formalized—and often dead—religious organization.

BURIAL: the practice of laying the dead in the ground rather than disposing of their bodies by CREMATION, exposure or some other means of rapid destruction. It is the traditional means of disposing of the dead in CHRISTIANITY and remains the only acceptable method in ISLAM because of beliefs associated with the RESURRECTION of the dead.

BURKE, Edmund (1729-1797): Anglo-Irish orator and founder of British CONSERVATISM who supported the American REVOLUTION and opposed SLAVERY. His best-known work is *Reflections on the French Revolution* (1790) which is a telling critique of revolutionary DOCTRINES based on a traditional CHRISTIAN ANTHROPOLOGY.

BURNS, Robert (1759-1796): national poet of Scotland whose poetry is highly skeptical and reflects ENLIGHTENMENT VALUES.

BUSHIDŌ: the way of the SAMURAI; a moral discipline and controlled life based on the SHINTŌ religion in Japan.

BUSHNELL, Horace (1802-1876): American CONGREGATIONALIST minister and theologian who argued in *Christian Nurture* (1874) that Christian CONVERSION is a result of education and upbringing in an environment of Christian community and not of sudden religious experience. In *The Vicarious Sacrifice* (1866) he argued for a moral-influence view of the ATONEMENT, in which the death of Christ was an illustration of the eternal principle of love rather than a satisfaction by which GOD was reconciled to humankind.

BUTLER, Joseph (1692-1752): English philosopher and ANGLICAN BISHOP who deplored "enthusiasm." His book *The Analogy of Religion* (1736) is a profound attack on DEISM and a thorough refutation of deistic views.

BYZANTIUM: Greek city founded 667 B.C. at the entrance to the Bosphorus. It became the "New Rome" of CONSTANTINE in A.D. 330 and after that date was called Constantinople. In 1453 it fell to the Turks and became known as Istanbul. Byzantium has come to be identified with the civilization developed by the EASTERN ORTHODOX CHURCH and has taken on semi-MYSTICAL connotations.

C

CABBALA: a medieval Jewish mystical system (*see* MYSTICISM) based on the HEBREW BIBLE but drawing on Platonism (*see* PLATO) and a variety of philosophical traditions. The major written source is known as the *Zohar*.

CADDY, Elaine (1917-): Egyptian-born English OCCULTIST and first wife of Peter CADDY. In 1953 she had a mystical experience (*see* MYSTICISM) in GLASTONBURY which led her to become a CHANNELER. In 1957 she helped establish the FINDHORN COMMUNITY which she continues to lead. She claims to be in constant communication with NATURE SPIRITS such as the god Pan and is important as a leader of the NEOPAGAN MOVEMENT.

CADDY, Peter (1917-): English OCCULTIST strongly influenced by THEOSOPHY who cofounded the FINDHORN COMMUNITY in the mid-1960s. He later divorced his wife, Elaine, who had acted as his CHANNELER, and moved to Mount Shasta, California, where he founded the Gathering of the Ways Center modeled after Findhorn.

CALENDAR: most traditional religions follow a liturgical calendar (*see* LITURGY). In ISLAM a lunar calendar is used to set the dates and times for religious festivals such as RAMADĀN; in CHRISTIANITY the fixed Gregorian calendar is used. There are differences in usage between Western and Eastern churches resulting in different dates for CHRISTMAS and EASTER. The purpose of a religious calendar is to instill in the minds of people the great events of a RELIGION by the repetition of religious acts and ceremonies spread throughout the year. Thus in Christianity there is ADVENT, or the time preceding the birth of JESUS, when the prophecies of the HEBREW BIBLE are remembered, followed by Christmas, which celebrates Jesus' birth. This leads on to LENT, when Jesus' temptations and earthly life are remembered, and then Easter, a time for meditation upon his DEATH and RESURRECTION. Finally, there is PENTECOST—or WHITSUN—when the ASCENSION and heavenly reign of CHRIST come into focus. Liturgical churches have also added various SAINTS' days to commemorate the life and death of outstanding CHRISTIANS.

CALIPH: the title given to the successor of MUHAMMAD, ABŪ BAKR, as the secular leader of ISLAM. The CALIPHATE has remained an important office in the SUNNĪ sect, but it is rejected by the SHI'ITES.

CALIPHATE: that aspect of ISLAM which recognizes a monarch who is seen as uniting the religious and SECULAR realms under his rule. The Ottoman Empire abolished the caliphate in 1924.

CALLAWAY, Henry (1817-1890): converted from QUAKERISM by the writings of F. D. MAURICE, Callaway trained as a medical doctor before becoming an ANGLICAN minister and missionary to Natal where he served under BISHOP COLENSO. As a MISSIONARY he opposed Colenso's views on POLYGAMY, arguing that, however fine in theory, the practice was demeaning to women. His sympathy for AFRICAN RELIGIONS is evident in his many writings, the best known of which are *Nursery Tales, Traditions, and Histories of the Zulus* (1868) and *The Religious System of the Ama-Zulu* (1870). Passionately interested in COMPARATIVE RELIGION, his contribution to religious studies has yet to be fully appreciated.

CALVIN, John (1509-1564): after LUTHER, Calvin is the greatest of the PROTESTANT REFORMERS and one of the most important CHRISTIAN theologians of all time. As a result of his CONVERSION and the influence of LUTHER he fled from France, arriving at Geneva in 1536. There he published the first edition of his *Institutes of the Christian Religion* (1536), the first systematic theological defense of the REFORMATION. In his consistently biblical theology the idea of the sovereignty, honor and glory of GOD is paramount. Calvin's influence spread throughout Switzerland to the French HUGUENOTS, the Dutch, the Scottish PRESBYTERIANS and the English PURITANS.

CALVINISM: originated with John CALVIN'S interpretation and exposition of SCRIPTURE found in his *Institutes of the Christian Religion* (1536). It emphasizes the sovereignty of GOD in SALVATION and was later closely associated with PURITANISM. The Five Points of Calvinism, referred to by the acronym "Tulip," were drawn up in response to ARMINIANISM. They are (1) TOTAL DEPRAVITY; (2) unconditional ELECTION; (3) limited ATONEMENT; (4) irresistible GRACE; (5) the perseverance of the saints. PRESBYTERIANS, various REFORMED churches, ANGLICANS and some BAPTIST CHURCHES have been strongly influenced by Calvinism as a theological system.

CALVINIST: someone who accepts the teaching of CALVINISM.

CAMBRIDGE PLATONISTS: a THEOLOGICAL movement which flourished at the University of Cambridge in the seventeenth century and advocated religious TOLERATION.

CAMPBELL, Alexander (1788-1866): born and educated in Ireland, he was the founder of the American restorationist movement known as the DISCIPLES OF CHRIST. His teachings, found in his magazines *The Christian Baptist* (1823-1830) and *The Millennial Harbinger* (1830-1866) and books like *The Christian System* (1839), gave birth to various CHURCHES OF CHRIST.

CAMPBELL, Joseph (1904-1987): American OCCULTIST and college teacher whose prolific but confused ideas about MYTHOLOGY made him a CULT figure for the COUNTERCULTURE of the 1960s and later for the NEW AGE MOVEMENT.

CAMPUS CRUSADE FOR CHRIST INTERNATIONAL: an EVANGELICAL CHRISTIAN EVANGELISTIC organization founded in 1951 by Bill BRIGHT as a means of spreading the gospel throughout the world, particularly on college campuses. Its popular booklet *Have You Heard of the Four Spiritual Laws?* gives the organization a simplistic image which fails to do full justice to its complex and innovative character. Campus Crusade has been a pioneer in Eastern European evangelism and various "covert" operations such as the founding of the Berkeley Christian Coalition, an organization connected to the JESUS MOVEMENT, in the 1960s.

CAMUS, Albert (1913-1960): French EXISTENTIALIST author, whose book *The Rebel* (1951) is a profound analysis of modern SOCIETY and the predicament of modern people living in a world without GOD.

CANAAN: the "promised land" of ancient JUDAISM which is identified with modern ISRAEL.

CANAANITES: a word of uncertain origin referring to a biblical people who occupied CANAAN before the arrival of either the PHILISTINES or the HEBREWS, who displaced them through armed conflict. They worshiped a variety of GODS, including BAAL, and probably practiced cultic prostitution and human sacrifice.

CANON: from the Greek meaning a "list," "rule" or "measure." It has come to mean an authoritative or officially received text. Christians refer to the collection of the books of the Bible as the CANON OF SCRIPTURE.

CANON LAW: a CHRISTIAN legal system regulating the conduct of the CHURCH. It has particular force within ROMAN CATHOLICISM.

CANON OF SCRIPTURE: those books of the BIBLE which are accepted as authoritative by a given religious tradition. ROMAN CATHOLICS include several books, known as the APOCRYPHA, which are not accepted as authoritative by PROTESTANTS, who generally restrict the canon to the thirty-three books of the OLD TESTAMENT and twenty-seven books of the NEW TESTAMENT. JUDAISM usually distinguishes between the first five books of MOSES, the *TORAH*, and the other books of the HEBREW BIBLE which are seen as of secondary importance, making a further division between the PROPHETS and the remaining books called the Writings. In ISLAM the QUR'ĀN is by definition canonical, leaving arguments about authenticity to questions about the ḤADĪTH. BUDDHISM recognizes several canons, such as the PALI CANON, based on the language of the text, but in general has a very flexible attitude toward such issues, as does HINDUISM where again there is a vast religious literature.

CANONIZATION: the practice of certain churches, especially the ROMAN CATHOLIC CHURCH, of declaring a deceased person to have been a SAINT (*see* BEATIFICATION), thus allowing for the VENERATION of their tomb or relics.

CANTERBURY: one of the oldest centers of CHRISTIANITY in Europe. It is the seat of the ARCHBISHOP of CANTERBURY who is the head of the ANGLICAN Communion. The CATHEDRAL dates from at least 1067, and a church has existed on the site from the sixth century.

CAPITALISM: an economic system which presupposes private property as the means of production, a market economy and the division of labor. It is often referred to as "free enterprise" or "the market system." According to MARX, capitalism is a transitional stage of human HISTORY leading to the communist SOCIETY of the future. WEBER suggested that democracy in its purest form can only occur in a capitalist society and that there is a complex relationship between capitalism and RELIGION, particularly CALVINISM.

CAPPADOCIAN FATHERS: this title is given to three theologians—BASIL THE GREAT, GREGORY OF NAZIANZUS and GREGORY OF NYSSA—who played a prominent role at the COUNCIL of CONSTANTINOPLE in defeating ARIANISM.

CAPRA, Fritjof (1931-): American physicist and author of the bestselling *Tao of Physics* (1975) who became a NEW AGE GURU because of his speculations about the relationship between modern physics and YOGIC RELIGIONS.

CARDINAL: a high ecclesiastical official in the ROMAN CATHOLIC CHURCH.

CAREY, William (1761-1834): an English shoemaker whose profound religious CONVERSION led him to write *An Enquiry into the Obligations of Christians to use Means for Conversion of the Heathen* (1792). This became the manifesto of the modern MISSIONARY movement. In 1793 he went to India where, because of opposition from the British East India Company, he lived in a Danish enclave. There he learned several

Indian languages, established a printing press and began the EVANGELIZATION of the subcontinent.

CARGO CULTS: Polynesian religious movements in which the followers of a PROPHET figure are promised "cargo" when the SAVIOR arrives to free the people from oppression and usher in a new order. The term is now commonly applied to all NEW RELIGIONS where earthly prosperity seems to be a major factor in making converts.

CARLYLE, Thomas (1795-1881): Scottish essayist who popularized GOETHE and German ROMANTICISM in England and profoundly influenced EMERSON'S TRANSCENDENTALISM. After a period of initial skepticism, during which time he influenced such people as George ELIOT, he promoted a generalized SPIRITUALITY opposed to all CREEDS and traditional theologies. Profoundly reactionary, he scorned industrialization, supported SLAVERY and objected to penal reform. He strongly attacked LIBERALISM and totally rejected the UTILITARIAN philosophy of John Stuart MILL. His views were popularized through a series of histories, such as *The French Revolution* (1837), and his essays *On Heroes, Hero-Worship, and the Heroic in History* (1841). Today his influence can be felt in the ECOLOGICAL MOVEMENT and other forms of anti-MODERNISM.

CARMELITE ORDER: founded in 1155 in Palestine by St. Berthold as the "Order of Our Lady of Mount Carmel," the order traced its origins to HERMITS who lived on Mount Carmel and ultimately to ELIJAH. The Order is extremely ASCETIC, concentrating on contemplation and missionary service. Following the defeat of the Crusader states most of its members retreated to Europe where it had a significant impact on Roman Catholic SPIRITUALITY. ST. JOHN OF THE CROSS is one of the order's best-known MYSTICS.

CARNEGIE, DALE (1888-1955): American public speaker and author of the immensely popular *How to Make Friends and Influence People* (1937). His success philosophy is a combination of homespun wisdom and basic Christian principles written in the framework of pop psychology. Although not a religious writer, Carnegie had a strong influence on such people as Norman Vincent PEALE, Robert SCHULLER and promoters of the "health and wealth gospel" such as Kenneth HAGIN.

CARNELL, Edward John (1919-1967): American theologian who played a significant role in the revitalization of post-war EVANGELICALISM and the foundation of Fuller Theological Seminary. His best-known books are *An Introduction to Christian Apologetics* (1948), *Christian Commitment* (1957) and *The Burden of Søren Kierkegaard* (1965).

CAROLINGIAN REVIVAL: the revival of learning encouraged by the emperor CHARLEMAGNE in the ninth century and directed by ALCUIN, which developed schools in conjunction with MONASTERIES in Western Europe.

CARTESIAN: the name applied to both the followers and the philosophy of the French philosopher René DESCARTES. It is a RATIONALIST system based on radical doubt.

CĀRVĀKA: the principal system of philosophical MATERIALISM in the Indian tradition. It flourished in the medieval period.

CASTANEDA, Carlos (1935-): the author of *The Teachings of Don Juan: A Yanqui Way of Knowledge* (1968) and a number of other books purporting to be ANTHROPOLOGICAL accounts of a Native American religious tradition. Although awarded a Ph.D. by the University of California for his first book, many scholars have doubted the authenticity of his work and question the appropriateness of his being awarded a doctorate.

CASTE: an integral part of HINDU religion and society. The word *caste* is normally used to refer to what in India is called Jāti, the social status, which is one's inheritance at birth. In Vedic times there were four castes: BRĀHMAṆA (priests), KṢATRIYAS (warriors), VAIŚYA (merchants) and ŚŪDRAS (farmers and manual workers). Members of the first three castes were called the "TWICE-BORN" and were identified largely on the basis of their color. Over time the caste system developed into a complex web of thousands of castes which came to embrace the whole of Indian society.

CASUISTRY: the application of ethical principles to specific cases. In theological ETHICS the practice developed in the eighth century and has continued until today under the name of "situation ethics."

CATACOMBS: caves in ROME and other cities used for the burial of the dead where the EARLY CHRISTIAN CHURCH found refuge from persecution.

CATECHISM: originally it meant instruction in the CHRISTIAN FAITH but later became identified with a book or teaching manual.

CATECHUMENS: people under instruction in the CHRISTIAN FAITH as preparation for BAPTISM.

CATEGORICAL IMPERATIVE: KANT's ethical theory that the absolute MORAL LAW, known by REASON, is unconditionally binding upon all people. He contrasted this view with ethical theories based upon pragmatic or prudential grounds (*see* ETHICS).

CATEGORIES: basic divisions of thought used to classify both ideas and objects. In the PHILOSOPHY of KANT, categories are held to mold our entire experience.

CATEGORY MISTAKE: an error of logic whereby two or more unrelated things or ideas are treated as though there were a necessary connection between them when in fact there is not; e.g., "I feel pink inside."

CATHARSIS: a Greek word meaning PURIFICATION or purging. It was applied to the emotions to explain theatrical performances, music and severe crises in daily life. In RELIGION the idea is applied to LITURGY and such things as CONVERSION experiences.

CATHEDRAL: a church containing the chair or throne (*cathedra*) of the BISHOP of the DIOCESE.

CATHERINE DE MEDICI (1519-1589): queen of France and persecutor of the HUGUENOTS, she is generally held responsible for the ST. BARTHOLOMEW'S DAY MASSACRE of 1572.

CATHERINE OF GENOA (1447-1510): Italian CHRISTIAN MYSTIC and author of the classic work *Vita e dottrina* (1551). Her good works spread her fame among the common people.

CATHOLIC APOSTOLIC CHURCH: sometimes known as "Irvingites," this group was founded in England by Edward IRVING (1792-1834) and originated as a CHARISMATIC group. It soon developed liturgical aspects (*see* LITURGY) similar to ROMAN CATHOLICISM and Greek Orthodoxy (*see* ORTHODOX CHURCH) but with a strong emphasis on the imminent return of CHRIST. As a movement it had some success in the late nineteenth century before entering a period of slow decline. Today its influence is felt mostly among new religious movements in the Third World, especially Africa.

CATHOLIC: from a Greek term meaning "in general" or "on the whole." In the EARLY CHURCH it was used to express the universal nature of CHRISTIANITY and to indicate that the belief and practice of a CHURCH was such that it had been "everywhere and always accepted by all." Thus it became identified with ORTHODOXY. Today the term is often used to mean "UNIVERSAL."

CAUSATION: the cause of anything. Traditionally it was argued that every event had a cause and that the first CAUSE was GOD. HUME rejected this notion, arguing instead that we observe many apparent relationships of succession but that this does not prove causation.

CAUSE: that which occasions or is the necessary condition for a given effect.

CAYCE, Edgar (1877-1945): American

psychic whose writings provided much of the impetus for "channelling" in the NEW AGE MOVEMENT as well as promoting belief in YOGIC RELIGION and such things as REINCARNATION. After experiencing HEALING as the result of a trance, he gradually became a popular psychic reader and lecturer. In 1931 he founded the Association for Research and Enlightenment and began issuing regular newsletters. After his death, his son turned these into a series of popular books which gained a wide following.

CELIBACY: the state of remaining unmarried for religious reasons. The practice is common to MONASTIC orders, and to the priesthood of BUDDHISM and ROMAN CATHOLICISM. In these and some other religions—such as ISLAM—sexual abstinence may be stressed for married persons on special occasions and at times of FASTING and REPENTANCE.

CHALCEDON, COUNCIL OF: the fourth ECUMENICAL COUNCIL, held in A.D. 451. The council arose from a dispute about the true NATURE of CHRIST's manhood and resulted in the Definition of CHALCEDON.

CHALCEDON, DEFINITION OF: the statement of FAITH affirmed by the COUNCIL of CHALCEDON in 451. It affirms the unity of the person of JESUS CHRIST, because both his NATURES, the divine and the human, are complete. He is "perfect," being consubstantial with God and humanity. Although as God he was preexistent, as a man he was born of the VIRGIN MARY. Christ is, therefore, said to be both fully God and fully man, making it possible for him to secure SALVATION for humans by his atoning death.

CHALICE: a goblet used to hold the communion wine in the MASS and holy communion (*see* EUCHARIST) in CHRISTIAN CHURCHES.

CHALMERS, Thomas (1780-1847): Scottish theologian and EVANGELICAL preacher whose intellectual defense of Christianity was linked with a strong concern for the poor. He pioneered popular education and modern social welfare. In 1843 he helped found the Free Church of Scotland and became a professor at its theological institution, New College, Edinburgh.

CH'AN: a Chinese school of BUDDHISM which aims at the immediate awareness of REALITY through the transcendence of objectivity and subjectivity to a nonduality which is a state of BEING. This school gave rise to the Japanese school of ZEN BUDDHISM.

CHANCE: "the unforeseen." In Greek RELIGION chance (*Tychē*) was deified and eventually venerated as "GOOD fortune."

CHANDAS: the meter used in chanting HINDU SACRIFICIAL RITUALS.

CHANNELER: see TRANSCHANNELER.

CHAOS: from the Greek word meaning "gap," "gasp" or "yawn." The poet Hesiod says, "In the beginning chaos came into being." In many Mesopotamian religious traditions the world was created out of a preexisting chaos. The HEBREW BIBLE appears to deny this, and traditionally CHRISTIANS have maintained a belief in CREATIO EX NIHILO ("creation from nothing"). Today some commentators argue that GOD created out of preexisting MATTER. Such a view has important philosophic implications for the origins of EVIL and is rejected by orthodox Christians.

CHAPTER AND VERSE: the BIBLE was first divided into chapters by Archbishop Stephen Langton in the thirteenth century. Verses were added to the HEBREW BIBLE and NEW TESTAMENT by RABBI Nathan and Robert Estienne, respectively, in the fifteenth century. The expression "chapter and verse" means to give a precise account or exact description such as is given when a biblical passage is located using this technique.

CHARISMA: from the Greek meaning "favor" or "grace." It was used by the SOCIOLOGIST Max WEBER to describe the attraction of a person with a magnetic personality or great gifts of leadership such as Alexander the Great or Napoleon.

Weber then applied this idea to religious leaders as a means of explaining the appeal of people like the BUDDHA, MOSES, JESUS, PAUL or MUHAMMAD. In this way it came to refer to the personal magnetism of leaders who are able to attract a devoted following. In popular CHRISTIANITY, charisma refers to the gifts of the HOLY SPIRIT which are believed to follow the baptism of the Spirit. Such gifts would include HEALING, SPEAKING IN TONGUES (see GLOSSOLALIA) and PROPHECY.

CHARISMATIC: a CHRISTIAN who identifies with the CHARISMATIC MOVEMENT by believing in the manifestation of the gifts (e.g., healing, tongues and prophecy) of the HOLY SPIRIT in contemporary Christianity.

CHARISMATIC MOVEMENT: a religious revival movement which started in the 1950s and took form in the early 1960s, spreading PENTECOSTAL-type experiences of the gifts of the HOLY SPIRIT from Pentecostal churches to mainline DENOMINATIONS. It is associated with the work of David Du Plessis, Dennis Bennett and Demos SHAKARIAN, the founder of the FULL GOSPEL BUSINESSMEN'S FELLOWSHIP INTERNATIONAL. The charismatic movement is a worldwide phenomenon and has served to bring many non-Western cultural practices, such as the emphasis on HEALING and the idea of "PRAYER MOUNTAINS," into Western CHRISTIANITY.

CHARLEMAGNE (742-814): King of the Franks (Germanic tribe of the Rhine region) and the first HOLY ROMAN EMPEROR. His conquests greatly extended his kingdom, and he was able to stem the spread of ISLAM, and, through enlightened reforms, revive learning in Western Europe.

CHARMS: magical formulas sung, recited or sometimes written down to bring GOOD luck or ward off EVIL.

CHASTITY: many religious orders in CHRISTIANITY, BUDDHISM and other religions require their members to take vows that they will abstain from intentional sexual activity. Chastity also implies a state of mind associated with purity and the renunciation of lust.

CHESTERTON, Gilbert Keith (1874-1936): English journalist and ROMAN CATHOLIC lay theologian whose writings, such as *Orthodoxy* (1908), provided a popular defense of CHRISTIANITY against modern RATIONALISM. He is best known for his "Father Brown" detective stories.

CHIH-I (538-597): Chinese religious leader and founder of the T'IEN T'AI school of BUDDHISM. He taught the illusory nature of matter based on the notion that only mind truly exists. For him ENLIGHTENMENT was the realization of the unity of the individual's consciousness with mind itself.

CHILDREN OF GOD: a new religious movement originating in the late 1960s and subsequently called "The Family of Love." It began as part of the JESUS MOVEMENT in California and was founded by David BERG, who became known as Moses David, or "Mo." Developing CHARISMATIC gifts, the group then began to encourage PROPHECY. This practice led to various OCCULT activities and a form of SPIRITUALISM through the invocation of spiritual guides such as "the Pied Piper" who Mo claimed communicated with him. Prophesying the imminent destruction of California and the whole American system, Mo told his followers to disperse throughout the world. Espousing what it called "godly socialism," the group's main theological reference became the *Mo Letters*. The Children of God were one of the first NEW RELIGIOUS MOVEMENTS to receive the attention of the ANTICULT MOVEMENT, and its activities led directly to the development of deprogramming by Ted PATRICK. One of the most highly publicized practices of the group is the use of "flirty-fishing," which involves prostitution as a CONVERSION technique. Today it is an essentially underground movement with an estimated 2,000 members worldwide.

CHILIASM: from the Greek word meaning 1,000. Speculations about the importance of a future thousand-year golden age occur in many religious traditions such as ZOROASTRIANISM, as well as in the work of Greek philosophers such as PLATO. In CHRISTIANITY belief in the millennium takes various forms (see MILLENNIALISM), and in the common EVANGELICAL premillennial tradition believers look for the imminent return of CHRIST.

CHINESE RELIGIONS: scholars have traditionally held the view that there were three major religious TRADITIONS in China: BUDDHISM, Confucianism (see CONFUCIUS) and TAOISM. Today this view is challenged by a much more complex one which sees the Chinese religious tradition dynamically incorporating various religious traditions within Chinese religion. The cult of ANCESTORS, SHAMAN and the WORSHIP of HEAVEN are important aspects of Chinese religion, which however took differing forms as political dynasties changed.

CH'ING MING: Chinese spring festival.

CHRIST: the most common title for JESUS OF NAZARETH, derived from *Christos*, a Greek equivalent for the Hebrew *Messiah*, meaning "anointed one."

CHRISTADELPHIANS: an American SECT founded in 1848 by John Thomas (1805-1871) who believed in the imminent RETURN OF CHRIST, denied his divinity and rejected the TRINITY. In many ways this group is similar to the JEHOVAH'S WITNESSES, who were influenced by its teachings.

CHRISTIAN: a follower of Jesus Christ. EVANGELICAL THEOLOGY would narrow the reference of this term to anyone who through FAITH in the atoning DEATH of JESUS CHRIST, the incarnate Son of God (see INCARNATION) has had their SINS forgiven by GOD and been BORN AGAIN by the HOLY SPIRIT.

CHRISTIAN MINISTRY: the offices within the CHRISTIAN CHURCH whereby individuals are appointed to preach, teach and care for members of the CONGREGA-TION or Christian community.

CHRISTIAN SCIENCE: The Church of Christ Scientist was founded by Mary Baker EDDY (1821-1910), who believed she had been healed after a severe injury in 1866. She dedicated her life to promoting a form of healing based on ideas taken from CHRISTIANITY, HINDUISM and BUDDHISM. In 1875 her book *Science and Health with Key to the Scriptures* was published, and on August 23, 1879, the CHURCH OF CHRIST SCIENTIST was incorporated in Boston. Christian Science teaches a confusing synthesis of ABRAMIC and YOGIC RELIGIONS on the premise that GOD is the "Divine Principle of all that really is."

CHRISTIAN SOCIALISM: a movement which developed in nineteenth-century Britain associated with Frederick MAURICE and Charles KINGSLEY that sought to promote social reform along SOCIALIST lines developed from Christian social teachings.

CHRISTIANITY: the RELIGION founded by JESUS OF NAZARETH, propagated by the apostle PAUL and dispersed throughout the world, where it has taken many forms. The three major groupings of Christian CHURCHES have traditionally been Eastern ORTHODOX, ROMAN CATHOLIC and PROTESTANT, to which a fourth group of PENTECOSTAL and CHARISMATIC churches can now be added.

CHRISTMAS: from the fourth century CHRISTIANS have celebrated December 25 as the date of the birth of JESUS. Today in North America the public holiday has become increasingly SECULAR with concerted efforts being made to remove all religious content from public celebrations.

CHRISTOLOGY: that branch of THEOLOGY which deals with questions about the PERSON and work of CHRIST. It covers such things as his INCARNATION and the meaning of his DEATH.

CHRYSOSTOM, John (A.D. 344/345-407): around 373 he became a HERMIT but was made a DEACON in Antioch in 381 and a PRIEST in 386. His brilliant preaching led to his becoming BISHOP of Constantinople in 398, but his criticism of the morals of the Imperial Court led to his banishment in 404 and his eventual death. His sermons and biblical exegesis had a profound effect on CALVIN and other PROTESTANT REFORMERS.

CHU HSI [Chu Tzu or Chu Yuan Hui Shushi] (1130-1200): A celebrated Chinese Confucian scholar (*see* CONFUCIUS) whose writings systematized the Confucian classics. He created a unified RATIONALISTIC PHILOSOPHY which remained the orthodox Confucian view until the twentieth century.

CHUANG-TZU [Chuang Chou] (369-286 B.C.): Chinese MYSTIC and TAOIST philosopher who taught that tranquility and spontaneous natural action were the goals of life. Happiness comes from knowing one's NATURE and living in harmony with the UNIVERSE. GOOD and EVIL are relative to one's own standards. Everything is part of a universal process of transformation. Pure experience arises when the individual becomes one with the Tao in a state of ABSOLUTE FREEDOM. Although a contemporary of MENCIUS, the two do not seem to have met and do not refer to each other's writings.

CH'UN-CH'IU: one of the five Confucian classics. It is traditionally attributed to CONFUCIUS himself and is a historical narrative used for instruction to encourage goodness and right living.

CHURCH: the word used to translate the Greek word *ekklēsia* that in the NEW TESTAMENT designates the community created by the preaching of the gospel of JESUS CHRIST. Theologically, *church members* are those people who participate in BAPTISM, receive the gift of the HOLY SPIRIT, and gather together for common WORSHIP and the celebration of the EUCHARIST. Sociologically, *church* is used to refer to a religious organization which is UNIVERSAL in its scope.

CHURCH FATHERS: the earliest CHRISTIAN writers and apologists whose work promoted the Christian FAITH in the Roman Empire.

CHURCH OF CHRIST SCIENTIST: See CHRISTIAN SCIENCE.

CHURCH(ES) OF CHRIST; DISCIPLES OF CHRIST: often described as "the most American" of CHRISTIAN CHURCHES, this family of churches is one of the largest DENOMINATIONS in America. They originated in the RESTORATION MOVEMENT of the nineteenth century and were inspired by Alexander CAMPBELL's monthly magazine *Millennial Harbinger* (1830-1866). A strongly anticreedal movement (*see* CREED), they sought to form independent CONGREGATIONS on the basis of SCRIPTURE and Scripture alone. Thus, although they are essentially orthodox, they reject the language of most doctrinal statements because it is derived from PHILOSOPHY and not found in the Bible.

CHURCH OF ENGLAND: also known as Anglicanism. The origins of English CHRISTIANITY are unknown, but the presence of British BISHOPS at the COUNCIL of Arles (A.D. 314) indicates the existence of an organized CHURCH. Following the Roman withdrawal and Teutonic invasions, Christianity retreated to the Celtic lands, but in the late sixth and early seventh centuries, Roman and Celtic missions began the reconversion of England. The Synod of Whitby (663-664) secured the observance of Roman forms. The English church was largely isolated from continental ECCLESIASTICAL affairs until the Norman invasion of 1066. Even afterwards distance from Rome, the conflict between England and France, and papal decline made English submission more nominal than real. It was an easy matter for King HENRY VIII (1491-1547) to use his divorce from Catherine of Aragon as grounds for detaching England from papal obedience. The parliament of 1532-1536 gave Henry the title "Supreme Head on Earth of the Church of England." Under EDWARD VI (1547-1553) the church underwent a LITURGICAL and doctrinal REFOR-

MATION. The accession of the Catholic Mary Tudor (1516-1558) inaugurated a period of reaction during which many of the Edwardian reformers were martyred. Elizabeth I (1558-1603) restored a PROTESTANT settlement, but her aim was a comprehensive, national, episcopal church, with the monarch as Supreme Governor. Moderate Protestantism, reflected in the church's doctrinal basis, the *Thirty-nine Articles*, and in the writings of Richard HOOKER, gave Anglicanism its classic *via media* statements, and the post-Restoration church had both High (inclined toward Catholicism) and Low (Protestant) wings.

Like most Protestant DENOMINATIONS, the Anglican Church was affected by DEISM in the eighteenth century, but the key movement of this period was the EVANGELICAL revival. Medieval spirituality was revived by the OXFORD MOVEMENT, led by John Henry NEWMAN and John KEBLE, with an emphasis on the church, APOSTOLIC SUCCESSION, sacramental GRACE (*see* SACRAMENT), and ASCETIC HOLINESS. The movement was seen by many people as a Romanizing tendency. Since the mid-nineteenth century, due to the activity of the CHRISTIAN SOCIALISTS, the church has become increasingly aware of its social responsibilities, and in the mid-1960s it witnessed the beginning of an evangelical revival among its clergy.

CICERO, Marcus Tullius (106-43 B.C.): probably the greatest Roman orator, whose prose profoundly affected Western literature. His political essays and high moral views have had a lasting influence on Western thought.

CIRCUMCISION: a practice, common in many CULTURES, of cutting away the foreskin as a SYMBOL of initiation or manhood. In JUDAISM it is practiced on infants and is the symbol of God's COVENANT with the people of ISRAEL (Genesis 17:9-11). The HEBREW BIBLE speaks about the "circumcision of the HEART" (Deuteronomy 10:16), an idea which is taken up in the NEW TESTAMENT as a spiritual state rather than an outward symbol, thus transforming a physical act into an inner, spiritual commitment (Philippians 3:3).

CISTERCIAN ORDER: founded in 1098 by Robert of Molesme as the White Monks, at Cîteaux in Burgundy. It is a strict religious order based on the RULE of Saint BENEDICT. Historically the Cistercians played an important role, especially in England, in the development of agriculture.

CITTA: BUDDHIST term translated as "consciousness" or "mind." It is believed to pertain to all entities superior to vegetable life.

CIVIL RELIGION: an idea developed by Jean-Jacques ROUSSEAU in *The Social Contract* and taken up by American sociologist Robert Bellah to explain the development of RELIGION in America. In Bellah's usage, civil religion is a vague religious sentiment promoted by STATE institutions on the basis of common ideas held by all citizens. As such it avoids DOGMA such as belief in the DEITY of CHRIST and emphasizes an undefined belief in GOD and PROVIDENCE.

CIVILIZATION: an achieved state or condition of organized social life which expresses a sense of historical process, associated with MODERNITY. Use of the term reflects the general spirit of the ENLIGHTENMENT, with its emphasis on secular and progressive human self-development.

CLAPHAM SECT: a group of influential Englishmen, including William WILBERFORCE and Lord SHAFTESBURY, whose activities centered on the EVANGELICAL religion preached at Clapham Parish Church in the late eighteenth and early nineteenth centuries. They toiled for the abolition of SLAVERY, the REFORM of child labor laws, and many other social innovations, in addition to supporting MISSIONARY work and evangelical Christianity generally.

CLEMENT OF ALEXANDRIA (A.D. 150-215): Greek Christian Platonist (*see* PLATO) whose works helped create ALEXANDRIAN THEOLOGY. He emphasized the idea that in CHRIST the LOGOS of the UNIVERSE was incarnate (*see* INCARNATION). He attempted to reconcile Greek PHILOSOPHY with CHRISTIANITY by teaching that Greek philosophy and the HEBREW BIBLE both lead to Christ. ALLEGORICAL INTERPRETATION of the BIBLE was an important tool in his APOLOGETICS. He is the author of *The Tutor, The Exhortation* and *Stromateis*.

CLEMENT OF ROME (1st century A.D.): one of the earliest BISHOPS of Rome. One of his letters dealing with the subject of the Christian ministry has survived, but the various other writings ascribed to him are considered unauthentic.

CLERIC, CLERGY: a minister of religion, originally used of those in the CHRISTIAN tradition, but increasingly used of any religion. A clergyman or woman is a person set aside, and often called a PRIEST, to perform religious rituals, pastoral care, etc.

CLOUD OF UNKNOWING: a fourteenth-century English MYSTICAL work which teaches that GOD cannot be known by REASON but only by LOVE.

CLOVIS (466-511): King of the Salian Franks who, after his CONVERSION to CHRISTIANITY, conquered large areas where he promoted the orthodox THEOLOGY of the ROMAN CATHOLIC CHURCH.

CLUNIAC ORDER: an offshoot of the BENEDICTINE ORDER originating in 910 with the monastery at Cluny in Burgundy, France, which profoundly affected the Western CHURCH in the tenth, eleventh and twelfth centuries.

COBBETT, William (1763-1835): English political journalist and essayist who used the pseudonym "Peter Porcupine." In his early pamphlets he attacked the FRENCH REVOLUTION, radicalism and American DEMOCRACY, but from 1804 he became a champion of radical causes.

CODEX ALEXANDRINUS: dating from the fifth century, this is one of the most important manuscripts of the GREEK BIBLE.

CODEX AMIATINUS: the oldest existing manuscript of the Latin VULGATE BIBLE, dating from the seventh century.

CODEX SINAITICUS: one of the two oldest complete manuscripts of the GREEK BIBLE, it dates from the fourth century. Earlier manuscripts of the Bible are fragmentary and incomplete.

CODEX VATICANUS: a fourth-century manuscript of the GREEK BIBLE which with CODEX SINAITICUS is the oldest complete surviving manuscript of the Bible.

COGITO ERGO SUM: "I think, therefore I am." The central anti-SKEPTICAL argument of Descartes.

COHERENCE THEORY OF TRUTH: the theory that TRUTH consists in coherence to a system of IDEAS as opposed to a relationship with EMPIRICAL REALITY. See CORRESPONDENCE THEORY OF TRUTH.

COHERENT: a system of thought where the major POSTULATES are both self-consistent and fit the facts of experience.

COLEBROOKE, Henry Thomas (1765-1837): English scholar who produced the first series of texts and translations from SANSKRIT based on scientific principles. His 1805 essay *On the Vedas* made a significant contribution to European interest in ancient Indian literature and religion.

COLENSO, John William (1814-1883): first ANGLICAN BISHOP of Natal and important pioneer of BIBLICAL CRITICISM. He gained the affection of the Zulus by refusing to compel polygamous Africans to divorce their additional wives, championing the black cause against white settler interests and writing the first Zulu grammar, dictionary and reading books. His interaction with PAGAN Zulus led him to write a series of books in the 1860s and 1870s challenging the literal truth of the SCRIPTURES. His correspondence with German theologians also helped stimulate many critical theories. In 1866 he was charged with HERESY and EXCOMMUNICATED by the Bishop of Cape Town.

COLERIDGE, Samuel Taylor (1772-1834): English poet, critic and philosopher whose early RATIONALISM gave way to a MYSTICAL religion influenced by BOEHME and SPINOZA. He preached against orthodox PROTESTANTISM in favor of a spiritualized religiosity unhampered by the constraints of biblical REVELATION. His ethical concerns led to his being seen as the "father" of the ANGLICAN Broad Church movement which rejected both EVANGELICAL PIETY (the Low Church) and the move toward ROMAN CATHOLICISM (the High Church).

COLET, John (1467-1519): English theologian and classical scholar whose CHRISTIAN HUMANISM had a profound effect on the English REFORMATION.

COLLINGWOOD, Robin George (1889-1943): English philosopher and historian who did important work on the HISTORY OF SCIENCE in which he stressed the importance of religious influences and CHRISTIANITY.

COLOR, LITURGICAL: around the twelfth century CHRISTIANS began using specific colors in church services to signify the divisions of the Christian Year (*see* CALENDAR), although general agreement on the color coding was never reached. In general, purple was used to signify DEATH and was also associated with Lent, white was used at CHRISTMAS for joy, and green for EASTER signified new life.

COMENIUS, Johann Amos (1592-1670): Moravian theologian and philosopher who pioneered in educational reform.

COMMUNION OF SAINTS: the Christian belief that all Christians—living or dead—share a common community and will eventually be united in the KINGDOM OF GOD. In the meantime, the deceased look on and intercede for the living as well as being MYSTICALLY present in the EUCHARIST and other acts of devotion. In the ROMAN CATHOLIC, Eastern ORTHODOX and various other CHURCHES, including many AFRICAN INDEPENDENT CHURCHES, this belief is the basis for offering prayers to the SAINTS.

COMMUNION TABLE: the table used in Christian churches for the celebration of the EUCHARIST. In the ROMAN CATHOLIC and ORTHODOX CHURCHES it is called an ALTAR.

COMMUNITY OF THE RESURRECTION: an ANGLICAN order of MONKS devoted to the deepening of spiritual life and the recovery of the CATHOLIC heritage of the CHURCH OF ENGLAND. Founded in 1892, the order has been active in missionary and educational work throughout the world.

COMPANIONS OF THE PROPHET: the earliest converts to ISLAM through the preaching of MUHAMMAD, they are the source of HADĪTH, or tradition, in SUNNI Islam. Their authority as teachers is rejected by SHI'ISM.

COMPARATIVE RELIGION: the study of comparative religion began with the Greek philosopher XENOPHANES in the sixth century B.C. when he observed that Thracians and Ethiopians both depicted their GODS after their own image. Although writers like Saint AUGUSTINE made some acute observations on the differences between religions, it was not until the THEORY of EVOLUTION gained popularity in the late nineteenth century that the serious study of comparative religion began. Under the influence of DARWIN, various scholars discovered what they believed to be evolutionary links between different religions. Max MÜLLER, E. B. Taylor and Sir James FRAZER were among the founders of the "new" science. In Britain the study of non-Christian religions tended to be linked to the needs of empire and had a more ANTHROPOLOGICAL bias than the theologically orientated Americans. In Germany it was the history of religions in an essentially evolutionary and Hegelian (*see* HEGEL) framework which predominated.

During the 1960s comparative religion, renamed "religious studies," became a popular course in many American universities, and the great increase in Asian immigration encouraged this trend. At its crudest, comparative religion teaches that all religions are essentially equal and originate from one underlying reality. Thus the TEN COMMANDMENTS, SERMON ON THE MOUNT, the FOUR NOBLE TRUTHS of BUDDHISM and HINDU teachings derived from the BHAGAVAD-GĪTA are sometimes seen as being essentially the same.

One fundamental problem for the more popular forms of comparative religion is that upon closer study the teachings of the major world religions are at least as different as they are similar. THERAVĀDA BUDDHISM presents a strong argument against the crudest forms of comparative religion because of its rejection of the importance of BELIEF in GOD, or gods, and denial of the existence of an individual self. Similarly, many religions, like ISLAM, do not separate religion and politics as JUDAISM and CHRISTIANITY do. The rise of NEW RELIGIOUS MOVEMENTS in Western society, often called CULTS, emphasizes the interconnectedness of the world. Today, for the first time since the Roman Empire, Western Christians live in a religiously plural world. See E. J. Sharpe, *Comparative Religion: A History;* N. Smart, *Reasons and Faiths;* H. G. Coward, *Pluralism: Challenge to World Religions;* J. H. Bavinck, *The Church Between Temple and Mosque;* and H. Kraemer, *World Cultures and World Religions.*

COMPASSION: a central DOCTRINE of BUDDHISM which expresses the basic Buddhist attitude to all sentient beings bound by the bonds of KARMA. In MAHĀYĀNA Buddhism it leads to doctrines about BODHISATTVAS who are able to offer release from KARMA through the transfer of MERIT accrued by their meritorious deeds.

COMTE, Auguste (1798-1857): French POSITIVIST philosopher and one of the founders of SOCIOLOGY. His major work is *The System of Positive Policy* (1875-1877, 4 vols.).

CONCEPT: an idea or MEANING which the mind gives to a UNIVERSAL term; e.g., justice.

CONCEPTUALISM: a medieval dispute between CHRISTIAN PHILOSOPHERS concerning the problem of UNIVERSALS. Conceptualists rejected the extremes of REALISM and NOMINALISM and attempted to mediate between the two by suggesting that universals exist in particular things and are therefore conceptualized by the activity of the observing mind.

CONCLAVE: a term used in the ROMAN CATHOLIC CHURCH for an official meeting of CARDINALS.

CONCORDANCE: a reference work which locates specific words in a text, frequently a religious text such as the BIBLE or QUR'ĀN.

CONCORDAT: an agreement between the ROMAN CATHOLIC CHURCH and SECULAR authorities.

CONDITIONAL IMMORTALITY: the belief that the SOUL is not intrinsically immortal but must prove its worth or be saved or be annihilated.

CONFESSING CHURCH: those churches which rejected the Church Union imposed on Germany and other acts of interference in Christian affairs by the Nazi regime. It was founded in 1934 and based its relations to the STATE on the Barmen Declaration which rejected TOTALITARIANISM. Among its prominent members were Karl BARTH and Dietrich BONHOEFFER.

CONFESSION: a religious RITUAL in which believers confess their SINS to a PRIEST or to other believers.

CONFIRMATION: the RITUAL by which individuals who were baptized as children are admitted into full communion in the CHURCH.

CONFUCIUS [Kung Fu Tzu] (551-479 B.C.): little is known about his background except that he was orphaned and grew up in poverty. He came to believe that he had a mission to bring peace and good government to China, but during his life he gained little success and died in obscurity. He is distinguished by his ethical rather than his religious teachings, the main idea of which is that the TAO, or Way of Heaven, should be followed by all men. He placed great emphasis on loyalty and the cultivation of humanity and taught that inner goodness finds expression in outward behavior. Following his death, his views became the basis of the Chinese understanding of the family, social and political life. His ideas are found in *The Analects of Confucius* compiled by his followers.

CONGREGATION: the gathered assembly of CHRISTIANS belonging to a local CHURCH.

CONGREGATIONAL CHURCH: the movement, sometimes called "Independents," arose out of the English REFORMATION and PURITANISM as a result of local CONGREGATIONS' separating from the CHURCH OF ENGLAND to choose their own ministers, ELDERS and DEACONS. Claiming autonomy for each local congregation, they argued that separate congregations must help and advise each other without imposing external authority on the local leadership. The congregational system of church government has been adopted by many other groups, including the BAPTISTS, many PENTECOSTAL denominations, and the United Reformed Church in England.

CONGREGATIONALISM: the theological DOCTRINE relating to church government which says that the local CONGREGATION ought to be the seat of authority, i.e., decisions such as the appointment of ministers should be decided at the local level by members of the congregation and not by BISHOPS or other centralized bodies such as PRESBYTERIES. The term can also be used of the movement represented by the CONGREGATIONAL CHURCH.

CONSERVATIVE: a person who seeks to conserve. Politically, conservatives are identified with Edmund BURKE, who advocated gradual REFORM rather than REVOLUTION. Theologically, conservatives seek to defend TRADITIONAL, historic ORTHODOXY. Conservatives in the Protestant Christian tradition accept the BIBLE as GOD'S REVELATION to humankind, share a SUPERNATURAL view of the UNIVERSE and are committed to a CHALCEDONIAN inter-

pretation of the PERSON of CHRIST.

CONSTANTINE THE GREAT (A.D. 288-337): the Roman emperor who in A.D. 313 accorded legal recognition to CHRISTIANITY and encouraged its acceptance as the RELIGION of the Roman Empire. In 325 he summoned the COUNCIL of Nicaea to discuss christological issues (*see* CHRISTOLOGY), and in 331 he moved the seat of the empire to Constantinople. He was baptized on his deathbed.

CONTINGENT: dependent, fortuitous, accidental.

CONTRADICTION, LAW OF: a proposition cannot be true and untrue at the same time. The same attribute cannot at the same time be affirmed and denied of the same subject. This is the basis of traditional logic as understood by ARISTOTLE (*see* EXCLUDED MIDDLE).

CONVERSION: a radical change, transformation, a turning around. In CHRISTIANITY it is often referred to as being "born again" or being "saved."

CONZE, Edward (b. 1904): English-born German Communist who fled Nazi Germany to take refuge in England in 1933. There he converted to BUDDHISM and became the greatest interpreter of Buddhism to the West. His book *Buddhism: Its Essence and Development* (1951) is the best single introduction to Buddhism, while his *Buddhist Thought in India* (1962) remains an undervalued classic. His autobiography, *The Memoirs of a Modern Gnostic* (1979), is interesting reading for anyone wishing to understand modern religious thought.

COPERNICUS, Nicholas (1473-1543): ROMAN CATHOLIC priest and astronomer known for his THEORY of the UNIVERSE which overturned the Ptolemaic system of antiquity (*see* PTOLEMY).

COPTIC CHURCH: an African form of CHRISTIANITY which has flourished in Egypt and Ethiopia since the earliest centuries of Christianity. The Copts often practiced communal BAPTISM and have at times been monophysite (*see* MONOPHYSITISM) in their CHRISTOLOGY. MONASTICISM has played an important role in Coptic religion.

CORRELATIVE: a thing which stands in reciprocal relation to another depending upon the other for its meaning; e.g., father and son, truth and error.

CORRESPONDENCE THEORY OF TRUTH: the view that truth consists of correspondence to REALITY and not in coherence of ABSTRACT IDEAS. See COHERENCE THEORY OF TRUTH.

COSMIC: of the cosmos or relating to the UNIVERSE. In the NEW AGE MOVEMENT and various modern forms of YOGIC RELIGION the term has become quite meaningless because it is used to give scientific legitimacy to various PSEUDO-SCIENTIFIC ideas.

COSMOLOGICAL ARGUMENT: an attempt to prove the existence of GOD from the EMPIRICAL fact that things exist. The argument is based on the view that being contingent the UNIVERSE requires the existence of a non-contingent God. Although the argument was attacked by David HUME and is generally neglected today, it has recently been revived by various philosophers, such as H. A. Meynell in his book *The Intelligible Universe* (1982).

COSMOLOGY: a series of related arguments and inquiries about the NATURE of the UNIVERSE in general and the world in particular. In RELIGION, cosmology refers to beliefs about the origins of things and the relationship between human affairs and the cosmos: How is GOD, or the gods, related to life and the world?

COUNCIL, BUDDHIST: all BUDDHISTS recognize three Great Councils. The first, held at Rājagṛha around 480 B.C., after the death of the GAUTAMA, set out to determine the authentic teachings of the BUDDHA as outlined in the early CANON. The second, held at Vaiśālī a century later, discussed specific practices, and the third, held at Pāṭaliputra around 250 B.C. during the reign of the emperor AŚOKA, set out to promote harmony and limit sectarian disputes. THERAVĀDIN BUDDHISTS recognize six councils in all, the last being held in Rangoon in 1956.

COUNCIL, CHURCH: throughout CHRISTIAN HISTORY councils of the CHURCH have been held to determine correct or orthodox DOCTRINE (*see* ORTHODOXY). The first recorded council of church leaders was held in JERUSALEM around A.D. 48 to discuss the admission of GENTILE converts into the Christian community. All Christians recognize four ECUMENICAL councils: Nicaea (A.D. 325); Constantinople (A.D. 381); EPHESUS (A.D. 431); and CHALCEDON (A.D. 451). The ROMAN CATHOLIC CHURCH claims a total of twenty-one councils while other churches count them differently. REFORMATION meetings which produced such documents as the AUGSBURG CONFESSION, BELGIC CONFESSION, WESTMINSTER CONFESSION and the Canon of DORT were, in effect, PROTESTANT councils. Similarly the ORTHODOX churches recognize a number of councils of their own, such as the Council of Trullan (A.D. 692).

COUNTERCULTURE: the social movement which emerged in the Haight Asbury district of San Francisco in 1967 in connection with the "HIPPIES." It was both a social protest against Western cultural values and a spiritual search for alternate realities. These were first found through the use of hallucinogenic drugs and later through YOGIC RELIGIONS. The counterculture paved the way for the NEW AGE MOVEMENT and is best summarized in *The Making of a Counter-Culture* (1970) by Theodore Roszak.

COUNTER-REFORMATION: a reform movement in ROMAN CATHOLICISM during the sixteenth century which sought to purify the church and combat the PROTESTANT REFORMATION.

COURSE IN MIRACLES, A: over 1,000 pages of text written between 1965 and 1973 in response to an "inner voice" which the author, Helen Schucman (d. 1981), an associate professor of psychology in New York, believed to be CHRIST. Published in 1975 without giving the author's name, the book became a best-seller in OCCULT and NEW AGE circles. The course has been criticized by some modern occultists for using language which is too CHRISTIAN, although, in fact, its teachings are really closer to CHRISTIAN SCIENCE. The message of the course is that we are what we believe, with the result that our false beliefs separate us from GOD who can be known when we recognize who we truly are.

COVENANT: a HEBREW religious idea which conceives of God's relationship to humankind in terms of an agreement in which God imposes conditions that humans are required to fulfill in return for blessings. In the HEBREW BIBLE the idea of covenant defines the relationship between Israel and God. In CHRISTIANITY the idea is developed in terms of a "new covenant" brought into existence by the life and DEATH of CHRIST.

COVENANTERS: Scottish PROTESTANTS who resisted the imposition of EPISCOPAL forms of church government on the Scottish Church by Charles I by signing a National Covenant to maintain Protestant forms of WORSHIP in Scotland. This action was important in terms of its influence on the development of DEMOCRACY and the American REVOLUTION.

COVERDALE, Miles (1488-1568): early translator of the English BIBLE and important PROTESTANT leader during the REFORMATION.

COW: the most SACRED animal in the HINDU tradition.

COWPER, William (1731-1800): English Christian poet who wrote such famous HYMNS as "O for a Closer Walk with God" and "God Moves in a Mysterious Way."

CRANMER, Thomas (1489-1556): ARCHBISHOP of CANTERBURY and prominent PROTESTANT REFORMER whose elegant prose in the BOOK OF COMMON PRAYER (1552) helped shape the English language. He was burned at the stake for HERESY during the reign of Mary Tudor.

CRAVING: the BUDDHIST HOLY TRUTH that through ignorance we are bound to the WHEEL OF EXISTENCE by craving.

CREATION: an important DOCTRINE in traditional CHRISTIANITY, JUDAISM and ISLAM where GOD is the sole CREATOR of the UNIVERSE. Some other religious traditions incorporate a view of creation, others deny it any special place in their BELIEF systems, while many see God, or the gods, as creating the universe out of preexisting matter, and some view it as an emanation of God. The doctrine of creation is important because of its implications for the related problems of EVIL and human SALVATION.

CREATIONISM: the belief that humans and the entire UNIVERSE owe their existence to GOD. In recent years the word has been taken over by certain groups of conservative Christians who, in the face of modern evolutionary theory, insist on a literal six-day CREATION which took place approximately 6,000 years ago. This view is claimed to be empirically supported by what is called creation science. In fact this restricted view appears to be the result of nineteenth-century RATIONALISM entering CHRISTIANITY and not supported by the BIBLE, where the creation story does not specify the time and date of creation.

CREATOR: a conscious agency, frequently a god, that brought into being the UNIVERSE or some aspect of it, perhaps only a particular nation or people. Various religious TRADITIONS affirm the existence of a Creator GOD. In ABRAMIC RELIGIONS the creator is the sole source of the origin of all things and both the maker and sustainer of the whole of REALITY. The Nicene creed expresses the CHRISTIAN version of this belief with the words "I believe in God the Father almighty, maker of heaven and earth and of all things visible and invisible." In the YOGIC TRADITION most HINDUS believe in some form of creator though not necessarily as the sole source of all things, while BUDDHISTS argue that questions about creation are unimportant when discussing ENLIGHTENMENT.

CREDO QUIA ABSURDUM EST: a Latin saying attributed to TERTULLIAN and translated as "I believe because it is absurd"; he intended it to mean that the gospel found in the NEW TESTAMENT is so astonishing that no human being could have invented it. The saying is often misused to imply anti-INTELLECTUALISM.

CREED: from the Latin *credo;* "I believe." Creeds are a distinctive feature of CHRISTIANITY. Although well-developed creeds do not occur in the BIBLE, rather rudimentary creedal forms found there provide models for later statements; e.g., Deuteronomy 26:5-9, 1 Corinthians 15:3-5, Romans 1:3-4 and 10:9-10. In Christian history three creeds have achieved particular prominence: (1) the APOSTLES' creed, supposedly written by the apostles; (2) the Nicene creed, which embodies in altered form, and without the anathemas, the CHRISTOLOGICAL teaching of the Council of Nicaea adopted in answer to ARIANISM, (3) the ATHANASIAN creed, popularly attributed to ATHANASIUS but thought by scholars to be a fourth- or fifth-century canticle of unknown authorship. As a direct statement of Trinitarian belief the latter became the test of ORTHODOXY and competence of the CLERGY in the West from the seventh century on. The REFORMERS valued it highly and the ANGLICANS made liturgical use of it, but the Eastern ORTHODOX CHURCH refused to recognize it.

CREMATION: the disposal of the corpse by burning. Although opposed by ROMAN CATHOLICISM and the MUSLIM religion, it was a religious RITE in HINDUISM.

CRISIS THEOLOGY: a term used for the DIALECTICAL THEOLOGY of twentieth-century theologians like Karl BARTH who were influenced by EXISTENTIALISM.

CROCE, Benedetto (1866-1952): Italian philosopher whose work on the philosophy of HISTORY strongly influenced R. J. COLLINGWOOD.

CROMWELL, Oliver (1599-1658): English PURITAN general and democrat who championed the rights of commoners against King Charles I and the aristocracy. He founded the New Model Army which he led to victory in the English Civil War. After Charles I threatened a second civil war, Cromwell supported his execution. He ruthlessly subdued the Royalist rebellion in Ireland (1649-1650), believing that his actions would prevent further bloodshed. He was made Lord Protector in 1653 and ruled by ordinances confirmed by Parliament. He reorganized the CHURCH OF ENGLAND, protected QUAKERS and JEWS, and favored religious TOLERATION. His actions ensured that England would be ruled by Parliament and not by absolute kings.

CROWLEY, Aleister (1875-1947): after growing up in a PLYMOUTH BRETHREN home he rejected CHRISTIANITY to become the leading English OCCULTIST of the twentieth century. A bisexual drug addict who scorned social convention, he proclaimed himself the ANTICHRIST and took the title "the Beast." After a wild life full of exaggerated deeds he died in abject poverty and despair.

CROWTHER, Samuel Ajayi (1806-1891): born in Nigeria and enslaved as a child, he was liberated by the British navy and taken to Sierra Leone where he became a CHRISTIAN in 1825. Ordained in 1843, he became the ANGLICAN BISHOP of West Africa in 1864 and led the Niger Mission which attempted to create a self-supporting black CHURCH. Conflict with white MISSIONARIES plagued his later years.

CRUCIFIX: an image of JESUS hanging on the cross.

CRUSADES: medieval religious wars in which CHRISTIANS sought to regain Jerusalem from its MUSLIM conquerors following its capture by the Turks in 1071.

CRUSIUS, Christian August (1712-1775): German PIETIST philosopher and theologian who opposed the RATIONALISM of WOLFF and LEIBNIZ and strongly influenced KANT. His books include *Sketch of Necessary Rational Truths* (1745).

CRYPTO: a prefix used to designate a

BELIEF which is so similar to another formally denied belief that in fact it represents a disguised form of the repudiated system. For example: some critics say that the HINDU scholar ŚAṄKARA was a "crypto-Buddhist," meaning that his teachings are so close to BUDDHISM that even though he denied being a Buddhist he *really* was one.

CULDEES: Irish monks originating in the eighth century who lived in groups of thirteen. In the nineteenth century they became the subject of NEOPAGAN speculation and were erroneously linked to the Druids. This usage has passed into various NEW RELIGIOUS MOVEMENTS of the twentieth century seeking to establish legitimacy for ESOTERIC BELIEFS.

CULLAVAMSA: the "Short Chronicle" which continues the "Long Chronicle" depicting the BUDDHIST HISTORY of Ceylon (Sri Lanka).

CULT: a controversial word greatly misused by the media to mean a group nobody likes due to its presumed association with BRAINWASHING. In THEOLOGY the term *cult* has been used to refer to forms of WORSHIP and the RITUALS associated with them such as those at the JERUSALEM TEMPLE in ANCIENT JUDAISM. Sociologically, it refers to small religious groups which are in tension with established religious traditions and society generally.

Rodney STARK and William Sims Bainbridge give an operational DEFINITION of cult as "a religious body which does not have a prior tie with another established religious body in the society in question. The cult may represent an alien (external) religion, or it may have originated in the host society, but through innovation, not fusion. Whether domestic or imported, the cult is something new vis-à-vis the other religious bodies in the society in question."

On the basis of this definition, they identify three types of cult: "Audience Cults," which resemble a very loose lecture circuit where people participate in lectures, seminars and workshops as well as buying books and magazines promoting a general spiritual point of view; "Client Cults," where mobilization is partial, rather than all-embracing, and people participate as clients, for example attending occasional SPIRITUALIST meetings when they have specific needs; and "Cult Movements" proper, where membership is required and there is a development toward the status of a SECT.

CULTURE: from the Latin "to till or cultivate." Generally it has come to mean the fabric of human endeavor in a society and as such embraces both arts and sciences. Sometimes it is contrasted with CIVILIZATION which is taken as a highly developed stage of culture.

CUNEIFORM: the ancient script used in the Near East which was invented by the Sumerians.

CUNNINGHAM, Loren (1935-): PENTECOSTAL PASTOR and American founder of Youth With A Mission. He is the author of *Is That Really Your God?* (1984).

CUSTOM: a habitual action; what has been passed on from the past or developed recently as a repetitive act, or series of actions, that underpins social life.

CUTHBERT (7th century A.D.): BISHOP of Lindisfarne and famous British SAINT.

CYNICISM: a school of Greek PHILOSOPHY dating to the fifth century B.C. which taught the value of a simple lifestyle and rigorous self-control. Because of their ridicule of social mores and personal follies, cynicism became associated with a general negative attitude of defeatism and scorn.

CYPRIAN (3rd century A.D.): early CHRISTIAN martyr who became BISHOP of Carthage. His book *On the Unity of the Catholic Church* (251) did much to promote the ascendancy of the ROMAN CATHOLIC CHURCH in the West. He is famous for his saying "He who does not have the Church as his Mother cannot have God as his Father."

CYRIL (826-869): known as "the APOSTLE to the Slavs," he played an important role in the CONVERSION of the Slavs to CHRISTIANITY.

D

DADHIKRĀ: HINDU DEITY depicted as a horse representing knowledge.

DADUPANTHIS: HINDU REVITALIZATION MOVEMENT which rejected or reformulated many TRADITIONAL Hindu BELIEFS. REBIRTH as an animal was considered impossible and reinterpreted as symbolic of the mood of the individual. BHAKTI played an important role in this movement, which was founded by a LAYMAN, Dādū (1544-1603). His followers included PRIESTS, and the movement shared many of the characteristics of SIKHISM.

DAITYAS: demonic figures in HINDU literature who are represented as giants opposed to the GODS.

DĀKINĪ: powerful spirits which may be GOOD or EVIL in TANTRIC BUDDHISM and HINDUISM.

DALAI LAMA: the title given to the head of the Yellow School of MONKS in TIBETAN BUDDHISM.

DAMASCUS: the ancient capital of Syria where PAUL of Tarsus lived after his CONVERSION to CHRISTIANITY.

DAMNATION: the belief found in most RELIGIOUS TRADITIONS that after DEATH humans may find themselves condemned to HELL rather than HEAVEN. This may be as a result of their deeds on earth and/or their relationship to GOD, the gods or a SAVIOR figure.

DANIEL: The only apocalyptic book (see APOCALYPTIC LITERATURE) of the HEBREW BIBLE. It tells the story of Daniel and his companions, who are taken as slaves to BABYLON, and it contains a series of visions depicting events which are to take place in the future. Traditionally the book is dated in the sixth century B.C., although most critical scholars date it to around 165 B.C.

DARBY, John Nelson (1800-1882): one of the founders of the PLYMOUTH BRETHREN who later went on to form his own group of EXCLUSIVE BRETHREN which excluded members that did not conform to Darby's conception of HOLINESS. Although a brilliant speaker and prolific writer, he appears to have had an unpleasant personality which led him to quarrel with other CHRISTIANS such as George MÜLLER. Darby's greatest importance was in his virtual creation of DISPENSATIONAL views of PREMILLENNIALISM later popularized in North America by C. I. SCOFIELD.

DARK AGES: a term used during the nineteenth century to refer to the medieval period in Europe. Today it is generally restricted to the period A.D. 500-800, which saw a sharp decline in the civilization of Western Europe.

DARSANAS: a philosophical system or viewpoint in HINDUISM. Traditionally there were six classical schools: NYAYA, Pūrva-Mīmāmsā, Sāmkhya, VAISESIKA, VEDĀNTA and YOGA.

DARWIN, Charles Robert (1809-1882): English scientist and author who is remembered for his seminal work *The Origin of Species* (1859), which purported to provide strong EMPIRICAL evidence for the theory of EVOLUTION. Darwin's views were shaped by his own observations while aboard the H.M.S. *Beagle*, where he worked as a naturalist, and by his reading of William PALEY and Charles LYELL. Following the publication of *Origins* Darwin was engaged in continuous controversy because, although he appears to have remained a THEIST, his views were seen as a frontal attack on Christian belief.

DATUM: the given, or what is offered, in an ARGUMENT or system of thought.

DAWSON, Christopher (1889-1970): Welsh historian and convert (in 1913) to ROMAN CATHOLICISM, whose writings on HISTORY and the PHILOSOPHY of history present a profound interpretation of the relationship between RELIGION, especially Christianity, and CULTURE. His books include *The Making of Europe* (1932), *Religion and Culture* (1948), *Dynamics of World History* (1958) and *Religion and World History* (1975).

DE FACTO: actually; as a matter of fact.

DEACON: the lowest rank of minister in the CHRISTIAN CHURCH. Their original function, in Acts 6:1-6, was to care for the poor and the needy in the Christian community.

DEAD SEA SCROLLS: a collection of manuscripts of Jewish texts, including books of the HEBREW BIBLE discovered in a cave in 1948 at Qumran, near the Dead Sea. In addition to biblical texts, the scrolls contain documents relating to the RITUALS and discipline of an unnamed religious

SECT often identified as that of the ESSENES. The dating of the texts is disputed, but none can be dated later than A.D. 68 when the site was abandoned. Controversy surrounds the interpretation of this material.

DEAN: originally a term used to refer to someone in charge of education and similar functions at a CATHEDRAL. Today it designates both an ECCLESIASTICAL office and an academic post.

DEATH: the end of life, it forms a central focus for most RELIGIOUS TRADITIONS. Ideas about the nature and significance of death reflect views about the human being. In CHRISTIANITY death is regarded as an intrusion into the divine order, the consequence of SIN which is a MORAL act of rebellion against GOD. The power of death is overcome in the death and RESURRECTION of CHRIST. For JUDAISM death is also an intrusion into God's original plan, but it is overcome through the LAW and life of the people of ISRAEL. ISLAM also shares the view that death is unnatural but overcomes it by obedience to God's will expressed in the QUR'ĀN and teachings of MUHAMMAD. Both HINDUISM and BUDDHISM view death as a METAPHYSICAL problem arising from the basic fact of human existence. Hindus seek to overcome death by a variety of paths which lead to one or another form of LIBERATION, while Buddhism offers release from the bonds of KARMA, and hence existence, through the attainment of NIRVANA.

DEATH OF GOD THEOLOGY: a trendy theological movement of the early 1960s predicated on the assumption of continued SECULARIZATION. It is associated with John A. T. ROBINSON, the BISHOP of Woolwich, whose book *Honest to God* caused a sensation when first published in 1963. The term originated with the German philosopher Friedrich NIETZSCHE in his story of the madman in *The Gay Science;* it was taken up by PROTESTANT theologians in the 1960s to express the REALITY of religion in a SECULAR SOCIETY. The leading exponents of this view were Paul M. van Buren in *The Secular Meaning of the Gospel* (1963), Thomas J. J. Altizer in *The Gospel of Christian Atheism* (1966) and William Hamilton (with Altizer), in *Radical Theology and the Death of God* (1966). All three writers appealed to Dietrich BONHOEFFER's *Letters and Papers from Prison* (1951)—particularly his phrase "religionless Christianity"—to support their views, although it is unlikely that Bonhoeffer would have agreed with their development of his thought.

DECALOGUE: the TEN COMMANDMENTS of the HEBREW BIBLE, which are found in Exodus 20:2-17.

DECONSTRUCTION: a modern literary and PHILOSOPHIC movement inspired by such French philosophers as DERRIDA, FOUCAULT and the literary critic Paul de Man, it attempts to go beyond normal literary or philosophic analysis to discover the TRUE, and previously hidden, meaning of a text or situation viewed as a text. Deconstruction has influenced many fields, from RELIGIOUS STUDIES to ANTHROPOLOGY, although many of its critics say that its only real insights are old truths of RHETORIC dressed up in modern form and confusing language. More radical criticism comes from scholars who point to what they see as a continuity between de Man's FASCISM and pro-NAZI activities and his later theoretical views. Such critics argue that by its very nature deconstruction encourages NIHILISM and eventually fascism. For a sympathetic interpretation see C. Norris, *Deconstruction: Theory and Practice* (1982).

DEDUCTION: a logical move from the general to the particular.

DEFINITION: the meaning of a term which indicates how it will be used in an argument or thesis.

DEIFICATION: the making of a person or thing into a DEITY. This was characteristic of many PAGAN religions and often involved the elevation of heroes to the rank of gods. In Eastern Orthodox theology (*see* ORTHODOX CHURCH) the term has

a technical meaning similar to SANCTIFICATION in Western theology. Through the work of the HOLY SPIRIT, humans are believed to regain those attributes belonging to the "likeness of GOD" lost at the FALL. Orthodox theologians are careful to point out that this process does not involve a blurring of the distinction between the creature and CREATOR such as is found in pagan religions.

DEISM: a PHILOSOPHY which regards GOD as the intelligent CREATOR of an independent and law-abiding world, but denies that he providentially guides it or intervenes in any way with its course or destiny. REASON is the sole instrument through which God's EXISTENCE and NATURE can be deduced from the orderly workings of the UNIVERSE. Deism flourished in England in the eighteenth century and strongly influenced the rise of BIBLICAL CRITICISM and MODERNISM in the nineteenth century.

DEITY: a god or GOD.

DELPHIC ORACLE: the famous PAGAN sanctuary on the slopes of Mount Parnassus in Greece which became a CULT center of the god Apollo. A priestess, in a state of frenzy, answered questions, and her answers were mediated to the questioner by a PROPHET. The cult center also developed the worship of DIONYSUS alongside Apollo. The cult was suppressed in A.D. 390 by the Emperor Theodosius.

DEMIURGE: the term used by PLATO for the CREATOR of the world (*see* CREATION). It was employed by PHILO and various early CHURCH FATHERS, as well as becoming an important term in GNOSTICISM.

DEMOCRACY: direct rule by the people. Only since the nineteenth and twentieth centuries have the majority of political parties and groups declared their belief in democracy, which was previously a very negative term connoting mob rule. In the thirteenth century AQUINAS defined democracy as popular power where ordinary people, by force of numbers, governed and oppressed all others, thus acting like a tyrant. Today democracy is usually confused with representative government in which people delegate AUTHORITY to elected officials to govern on their behalf.

DEMONS: EVIL SPIRITS who seek to harm humans, sometimes called "DEVILS." They are fallen ANGELS, whose leader is known as SATAN or the Devil. Demons are in rebellion against GOD and seek to lure humans into their service, and they are depicted as the cause of much suffering, illness, strife and EVIL.

DEMYTHOLOGIZATION: a type of NEW TESTAMENT interpretation systematically proposed by Rudolf BULTMANN, who argued that the message of the New Testament is couched in the language of MYTH and is primitive and prescientific. According to Bultmann, the New Testament portrays DEMONS, ANGELS, apocalyptic events at the end of the age, and testifies to miracles directly caused by SUPERNATURAL powers. Theologians, Bultmann argued, should understand the New Testament as having a mythological form and should seek to interpret its existential message in a form acceptable to modern, scientific people.

DENOMINATION: a term derived from the Latin word meaning "to name." It is used to distinguish religious organizations that are not CHURCHES in the sociological sense that their membership encompasses everyone in a given geographical area. Nor are they SECTS with exclusivistic tendencies that demand a profession of FAITH or acceptance of particular teachings before granting membership. Many denominations, however, began as NEW RELIGIOUS MOVEMENTS which displayed sectlike qualities which lessened over time. Therefore, some writers describe a denomination as "a sect on the way to becoming a church." The classic discussion of this issue is in H. Richard NIEBUHR's *The Social Sources of Denominationalism* (1929).

DEONTOLOGY: any ethical system which seeks to determine correct action without reference to the consequences.

DERRIDA, Jacques (1930-): Algerian JEWISH writer, critic and major exponent of DECONSTRUCTION which some see as a SECULAR development of his RABBINIC heritage. A scholar of HEGEL, his work has had a major influence on literary criticism in North America and increasingly on other academic disciplines. Opponents of his views, however, point to their NIHILISTIC tendencies which they see confirmed by his failure to condemn the clear FASCISM and pro-NAZI activities of another deconstructionist, Paul de Man.

DERVISH: a member of a ṢŪFĪ order, usually a mendicant or beggar.

DESCARTES, René (1596-1650): French RATIONALIST PHILOSOPHER whose method of radical doubt, *cogito ergo sum* ("I think, therefore I am"), made him "the father of modern philosophy." Educated by the JESUITS, he travelled widely, eventually settling in the Netherlands. Descartes stressed the importance of mathematics for all true scholarship and constructed a mechanistic model of the UNIVERSE. From his initial deduction about his own existence he went on to develop an ONTOLOGICAL argument for the existence of GOD which he reinforced by his own form of the COSMOLOGICAL argument. Making a radical distinction between mind and MATTER, he promoted DUALISM and a sharp distinction between the body and SOUL. His philosophy, known as CARTESIANISM, provoked many responses and stimulated the development of work by HOBBES, LOCKE and HUME.

DETERMINISM: the view that all events are to be understood as the necessary outcome of certain CAUSES and so may be regarded as instances of laws.

DEUTERO-ISAIAH: chapters 40—55, or sometimes 40—66, of the book of Isaiah in the HEBREW BIBLE, which are ascribed by some biblical critics (*see* BIBLICAL CRITICISM) to an unknown author.

DEVA: a PALI and SANSKRIT term meaning "Heavenly Being" or "Shining One."

Devas are not GODS because they are not eternal and are therefore subject to the law of REBIRTH. Nevertheless, they are powerful BEINGS living on a high spiritual plane.

DEVA-DŪTA: the three messengers of age, disease and death sent to humans to remind them of their mortality.

DEVADĀSĪS: a class of women in HINDU practice who were dedicated to the service of a god and lived within a TEMPLE complex. Although they often included dancers and other artists, they were essentially temple prostitutes.

DEVIL: an anglicized Greek term (*diabolos*), meaning "slanderer," used in the Greek translation of Hebrew Scripture and pseudepigrapha, and in the New Testament and CHRISTIAN THEOLOGY as an equivalent to the Hebrew-derived term SATAN. In traditional Christian theology the Devil is a created but fallen and evil, personal, spiritual being actively opposed to the purposes of God. The plural, "devils," is sometimes used to refer to DEMONS.

DEVOTEES: followers of a RELIGIOUS TRADITION whose PIETY is expressed in devotion, or a strong personal commitment, to a GOD or gods.

DHAMMAPADA: an anthology of sayings of the BUDDHA found in the PALI CANON containing some 423 verses. It was translated into English by Max MÜLLER in 1898.

DHARMA: literally, that which is established law, the WHEEL OF EXISTENCE, ultimate TRUTH. A term used by BUDDHISTS, HINDUS and JAINS to describe the human situation and the way or means of SALVATION. It is a complex concept which is often misunderstood and needs to be seen in the context of Indian religious and philosophical thought. Among other things, *dharma* implies a moral order expressed through the network of human rights and obligations supported by a cosmic order and the CASTE system.

DIALECTIC: a form of reasoning originally used by PLATO in his early dialogues.

In medieval THEOLOGY the dialectical method took the form of first stating an opinion from an established authority, then a different opinion from another authority, and finally proposing a solution to reconcile the two contradictory opinions. In modern PHILOSOPHY the term is associated with the logic of HEGEL. He argued that the very nature of REASON leads us to posit a THESIS which generates its ANTITHESIS, or opposite. This process, in turn, leads to a synthesis or reconciling of the two theses. Karl MARX claimed to see the laws of Hegelian dialectics at work in history and the economic affairs of humans. This led him to develop his materialistic interpretation of history (*see* DIALECTICAL MATERIALISM). The term was used in a religious framework by Søren KIERKEGAARD who saw the dialectic as two apparent opposites with profound EXISTENTIAL significance. Kierkegaard's ideas, in turn, influenced NEO-ORTHODOX theologians in the twentieth century.

DIALECTICAL MATERIALISM: the Marxist theory of knowledge which seeks to explain the development of human society and thought in terms of a DIALECTIC based entirely on MATERIALISM without reference to spiritual factors. The term is often used as a synonym for Marxism (*see* MARX).

DIALECTICAL THEOLOGY: See NEO-ORTHODOXY.

DIAMOND SŪTRA: a MAHĀYĀNA BUDDHIST text dedicated to the attainment of the perfection of WISDOM.

DIANETICS: a theory, book and later therapy, developed by Ron L. HUBBARD, the founder of SCIENTOLOGY, who taught that psychological and other problems result from *engrams*, or bad impressions in the subconscious mind. Negative engrams must be eliminated to enable the individual to recognize and realize his or her natural and spiritual potential.

DIASPORA: a term used to refer to the scattering of a people among many nations. This has particular relevance for

Jewish history, referring to Jews living outside Palestine following the destruction of JERUSALEM in 597 B.C. and in A.D. 70 (*see* JUDAISM, ANCIENT).

DIGGERS: a radical SECT led by Gerrard Winstanley (1609-1660) which emerged during the English Civil War to advocate agrarian communism and egalitarianism.

DING AN SICH: literally the "thing-in-itself." A term used by KANT to speak about REALITY as opposed to APPEARANCE or the phenomenal.

DIOCESE: an administrative area of the CHRISTIAN CHURCH which is under the authority of a BISHOP.

DIONYSUS: Greek GOD of wine around whom an ecstatic CULT developed that held special appeal for women. Accounts of orgies and frenzied DEVOTEES whirling in dance prior to devouring live animals and even children characterize the cult's wilder aspects. In its milder form it eventually became associated with the Orphic Mysteries (*see* ORPHISM).

DĪPAMKARA: the name of a legendary BUDDHA said to have been the first of twenty-four Buddhas to have preceded GAUTAMA (Buddha), who founded BUDDHISM.

DIPAVAMŚA: the oldest historical chronicles of the PALI CANON which consists of a history of Ceylon (modern Sri Lanka) and of the introduction of BUDDHISM to the island. It was probably written between A.D. 350 and 450 using older sources.

DISCIPLES OF CHRIST: a North American religious movement which began to develop in 1811 out of PRESBYTERIANISM through the work of Alexander CAMPBELL. CONGREGATIONAL in form, it stressed ECUMENICAL fellowship among CHRISTIANS and eventually became an independent DENOMINATION in 1827. Today there are over 3 million members of this denomination.

DISPENSATIONALISM: a type of biblical interpretation found among conservative Protestant CHRISTIANS which divides GOD's dealings with humans into "times" or "dispensations" characterized by unique opportunities and responsibilities. This view was held by the PLYMOUTH BRETHREN and was popularized in the *Scofield Reference Bible* published in 1910. It is very popular among FUNDAMENTALISTS and EVANGELICALS in North America.

DIVINATION: the foretelling of the future using such means as ASTROLOGY, augury and auspices. In principle the future course of events is read from patterns found in the stars, the entrails of animals and such things as the way bones or sticks fall when thrown. Divination plays an important role in many religious systems and is central to many FOLK RELIGIONS.

DIVINE KINGSHIP: a belief found in many religions that the monarch is SACRED and in some sense responsible for the welfare of the land and people.

DIVINE LIGHT MISSION: a modern HINDU MISSIONARY movement founded by Shri Hans Maharajji (d. 1966). It came to the West in 1971 under the leadership of his son, the thirteen-year-old GURU Maharaj Ji (1959-). After initial success and extensive media coverage the movement floundered due to mounting debts and internal strife. The movement is an offshoot of the Sant Mat, a SIKH SECT strongly influenced by Hinduism.

DIVINE RIGHT OF KINGS: a CHRISTIAN version of DIVINE KINGSHIP which makes the monarch God's anointed leader to whom loyalty and obedience are therefore due. In the seventeenth century the PURITANS rejected such arguments on biblical grounds, resulting in the English Civil War and, eventually, the establishment of representative government.

DIVORCE: the dissolution of a marriage. Traditional Judaism has been permitted divorce for a number of reasons, but it is largely the husband's prerogative. Likewise, in Islam divorce is permitted, though it is easier to initiate by the husband. Within CHRISTIANITY there are a number of views regarding the acceptability of divorce, due largely to disagreements over the interpretation of various sayings of JESUS and PAUL, and to sacramental (*see* SACRAMENT) views of marriage. In theory the ROMAN CATHOLIC CHURCH forbids divorce, although exceptions can be made through annulment of the marriage. The Eastern ORTHODOX CHURCH allows divorce for a number of reasons, while PROTESTANTS are divided about the issue. Mainline Protestants tend to permit divorce for many reasons, including incompatibility. Many FUNDAMENTALIST groups forbid or strongly discourage the practice except in cases of adultery, and some in North America argue that not only must a Christian not divorce but anyone who is divorced and subsequently becomes a Christian must remarry the original marriage partner, regardless of any later marriages that may have been contracted.

DOCETISM: a CHRISTIAN HERESY which maintained that CHRIST was not a real human who actually suffered and died on the cross, but only seemed to do so. Docetists therefore deny the INCARNATION, maintaining that Christ was a SPIRIT whose incarnate FORM was unreal. This view seems to have influenced MUḤAMMAD and is found in the QUR'ÂN, *Sūra* IV, 156-157.

DOCTRINE: that which is believed, a dogma. The teachings or official beliefs of a religious group. A set of principles, creed or theory of a religious, social or political movement.

DOGMA: a Greek term meaning "that which seems GOOD." It was used in antiquity to refer to such things as the decrees of kings and principles regarded as axiomatic by various PHILOSOPHICAL schools. DOGMA is now applied somewhat generally to those official beliefs which are considered to be fundamental to a church and the acceptance of which is a necessary condition of membership.

DOME OF THE ROCK: the site of a beautiful MOSQUE which is one of the holiest sites in ISLAM due to its association with ABRAHAM, JESUS and MUḤAMMAD. It is located within the site of the former Jewish TEMPLE in JERUSALEM and is thus a source of friction between MUSLIMS and Jews.

DOMINICANS: a ROMAN CATHOLIC religious order also known as the BLACK FRIARS, and sometimes Friars or Preachers, they are recognized by their black mantle covering a white habit. They were formed in 1220 by ST. DOMINIC (1171-1221) as a preaching and teaching ORDER based on the RULE OF ST. AUGUSTINE. Historically, their most notable members have been scholars like Albertus MAGNUS and Thomas AQUINAS. Yet they also took an active part in promoting crusades and running the INQUISITION to combat HERESY.

DOMINIC (1170-1221): Spanish ROMAN CATHOLIC SAINT and founder of the ORDER of PREACHERS known as the DOMINICANS. He was a devoted CATHOLIC and fanatical opponent of HERETICS, especially the ALBIGENSES.

DONATION OF CONSTANTINE: forged in the eighth or ninth century A.D., this document was supposedly written by the Roman emperor CONSTANTINE to confirm the religious AUTHORITY of the POPE. It was exposed as a forgery in the fifteenth century.

DONATISM: a religious movement named after Donatus, bishop of Carthage. It developed during the fourth century in North Africa in response to perceived laxity in the church of Carthage. It was characterized by terrorist activity and highly exclusivistic BELIEFS which stressed the ideal of martyrdom, a pure CLERGY and the necessity of their members being rebaptized. It was strongly opposed by AUGUSTINE who emphasized the catholicity (*see* CATHOLIC) of the church.

DOOYEWEERD, Herman (1894-1977): Dutch Christian PHILOSOPHER whose seminal four-volume work *New Critique of Theoretical Thought* (1953-1958) was written in the tradition of Abraham KUYPER and GROEN VAN PRINSTERER as a radical reformation of philosophic thought inspired by CALVINISM. Dooyeweerd seeks to go beyond KANT by claiming to discover the ultimate root of human reasoning in religious GROUND MOTIVES which reflect both individual and communal relationships to GOD or an IDOL. Although generally neglected by philosophers, Dooyeweerd's work is remarkable in its anticipation of many of the ideas of thinkers like W. V. O. QUINE and Thomas KUHN.

DORT, SYNOD OF: held in 1618-1619 in the Netherlands in the town of Dortrecht, the Synod produced the "Canon of Dort" defining their understanding of orthodox CALVINISM. The Synod also produced the so-called Five Points of Calvinism.

DOUBLE EFFECT: an ethical theory which states that when a GOOD action may only be achieved by causing harm, it is permissible, if the good outweighs the harm that may result.

DOUBLE PROCESSION: in the Eastern ORTHODOX CHURCH the HOLY SPIRIT is said to proceed "from GOD the Father through CHRIST His Son." In the WESTERN CHURCH it was maintained that the Holy Spirit "proceeds from the Father and the Son."

DOUBLE TRUTH: the idea that religious TRUTH can be different from scientific or other truth. The theory was advocated by the ISLAMIC philosopher AVERROES and was rejected by orthodox Christians, although it has been popular since the nineteenth century as a means of escaping problems arising from challenges like the theory of EVOLUTION. EVANGELICAL apologist Francis SCHAEFFER rejected the notion, referring to it in terms of "upper and lower story" theories of truth.

DOUBT: although often contrasted with FAITH it really means uncertainty and has traditionally been seen as a means of strengthening faith through the need to search for TRUTH and make moral decisions.

DOUKHOBORS: literally "spirit wrestlers." A Russian religious SECT founded in the eighteenth century which is characterized by a rejection of civic authority and tendency toward communalism. Persecuted during the nineteenth century, they emigrated to Canada where small communities still exist.

DRĀVIDIANS: probably the original inhabitants of India. These darker-skinned peoples of Southern India occupy a low position in the CASTE SYSTEM. They are believed to have made a significant contribution to HINDUISM and have certainly led the way in the development of various egalitarian religious movements of a pietistic type (see PIETISM) associated with BHAKTI.

DREYFUS CASE: the trial for treason, condemnation, retrial and eventual exoneration of a Jewish Captain of the French General Staff, Alfred Dreyfus (1859-1935). The case divided France into anti-Dreyfusard groups, which were nationalist, monarchist and CATHOLIC, and the republican anticlerical Dreyfusards. It is important because of its place in the history of ANTI-SEMITISM.

DRUCKER, Peter F. (1909-): Austrian-American thinker best known for his many books on modern business, including *Management* (1973). His work on management arose out of a strong opposition to FASCISM and the NAZIS based on deep CHRISTIAN convictions. His first English book *The End of Economic Man* (1939) is a brilliant analysis of the intellectual, moral and social crisis facing the modern world. He has also written *The Future of Industrial Man* (1942), *The Concept of the Corporation* (1946) and *The Adventures of a Bystander* (1979).

DRUZE: a sectarian religious movement (see SECT) within ISLAM regarded as heretical by the orthodox. Its founder was Caliph al-Ḥākim Bi-amr Allah (A.D. 985-1021), who proclaimed himself an INCARNATION of the divine. Today there are around 200,000 Druzes, the majority of whom live in Lebanon.

DUALISM: a term describing worldviews that explain the FACTS of the world, or even particular facts encountered in daily life, in light of two different, ultimate and irreducible principles. There are two major forms of dualism: the first offers an interpretation of the universe which sees it as a cosmic battleground between the principles of GOOD and EVIL: ZOROASTRIANISM is a classic example of this view within a religious movement. The second form argues for the strict division of human nature into SPIRIT and MATTER. This view first emerged in Indian religions and entered the West with Pythagoreans (*see* PYTHAGORAS) and ORPHISM in the sixth century B.C. Both forms of dualism have influenced certain developments of CHRISTIAN THEOLOGY. Although many philosophers have maintained that the idea of GOD as the CREATOR of the UNIVERSE implies a form of MONISM, Christian theology has generally emphasized the distinction between the Creator and his creation. Christian theology may be viewed as a limited dualism, however, in terms of its emphasis on the cosmic conflict between good and evil, God and SATAN. But, unlike MANICHAEISTS, Christians view this conflict as temporary and not eternal.

DUKKHA (Pali) or DUHKHA (Sanskrit): one of the three characteristic marks of EXISTENCE in BUDDHISM. It is usually translated "suffering," but this should be understood as a radical suffering which characterizes the whole of existence.

DUNS SCOTUS, Johannes (1264-1308): Scottish medieval FRANCISCAN PHILOSOPHER who taught at the University of Paris from 1302 to 1307 before moving to Köln where he died suddenly. He combined elements of ARISTOTELIANISM with AUGUSTINIAN philosophy giving primacy to the will and love over REASON. His greatest work is his *Commentary on the Sentences of Peter Lombard*. Although ridiculed by RENAISSANCE scholars who coined the word *dunce* from his name, his work has been greatly appreciated by such modern figures as Charles PEIRCE, Martin HEIDEGGER and Gerald Manley HOPKINS.

DURGĀ: the HINDU GODDESS depicted as a warrior who is often identified with KĀLĪ. She rides on a tiger and is the slayer of DEMONS.

DURKHEIM, Émile (1858-1917): alongside COMTE, SPENCER, MARX and WEBER, Durkheim is one of the great founders of SOCIOLOGY. He had a lifelong preoccupation with the problem of RELIGION in MODERN SOCIETY and the ALIENATION he observed, which he attributed to a loss of FAITH and of an overarching BELIEF system. The notion of SACRED and PROFANE as a basic category of religious thought was popularized through his writings as an empirically observable FACT, although closer examination reveals that it was based on his underlying commitment to neo-KANTIAN PHILOSOPHY. His greatest works are *The Division of Labour in Society* (1893), *The Rules of Sociological Method* (1895), *Suicide* (1897) and *The Elementary Forms of Religious Life* (1912).

DUTCH REFORMED CHURCH: that branch of the PROTESTANT tradition which originated in the Netherlands during the REFORMATION. Today there are various splinter groups in the Netherlands, all claiming that the official, STATE church has departed from its original DOCTRINES. Offshoots from the Dutch Reformed Church are to be found in North America in such DENOMINATIONS as the Christian Reformed Church and Reformed Church in America, and in South Africa where again there are several branches of the REFORMED TRADITION, each claiming to be its true representative. In South Africa the largest of these CHURCHES, the Nederduits Gereformeerde Kerk, has often been accused of both originating and promoting apartheid. The relationship between Afrikaner Nationalism, Afrikaans churches and both the policy and IDEOLOGY of apartheid is a complex one, subject to intense historical debate. Today most leading historians, such as T. R. H. Davenport, would agree that after the rise of Afrikaner Nationalism ministers of all three major Dutch Reformed churches did promote Afrikaner Nationalism. But their role in its origin and in the evil of apartheid is more complex. To its credit the Dutch Reformed Church produced many critics of South African government policy and eventually condemned the theological justification of apartheid as a heresy.

E

EARLY CHURCH: the formative period of the Christian CHURCH before the emergence of the centralized authority of the ROMAN CATHOLIC Church in the West. Usually the term refers to CHRISTIANITY during its first few centuries.

EASTER: the oldest and most important CHRISTIAN celebration, which commemorates the RESURRECTION of JESUS CHRIST.

EASTERN ORTHODOX CHURCH: *see* ORTHODOX CHURCH.

EBIONITES: an early CHRISTIAN HERESY referred to by IRENAEUS. Their beliefs are obscure, but they are thought to have been a poor Jewish-Christian SECT which rejected Pauline Christianity (*see* PAUL) and affirmed the Gospel of Matthew, but rejected the VIRGIN BIRTH.

ECCLESIASTES: part of the WISDOM LITERATURE of the HEBREW BIBLE; ascribed to King Solomon. Famous phrases from this book include: "To everything there is a season. . . . A time to be born, and a time to die" and "Vanity of vanities, all is vanity" (KJV).

ECCLESIASTICAL: of, or relating to, the CHURCH.

ECCLESIASTICUS: the Latin title of a work otherwise known as The Wisdom of Jesus Ben Sirach, one of the books of the APOCRYPHA. This is an example of Hebrew WISDOM LITERATURE and contains many proverbs.

ECK, John (1486-1543): German ROMAN CATHOLIC THEOLOGIAN remembered for his role in the EXCOMMUNICATION of Martin LUTHER and his strong opposition to the PROTESTANT REFORMATION.

ECKANKAR: a new religious movement founded in 1965 by Paul Tritchell (1908-1971), who popularized his ideas through his books *The Tiger's Fang* (1967), *Eckankar* (1969) and Brad Steiger's biography *In My Soul I Am Free* (1968). Tritchell claimed to be the 971st ECK Master who was revealing a long-secret tradition to the world. His teachings included REINCARNATION, soul travel and a variety of YOGIC and OCCULT beliefs and practices. After Tritchell's death he was succeeded by Darwin Gross as the 972nd ECK Master. Gross married Tritchell's widow, but following the couple's divorce in 1978 the group split, and Gross was succeeded by Harold Klemp. In origin Eckankar is an offshoot of Kirpal Singh's Ruhani Satsang and the Self-Revelation Church and owes many of its ideas to the Indian Sant Mat tradition.

ECLECTIC: to take ideas and practices from various TRADITIONS and join them together as though they belonged to a unified system. The term is used in RELIGION and PHILOSOPHY to describe people and systems which borrow widely without any real unified structure.

ECOLOGICAL MOVEMENT: a complex development of environmentalism which has roots in nineteenth-century ROMANTICISM and GENERAL SYSTEMS THEORY. At its source is a desire to preserve NATURE, especially wild or natural environments. In Britain early ecologists were involved in groups like The National Trust, while North Americans formed the Sierra Club. National parks and other forms of nature parks resulted from these early environmental movements. In the 1960s books like Rachel Carson's *Silent Spring* (1962) warned about the dangers of DDT and other chemicals being absorbed into the food chain. These warnings were taken seriously by various CHRISTIAN writers such as Francis SCHAEFFER in his book *Pollution and the Death of Man* (1970) and John V. Taylor in *Enough Is Enough* (1975). Both of these writers were, however, concerned for the poor and the economic development of the Third World. The ecological movement as such developed around 1970 following the publication of Barry Commoner's *Science and Survival* (1968), Paul Ehrlich's *The Population Bomb* (1969) and the trilogy of *Limits to Growth* (1973), *Blueprint for Survival* (1972) and E. F. Schumacher's *Small Is Beautiful* (1973). Of these works only Schumacher's had a strong religious message, a result of his commitment to BUDDHISM under the influence of Edward CONZE. This new movement was soon influenced by Gerrit Hardin who had already argued in his book *Population, Evolution and Birth Control: A Collage of Controversial Ideas* (1964) that the West must adopt a "lifeboat ethic" which meant leaving the Third World to starve. Similar views were also found in *The Ecologist* and the work of the systems-theory pioneer Jay Forrester. Essentially, this form of ecological thinking was a return to the views of MALTHUS about the ability of the world to feed a growing human population. The ecological movement took an increasingly religious turn during the 1980s when its systems approach was linked to the theory of EVOLUTION to form a grand interpretive scheme resulting in what Bill Devall and others call *Deep Ecology* (1985). This scheme blends various forms of spirituality from BUDDHISM to WICCA and NEOPAGANISM with environmental concerns. The history of the ecological movement is documented by David Pepper in *The Roots of Modern Environmentalism* (1984), while its basic scientific assumptions have been challenged by John Maddox in *The Doomsday Syndrome* (1972) and later by Julian L. Simon and Herman Kahn, eds., in *The Resourceful Earth* (1984). A more worrying analysis of the roots of the ecological movement is to be found in Anna Bramwell's *Blood and Soil: Walther Darre & Hitler's "Green Party"* (1985).

ECSTASY: literally means "standing outside of oneself" and has traditionally been applied to those psychic or spiritual states which are supposed to seize MYSTICS and PROPHETS.

ECUMENICAL: derived from the Greek *oikoumenē*, which meant the "entire inhabited world." While describing any effort to unite religious bodies, today it primarily refers to the worldwide ECUMENICAL MOVEMENT to unite various CHRISTIAN DENOMINATIONS into one CHURCH or church association such as the WORLD COUNCIL OF CHURCHES.

ECUMENICAL MOVEMENT: the twentieth-century movement to unite worldwide CHRISTIAN CHURCHES. Its roots are found in the World Missionary Conference held in Edinburgh in 1910, which led to the formation of a Provisional Committee in 1938 and the founding of the WORLD COUNCIL OF CHURCHES in 1948.

EDDINGTON, Sir Arthur Stanley (1882-

1944): British physicist and astronomer who contributed to the general theory of RELATIVITY. He was very interested in the PHILOSOPHICAL implications of SCIENCE and speculated about BELIEF in GOD.

EDDY, Mary Baker (1821-1910): the founder of the CHURCH OF CHRIST SCIENTIST, popularly known as CHRISTIAN SCIENCE, and the author of *Science and Health with Key to the Scriptures* (1875). She was a physically weak woman but experienced a profound physical HEALING which she attributed to the work of GOD. Her teachings consist of a CHRISTIANIZED form of HINDUISM which draws inspiration from many other religious and metaphysical sources. Probably her most lasting achievement outside her church was the establishment of the *Christian Science Monitor* as a world-class newspaper with extremely high standards of journalism.

EDEN: the place described in the HEBREW BIBLE where the first humans, ADAM and EVE, lived in PARADISE before the FALL.

EDERSHEIM, Alfred (1825-1889): Austrian Jewish BIBLICAL scholar who converted to CHRISTIANITY. His works included *The Life and Times of Jesus the Messiah* (1883).

EDHAS: SACRED wood burnt for SACRIFICIAL fires in HINDUISM.

EDWARD VI (1537-1553): the only son of King HENRY VIII. His reign saw the continuation of the REFORMATION of the church in England.

EDWARDS, Jonathan (1703-1758): a staunch CALVINIST and probably the greatest of all American philosophers, he was also an outstanding revivalist preacher (*see* REVIVALISM) and theologian who played the key role in the GREAT AWAKENING of 1734-1735. His early writings covered various subjects, including SOCIOLOGY and the PSYCHOLOGY OF RELIGION, in *Concerning Religious Affections* (1746); PHILOSOPHY, in *The Freedom of the Will* (1754), which was a reply to John LOCKE; and THEOLOGY, in *Original Sin* (1758). Like

AUGUSTINE, he combined a highly intellectual speculative outlook with personal PIETY and devotion to GOD.

EFFABLE: capable of being expressed in words. It is the opposite of INEFFABLE, which means that which cannot be expressed.

EGOTISM: the teaching that in reality all actions are performed out of self-interest. Ayn RAND and others have developed this viewpoint into a systematic theory that all actions *ought* to be performed out of self-interest. Traditionally the great world religions have condemned egotism as either sinful or undesirable.

EGYPTIAN RELIGION: the religions of ancient Egypt developed over several millennia and are now known only from ancient texts and archeological evidence. They involved belief in various gods and maintained a strong emphasis on the afterlife and judgment after DEATH.

EIGHTFOLD PATH: the BUDDHIST exposition of the means by which a believer may gain ENLIGHTENMENT. Although not found in the earliest Buddhist texts, it is generally accepted as a basic tenet of Buddhism. The Path can be divided into the three parts of FAITH, morality and MEDITATION. It consists of right understanding and right thought which refer to faith; right speech, right bodily action and right livelihood which refer to morality; and right effort, right mindfulness and right concentration which refer to meditation. It is thus a systematic summary of Buddhist BELIEF which may be expanded into much longer treatises.

EINHEITLICHE WELTANSCHAUUNG: German philosophical term meaning "unified WORLDVIEW."

EINSTEIN, Albert (1879-1955): German Jewish mathematician and physicist who immigrated to America and whose work radically changed scientific understanding of space and time. Together with Max PLANCK'S quantum theory, Einstein's work on RELATIVITY laid the foundations for modern physics. Popular misunderstandings of his work have promoted the idea that everything, including morals and truth, is RELATIVE and have helped boost religious developments like the NEW AGE MOVEMENT.

ELDERS: generally, any learned or authoritative figures in religious traditions. Within CHRISTIANITY it specifically refers to LAITY who assist the minister in running the congregation in PRESBYTERIAN and CONGREGATIONAL forms of CHURCH government.

ELEATIC SCHOOL: an early school of Greek PHILOSOPHY which promoted a form of MONISM similar to Indian VEDANTA. The leading figure in this school, which flourished in the sixth and fifth centuries B.C., was PARMENIDES.

ELECTION: the teaching found in both the HEBREW BIBLE and the NEW TESTAMENT that human SALVATION ultimately depends on an act of GOD who, in his mercy, chooses peoples and individuals to fulfill his purpose, and leads them to salvation.

ELEUSINIAN MYSTERIES: information about these RITES, which took place as part of a MYSTERY RELIGION at Eleusis near Athens, is fragmentary and unreliable. Initiation lasted two years and involved vows of secrecy. The CULT was suppressed in the fourth century A.D.

ELIADE, Mircea (1907-1988): Romanian historian of RELIGION whose original ambition was to be a novelist. He became professor of RELIGIOUS STUDIES at the University of Chicago in 1956 from where he exercised a vast influence on the development of religious studies. Eliade's early novels, only recently translated into English, are said to have a FASCIST tinge, raising doubts about some of his philosophical assumptions. His work reflects an interest in a highly MYTHICAL, abstract spirituality which has been strongly criticized by anthropologists and historians for its detachment from EMPIRICAL reality. It includes *Yoga, Immortality and Freedom* (1936), *The Myth of the Eternal Return* (1954) and *Patterns in Comparative Religion* (1958).

ELIOT, Thomas Stearns (1888-1965): an American who became a British citizen, Eliot was a poet, critic and playwright, and a staunch ANGLICAN. His poem *The Waste Land* (1922) crystallized the spiritual desolation and alienation that followed World War I. His most successful play was *Murder in the Cathedral* (1935) which depicted the martyrdom of Thomas à BECKET. His essays include *The Idea of a Christian Society* (1939).

ELOHIST: term used by critical scholars of the HEBREW BIBLE to refer to the "author" of one of the sources, referred to as E, used in the composition of the Pentateuch. Among other characteristics, this hypothetical source is distinguished by its use of the Hebrew word ELOHIM to refer to GOD (*see* YAHWIST).

EMANATIONISM: the view that the UNIVERSE flows from the BEING of GOD rather like the rays of the sun shine forth from the sun. This viewpoint is found in YOGIC philosophies and such Western systems as NEOPLATONISM and GNOSTICISM.

EMERGENT EVOLUTION: the idea that life and consciousness have emerged out of inert matter and will ultimately evolve to a godlike state. This theory finds expression in the philosophy of Henri BERGSON.

EMERSON, Ralph Waldo (1803-1882): American essayist and leader of the TRANSCENDENTALIST movement. He was minister of the Unitarian Second Church of Boston (*see* UNITARIANISM) from 1829 to 1832, but resigned over theological issues to become an independent lecturer and writer. His PHILOSOPHY drew on YOGIC religions to combine RATIONALISM and MYSTICISM. It also encouraged a strong emphasis on self-reliance and a belief in the ability of the individual to overcome all problems. Although much more profound, he was the forerunner of Dale CARNEGIE and POSITIVE THINKING, which characterizes much American popular PIETY. His influence can be seen in the NEW

AGE MOVEMENT and a host of other popular spiritual movements seeking inner truth.

EMPIRICAL: knowledge founded on observation, FACTS, experience and sense perception. That which can be known directly by the senses.

EMPIRICISM: the view that all knowledge is ultimately derived from experience. It is contrasted with RATIONALISM, which is the view that the mind may arrive at true knowledge by the use of reason alone without appeal to experience.

ENCYCLOPEDISTS: the eighteenth-century French INTELLECTUALS who contributed to the *Encyclopédie*, which became a thirty-five-volume work designed to record all human knowledge. Edited by Denis Diderot, the project was highly SKEPTICAL and strongly critical of both the existing political order and RELIGION.

ENGELS, Friedrich (1820-1895): German industrialist who became patron, close friend and collaborator to Karl MARX in founding Marxism. Engels contributed many ideas to the Marxist movement, including what was to become known as DIALECTICAL MATERIALISM. From 1842 he ran his family's factory in Manchester, England, where he was also a rapacious landlord. While in Manchester he wrote *The Condition of the Working Class in England* (1845), supposedly based on his own experiences but actually written from outdated *Poor Law Reports*. This work is full of factual errors and deliberate attempts to exaggerate the true situation. As a militant ATHEIST, he welcomed DARWIN's theory of EVOLUTION as proof for his own anti-religious views.

ENLIGHTENMENT [1]: a movement characterized by the historian Ernst TROELTSCH (1865-1923) as the beginning of the really modern period of European CULTURE. It had its roots in PROTESTANT CHRISTIANITY and was strongly influenced by PIETISM. It found its clearest expression in the work of KANT who, in his book

Religion Within the Limits of Reason (1793), defined "the Enlightenment" as man's emergence from a self-inflicted state of minority. Kant wrote: "Have the courage to make use of your own understanding is therefore the watchword of the Enlightenment." The Enlightenment originated in the Netherlands and England in the mid-seventeenth century but reached its high-water mark in French RATIONALISM and MATERIALISM, finding political expression in the FRENCH REVOLUTION. Its richest philosophical and political results were achieved in Germany under the influence of Kant. Although many branches of the Enlightenment were consciously anti-Christian, a distinctive form of Enlightenment Christianity developed in Protestant countries that was influential in promoting concerns similar to those of the Rationalists. Enlightenment Christianity as such was characterized by a retreat from DOGMAS, SACRAMENTS and CEREMONIES, by FAITH in PROVIDENCE, obligation to "VIRTUE" and a tendency to subordinate Christian dogmas to current ideas from SCIENCE and culture.

ENLIGHTENMENT [2]: in YOGIC RELIGIONS, the attainment of a state of spiritual knowledge, awareness or bliss; in BUDDHISM, the revelatory experience of the BUDDHA and the attaining of NIRVĀNA.

ENTHUSIASM: the original Greek word means "rapture" or being possessed by a GOD. The word was used disparagingly in the seventeenth century to depict the religious attitude of the PURITANS and, in the eighteenth century, the METHODISTS. Today the word has the general sense of a passionate eagerness in any pursuit.

EPHESUS: one of the great cities of the ancient world, located in what is now Turkey. It was famous for its temple of the GODDESS Diana, and it featured prominently in the HISTORY of early CHRISTIANITY.

EPHESUS, COUNCIL OF: known as the Third ECUMENICAL COUNCIL, the Council of Ephesus was held in A.D. 431. It approved the VENERATION of the virgin MARY.

EPICTETUS (138-60 B.C.): STOIC philosopher whose work greatly influenced MARCUS AURELIUS and some early CHRISTIAN thinkers.

EPICUREANISM: a Greek PHILOSOPHICAL school, founded by EPICURUS, which taught detachment from the world through contentment and the attainment of happiness through the recognition that the absence of pain and distress is the greatest pleasure. The Epicureans rejected the idea of life after death and sought the GOOD life on earth through the cultivation of WISDOM.

EPICURUS (341-270 B.C.): Greek philosopher who cultivated friendship and rejected both SKEPTICISM and IDEALISM in favor of an emphasis on immediate experience. In his thought SENSE DATA is the basis of knowledge, the feeling of pleasure and the ultimate GOOD. He held to a form of atomic theory of the physical world and argued that body and SOUL are interdependent and that neither can survive without the other.

EPIPHANY: from the Greek, meaning "manifestation." It became a celebration in the CHRISTIAN CHURCH marking the appearance of CHRIST to the world and was celebrated on the sixth day of January.

EPIPHENOMENALISM: the theory that physical PHENOMENA are entirely responsible for our mental states and actions, so that thoughts in the brain are entirely determined by physical and not mental causes. The theory undermines traditional religious teaching about FREE WILL and moral responsibility.

EPISCOPALIAN: the North American term for ANGLICAN, it is derived from the Episcopal system of CHURCH government of the Anglican Church which involves the hierarchical organization of CLERGY and supervision of local churches by a BISHOP.

EPISTEMOLOGY: comes from the Greek words *epistēmē* meaning "knowledge" and LOGOS meaning "discourse." It is applied to that part of PHILOSOPHY concerned with issues surrounding the origins and nature of human cognition and knowledge.

EQUALITY: the idea that humans are "created equal." A popular religious-based idea, particularly in Western cultures, it is fraught with difficulties. Some would maintain that the notion needs to be interpreted in terms of equality of opportunity rather than a crude determination to make everyone equal despite natural talents and abilities.

EQUIVOCATION: using a term with two meanings as if it had only one. In other words, the misleading use of language, or ambiguity.

ERASMUS, Desiderius (1469-1536): Dutch CHRISTIAN HUMANIST who exercised a profound influence on the PROTESTANT REFORMERS although he never left the ROMAN CATHOLIC CHURCH and, after first encouraging LUTHER, became a strong critic of his THEOLOGY. His most famous books are *The Praise of Folly* (1509), *Education of a Christian Prince* (1516) and *Diatribe on Free Will* (1524), which was an attack on Luther's views.

ERHARD SEMINAR TRAINING: See EST.

ERHARD, Werner (1935-): born Jack Rosenberg, an American OCCULTIST and the founder of EST (Erhard Seminar Training). This involves an ECLECTIC type of self-development and spiritual technology based largely on ideas and practices derived from ZEN BUDDHISM and SCIENTOLOGY.

ERIGENA, Johannes Scotus (c. 815-877): Irish SCHOLASTIC philosopher who translated the works of Pseudo-Dionysus from Greek and promoted a form of Christian PANTHEISM. His works strongly influenced later medieval thinkers.

ESCHATOLOGY: literally meaning "discourse about the last things," it refers to that part of the THEOLOGY of a RELIGION which deals with the final end of humankind and of the world.

ESOTERIC: from the Greek term meaning "inner" or "hidden." Today it refers to secret teachings which either belong to secret societies or lie behind the official BELIEFS which a religious group proclaims to the world. Thus many NEW RELIGIOUS MOVEMENTS are based upon claims that they and they alone know the "true" meaning of a religious teacher's message, and that the apparent teaching conceals its real meaning.

ESP: extrasensory perception; claims by individuals to experience paranormal PHENOMENA such as TELEPATHY, PROPHECIES, significant or prophetic dreams, visions, powers to levitate and affect physical objects by mental power. Although most claims of this nature clearly belong to the realm of PSEUDOSCIENCE, sufficient examples exist in the experience of many people to leave open the possibility that some powers of this nature do exist. But there are two main problems with such claims: first, they clearly violate the known laws of MODERN SCIENCE; second, they are often made in connection with bizarre theories derived from YOGIC RELIGIONS and SPIRITUALISM devoid of all RATIONAL justification.

ESSENCE: the sum total of those ATTRIBUTES which cannot be removed from a BEING without destroying the being itself; e.g., rationality (*see* RATIONAL) is the traditional definition of human beings.

ESSENES: an ancient Jewish SECT dwelling in the vicinity of the Dead Sea about which little is known despite much speculation. They are generally believed to be associated with the DEAD SEA SCROLLS, although some scholars question this assumption. Since the nineteenth century various ESOTERIC religious movements have claimed continuity with the Essenes and used their name to propagate their own views. Such groups must be recognized as NEW RELIGIOUS MOVEMENTS lacking historical justifications for their claims, which are unfounded speculations.

EST: Erhard Seminar Training, founded in 1971 by Werner ERHARD on the basis of spiritual practices derived from ZEN BUDDHISM and SCIENTOLOGY. The movement, which has operated under a variety of names, organizes intense weekend seminars intended to break down inhibitions and bring individuals into touch with their true selves. Many participants report OCCULT experiences and encounters with SPIRIT BEINGS toward the end of the seminar, which is officially non-religious. Generally EST has helped promote a type of self-ENLIGHTENMENT and thus the NEW AGE MOVEMENT.

ETERNAL LIFE: in CHRISTIANITY, participation in the life of GOD through the NEW BIRTH is referred to as "eternal life." What is important here is the quality of life, not its timelessness. Eternal life is the gift of God to believers in response to their acceptance of forgiveness of SIN through the work of CHRIST.

ETERNAL PROGRESSION: the MORMON DOCTRINE of existence, which theorizes a spiritual EVOLUTION for humanity, resulting in their DEIFICATION to become "gods." The idea was summed up by the Mormon APOSTLE Lorenzo Snow, who said: "As man is, God was. As God is, man will become."

ETERNAL RECURRENCE: the idea that time is cyclic and all events ultimately repeat themselves.

ETERNITY: the opposite of time, what is timeless. In CHRISTIAN teaching "eternity" is associated with life after death and the realm of GOD or HEAVEN.

ETHICS: a theory of conduct and correct action. It answers questions such as: How can I know what is right and wrong? How should I act in this situation? What do we mean by the term "GOOD"?

ETHIOPIAN CHURCH: the ancient CHRISTIAN CHURCH of Ethiopia, which was founded by at least the third century and flourished for centuries as a genuine African expression of Christianity, though cut off from contact with the West by ISLAM.

EUCHARIST: a term derived from the Greek word meaning "to give thanks," which is applied to the SACRAMENT of the Lord's Supper, also known as Communion or "the Breaking of Bread."

EUCLID (c. 300 B.C.): Greek mathematician and "father" of geometry.

EUHEMERISM: the idea that the ancient GODS were originally CULTURE heroes elevated to divine status by popular sentiment.

EUNUCH: in the ancient Orient there was a cruel practice of castrating males to use them as slaves, often in attendance upon the wives of a king.

EUPHRATES: the great river of the ancient world, which runs from its source in Armenia to the Persian Gulf. Many biblical stories and allusions refer to the Euphrates.

EVANGEL: the gospel, or "good news," of CHRISTIANITY.

EVANGELICAL: pertaining to the gospel; one who is devoted to the good news, or "EVANGEL," of GOD's REDEMPTION in JESUS CHRIST. Evangelical Christians believe in the INSPIRATION OF THE BIBLE, to which they hold as the divine rule of FAITH and practice. They affirm the fundamental DOCTRINES of the gospel, including the INCARNATION, VIRGIN BIRTH of Christ, his sinless life, substitutionary ATONEMENT and bodily RESURRECTION as the grounds of God's forgiveness of SIN, JUSTIFICATION BY FAITH alone, and the spiritual REGENERATION of all who trust in Jesus Christ.

EVANGELIST: originally someone who spread the CHRISTIAN gospel. More recently the term has also been applied more generally to anyone who has a message—religious, political or social—to spread and who does so with zeal.

EVANGELIZATION: originally the propagation of the CHRISTIAN gospel. More recently the term has been generally applied to any form of propaganda aimed at making converts (see CONVERSION).

EVANS-PRITCHARD, Edward Evan (1902-1973): British anthropologist (see ANTHROPOLOGY) who, along with Raymond Firth, trained under Bronislaw Kasper MALINOWSKI. His first book *Witchcraft, Oracles and Magic Amongst the Azande* (1937) is a masterpiece which demonstrates the inner coherence of seemingly IRRATIONAL BELIEF systems. Its publication led to a bitter dispute with Malinowski who disassociated himself from Evans-Pritchard's views and attempted to prevent him from obtaining an academic post. Evans-Pritchard's CONVERSION to ROMAN CATHOLICISM in 1944 further raised the ire of the academic community but, with the help of RADCLIFFE-BROWN, in 1946 he obtained the chair of social anthropology at the University of Oxford and went on to establish the influential Oxford School of Social Anthropology.

EVE: the first woman and wife of ADAM in the BIBLE. Genesis 3:20 describes Eve as "the mother of all the living." The social significance of the story of Eve is that it emphasizes the unity of the human race which is described as springing from a common ancestor.

EVIL: either frustration of human values, or SIN—a want of conformity to, or transgression of, the law of GOD. All EVIL is either sin or God's punishment for sin.

EVIL EYE: a popular folk belief (see FOLK RELIGION), found in many cultures, which attributes powers of EVIL to the look of certain individuals.

EVOLUTION: in modern times the theory of evolution was first advanced by Charles BONNET (1720-1793) who argued that an embryo already contains all the parts of the mature organism. Charles LYELL speculated on the evolution of land animals in 1832, and his work influenced Charles DARWIN, who wrote *The Origin of Species* (1859). Prior to that, Herbert SPENCER in 1852 had defined a general theory of evolution from lower to higher forms of life and organization. What Darwin did was new; he described some of the processes by which new species developed and generalized these as "natural selection." In the development of social Darwinism, the generalized natural history provided images for social action and change and came to justify ruthless competition on the basis of "natural selection" and "the survival of the fittest."

EX CATHEDRA: literally, "from the chair." Refers to the POPE in his official office as head of the ROMAN CATHOLIC CHURCH. When the pope speaks ex cathedra his judgments in matters pertaining to FAITH and practice are assumed by his followers to be infallible.

EX NIHILO: literally, "out of nothing." The traditional CHRISTIAN BELIEF that GOD created the UNIVERSE without recourse to preexisting MATTER entirely by and from his own power and BEING. The DOCTRINE thus denies the possibility that CREATION might have been ontologically flawed (*see* ONTOLOGY) from the very beginning; instead, the presence of EVIL is attributed to the FALL.

EX OPERE OPERATO: a medieval CHRISTIAN theological CONCEPT expressing the idea that the SACRAMENTS are effective regardless of the worthiness of either the minister or the recipient. Critics of this view have pointed out the danger that the sacraments thereby come to be regarded as at best mechanical, at worst MAGICAL. BAPTISM, for example, can be perceived to result in the SALVATION of individuals regardless of the personal FAITH or lifestyle of the person concerned. The idea was rejected by PROTESTANTS who insisted on the importance of personal FAITH and individual commitment.

EXCLUDED MIDDLE: the law of logic which states that "A" is either "B" or not "B" (*see* CONTRADICTION, LAW OF).

EXCLUSIVE BRETHREN: a breakaway branch of the PLYMOUTH BRETHREN which followed John Nelson DARBY in insisting on high degrees of personal HOLINESS as expressed in a complete separation from "the world." Eventually the movement came under the control of leaders who imposed a growing number of regulations on their followers. The movement declined dramatically in the 1980s after a series of scandals involving suicides among members and the exposure of alcoholism and sexual abuse among some of its leaders.

EXCOMMUNICATE: to exclude or expel. Originally a form of discipline within the Christian CHURCH whereby persistent offenders against Christian ethical standards or people who rejected ORTHODOXY were disfellowshiped from the CONGREGATION and publicly censured by the CLERGY. Excommunication involved the denial of the SACRAMENTS and, by implication, the loss of SALVATION.

EXEGESIS: refers to the process of interpreting a text. It is to be distinguished from translation, on the one hand, and from inquiry into the principles of interpretation, or HERMENEUTICS, on the other.

EXISTENCE: usually contrasted with ESSENCE in classical THEOLOGY, and refers to the actuality in time and space of any subject, in contrast to its mere possibility or potentiality. In EXISTENTIALISM, the word *existence* refers to the unique way in which humans live their lives. Since the distinctive nature of human existence is choice of freedom, and freedom in turn cannot be defined as a "thing," Jean-Paul SARTRE has argued that "man has no essence" or "existence precedes essence."

EXISTENTIAL: an adjective frequently used in contemporary theological and religious literature to signify something that is of ultimate significance for one's BEING.

EXISTENTIALISM: a philosophical movement which emerged shortly before World War II united by common concerns, motifs and emphases. The most influential exponents were Martin HEIDEGGER, whose *Being and Time* appeared in 1927; Karl JASPERS, whose second volume of *Philosophie* appeared in 1932; and Jean-Paul SARTRE. All of the important leaders were indebted to the writings of Søren KIERKEGAARD (1813-1855), a once-neglected

Danish author whose works were not translated into German until early in this century and into English even later.

The movement may be characterized as follows. It begins with the conviction that Western PHILOSOPHY since the Greeks has been preoccupied with the idea of ESSENCE, that is with the general and UNIVERSAL features of anything, rather than with concrete, INDIVIDUAL essence being counted more real than EXISTENCE because it is unchanging. Consequently, Western philosophy has been INTELLECTUALISTIC and RATIONALISTIC. It is, therefore, irrelevant as far as illuminating life is concerned, because it has obscured the TRUTH about human existence instead of illuminating REALITY. Existentialism had a profound impact on NEO-ORTHODOX Christian theologians like Karl BARTH, and strongly influenced Rudolf BULTMANN, Paul TILLICH and Reinhold NIEBUHR, as well as some Roman Catholics like Gabriel MARCEL and Karl RAHNER. Broadly speaking, an existentialist Christian theology argues that the self is a unity of radical FREEDOM and limitedness. FAITH, therefore, is acceptance of this paradoxical unity. But faith is not the possession of a CREED, DOCTRINE or BELIEF; rather, it is the decision to be oneself as this person in this specific situation. This decision is made possible by the unconditioned acceptance of the person by GOD which enables each individual to have the courage to be.

EXODUS: the "coming out" of ISRAEL from Egyptian bondage and the name of the second book of the TORAH in the HEBREW BIBLE which relates this story; it has the powerful connotation of freedom from slavery.

EXORCISM: the act of casting out DEMONS in a RITUAL designed to free the individual from EVIL influences. In the ORTHODOX CHURCH exorcism is practiced prior to BAPTISM. As a result of RATIONALISM, during the nineteenth century belief in evil spirits was largely discarded by most Western churches. In recent years there has been a revival of the practice of exorcism and an increasing demand for the services of exorcists by troubled individuals.

EXPLANATION: to explain, clarify or describe something so that it is understood.

EXTINCTION OF OUTFLOWS: a synonym of ARAHANT in BUDDHISM signifying a person who has overcome worldly desires.

EZEKIEL (6th century B.C.): biblical PROPHET and author of the book of Ezekiel in the HEBREW BIBLE. His work is noted for its VISION of GOD and positive interpretation of the BABYLONIAN CAPTIVITY of the Jewish people in terms of the sovereignty of God.

EZRA (5th to 4th century B.C.): Jewish priest and scribe whose activities are recorded in the books of Ezra and Nehemiah in the HEBREW BIBLE. Under commission by Artaxerxes I, he returned from Babylon to Jerusalem and was responsible for reestablishing the Jewish community in Jerusalem and reenforcing Mosaic Law, including the racial purity of the Jewish people.

F

FA HSIEN (late 4th and early 5th centuries): famous Chinese BUDDHIST MONK who left China in A.D. 399 to visit India in search of Buddhist SCRIPTURES. Returning to China in A.D. 414, he initiated a period of intense translation of the manuscripts he had collected. His adventures were recorded in *The Narrative of Fa Hsien*, which was translated into English in 1869.

FABIANS: members of the Fabian Society, an important British SOCIALIST society, founded in 1883, which favored an evolutionary socialist "permeation" of CAPITALIST institutions and opposed the REVOLUTIONARY DOCTRINE of MARX. The society was named after the Roman general Fabius Cunctator, who defeated his enemies by wearing them down with long campaigns rather than pitched battles.

FACT: any unit of BEING which is capable of bearing MEANING.

FAITH: In CHRISTIAN thought two tendencies concerning faith may be observed: first, faith is regarded as BELIEF or mental assent to the TRUTH; and second, faith is understood as the orientation of the total person best described as trust, confidence or loyalty. The THEOLOGICAL system of Thomas AQUINAS was based on an intellectualistic model of faith. His teachings are basic to the DOCTRINE of ROMAN CATHOLICISM in which faith is to be regarded as an act of intellectual assent to SUPERNATURAL truths based on their divine AUTHORITY. LUTHER rejected this view of faith, arguing instead that faith is the response of the total person to the gospel. Other religious systems sometimes make use of the word *faith* when translating texts into English, but only PURE LAND BUDDHISM has a view of faith similar to the Christian one. The other usages distort both the meaning of faith and the beliefs of the religion concerned. It is possible to speak about "the faith" of a group, meaning the complex of beliefs and practices belonging to a particular RELIGION. But in general faith refers to Christianity.

FALL: a term used in CHRISTIAN THEOLOGY to denote humanity's original rebellion against GOD as described in the biblical story of ADAM and EVE, found in Genesis 2—3. Theologians argue about whether the story is to be taken literally or whether it is symbolic of the human condition. Most agree that the essential point of the Christian understanding of the human situation is that suffering and EVIL entered the world as a result of a wrong moral choice on the part of human beings. Other religious traditions either do not share this view of the human condition or view it as an ONTOLOGICAL and not a moral problem. JUDAISM does not see the human condition as resulting from an act of rebellion, while HINDUISM expresses a far more radical pessimism based on the essential nature of existence within the bounds of KARMA.

FALLACY: arguments which seem correct but upon examination prove false. They are arguments which are psychologically persuasive but logically wrong because of mistakes in relating, inferring or concluding. Traditional logic identified fallacies as either "formal" or "informal." A formal fallacy appears valid but actually breaks the rules of reasoning. Informal fallacies are harder to discover but can usually be exposed by counterexamples. They result from either carelessness and inattention to the subject matter or through ambiguity in the language used. As a result, informal fallacies may be classified as fallacies of relevance and fallacies of ambiguity.

FALSIFIABILITY: a variant of the VERIFICATION PRINCIPLE developed by Sir Karl POPPER, who argued that while we cannot absolutely prove that something is true, it is possible to falsify theories and beliefs, thus eliminating error. He made falsification the test of TRUTH in his theory of SCIENCE and used it to distinguish between science and PSEUDOSCIENCE.

FALWELL, Jerry (1934-): American FUNDAMENTALIST leader, pastor of Thomas Road BAPTIST CHURCH and founder of Liberty University. He achieved national attention through his involvement with the MORAL MAJORITY movement of which he was the founder. He is the author of *The Fundamentalist Phenomenon* (1981).

FAMILY OF LOVE: *see* CHILDREN OF GOD.

FANON, Franz (1925-1961): French-speaking psychoanalyst and political philosopher from Martinique who developed the idea of "negritude" and a theory of violence as a therapeutic process of religious intensity. He is the author of various books, including *Black Skin, White Masks* (1952) and *The Wretched of the Earth* (1961), both of which contributed to the theory of terrorism and LIBERATION THEOLOGY.

FĀRĀBĪ, Abū Naṣr Muḥammad al- (870?-950): famous Turkish philosopher who settled in Baghdad and wrote commentaries on ARISTOTLE, his "teacher." He was also influenced by NEOPLATONISM and PLATO's *Republic*. He argued that REASON is superior to FAITH and that PROPHECY is a gift which supplements RATIONAL faculties.

FARD, Wallace D. (? -1934 ?): (also Wali Farad Muhammad) a clothes peddler of unknown origin, he appeared in Detroit in 1930 claiming to have come from MECCA with a mission to found the NATION OF ISLAM IN THE WEST. He wrote *The Secret Ritual of the Nation of Islam* and *Teaching for the Lost-Found Nation of Islam in a Mathematical Way* and was regarded as a PROPHET by his followers. He vanished mysteriously in 1934 and was succeeded by Elijah Muhammad.

FAREL, Guillaume (1489-1565): French PROTESTANT REFORMER who worked closely with John CALVIN in Geneva.

FARRER, Austin Marsden (1904-1968): English ANGLO-CATHOLIC theologian philosopher and close friend of C. S. LEWIS. His best-known book is *The Glass of Vision* (1948).

FARRER, Frederick William (1831-1903): English ANGLICAN theologian who wrote a popular book titled *Life of Christ* (1874) and strongly influenced F. D. MAURICE.

FASCISM: a name derived from the Latin word *fasces* which means a bundle of rods carried by a Roman consul as a sign of authority. The word was used by the Italian dictator Mussolini (1883-1945) to describe the political movement he led to power in 1922. Later it was applied to the NAZIS in Germany and various other political movements which emphasized the role of the leader in national SALVATION. All forms of fascism have strong CULTIC overtones and draw upon religious symbolism to create essentially SECULAR forms of RELIGION. The best analysis of fascism in terms of its religious motivation is to be found in Peter F. DRUCKER's *The End of Economic Man* (1939).

FASTING: the practice of abstaining from food and/or other physical necessities and pleasures for religious purposes. Through fasting humans are believed to gain a clearer understanding of the ways of God and to be able to offer more meaningful PRAYER. In addition to being used as an exercise to increase SPIRITUALITY fasting is also often used as a form of PENANCE to express REPENTANCE.

FATE: the BELIEF that human affairs are destined by COSMIC powers, either GOD or gods or the workings of the UNIVERSE.

FATHERHOOD OF GOD: an idea implicit in the HEBREW BIBLE and clearly stated in the NEW TESTAMENT that GOD is like a loving father to Jesus the Son of God and to believers as sons of God.

FĀTIḤAH: the title of the opening *Sūra* of the QUR'ĀN.

FĀṬIMA (7th century): daughter of MUḤAMMAD who married Ali ibn Abī Ṭālib. SHI'A IMĀMS claim descent from Muhammad through her sons. In some Shi'a circles, Fātima has become an object of devotion similar to the Virgin MARY in ROMAN CATHOLICISM.

FATWĀ: a decree or ruling given by a muftī, or legal scholar, on a point of law in ISLAM.

FEMINIST THEOLOGY: a recent development in North American THEOLOGY inspired by the Women's Movement, feminist theology seeks to emphasize the contribution of women and their unique SPIRITUALITY within the CHRISTIAN TRADITION. In its mild and ORTHODOX forms feminist theology is simply an attempt to recognize the role of women in the Bible and Christian history. More radical versions of feminist theology concentrate on the GODDESS RELIGION and other forms of NEOPAGANISM. The most far-reaching influence of feminist theology has been its insistence on inclusive language, which avoids the use of masculine terms, in CHURCH WORSHIP and in the translation of the Bible.

FERGUSON, Marilyn Grasso (1938-): popular American publicist and advocate of the OCCULT and YOGIC RELIGION, which she first encountered through TRANSCENDENTAL MEDITATION. Her best-selling book, *The Aquarian Conspiracy* (1980), was largely responsible for giving form to the NEW AGE MOVEMENT and creating a consensus about its reality and importance as a spiritual force.

FESTIVALS: all religious TRADITIONS celebrate various feast days or festivals. These usually recall events associated with the HISTORY of the religion and are intended to inspire DEVOTEES to greater devotion.

FETISH: a term derived from the Portuguese *feitico*, meaning "skillfully made," and originally applied by sailors to objects of devotion found in West Africa. Later it came to be applied to any object believed to have SACRED significance and the ability to protect its owner from EVIL.

FEUERBACH, Ludwig Andreas (1804-1872): German materialist philosopher (*see* MATERIALISM) famous for his statement "A man is what he eats," which he used to explain English victories over Irish rebels. He studied under HEGEL, whose idealism he rejected in favor of a thoroughgoing materialism. Subsequently he strongly attacked religious beliefs, especially those of PROTESTANT CHRISTIANITY as represented by Friedrich SCHLEIERMACHER, by arguing that the idea of GOD is an outward projection of man's inner nature. Thus the Holy Family reflects the inadequacies of actual human families and subconsciously compensates for them in the imagination of the believer. His work had a profound influence on Karl MARX, who accepted and improved upon his basic criticisms of religion. His most important works are *The Essence of Christianity* (1840) and *The Essence of Religion* (1846).

FICHTE, Johann Gottlieb (1762-1814): German philosopher who promoted his own version of KANTIAN thought and a rabid NATIONALISM which found expression in his *Address to the German Nation* (1808-1809). His writings are seen by many as one of the intellectual roots of modern RACISM.

FIDEISM: BELIEFS that rest entirely on FAITH without RATIONAL support and often use arguments that deny the VALIDITY of rationality.

FILIAL PIETY: the supreme VIRTUE in Confucian ETHICS (*see* CONFUCIUS), associated with the honoring of elders and the ANCESTORS.

FILIOQUE CLAUSE: the doctrinal formula found in Western Christian CREEDS meaning "and the Son," which affirms the DOUBLE PROCESSION of the HOLY SPIRIT from "the Father and the Son."

FINAL CAUSE: the end REASON for a process, as the purpose which GOD had in mind in creating the UNIVERSE.

FINDHORN COMMUNITY: one of the most influential NEW AGE communities and sources for modern NEOPAGANISM. Founded in 1965 by Eileen and Peter CADDY as a trailer park in northern Scotland, the community ascribed its success to the intervention of NATURE SPIRITS. In 1970 David SPANGLER joined the community to eventually become its leading theorist and advocate. The community is deeply influenced by and promotes various forms of OCCULTISM of THEOSOPHICAL origin.

FINITE: having specific limits or boundaries; opposed to infinite.

FINNEY, Charles Grandison (1792-1875): American CLERGYMAN, educator and creator of modern EVANGELISM. Following a profound conversion experience he abandoned a legal career to become a PRESBYTERIAN minister and revivalist

preacher. Later he abandoned many CALVINIST teachings and moved toward an ARMINIAN theology. He founded Oberlin College, where he was professor of theology from 1837 to 1875 and president from 1851 to 1866. In his *Lectures on Revival* (1835) he stressed the techniques needed to create REVIVALS. A tendency to psychologize Christian experience is also found in his *Systematic Theology* (1847).

FIQH: the legal order of ISLAM as exercised in the courts and expounded by the various legal schools; jurisprudence.

FISH: the symbol of the EARLY CHURCH, derived from the acronym of the Greek word *ichthys*, which represents the Greek words for JESUS CHRIST, SON OF GOD, Savior.

FITNA: originally a term used to speak about the persecution borne by the early followers of MUHAMMAD. In time it came to be applied to sedition or conspiracy against an Islamic STATE and eventually hostility to ISLAM.

FLAGELLATION: whipping or other harsh punishment for the purpose of mortifying the flesh and promoting spiritual well-being. The practice is found in many religious traditions. It was popular in medieval Christian MONASTICISM but has fallen into disuse among most Christian groups today.

FLEW, Anthony (1923-): probably the leading British AGNOSTIC, HUMANIST and philosopher of the 1960s and 1970s. The author of many books on RELIGION and PHILOSOPHY, including *God and Philosophy* (1966) and *The Presumption of Atheism* (1972). His work presents a strong and yet academically fair challenge to CHRISTIAN BELIEF.

FLOOD: the story of a universal flood is found in Genesis 6—9, as well as in many other ancient documents, and also in the mythologies (*see* MYTH) of Native Americans and many other peoples.

FLORENCE, COUNCIL OF: a general COUNCIL of the CHRISTIAN CHURCH held in Florence from 1438 to 1445 to heal the rift between the ROMAN CATHOLIC and ORTHODOX CHURCHES. It established the important principle that unity does not depend on uniform LITURGICAL styles, but collapsed without agreement on doctrinal issues.

FLUX: change, becoming, movement; e.g., as a flowing river.

FOLK RELIGION: popular RELIGIONS, BELIEFS and practices—sometimes referred to as "little traditions"—which operate alongside and often in opposition to the dominant religious TRADITION of a SOCIETY. Such religions often involve MAGIC, HEALING, prophetic movements (*see* PROPHECY) and local charismatic leaders (*see* CHARISMA) or healers. Folk religion is often regarded as a threat by the dominant tradition, which may take active steps to suppress its practice.

FOOD: many religions have strict food laws which create social barriers or boundaries between believers and non-believers. The most obvious example is to be found in JUDAISM, where the priestly laws of the book of Leviticus are applied to daily life in the Mishnah and TALMUD. Similar rules are found in ISLAM, and other rules apply to PRIESTS in BUDDHISM, HINDUISM and MONASTIC orders in CHRISTIANITY.

FORD, Henry (1863-1947): American inventor and automobile manufacturer, who is credited with the expression "History is bunk."

FOREKNOWLEDGE: the CHRISTIAN BELIEF that in one simple and eternal act of cognition GOD knows the past, present and future.

FORM: an important philosophical term referring to the essential REALITY of things. It is particularly important in Platonism (*see* PLATO), where form, which is true and eternal, is contrasted with APPEARANCE, which is temporal and deceptive.

FORM CRITICISM: from the German *Formgeschichte;* a method of analysis and interpretation of preliterary oral TRADI-

TIONS based on the conviction that ancient writers frequently collected, arranged and edited materials, stories and legends already circulating in the CULTURE in which they lived. Form criticism was first applied to the HEBREW BIBLE before being applied to the NEW TESTAMENT. It seeks to discover the "original" oral tradition behind the literary documents.

FORM-MATTER GROUND MOTIVE: a term used in the Christian PHILOSOPHY of Herman DOOYEWEERD to signify the encounter between the old pre-Homeric Greek RELIGION of life and the later cultural religion of the Olympian GODS. The older religion deified the eternally flowing stream of life, which is unable to fix itself in any individual form, but out of which transitory beings are generated whose existence is limited by an individual form, with the result that they are subjected to the fate of death. This is the MATTER motive of Greek thought, which found its most pregnant expression in the worship of DIONYSUS. The form motive, found in the later Olympian religion, valued measure and harmony and rested on the essential DEIFICATION of the CULTURAL aspect of Greek society and the personification of cultural powers through the Olympian gods. Its greatest expression was in the WORSHIP of the lawgiver, the Delphic god APOLLO.

FORMAL: pertaining to the theory of logical validity; not material or concrete.

FORMGESCHICHTE: *see* FORM CRITICISM.

FORMLESS: an Indian religious CONCEPT signifying those levels of the UNIVERSE where MATTER is absent. It is the higher form of trance.

FOSDICK, Harry Emerson (1878-1969): American BAPTIST minister who taught practical THEOLOGY and played a prominent role in promoting theological LIBERALISM in the FUNDAMENTALIST controversy. He was a great popularizer and promoted BIBLICAL CRITICISM, the PSYCHOLOGY OF RELIGION and a psychologically orientated personal PIETY. He influenced American preaching through his "problem orientated" homiletical style. His works include *The Modern Use of the Bible* (1924) and *On Being a Real Person* (1943).

FOUCAULT, Michel (1926-1988): influential French philosopher who promoted a highly RELATIVISTIC conception of the prevailing assumptions about what is to count as knowledge and as acceptable discourse. His views are expounded in *The Order of Things* (1970), *The Archaeology of Knowledge* (1972) and various other works.

FOUR HOLY TRUTHS: the four principles of existence discovered by the BUDDHA. They are: suffering, the cause of suffering, the cessation of suffering, and the path which leads to the cessation of suffering. See DUKKHA.

FOUR NOBLE TRUTHS: see FOUR HOLY TRUTHS.

FOX, George (1624-1691): English MYSTIC and prophetic figure who suffered considerable persecution for his faith and founded the QUAKERS or Society of FRIENDS in 1652. Disillusioned by existing CHURCHES and systems of THEOLOGY, he stressed the need for direct communion with GOD through what he called the "INNER LIGHT." His essentially CHRISTIAN ORTHODOXY and personal PIETY can be seen from his published *Journal*.

FOX, Matthew (1940-): ROMAN CATHOLIC PRIEST and speculative theologian of doubtful ORTHODOXY whose works have been censured by his CHURCH but taken up by the NEW AGE MOVEMENT. In 1977 he founded the Institute in Culture and Creation Spirituality in Chicago, which he moved to California in 1981. Through this Institute he propagated his views and gave a platform to such people as the self-styled "witch Starhawk" and other NEO-PAGAN leaders like the self-proclaimed VOODOO priestess Luisha Teish and various neo-SHAMAN and YOGA practitioners.

FOXE, John (1516-1587): English Protestant and author of *Acts and Monuments of Matters Happening in the Church*—popularly known as *Foxe's Book of Martyrs*—which documented ROMAN CATHOLIC persecution of PROTESTANTS. For at least two centuries this book was the most important and widely read religious work in English after the BIBLE and *The Pilgrim's Progress*.

FRANCIS OF ASSISI (c.1181-1226): founder of the FRANCISCAN Order and son of a wealthy textile merchant. In 1202, after taking part in a feud in a nearby city, he was imprisoned for over a year. This experience led him to reflect on life and make a PILGRIMAGE to Rome in 1205. After a vision, he began to rebuild the church of Saint Damian near Assisi. His father, assisted by the local bishop, attempted to forcibly restore him to a secular vocation, but he persisted in his religious convictions, whereupon his father disowned him. In 1209 he began preaching brotherly love, apostolic poverty and repentance. This led to the founding of his order and his original Rule. In 1224 he retired to a hermitage (*see* HERMIT) to spend the remainder of his life in PRAYER. During this time he composed his *Canticle to the Sun* and is alleged to have borne the STIGMATA, the marks of the crucifixion of CHRIST. He was canonized two years after his death (*see* CANONIZATION).

FRANCIS OF SALES (1567-1622): French ROMAN CATHOLIC PRIEST and MYSTIC, whose book *Introduction to the Devout Life* (1607) is a classic of Catholic spirituality.

FRANCISCANS: the MONASTIC order founded by FRANCIS OF ASSISI in 1209 based on the Rule of poverty, preaching and penance. Two modified versions of the original Rule followed. They relaxed its stricter obligations and opened the order to a wider selection of candidates. Francis always preferred his original, stricter Rule. For four centuries after his death conflict divided the order over which Rule ought to be followed. The order is noted for its charitable works, hospitals, schools and MISSIONARY endeavors. Five members of the order have become popes, and it has produced such outstanding philosophers as BONAVENTURE, DUNS SCOTUS and William of OCKHAM.

FRAZER, Sir James George (1854-1941): a British lawyer, influenced by William Robertson SMITH, who in 1907 became the first professor of social anthropology at the University of Liverpool, England. He quickly retired from this post and devoted his life to writing. Although a prolific writer, his anthropology was decidedly of the "armchair" variety, based on interpretations of works by MISSIONARIES, traders and travellers. He tended to take BELIEFS and practices totally out of their social and historical context to create a grand theory. His influence on the development of COMPARATIVE RELIGION and popular religious ideas was considerable, as can be seen by the continuing popularity of his major work *The Golden Bough* (published in twelve volumes between 1890 and 1915), which attempts to show underlying themes common to all religions. His other works include *Folklore of the Old Testament* (1918) and *The Fear of Death in Primitive Religion* (1933-1936). While his work remains popular with the public, it has little scholarly value.

FREE CHURCHES: those English CHURCHES and by extension churches in former British colonies, sometimes called nonconformist, which rejected ANGLICANISM and sought to remain independent of STATE control. The term is also used more broadly to refer to churches that historically reject governmental affiliation, such as ANABAPTISTS.

FREE THINKERS: people who reject the AUTHORITY of RELIGION in favor of a belief in REASON as the ultimate and only authority in human affairs. Free thinkers have tended to be violently anti-religious, though there is nothing in their position that demands such an attitude.

FREE WILL: the belief and feeling that the individual is capable of making uncaused decisions and actions which are devoid of external compulsion. The belief that the will is not determined or caused by anything but itself. The notion of free will has been challenged by various forms of DETERMINISM which point to social, psychological and other factors which influence human action. Theologically, the freedom of the will raises questions about GOD'S OMNISCIENCE and FOREKNOWLEDGE. The question of SIN in CHRISTIAN THEOLOGY also poses the problem of the extent to which human decisions are biased as a result of the FALL and disobedience to God's LAW. Arguments around this topic have centered on LUTHER's book *The Bondage of the Will*, and the theological conflict between CALVINISM and ARMINIANISM.

FREEDOM: an important concept in Western PHILOSOPHY, where it becomes the basis for moral choice and the foundation of traditional legal thought. It is characterized by a lack of restraint and the ability to make one's own decisions without interference. The concept runs into difficulties when we try to understand what is meant by "restraint" and what limits exist that inhibit our ability to act freely. As a result, intense debate rages around the concept. In RELIGION it becomes an important issue in terms of the justice of GOD. Can humans freely choose to serve God, or do they require divine assistance? If God's GRACE is needed to bring men and women into his service, is it fair for God to judge those who do not respond, when they lack the grace needed to enable them to respond? The issue is complex and has plagued both philosophers and theologians for centuries.

FREEMASONRY: an international organization whose principles are embodied in SYMBOLS and ALLEGORIES connected with the art of building and involving an oath of secrecy. The origins of the movement probably lie in twelfth-century Europe. There are two major divisions: the Old Charges, which date from 1390 and 1400, and The Masonic Word, which is a Scottish institution of obscure origin. From the eighteenth century there developed "Speculative Masonry" or modern Freemasonry. The Grand Lodge was formed in 1717 to coordinate other Lodges. The origins of most Masonic ceremonies are obscure and probably date to the seventeenth century. The movement places considerable emphasis on social welfare activities and claims to be based on the fundamentals of all religions. In the eighteenth century it was closely associated with DEISM and even today a general deistic ethos generally prevails, modified by the incorporation of religious symbols derived from Assyrian and Egyptian beliefs. The CHURCH OF ENGLAND, ROMAN CATHOLIC CHURCH and many EVANGELICAL denominations have condemned Freemasonry as un-Christian. Recently various sensationalist journals have published exposés, claiming that Freemasonry is a closed club which often breaks the law to promote the interests of its members. Such claims are, of course, vehemently denied by Masons.

FRENCH REVOLUTION: one of the great events of modern history, it began in 1789 and led to the overthrow of monarchical government in France by republican forces followed by a reign of terror and the eventual triumph of Napoleon Bonaparte.

FREUD, Sigmund (1856-1940): Austrian neurologist and founder of psychoanalysis. He worked on the treatment of hysteria by hypnosis but later developed a method of treatment in which he replaced hypnosis by free association of ideas. He believed that a complex of repressed and forgotten impressions underlies all abnormal mental states such as hysteria, and he developed the theory that dreams are an unconscious representation of repressed desires, especially sexual desires. Strongly anti-Christian, he authored *The Future of an Illusion* (1927) and *Moses and Monotheism* (1939), works which develop projectionist theories similar to those of FEUERBACH. In

many respects his technique of psychoanalysis can be seen as a form of SECULAR MYSTICISM reminiscent of Jewish mystical thought.

FRIENDS, SOCIETY OF: known as QUAKERS. Their beliefs may be traced to R. Barclay's (1648-1690) book *Theologiae Verae Christianae Apologia* (1676), which argued that CHRISTIANS ought to be guided by an "INNER LIGHT." The founder of the movement proper was George FOX, who experienced a profound religious CONVERSION in 1647 followed by a VISION in 1652. His first converts were called "Friends in Truth," but quickly acquired the derogatory nickname "Quaker" because of the trembling which characterized their WORSHIP. Quakers emphasize simplicity of worship and direct guidance from GOD. Over the centuries the role of the BIBLE has tended to diminish in Quaker congregations, although a small group has remained faithful to biblical authority. The Quakers have produced some outstanding leaders and social reformers such as William PENN and Elizabeth FRY.

FROBENIUS, Leo (1873-1938): German anthropologist (*see* ANTHROPOLOGY) and student of Ratzel who developed a THEORY of cultural areas of human civilization. He emphasized the importance of fieldwork and was in many ways the forerunner of MALINOWSKI. His works include *Kulturgeschichte Afrikas* (1933).

FROEBEL, Friedrich Wilhelm August (1782-1852): German educationalist and originator of the "Kindergarten."

FROMM, Erich (1900-1980): German-American PSYCHOLOGIST who developed his ideas in terms of the work of both FREUD and MARX to apply psychoanalysis to society generally in the form of a new HUMANISM. He drew inspiration from BUDDHISM and the CHRISTIAN mystical tradition and is well known for his psychological character studies of famous historical personalities. His books include *The Fear of Freedom* (1941) and *The Anatomy of Human Destructiveness* (1973).

FRY, Elizabeth (1780-1845): English QUAKER and advocate of prison reform and practical help for the poor.

FULL GOSPEL BUSINESSMEN'S FELLOWSHIP INTERNATIONAL: a highly successful inter-DENOMINATIONAL, EVANGELISTIC lay organization promoting CHARISMATIC CHRISTIANITY founded in 1951 by Demos SHAKARIAN.

FUNCTIONALISM: the ANTHROPOLOGICAL and SOCIOLOGICAL THEORY which attempts to explain social reality in terms of an interrelated system where in order to explain one part of the system, its consequences, or functions, for other parts must be shown.

FUNDAMENTALISM: a CONSERVATIVE theological movement which arose in American PROTESTANTISM in the 1920s in opposition to "MODERNISM." Fundamentalism should be understood primarily as an attempt to protect the essential DOCTRINES, or "fundamentals," of the CHRISTIAN FAITH from the eroding effects of modern thought. The doctrines considered essential by fundamentalists include: the VIRGIN BIRTH of JESUS, his RESURRECTION and DEITY, his substitutionary ATONEMENT and Second Coming. Finally, they lay great stress on the authority of the BIBLE, which is usually expressed in terms of its INFALLIBILITY and INERRANCY.

The roots of fundamentalism go back to the nineteenth century, when EVOLUTION, BIBLICAL CRITICISM and COMPARATIVE RELIGION began to challenge the authority of the biblical REVELATION. A significant offensive against modernism was launched in 1910 with the publication of *The Fundamentals,* a series of tracts written by conservative scholars to counter theological tendencies they considered dangerous. In a relatively short time the fundamentalist image became stereotyped as closed-minded, belligerent, separatist and uncultured. Even though the original fundamentalists included some well-educated scholars—some from leading universities, such of J. Gresham MACHEN at Princeton—the movement as a whole quickly became identified with a rejection of education and a reactionary rural nostalgia.

Recently the term "fundamentalism" has been applied to MUSLIMS and members of other faiths who wish to retain their TRADITIONAL BELIEFS. Although there may be some merit in such usage, it is very misleading because many people identified thus are simply anti-Western. For example, the Iranian REVOLUTION is usually described as "fundamentalist Islam," while the Saudis are seen as pro-Western and therefore more LIBERAL. In reality the Iranians interpret the QUR'ĀN in a far more liberal and open manner than the Saudis, who are much closer to Christian fundamentalists in their religious beliefs and practices than the Iranians. The use of "fundamentalism" in this context is, therefore, not very helpful.

FUNDAMENTALIST: a CONSERVATIVE CHRISTIAN who affirms "the fundamentals" of the Christian faith (*see* FUNDAMENTALISM).

FURQĀN: a title of the QUR'ĀN meaning "the distinguisher" or the criterion.

G

GABLER, Johann Philipp (1753-1826): German theologian and pioneer of BIBLICAL CRITICISM. He was one of the earliest scholars to make a sharp distinction between the historical investigation of the BIBLE and the theological, or dogmatic, task of articulating Christian belief from Scripture.

GABRIEL: The name of a heavenly messenger or ANGEL of great power and holiness in the Bible, who interprets DANIEL's dreams and announces the births of JOHN THE BAPTIST and JESUS. In ISLAM, he is said to have revealed the QUR'ĀN to MUHAMMAD.

GAIA: the name, taken from that of the Greek earth GODDESS Gē or Gaia, given by the NEW AGE MOVEMENT to the belief that the earth is a living organism. Although justified in terms of ecology, this is the revival of a medieval OCCULT idea which has been popularized by NEOPAGANISM and groups like the FINDHORN COMMUNITY. The idea that NATURE is alive is often connected with belief in such beings as fairies and nature SPIRITS.

GALBRAITH, John Kenneth (1908-): Canadian-American, "Keynesian" (*see* John Maynard KEYNES) economist, and advisor to the American Democratic Party. In 1961 he was appointed American ambassador to India. He shaped the thoughts of many people about modern society through such books as *The Affluent Society* (1958) and *The New Industrial State* (1967).

GALEN, Claudius (130-200): Greek physician and author whose works, especially on medicine, deeply influenced both CHRISTIAN and ISLAMIC thought.

GALILEO, Galilei (1564-1642): Italian astronomer whose theories about the universality of motion and mechanistic nature of the universe, attack on the philosophy of Aristotle, and confrontational personality brought him into conflict with the ROMAN CATHOLIC CHURCH. In the nineteenth century he became a popular, rationalist hero who was seen as a MARTYR for SCIENCE against the dogmatism of RELIGION. In reality he went out of his way to provoke the church and was as dogmatic and intolerant as his opponents.

GALLICANISM: the theory developed by French theologians in the fourteenth century and popular until at least the late nineteenth century that the ROMAN CATHOLIC CHURCH in France ought to be free from PAPAL AUTHORITY.

GANDHABBAS (Pali); GANDHARVAS (Sanskrit): a class of heavenly BEINGS whose existence is taken for granted in BUDDHIST cosmology. They are the lowest of the DEVAS and subject to the law of REBIRTH.

GANDHI, Mohandas Karamchand (1869-1948): Indian political leader and MYSTIC who developed a technique of spiritual/political action which he called "Satyāgraha" (truth-force). Today he is remembered as an advocate of nonviolent resistance. Gandhi was opposed to modern technology and sought to return India to its spiritual roots.

GAŅEŚA: a popular HINDU GOD who was the son of Śiva and KĀLĪ. He is represented as an elephant-headed being and is regarded as the union of opposites, being partly human, partly elephant. Thus he is seen as symbolizing the identity between God and man.

GARBHAGŖHA: from the SANSKRIT term referring to the home, womb or seed. It is used to refer to the inner sanctum of a TEMPLE.

GARDNER, Gerald Brousseau (1884-1964): English Mason, OCCULTIST and creator of modern WITCHCRAFT, or WICCA. Gardner was sickly as a child and consequently received very little formal education. In 1900 he moved to Sri Lanka to work on a plantation, and later his work as a civil servant led him to travel widely. In the process he absorbed local Eastern CULTURES and FOLK BELIEFS. Retiring to England in 1938, he joined a THEOSOPHICAL group, led by the daughter of Annie BESANT, and met Dorothy Clutterbuck who initiated him into WITCHCRAFT. Under the name Scire, he published a novel, *High Magic's Aid* (1948), outlining ideas about MAGICAL RITUAL. When England's Witchcraft Laws were repealed in 1951, he published *Witchcraft Today* (1954) and numerous other OCCULT books.

GARDNERIAN WITCHCRAFT: a very influential NEW RELIGIOUS MOVEMENT which has influenced WICCA and many NEOPAGAN groups. Gardner's system is a mishmash of Masonic ritual, Eastern FOLK CULTURE, YOGIC RELIGION and his own vivid imagination, all designed to appeal to a popular audience on the basis of its alleged historical roots. He tried to re-create the type of WITCHCRAFT discussed by Margaret A. MURRAY in her various books by creating RITUALS and BELIEFS to integrate OCCULT, SPIRITUALIST and YOGIC RELIGIONS into a Gothic-type MYTHOLOGY. Central to his ideas is the creation of a CULT of the Mother GODDESS. In 1963 Gardner initiated Raymond and Rosemary Buckland, who spread his CREED to North America. Gardner almost single-handedly created and supplied the NEOPAGAN Movement with pseudohistorical justifications leading many to falsely believe that they were joining an ancient religion which had flourished underground for centuries while being officially suppressed by CHRISTIANITY.

GĀTHĀS: the oldest writings of the ZOROASTRIAN SCRIPTURES, the Avesta, which form a liturgy of seventeen HYMNS.

GAUTAMA (563-483 B.C.?): the SANSKRIT name for the founder of BUDDHISM, known in PALI as Gotama. In traditional stories he appears as a wealthy North Indian prince who lived about 100 years before AŚOKA. The details of his life are legendary and MYTHOLOGICAL. We do not even know the language he spoke, although it is generally believed to be Ardhamagadhi. Thus none of his sayings have been preserved in their original form and of his actual words nothing survives. Our earliest surviving written texts are fragmentary and were written several centuries after his death. Modern scholarship dates his death at 483 B.C., although Indian Buddhists argue for a variety of dates, including one as early as 852 B.C.

GĀYĀ: a small town in Bihar, northern India, which is where the BUDDHA is believed to have received ENLIGHTENMENT. It is one of the four SACRED places for BUD-

DHIST pilgrims (*see* PILGRIMAGE).

GEERTZ, Clifford (1926-): American anthropologist (*see* ANTHROPOLOGY) and strong advocate of cultural RELATIVISM. His works include *Islam Observed* (1968) and *The Interpretation of Cultures* (1973).

GEHENNA: a valley between JERUSALEM and the hills to the south and west which gained an evil reputation due to its CULTIC associations with human SACRIFICE. In later Jewish literature it is equated with the place of punishment of the wicked by fire, and in the NEW TESTAMENT it is described as a pit into which the evil are cast. As a result it became synonymous with HELL.

GEISTESWISSENSCHAFTEN: a German word meaning "spiritual sciences" as distinct from the "physical sciences." The term includes such things as AESTHETICS, ETHICS and RELIGION.

GENERAL SYSTEMS THEORY: an influential interpretation of REALITY in terms of inter-related systems developed by Jay Forester (*Principles of Systems*, 1968), Ludwig von Bertalanffy (*Robots, Men and Minds*, 1967), Immanuel Wallerstein (*The Modern World-System*, 1974) and others which among other things led to the development of ideas about ecology and eventually to the ECOLOGICAL MOVEMENT.

GENESIS: a Greek word meaning "origins" or "beginnings"; it is the name given to the first book of the BIBLE in the Greek and Latin translations.

GENEVA: the Swiss city which became the center of the CALVINIST REFORMATION.

GENEVA BIBLE: the first English translation of the BIBLE to use CHAPTER AND VERSE markings. It was favored by the English PURITANS and used by Shakespeare. It is also known as the "Breeches Bible" because of its translation of Genesis 3:7, which normally reads "garments" (or "aprons"), as "breeches."

GENKU (12th century): *see* HŌNEN.

GENSHIN (942-1017): Japanese BUDDHIST scholar and exponent of the PURE LAND SCHOOL whose art was greatly admired for his depiction of TRANSMIGRATION and the AMIDA BUDDHA.

GENTILE: a non-JEW.

GENUFLECTION: the RITUAL act of kneeling on the right knee while holding the head erect during specific parts of the MASS or while approaching the SACRAMENTS.

GENUS: a general class of objects which possess the same qualities; e.g., dog, cat, tree.

GENUS AND SPECIES: a form of classification used in the logic of ARISTOTLE which greatly influenced the development of Western thought and SCIENCE. A "genus" is a class which may be divided into subclasses or "species"; e.g., *Felis* is the genus, while domestic cat is the species.

GHAZĀLĪ, al- (1058-1111): the most original thinker and greatest theologian that ISLAM has produced. During his youth, ṢŪFĪ exercises made no impression on him, and he tended toward RATIONALISM, eventually becoming an absolute SKEPTIC. Finally, although he never overcame his PHILOSOPHICAL skepticism, he returned to Ṣūfism. Intellectualism failed, so he returned to a belief in GOD, PROPHECY and the last JUDGMENT based on religious experience.

GHETTO: the segregated part of a town or city set aside for JEWS, often involving curfews and other restrictions on movement. European ghettos were self-governing, usually under the control of RABBIS, in what was a form of apartheid.

GIBBON, Edward (1737-1794): English historian famed for his book *The Decline and Fall of the Roman Empire* (1776-1781). A youthful convert to ROMAN CATHOLICISM, he later rejected CHRISTIANITY and presented a hostile interpretation of the rise of the CHRISTIAN CHURCH in his classic work.

GIBRAN, Kahlil (1883-1931): Lebanese MYSTIC, poet and playwright, who abandoned Arabic for English to express his mystical VISION in a series of books with CHRISTIAN themes with titles such as *Jesus,* *the Son of Man* (1928) and *The Prophet* (1923). In recent years his works have been popular with people in the NEW AGE MOVEMENT.

GIFTS OF THE SPIRIT: a popular term used in CHARISMATIC CHRISTIANITY to refer to such things as HEALING, PROPHECY and SPEAKING IN TONGUES which are believed to be SUPERNATURAL gifts which GOD endows upon individuals and thereby shows his presence in today's world. A close examination of the NEW TESTAMENT shows that the biblical meaning of "gifts of the Spirit" is complex and not restricted to such dramatic signs.

GILGAMESH, EPIC OF: an ancient Sumerian epic tale of a legendary king, Gilgamesh. The moral of the epic is that men must accept their lot and not seek the impossible. The story itself contains a FLOOD LEGEND and a form of the CREATION story. It is best described as a MEDITATION on death in the form of a tragedy.

GILSON, Étienne Henry (1884-1978): French Thomist philosopher who played an important role in the revitalization of Thomism during the twentieth century. His works include *The Christian Philosophy of St. Thomas Aquinas* (1956) and *Elements of Christian Philosophy* (1960).

GIOTTO di Bondone (1267-1337): Italian artist who played an important role in the RENAISSANCE and the rediscovery of REALISM in art.

GLADSTONE, William Ewart (1809-1898): British LIBERAL leader and statesman whose policies were based on his attempt to apply CHRISTIAN principles to politics.

GLASTONBURY: the ancient English town and MONASTIC site where King Arthur was said to be buried. The BENEDICTINE monastery was the largest in England and traced its ancestry to a church which the monks claimed had been built by Joseph of Arimathea. Many medieval LEGENDS, including ones about visits by the child JESUS, are associated with the town. It became a center for the COUNTERCULTURE in the 1960s and has played a prominent role in the MYTHOLOGY of the NEW AGE MOVEMENT.

GLOCK, Charles Y. (1924-): American SOCIOLOGIST and survey researcher who has done extensive work on religion and RACISM. His works include *Religion and Society in Tension* (1965) and *Christian Belief and Anti-Semitism* (1966), both of which were coauthored by Rodney STARK.

GLOSSOLALIA: literally "speaking in tongues." It refers to an ecstatic spiritual state that manifests itself in utterances. Glossolalia is found among many CHARISMATIC and PENTECOSTAL groups, who claim to derive the practice from verses in the NEW TESTAMENT such as Acts 2:1-6, 10:44-47 and 1 Corinthians 12:1-11.

GNOSTICISM: a religious and philosophical movement which was popular in the Greco-Roman world and found expression in many different SECTS and settings. Gnostic groups were characterized by their claim to possess secret knowledge, "gnosis," about the NATURE of the UNIVERSE and human existence. Despite what seem to be clear criticisms of Gnostic ideas in the NEW TESTAMENT, many writers have attempted to prove a link between the EARLY CHURCH and Gnosticism. This view has been increasingly discredited as our knowledge of both Gnosticism and the Early Church has increased through archaeological and other discoveries. Today, many NEW AGE groups claim links to ancient Gnosticism, although such claims are pure fabrication (*see* NAG HAMMADI).

GOBIND SINGH (1666-1708): the tenth SIKH GURU, who gave the community its present form. He organized the Sikhs as an effective military force and ordained the "Five emblems" or "Five K's" of SIKHISM. Before he was assassinated in 1708, he made his followers accept that he was the last human guru and that after his death they would look to their SACRED writings, the *Granth*, as their guru.

GOBINEAU, Joseph Arthur, Comte de (1816-1882): French diplomat and "father" of modern RACISM, whose theories, which involved a rejection of orthodox CHRISTIANITY, have had a disastrous effect on European HISTORY.

GOD: although many people claim that all RELIGIONS share the idea of God, in fact only CHRISTIANITY, ISLAM and JUDAISM have a similar understanding of the term. This understanding probably comes from a common source in the religion of ABRAHAM, with the result that these religions may be identified as ABRAMIC RELIGIONS. Traditionally, the Abramic religions understand God as the CREATOR of the UNIVERSE and everything that exists. All three religions see God as a personal BEING who demands obedience from humans, but it was in Christianity that the personal relationship between God and humans was given its highest expression; the DOCTRINE of the INCARNATION teaches that God became human in the person of JESUS CHRIST. Islam and Judaism place greater stress on God as lawgiver and our responsibility to respond to him by obeying his law. Many INDIAN religions developed highly personal versions of the DEITY, but usually limited the powers of each deity through the acceptance of a vast pantheon of over three million gods. The concept of a creator God in the Abramic sense is, however, missing from Indian religions. CHINESE and JAPANESE religions recognized an impersonal force behind the universe but never developed a concept of God similar to the Abramic one. In other religious traditions God or gods may play important roles for specific tasks, such as healing, but their power and role as creator or their personality is severely limited. BUDDHISM is unique in recognizing the existence of gods in the affairs of daily life, but in declaring in no uncertain terms that as a religion or practice, Buddhism has nothing to do with God. Indeed, Buddhism explicitly denies the Abramic concept of God and is therefore often described as a form of ATHEISM.

GODDESS: a very popular focus for worship in modern NEOPAGAN RELIGIONS, especially those associated with FEMINISM. Advocates of this view, influenced by GARDNERIAN WITCHCRAFT and books like Margaret Murray's *The Witch-Cult in Western Europe* (1921), claim to belong to an ancient pre-Christian religion of goodness and light which lived in harmony with NATURE. The rise of goddess religion is discussed in *Goddesses in Religious and Modern Debate*, edited by Larry W. Hurtado (1990), where anthropologist Joan Townsend offers a thorough refutation of the more absurd claims of many followers of the goddess.

GODPARENTS: in CHRISTIAN CHURCHES which practice INFANT BAPTISM it is common to appoint sponsors who assume responsibility for the spiritual welfare of the child and promise to assist the parents in fulfilling their role in religious education.

GOETHE, Johann Wolfgang von (1749-1832): arguably the greatest German poet, philosopher and man of letters. In his early work he was an exponent of ROMANTICISM, but later he took a more critical attitude toward the Romantic movement and developed his own unique insights and spirituality. He was a lover of nature and a religious HUMANIST who strongly influenced German CULTURE.

GOG AND MAGOG: symbolic enemies of GOD in the BIBLE. In APOCALYPTIC LITERATURE they are identified with specific peoples and figure prominently in attempts by modern writers to interpret biblical PROPHECY.

GOLDEN AGE: the idea that in the far distant past there was a time of peace and prosperity which was lost through some human act. The idea features in many RELIGIONS and is often linked with the related notion of the "decline of the ages."

GOLDEN CALF: in Exodus 32, MOSES descends from Mount Sinai with the TEN COMMANDMENTS to discover that the people of ISRAEL have created a golden idol in the image of a calf. The expression has come to represent APOSTASY and anything which lures believers from worshiping GOD.

GOLDEN RULE: taken from the SERMON ON THE MOUNT where JESUS tells his followers, "Do to others as you would have them do to you" (Matthew 7:12). The term has become the basis for a SECULAR morality which essentially says that we ought to act toward others as we would like them to act toward us.

GOOD: theologically, that which is approved by GOD or the divine. In SECULAR ETHICS defining "the good" becomes a major problem to which many solutions are offered.

GOOD FRIDAY: the Friday before EASTER which commemorates the DEATH of JESUS. It is called "Good Friday" because CHRISTIANS believe that on that day, through his obedience to GOD and SACRIFICIAL death, Jesus obtained the SALVATION of mankind. Christians usually celebrate the day with penitence and FASTING.

GORE, Charles (1853-1932): English ANGLO-CATHOLIC theologian, BISHOP of Oxford and one of the founders of the ANGLICAN MONASTIC order THE COMMUNITY OF THE RESURRECTION. He was the editor of the controversial book *Lux Mundi* (1889), and the author of numerous works, including *The Reconstruction of Belief* (1924).

GOTAMA: the name of a famous RISHI, or seer, in HINDU MYTHOLOGY whose beautiful wife was seduced by the god INDRA. In PALI, Gotama is also the name given the founder of BUDDHISM, who is known in SANSKRIT as GAUTAMA.

GOTHARD, Bill (1944-). American FUNDAMENTALIST Bible teacher and founder of the Institute of Basic Life Principles (originally Institute of Basic Youth Conflicts). He teaches a highly authoritarian view of the family promoting the view that children, regardless of age, must remain obedient to the wishes of their parents.

GRACE: in CHRISTIAN THEOLOGY grace is the loving action of GOD in an individual's life, making possible their SANCTIFICATION. It is by grace that God makes SALVATION possible and through grace that he sustains the CHURCH.

GRAF-WELLHAUSEN HYPOTHESIS: the major explanation of the origins of the Pentateuch, the first five books of the HEBREW BIBLE, in terms of EVOLUTIONARY development based upon the identification of supposed documentary sources. These sources were identified as J or Jahwist, E or Elohist, D or Deuteronomist, and P or Priestly. The theory marked the beginning of the influence of HIGHER CRITICISM in the nineteenth century and revolutionized the study of the Bible among PROTESTANTS.

GRAHAM, William Franklin, "Billy" (1918-): American mass EVANGELIST and Southern BAPTIST preacher whose citywide evangelistic crusades and radio and television broadcasts did much to revive evangelical Christianity in America. His many achievements include leadership in international congresses on evangelism, the founding of a significant magazine, *Christianity Today* (1956), and the encouragement of solid evangelical scholarship. His ideas and appeal are summed up in his book *Peace with God* (1953).

GRAIL, THE HOLY: in LEGENDS originating from the twelfth century the CHALICE, or cup, used at the Last Supper was said to have MYSTICAL powers. Stories about the Holy Grail are associated with King Arthur and the Knights of the Round Table as well as with GLASTONBURY and Joseph of Arimathea.

GRAMSCI, Antonio (1891-1937): Italian Communist leader and theoretical Marxist (*see* MARX) who is viewed by many as the most important European Communist since LENIN. His works became fashionable among left-wing intellectuals in Britain and America because they appeared to offer a viable form of Marxist HUMANISM.

GREAT AWAKENING: a series of spiritual REVIVALS in the American colonies between 1725 and 1760. They reached a peak in 1726, but fresh CONVERSIONS and excitement occurred in New England in 1734-1735 through the preaching of Jonathan EDWARDS. The English EVANGELIST George WHITEFIELD linked these regional awakenings into a "Great Awakening" through his itinerant preaching tours. The established CLERGY soon criticized the revivalists' preaching and practices, and Edwards became their vigorous defender. In his book *Some Thoughts Concerning the Present Revival* (1743), and later work *A Treatise on Religious Affections* (1746), Edwards distinguishes between the beneficial and detrimental effects of revivals. New England defenders of the Great Awakening were known as the "New Lights," while those who opposed it were known as "Old Lights." The movement made a great contribution to education and led to the founding of Princeton University, the University of Pennsylvania, and Rutgers, Brown and Dartmouth Colleges. Equally important was the mood of tolerance that led to ECUMENICAL ventures among clergy supporting the movement.

GREAT MOTHER: a CULT figure in ancient Greece who became important in the Roman Empire before dying out around the fourth century. Many WICCA-type movements have sought to revive the cult by giving it modern interpretations in terms of a FEMINIST THEOLOGY (*see* GAIA).

GREAT WHITE BROTHERHOOD: an imaginary hierarchy of spiritual beings, who were said by Helena BLAVATSKY to oversee human development. The idea is very important in THEOSOPHY and many of its offshoots such as the I-AM MOVEMENT. According to Blavatsky, the brotherhood is based in Tibet, from where it contacts initiates by TELEPATHY.

GREBEL, Conrad (1498-1526): leader of the Swiss Brethren movement, out of which the MENNONITES emerged. He was converted to LUTHERAN views around

1522, and in 1525 founded the ANABAPTIST movement which preached adult BAPTISM and advocated what is now known as a "Believer's Church."

GREEK: the trade language of the Mediterranean world in the first century A.D.; this is the language used in the NEW TESTAMENT.

GREEN, T. H. (1836-1882): English philosopher and leading champion of Hegelianism (*see* HEGEL) in Britain during the nineteenth century.

GREENPEACE: founded in 1971 as an environmental protection lobby, the movement has maintained a REVOLUTIONARY edge and APOCALYPTIC spiritual flavor, probably derived from YOGIC RELIGIONS and the prophetic fringe of CHRISTIAN FUNDAMENTALISM of its early members. Today it is the second-largest environmental organization in the world.

GREGORIAN CHANT: *see* PLAINSONG.

GREGORY OF NAZIANZUS (329-389): CHRISTIAN THEOLOGIAN and "Cappadocian Father" who was a strong defender of ORTHODOXY. His work, *Five Theological Orations*, contains a long section on the DOCTRINE of the HOLY SPIRIT.

GREGORY OF NYSSA (330-395): one of the CAPPADOCIAN FATHERS and a notable CHRISTIAN philosopher and theologian strongly influenced by PLATO and ORIGEN. He was a defender of the NICENE CREED and Christian ORTHODOXY.

GREGORY OF TOURS (538-594): BISHOP of Tours, France, who wrote *The History of the Franks*.

GREGORY THE GREAT (540-604): one of the greatest of the POPES. At a time when civilized life in Western Europe was collapsing, he used his genius for administration to strengthen the church. He founded many MONASTERIES, sent MISSIONARIES all over Northern Europe, including AUGUSTINE (OF CANTERBURY) to England, and played an important role in shaping the LITURGY of the ROMAN CATHOLIC CHURCH.

GREGORY VII (1021-1085): a dynamic

POPE, also known as Hildebrand, he was responsible for many REFORMS in the ROMAN CATHOLIC CHURCH and insisted on the separation of the church from the power of SECULAR authorities.

GRHA SŪTRA: a BUDDHIST text which discusses the "science of household behavior."

GRID: a term used by anthropologist Mary Douglas (*see* ANTHROPOLOGY) in her GROUP-GRID ANALYSIS. A grid exists when the roles of individuals are "allocated on principles of sex, age and seniority" and represent ego-centered CATEGORIES which are capable of varying independently of the GROUP. In other words, a grid represents SOCIAL relationships which are controlled by sets of rules and impersonal criteria.

GROEN VAN PRINSTERER, Guillaume (1801-1876): Dutch historian, political theorist and CHRISTIAN philosopher who founded the Dutch Anti-Revolutionary Movement to oppose the ideology of the ENLIGHTENMENT and FRENCH REVOLUTION. An outline of his system is to be found in his greatest work, *Unbelief and Revolution* (1847). As a member of the Dutch Parliament, he argued vigorously for Christian schools, which he saw as distinct from both CHURCH and STATE schools. The reasons he gave for his position are used today by many supporters of Christian education, even though few recognize the origins of their arguments.

GROTIUS, Hugo (1583-1645): Dutch theologian and jurist who pioneered BIBLICAL CRITICISM and religious liberty. His greatest theological work was *De Veritate Religionis Christianae* (1622), which was intended as a handbook for MISSIONARIES to refute all other religious claims and was admired by ROMAN CATHOLICS and PROTESTANTS alike.

GROUND MOTIVE: a term used in the PHILOSOPHY of Herman DOOYEWEERD. A ground motive represents the fundamental motivation or driving force of a CULTURE. It is the common spirit which gives

a community its dynamics and controls its entire attitude to life. Ground motives exercise unconscious influence on individuals and societies. Dooyeweerd recognizes four basic ground motives in the development of Western society: form-matter; creation-fall-redemption; nature-grace; and nature-freedom. In his view only the Christian ground motive of creation-fall-redemption exists as a radical unity that avoids dialectical tensions. The others are plagued by reductionist tendencies which force a choice between one or the other poles of the ground motive. According to Dooyeweerd these conflicts reflect the influence of the polar tensions of the modern Western ground motive of nature-freedom and not, as most practitioners think, different interpretations of "the facts."

GROUP: in Mary Douglas's GROUP-GRID ANALYSIS, "To the extent that the family is a bound unit, contained in a set of rooms, known by a common name, sharing common property, it is a group." In other words, a group can be seen as a set of SOCIAL relationships governed by personal interactions.

GROUP-GRID ANALYSIS: a method of social analysis developed by anthropologist Mary Douglas as a means of comparing societies and their cosmologies. Douglas argues that similar social structures will produce similar cosmologies. Thus an observer ought to be able to deduce the cosmology of a society from information about its social structure and to re-create its social structure on the basis of a knowledge of its cosmology. The technique is based on the concept of positional control or the social restraints, physical or otherwise, which limit the ability of people to act.

GURDWARA: a SIKH temple which houses the *Granth*, or HOLY SCRIPTURES of the Sikh religion.

GURU: a spiritual teacher. Traditionally a guru occupied a hermitage and the student lived with him to serve him and learn from him. The guru is important in HIN-DUISM as a communicator of divine TRUTH. The term is also used by the SIKHS to denote the founders and leaders of their RELIGION.

GUYARD, Marie (1599-1672): ROMAN CATHOLIC MYSTIC and the first Mother Superior of the URSULINE order of NUNS in Quebec, Canada.

GUYON, Madame Jeanne Marie Bouvier de la Mothe (1648-1717): ROMAN CATHO-LIC PIETIST writer and MYSTIC who was several times imprisoned for HERESY and supposed immorality. Her works include *A Short and Easy Method of Prayer* and her *Autobiography.*

H

HACHIMAN: SHINTŌ war GOD who is also a protector of human life and a god of agriculture who gives peace and happiness to Japan.

HADES: the name of the LORD of the underworld, or House of Hades. In Greek mythology it means "to where the dead descend." In the New Testament it is used to refer to the place of the dead (Rev 20:13), and as a place of future punishment (Lk 16:23).

HADĪTH: a TRADITION, communication or narrative, which in ISLAM has the particular meaning of a record of the actions and sayings of the PROPHET MUHAMMAD and his companions. The whole body of the SACRED tradition of MUSLIMS is called "the Hadīth."

HAGGADAH: a HEBREW term meaning "narrative" which is used in RABBINIC studies to describe the exposition or interpretation of SCRIPTURE, mainly narrative portions, and reflection on its ETHICAL and THEOLOGICAL import.

HAGIN, Kenneth (1934-): PENTECOSTAL religious leader who developed "WORD OF FAITH" DOCTRINES.

HAJJ: PILGRIMAGE to MECCA and its environs in the month of Dhū-l-Hijjah, the last month of the Muslim year. This is the fifth PILLAR OF ISLAM.

HAKUIN EKAKU (1685-1768): the greatest Japanese ZEN master after Dogen. He led a major religious REVIVAL and laid the foundations for modern Zen. His DOCTRINE can be summed up in terms of a progression through MEDITATION from the Great DOUBT to the Great ENLIGHTENMENT to the Great Joy.

HALAKHAH: JEWISH law which forms part of the TALMUD. The basic meaning of the term is "the way" and is a means of interpretation and applying the legal portions, or TORAH, of HEBREW SCRIPTURE.

HALAL: the ISLAMIC equivalent of Kosher; it involves strict dietary laws and regulations for the slaughter of animals.

HALDANE, Robert (1764-1842): Scottish writer and philanthropist whose CONVERSION led him to give away his fortune to become an EVANGELIST. During a stay in Geneva (1816), his private BIBLE studies for theological students led to a religious REVIVAL which greatly influenced the European revival movement known as the "reveil." His works include *Evidences and Authority of Divine Revelation* (1816) and *A Commentary on the Epistle to the Romans* (1818).

HALÉVY, Elie (1870-1937): French historian and social philosopher whose work on English history led him to argue that METHODISM saved England from REVOLUTION, especially in 1815. His thesis, known as "the Halévy thesis," is similar to that of WEBER in emphasizing the role of ideas and religious convictions in shaping SOCIAL REALITY.

HALO: a circle of light surrounding the head or even the entire body. The use of halos in art is found in Greek RELIGION and was taken over by the Romans. In the third century it was adopted by CHRISTIANS in representations of CHRIST and the SAINTS.

HAMANN, Johann Georg (1730-1788): contemporary of KANT who rejected the RATIONALISM of his age and, following an EVANGELICAL CONVERSION, became a leader of the "Storm and Stress" (*Sturm und Drang)* movement, which emphasized the immediacy of religious experience. An essentially CONSERVATIVE thinker, he greatly influenced KIERKEGAARD, SCHLEIERMACHER and RITSCHL.

HAMILTON, Alexander (1765-1824): English scholar and popularizer of SANSKRIT who taught the language to SCHLEGEL while imprisoned in Paris during the Napoleonic Wars.

HAMMURABI, CODE OF: one of the most ancient legal codes, it was composed by the Babylonian king Hammurabi around 1750 B.C. and consists of 282 laws.

HANDEL, George Frederick (1685-1759): German musician who became a British citizen in 1726. He is the composer of *Messiah* and many other religious and SECULAR works.

ḤANĪF: in ISLAM, any seeker after TRUTH, such as ABRAHAM, who opposed IDOLATRY before the coming of the PROPHET MUḤAMMAD.

HARDY, Thomas (1840-1928): English novelist and poet whose works contain biting attacks on Christian ORTHODOXY.

HARE KRISHNA MOVEMENT: the International Society for Krishna Consciousness, founded on his arrival in America in 1965 by His Divine Grace SWAMI A. C. Bhaktivedanta PRABHUPADA, is one of the most visible of the NEW RELIGIOUS MOVEMENTS. DEVOTEES sing, dance, sell records, books or the magazine *Back to Godhead*, and wear saffron-colored robes. The young men have their heads shaved, apart from a topknot by which they believe KRISHNA will pluck them up when he rescues them at the time of the deliverance of the world. It is through the frequent chanting of their MANTRA—Hare Krishna, Hare Krishna—that the devotees have become popularly known as Hare Krishnas. The theological basis of the movement is the BHAGAVAD-GĪTA as translated by their Master.

HARMONIC CONVERGENCE: an idea said to have originated with Jose Arguelles in his book *The Transformative Vision* (1975). It is based on "prophecies" from ancient Mayan writings which predicted the release of COSMIC energies due to a cyclic alignment of various stars and planets. Arguelles predicted that this would occur on August 16 and 17, 1987. Many people in the NEW AGE MOVEMENT accepted this idea, which since then has been closely linked with the GAIA hypothesis and an expectation of imminent spiritual and social change.

HARNACK, Adolf von (1851-1930): one of the greatest German LIBERAL Christian theologians and church historians. He saw RELIGION as reconciling CULTURE and CHRISTIANITY for the proper ordering of daily life. To him DOGMA in the EARLY CHURCH obscured the practical thrust of JESUS' teachings. He argued that we must separate the permanently valid kernel of the gospel from the culturally conditioned husk. In *What Is Christianity?* (1901) he argues that Jesus' message was his ethical preaching about the KINGDOM OF GOD. Harnack's other works include *The History of Dogma* (1894-1899, 7 vols.), *The Mission and Expansion of Christianity in the First Three Centuries* (1904-1905, 2 vols.), and *The*

Constitution and Law of the Church in the First Two Centuries (1910).

HARRINGTON, Michael (1928-1989): leading American SOCIALIST economist and political commentator whose *The Other America* (1963) was a stunning indictment of poverty in America. One of his last books, *Politics at the Funeral of God: The Spiritual Crisis of Western Civilization* (1983), is a remarkable critique of Western society and a lament for the loss of spiritual values.

HARRIS, THE PROPHET (1865-1929): Liberian EVANGELIST, CHURCH founder and ANGLICAN lay preacher. He traveled to the Ivory Coast in 1913 wearing a white gown with black bands crossed across the chest, carrying a gourd for baptismal water, a rattle and a large staff in the form of a cross. His dynamic preaching and call for the people to forsake their traditional beliefs and accept CHRIST led to a major REVIVAL and the foundation of many HARRIST CHURCHES. At the end of 1914 he was deported from the Ivory Coast by the French authorities after having BAPTIZED over 120,000 people whom he had begun to organize into a church with the help of the Methodists (*see* METHODISM). After his expulsion he returned to Liberia, from where he continued to guide, though not direct, his followers.

HARRIST CHURCHES: in 1913 and 1914 a REVIVAL broke out in the Ivory Coast, West Africa, in response to the preaching of the prophet HARRIS. As a result the French colonial authorities deported the prophet to his native Liberia at the end of 1914, and his followers were left leaderless, with only a rudimentary organization based on METHODISM. Harris had, however, made a PROPHECY about the arrival of "Bible teachers." In 1924 the long-awaited teachers arrived in the form of PROTESTANT MISSIONARIES. They were welcomed by Harris's followers, but tensions soon developed over African CULTURAL TRADITIONS, especially POLYGAMY. With the blessing of the Prophet his followers then formed their own churches. Today the Harrist Churches form a large family in a number of different church groups. Their theology is orthodox in intent (*see* ORTHODOXY), although it is deeply colored by their experience of colonialism and African culture.

ḤASAN, 'Ali (d. 669): grandson of MUḤAMMAD, who succeeded as CALIPH after the assassination of his father but abdicated in favor of Muʿāwiya ibn Abī Sufyān.

ḤASAN AL-BASRĪ, al- (d. 728): influential ISLAMIC religious scholar whose name became associated with many later religious movements due to his great reputation for PIETY and learning.

HASIDIC JEWS: followers of HASIDISM or Hasidic practices.

HASIDISM: Hebrew term for "PIETY" or "the pious." In the eighteenth century it became associated with an Eastern European JEWISH sect founded by RABBI Israel ben Eliezer. It reacted against what it saw as the arid interpretation of the TALMUD by rabbis and drew upon the CABBALA to develop a rich MYSTICAL tradition. Union with GOD was sought through ECSTATIC PRAYER, and the coming of the MESSIAH was earnestly desired. Today Martin BUBER is the best-known interpreter of Hasidism, even though many scholars question his understanding of the tradition.

HASTINGS, Warren (1732-1818): servant of the British East India Company and first governor general of Bengal, who in 1788 was impeached by the British Parliament for his mismanagement of India. He encouraged the study of SANSKRIT and in 1785 produced his own translation of the BHAGAVAD-GITA.

HAṬHA YOGA: that branch of YOGA which seeks to establish conscious control over the automatic processes of the body. This is the most popular form of Yoga in the West, where it is taught in terms of physical health and exercise. It is often mistakenly thought by Westerners to be the only form of Yoga.

HEALING: most RELIGIOUS TRADITIONS involve BELIEF in the power of GOD or gods to heal humans of both physical and psychological disorders. Such healings may take place through PRAYER, FASTING or a variety of other specific means to achieve the desired end. FAITH HEALING is a modern development of the CHRISTIAN healing tradition which emphasizes the role of FAITH in the healing process. CHRISTIAN SCIENCE is a nineteenth-century NEW RELIGIOUS MOVEMENT which concentrated on SPIRITUAL healing through a combination of Christian themes and an essentially YOGIC PHILOSOPHY derived from HINDUISM. Today the most common expression of religious healing in the West is to be found in CHARISMATIC and PENTECOSTAL CHURCHES. Good discussions of healing are to be found in Martin E. Marty and Kenneth L. Vaux, eds., *Health/Medicine and the Faith Traditions* (1982); Meredith B. McGuire, *Ritual Healing in Suburban America* (1988); and Sudhir Kakar, *Shamans, Mystics and Doctors* (1982).

HEART: in many CULTURES the heart is regarded as the center of emotional and spiritual life.

HEAVEN: many religions separate the heavens and the earth, making the heavens the realm of the gods. In HINDU MYTHOLOGY there are many heavens in a multilayered UNIVERSE. Similarly in JAINISM and BUDDHISM many heavens exist, although the aim of SALVATION is to avoid REBIRTH, even in heaven. JUDAISM, ISLAM and CHRISTIANITY share a common conception of heaven as the realm of GOD and the destiny of believers after the last JUDGMENT.

HEBREW: the ancient language of the JEWISH people in which almost all of the HEBREW BIBLE is written.

HEBREW BIBLE: the ancient SCRIPTURES of the JEWISH people known as the OLD TESTAMENT by CHRISTIANS. Traditionally the books of the Hebrew Bible were held to have been written at different times in JEWISH HISTORY, from as early as 1400 to 400 B.C. The earliest extant manuscripts of the Hebrew Bible, dated to the first century A.D., are found among the DEAD SEA SCROLLS. The earliest complete HEBREW manuscript is the Leningrad Codex dated A.D. 895, although translations of the text exist in manuscript form from as early as the third century A.D., and many fragments of the Hebrew text are also dated to this period.

HEBREWS: members of the Jewish people; ISRAELITES.

HEDONISM: a word derived from a Greek term meaning pleasure or enjoyment. The term is used to refer to ETHICAL systems which understand pleasure to be the ultimate GOOD.

HEGEL, George Wilhelm Friedrich (1770-1831): German philosopher whose system is commonly known as "Hegelianism." His complex idealist philosophy contains many elements, the most influential of which are: (1) the DIALECTIC, which is generally interpreted to mean that all reasoning is dialectical, proceeding from a CONCEPT to a new and contradictory concept, which gives way to a third concept that transcends and synthesizes both earlier concepts. This is usually stated as thesis-ANTITHESIS and synthesis; (2) the theory of self-realization, by which the dialectical process in the individual leads to a determinate "SELF" which is "for itself"; (3) the theory of history, which is a dialectical process leading to the manifestation of the ABSOLUTE SPIRIT which in every specific age manifests itself in the *Zeitgeist* or the "spirit-of-the-age," which determines social and political life, knowledge, religion and art. Hegel's work strongly influenced such people as FEUERBACH and MARX. Critics contend that it leads to TOTALITARIANISM and is so obscure as to bewitch the intellect.

HEIDEGGER, Martin (1884-1976): a central figure in contemporary continental PHILOSOPHY, the development of EXISTENTIALISM and new directions in HERMENEU-

TICS. In *Being and Time* (1927) he characterized everyday existence as unauthentic because we are "thrown" into our world, or mental UNIVERSE, which makes our SELF inseparable from our world, and as a result genuine being remains undiscovered. Although his philosophy was deeply spiritual, he attacked CHRISTIANITY for contributing to our self-betrayal and to the destruction of genuine CULTURE. As early as 1946 Karl Lowith pointed out Heidegger's enthusiasm for the NAZIS: this was vigorously denied by his followers but now seems established beyond all doubt.

HEIDELBERG CATECHISM: a CALVINIST confession of FAITH written in 1562 in Heidelberg. It has become one of the most popular statements of faith for REFORMED churches throughout the world.

HEILSGESCHICHTE: a German term meaning "SALVATION history." It is used to express the idea that GOD declares his purposes through his actions in HISTORY which are interpreted by FAITH or the revealed word of God.

HEISENBERG, Werner (1901-1976): German physicist who developed the principle of indeterminacy and worked on the QUANTUM THEORY. His principle, known as the "Heisenberg" or Uncertainty Principle, says that at the subatomic level one cannot know both the momentum and position of a particle.

HELL: an old English term used to translate the HEBREW terms SHE'ÓL and GEHENNA. In most religions hell is the place of the damned. In the YOGIC religions escape from hell is ultimately possible through eventual REBIRTH. In traditional ABRAMIC religions, however, hell appears to be the permanent abode of the wicked, where they are eternally separated from GOD.

HENOTHEISM: from the Greek words *henos* meaning "one" and *theos* meaning "God." The term was coined by Max MÜLLER for a form of RELIGION which accepts the WORSHIP of one GOD by a particular individual or group but does not deny the existence of different gods worshiped by other people. It is sometimes described as "one-God-at-a-timeism." Müller suggested that originally the ancient HEBREWS and many other peoples were henotheists.

HENRY VIII (1491-1547): English king who was declared "Defender of the Faith" by the POPE for his critique of LUTHER in 1521. He was excommunicated in 1533 as a result of his divorce—an act which initiated the first political phase of the English REFORMATION.

HERACLITUS of Ephesus (540-475 B.C.): Greek philosopher who withdrew from SOCIETY and in obscure terms attacked the Ephesians and humankind in general for their stupidity. He argued that the unity of the world rested in its structure, not its material, and that fire was the primary element. FLUX characterizes existence, and strife is necessary for the continued unification of opposites.

HERBERT, Edward, Lord of Cherbury (1583-1648): one of the intellectual sources of DEISM, he rejected REVELATION and taught that RELIGION is based on a BELIEF in GOD who should be WORSHIPED through virtuous action. Humans are responsible to REPENT from SIN and ought to believe in life after death.

HERBERT, George (1593-1633): English ANGLICAN CLERGYMAN, poet and HYMN writer. He is the author of such popular hymns as "The King of Love My Shepherd Is."

HERDER, Johann Gottfried von (1744-1803): German LUTHERAN scholar and leader of the ROMANTIC movement, who was influenced by the philosophy of KANT. His studies of the Synoptic Gospels (1796) and the Gospel of John (1797) led him to conclude that they could not be harmonized, and helped launch German BIBLICAL CRITICISM. In his philosophy of language he argued that the language of a people encapsulates its historical identity and underlying unity. This view greatly influenced German NATIONALISM, although

Herder himself was essentially LIBERAL and cosmopolitan in his outlook. His most influential works were his *Outlines of a Philosophy of History of Man* (1800) and *Treatise upon the Origin of Language* (1827).

HERESY: in its loose sense it refers to the conscious, willful rejection of any DOCTRINE held to be normative by a group or institution. ROMAN CATHOLICISM defines a heretic as any BAPTIZED person who, wishing to be identified as a CHRISTIAN, denies the TRUTH revealed to the CHURCH. Until the nineteenth century, PROTESTANTS generally regarded heresy as the willful rejection of any truth taught in the BIBLE. With the rise of BIBLICAL CRITICISM, defining heresy became a problem because the notion of a CANON and ORTHODOXY itself came under increasing criticism. Although originally a religious term, it is common today to talk about political, scientific and other forms of heresy, meaning deviation from the *status quo* or accepted orthodoxy.

HERMAS (2nd century): an otherwise unknown CHRISTIAN author who wrote the influential *Shepherd of Hermas* which recorded visions about the CHURCH.

HERMENEUTICS: an inquiry concerning the presuppositions and rules of interpreting a text. The text is usually a written document, although it could be some other form of artistic or social expression.

HERMETIC LITERATURE (Corpus Hermeticum): a series of GNOSTIC-like writings, probably dating from the second century, which claimed an ancient Egyptian origin in the god Hermes Trismegistus. Today they are appealed to by many NEW RELIGIOUS MOVEMENTS seeking to legitimize themselves historically.

HERMIT: a word, derived from the Greek word for "desert," used to describe people who, for religious reasons, went into the desert to dwell alone. It was later applied to anyone who lived a solitary life.

HEROD ANTIPAS (d. A.D. 39): ruler, or Tetrarch, of Galilee and Peraea; he ordered the execution of JOHN THE BAPTIST.

HESIOD (8th century B.C.): Greek poet whose *Works and Days* gives vivid insights into traditional Greek RELIGION. He ascribes the wretchedness of life to the enmity of ZEUS and offers an interpretation of HISTORY as a process of decline in five stages or ages.

HESSE, Herman (1877-1962): German poet and novelist born of a MISSIONARY family in India. Deeply influenced by KIERKEGAARD, NIETZSCHE and BUDDHISM, he rejected CHRISTIANITY. His works became CULT readings among the West Coast HIPPIES in America during the 1960s. The hallmark of his work is a desire for experience untrammeled by the inhibitions of institutionalized society, and the LIBERATION of thought and behavior. His most famous works are *Siddhartha* (1922, translated 1951), *Steppenwolf* (1927, translated 1929) and *The Glass Bead Game* (1943, translated 1970).

HEXAGRAM: a six-pointed star developed out of a hexagon or from the use of equilateral triangles used for DIVINATION. The most common form of hexagram is found in the I-CHING.

HEYNE, Christian Gottlob (1729-1812): German PHILOLOGIST and professor at Göttingen whose work on ancient literatures played an important role in developing the tools used by BIBLICAL CRITICISM. He was a pioneer in the study of MYTH, which he understood as the ideas and beliefs of "primitive man."

HIERARCHY: an organized body of PRIESTS or CLERGY with specialized offices based on a ranked order. One can also speak of a hierarchy of such things as ideas and principles; this implies that some are more important than others.

ḤIFẒ AL-QUR'ĀN: the memorizing and recitation of the QUR'ĀN. The believer does this as a way of participating in the God-given words.

HIGH CHURCH: a term used to identify PROTESTANTS—usually ANGLICANS—with leanings toward ROMAN CATHOLICISM. The name is derived from their view that the CHURCH or CHRISTIAN community is of greater importance than the individual.

HIGH GODS: some scholars argue that a primitive MONOTHEISM lies behind most religious movements, even though the people concerned appear to WORSHIP many gods. The idea is that behind the lesser gods of everyday life lies a more remote High God who is the true GOD and source of their religious ideas. This concept originated as a form of Christian APOLOGETICS and is particularly associated with the work of Father Wilhelm SCHMIDT. His ideas are rejected by many modern scholars.

HIGHER CRITICISM: that part of BIBLICAL CRITICISM which seeks to discover the "sources" used by biblical authors and in doing so traces the ideas involved to their religious and historical roots. In general, though not necessarily, it is carried out with highly RATIONALISTIC presuppositions which undermine the credibility of SUPERNATURAL events presented in the BIBLE.

HIPPIE: a popular term coined in 1967 by *San Francisco Chronicle* journalist Herb Caen to describe the young people who gathered in the Haight-Ashbury district of San Francisco wearing long hair, a distinctive clothing and using soft drugs and LSD. In Britain many people preferred the term "Freaks" to hippie, which they deemed "too American."

ḤIJRAH: the emigration of MUḤAMMAD and his followers from MECCA to MEDINA in 622. This marked a turning point in his career and marks the date from which the ISLAMIC calendar begins.

HILLEL (1st century): JEWISH RABBI whose disciples taught a LIBERAL and less austere interpretation of the *Torah*, in opposition to the school of Shammai.

HĪNĀYĀNA: literally the "lesser vehicle"; one of the major schools of BUDDHISM, it stresses intellectual understanding. It thrives in Sri Lanka and Southeast Asia, where it places its emphasis upon the role of the priesthood and attainment of EN-LIGHTENMENT through strenuous SPIRITUAL EXERCISES within the MONASTIC community. It first became known in the West during the late nineteenth century, giving the false impression that Buddhism is simply a form of HUMANISM devoid of SUPERNATURAL BELIEFS.

HINDRANCES: those mental stages identified by BUDDHISM as preventing trance.

HINDUISM: a diverse group of RELIGIOUS TRADITIONS consisting of numerous CULT movements, BELIEFS, RITUAL practices and the CASTE system, which often have little in common but their origin and location within the Indian subcontinent. In the nineteenth century, as a result of the HINDU RENAISSANCE, these traditions were reinterpreted as a unified whole that formed a NATIONAL religion. This included the DOCTRINES found in the UPANISHADS, the VEDAS and popular devotion to GODS like VĀSUDEVA, VISHNU and SIVA. This interpretation saw the religious history of India in terms of an amalgamation of earlier VEDIC and BRAHMANICAL religions, mediated by PRIESTS, or BRAHMINS, and represents the triumph of a GREAT TRADITION, VEDANTA, over thousands of local LITTLE TRADITIONS.

Following the example set by nineteenth-century interpreters, five periods in the development of Hinduism are commonly recognized: (1) the early, or VEDIC religion, which centered on ritual SACRIFICE, during which VEDIC HYMNS are said to have been composed and collected. This period lasted from the second millennium B.C. to around 800 B.C.; (2) the UPANISHADIC period during which a MONISTIC, MONOTHEISTIC religion is believed to have grown up in reaction to the crudity of Vedic sacrifices and the domination of PRIESTS; (3) the classical period lasting from 500 B.C. to A.D. 500 during which, it is claimed, Hinduism acquired its distinctive form; (4) the MEDIEVAL period which saw the evolution of devotional BHAKTI cults; and (5) finally, the MODERN period, identified with Vedanta, when Indian INTELLECTUALS came to grips with the impact of Western thought and British domination. Hinduism is not usually thought of as a MISSIONARY religion, though organizations like the RAMAKRISHNA and HARE KRISHNA increasingly make UNIVERSAL claims and seek non-Indian CONVERTS, especially in Europe and North America. In attempting to understand Hinduism it is important to realize that very little written evidence, except passing observations by BUDDHIST and later MUSLIM scholars and a few inscriptions, exists before the eighteenth century and that the earliest extant copies of Hindu scriptures are no older than the fifteenth century.

HIPPOCRATES (460?-370? B.C.): Greek physician and "father" of medicine.

HIPPOLYTUS (165-236): Roman theologian who was an exponent of the LOGOS DOCTRINE in the EARLY CHURCH.

HISTORY: the study of the past. As an academic discipline, history emerged in the late nineteenth century, although there have been many great historians in Western civilization since the time of the early Greeks. The ABRAMIC RELIGIONS are essentially historical and encourage the study of history because they believe GOD has revealed himself in time. By contrast, history is essentially disregarded by YOGIC RELIGIONS. Fundamentally history involves a process of interpreting the past based on evidence available in the present and accounts inherited from earlier times. Although each generation reinterprets history in light of contemporary questions, history claims a scientific status through its careful use of sources and weighing of evidence.

HITLER, Adolf (1889-1945): Austrian OCCULTIST who became the leader of the NAZI party in Germany and rivals STALIN as a mass murderer. More than any other person, he bears responsibility for World War II, the destruction of much of Germany, and the HOLOCAUST. His interest in

NEOPAGANISM is often overlooked by secular biographers. Cf. Sebastian Haffner, *The Meaning of Hitler* (1979); Joachim Fest, *Hitler* (1973); and Nicholas Goodrick-Clarke, *The Occult Roots of Nazism* (1985).

HITTITES: an ancient Indo-European people who settled in Asia Minor prior to 2000 B.C. and are mentioned in the HEBREW BIBLE.

HO YEN (3rd century A.D.): Chinese TAOIST philosopher, Confucian scholar (*see* CONFUCIUS) and author of *Treatise on the Tao.*

HOBBES, Thomas (1588-1679): English philosopher and author of the *Leviathan* (1651), a work dedicated to both political theory and the interpretation of SCRIPTURE. For practical purposes he developed a DOCTRINE of mechanistic MATERIALISM and defended the theory of a social contract as a basis for political obligation. Although a monarchist, he rejected DIVINE RIGHT doctrines of the state. Often described as a DEIST, he considered himself a CHRISTIAN and wrote at length about GOD's providential care for humans.

HODGE, Charles (1797-1878): PRESBYTERIAN theologian who taught at Princeton Theological Seminary. As editor of the *Biblical Repertory* and *Princeton Review* (founded 1825), he expounded his own version of CALVINISM which exercised a great influence over American PROTESTANTISM. His *Systematic Theology* (1872-1873, 3 vols.) is still a standard work in many conservative theological schools.

HOLBACH, Paul Henri Thyry, Baron d' **(1723-1789):** French RATIONALIST philosopher and ENCYCLOPEDIST.

HOLINESS: the essential character of GOD. In humans and human institutions holiness is a quality conveyed by God upon his creatures and creation.

HOLINESS MOVEMENT: any religious movement within CHRISTIANITY which seeks to promote personal HOLINESS. Such movements became particularly important in the late nineteenth century and contributed to the growth of both EVAN-

GELICAL and FUNDAMENTALIST Christianity.

HOLISM: a term used by General Jan SMUTS in his book *Holism and Evolution* (1926) to express his belief in EMERGENT EVOLUTION. The idea comes from IDEALIST PHILOSOPHY and expresses the notion of wholeness. In recent years it has become a buzz word in various alternative health movements and the NEW AGE MOVEMENT.

HOLISTIC MEDICINE: a wide spectrum of alternative medical practices from simple herbalism and homeopathic treatments to highly RELIGIOUS practices involving TANTRA and other techniques derived from the YOGIC TRADITION. Holistic medicine expresses a desire to treat the whole person and not simply the symptoms of disease. As such it may be quite compatible with modern, Western medical practice. Herbal medicines and many other forms of holistic medicine, including homeopathy and chiropractic treatments, have no necessary SPIRITUAL significance. In many circles, however, all of these alternate forms of HEALING are given an OCCULT interpretation and developed in conjunction with the beliefs and practices of NEW RELIGIOUS MOVEMENTS.

HOLMES, John Haynes (1879-1959): American LIBERAL churchman and one of the founders of the American Civil Liberties Union.

HOLOCAUST: a Jewish term meaning "catastrophic destruction" which is derived from *holokautoma*, a word in the SEPTUAGINT meaning "complete burning" or "sacrifice by fire." After World War II the term was applied to what the NAZIS called "the final solution": the attempt during World War II by the Nazi regime to exterminate the Jews by systematically putting to death almost 6 million Jews. Although something like 20 million people in all were murdered in Nazi concentration camps, the Holocaust is unique in that it involved an entire people defined by racial origin. This event is something with which even now JEWISH and CHRIS-TIAN THEOLOGIANS struggle to come to terms. Cf. Martin Gilbert, *The Holocaust: A History of the Jews of Europe During the Second World War* (1985); Richard L. Rubenstein, *After Auschwitz* (1966); Richard Rubenstein and John K. Roth, *Approaches to Auschwitz: The Holocaust and Its Legacy* (1987).

HOLY: a basic religious concept understood in various ways in different religions. In religious HISTORY, anything men and women worship may be called holy and especially the powers that manifest themselves in any sphere of life. In Christianity, the holy also refers to that which is set apart and belongs to GOD because it possesses the character of HOLINESS which is derived from God. See R. OTTO, *The Idea of the Holy* (1923).

HOLY BOOKS: many RELIGIOUS TRADITIONS possess SACRED SCRIPTURES and other books which are regarded as INSPIRED by GOD and hence holy. These works lend authority to the tradition and provide inspiration to followers.

HOLY PLACES: most religions emphasize the importance of certain places which are viewed as HOLY. Inevitably these places become centers of PILGRIMAGE. PROTESTANT CHRISTIANITY appears unique in its theological rejection of holy places and insistence that the whole of life has a SACRED dimension.

HOLY ROMAN EMPIRE: established by CHARLEMAGNE by his coronation on Christmas Day, A.D. 800, as the Western successor to the Roman Empire. The Holy Roman Empire provided a loose confederation and more importantly an ideal of order for much of western Europe, especially Germany, until it was finally abolished by Napoleon in 1806.

HOLY SPIRIT: the Third Person in the Christian Godhead or TRINITY. The Holy Spirit is believed by Christians to have been active in creation and throughout history, to indwell believers, guide the CHURCH, and be the source of the INSPIRATION of SCRIPTURE. In the twentieth century the THEOLOGY of the Holy Spirit has become a central issue in the CHARISMATIC MOVEMENT.

HOMER (before 700 B.C.): Greek POET to whom the *Iliad* and the *Odyssey* are traditionally attributed.

HŌNEN (1133-1212): founder of JŌDŌ BUDDHISM in Japan in 1175. His fundamental thesis was BELIEF in the saving power and GRACE of Aida, the Lord of Sukhāvatī, the Western paradise. SHINRAN was his greatest disciple.

HOOKER, Richard (1554-1600): moderate English ANGLICAN theologian who defended episcopacy, the institution of BISHOPS, and attacked what he saw as the excesses of PURITAN enthusiasm. His greatest work is his seven-volume *Of the Laws of Ecclesiastical Polity* (1593-1662).

HOPKINS, Gerald Manley (1844-1889): English ROMAN CATHOLIC CONVERT, a JESUIT and poet who became professor of Greek at the University of Dublin in 1884. His greatest works are thought to be "The Wreck of the Deutschland" and "The Windhover: To Christ Our Lord."

HORT, Fenton John Anthony (1828-1892): English biblical scholar who, with B. F. WESTCOTT, was responsible for the production of a standard GREEK text of the NEW TESTAMENT.

HORTON, Robin (b. 1932): British anthropologist (*see* ANTHROPOLOGY) whose work on the relationship between TRADITIONAL AFRICAN and scientific thought and on the nature of CONVERSION in an African society has provoked heated debate. His major book is *Kalabari Sculpture* (1966).

HOUSE-CHURCH MOVEMENT: a complex and highly diverse NEW RELIGIOUS MOVEMENT within CHRISTIANITY which traces its origins to the NEW TESTAMENT where CHRISTIANS are depicted as meeting in people's homes rather than CHURCH buildings. The modern movement originated in Ireland in the early nineteenth century giving rise to the growth of the PLYMOUTH BRETHREN. In this century Brethren-inspired groups emerged in China and Japan before being reexported back

to Britain and North America where the movement gained momentum during the 1980s. Inevitably, however, as with the JEHOVAH'S WITNESSES, who were also a house-church movement, most groups tend toward DENOMINATIONALISM and the acquisition of special buildings for WORSHIP.

HSŪAN-HSŪEH: "mysterious and profound learning" was the name given to a neo-TAOIST movement that arose in China in the third century A.D. The movement honored CONFUCIUS and taught that NONBEING is the ultimate REALITY underlying all visible things.

HSŪAN T'SANT (596-664): the greatest Chinese philosopher and pilgrim to visit India, and one of the most important figures in Chinese BUDDHISM. He translated over seventy-five Buddhist works into Chinese and published an account of his journeys, which is regarded as a classic of Chinese literature. It was translated into English as *Si-yu-ki Buddhist Records of the Western World* in 1884.

HUA YEN: an important school of Chinese BUDDHISM which taught that BEING and NONBEING are equally illusory and are negated in the Void. Mind is the basis of all phenomena and permeates all things.

HUANG-LAS CHŪN: an important TAOIST DEITY who was believed to be the supreme instructor and chief of the gods.

HUBBARD, Ron L. (1911-1976): brilliant SCIENCE FICTION writer and adventurer who founded SCIENTOLOGY in 1955, after the publication of his bestselling *Dianetics: The Modern Science of Mental Health* (1951).

HUBRIS: in Greek thought, the capital SIN of self-assertion, which was bound to arouse the anger of the GODS.

HÜGEL, Frederick, Baron von (1852-1925): Italian-born ROMAN CATHOLIC theologian who settled in England where he was a close associate of various Roman Catholic MODERNIST leaders. His major work, *The Mystical Elements of Religion* (1908), is a study of the writings of CATHERINE OF GENOA.

HUGUENOTS: French PROTESTANTS who were followers of John CALVIN. After two civil wars in which they fought for the freedom of religion, many of them were slaughtered in the ST. BARTHOLOMEW'S DAY MASSACRE in 1572. After a third civil war and eventual peace they were finally expelled from France when the Edict of Nanté, which granted them TOLERATION in 1598, was revoked in 1685. Many fled to England, Germany, Holland, Prussia and South Africa, where they made significant contributions to the development of local industry and culture.

HUI-NENG (628-713): known in China as Wei Lang and in Japan as Eno, he was the sixth and last patriarch of CH'AN BUDDHISM in China. He promoted the DOCTRINE of spontaneous realization or sudden ENLIGHTENMENT.

HUI-YÜAN (334-417): a convert from TAOISM and Confucianism (*see* CONFUCIUS) to BUDDHISM. He founded the famous MONASTERY of Tung-lin and through his White Lotus Society is seen as one of the founders of PURE LAND BUDDHISM.

HUMAN SACRIFICE: although some anthropologists have attempted to deny its REALITY, there seems no doubt that human sacrifice has played an important role in many religious systems and continues to this day to exercise remarkable appeal throughout both Africa and India.

HUMANISM: that philosophic-religious system which has as its central controlling interest the values of man. CHRISTIAN humanism, as practiced by such important figures as ERASMUS, must be carefully distinguished from modern SECULAR humanism which is anti-Christian.

HUME, David (1711-1776): Scottish skeptical philosopher, historian and essayist, whose radical empiricism has had a profound influence on modern thought. KANT claimed that Hume "awoke" him "from dogmatic slumber" through his *A Treatise on Human Nature* (1739). Hume's *Dialogues on Natural Religion* (1779), published posthumously, is a sustained attack on CHRISTIANITY and an attempt to prove the existence of GOD. In his lesser-known work *The Natural History of Religion* (1757), he argued that POLYTHEISM was both the natural and original RELIGION of mankind.

HUNG HSIU-CH'ÜAN (1812-1864): influenced by CHRISTIANITY, he joined the Society of God and in 1836 announced that he was a younger brother of JESUS CHRIST. In 1850 he began the T'ai P'ing rebellion to establish a theocratic state and destroy the opium trade. He denounced the IDOLATRY of BUDDHISM and TAOISM and replaced the Confucian classics with Christian Gospels. Despite his sweeping social REFORMS and desire to cooperate with Western powers, his movement was eventually destroyed with appalling loss of life by Western armies.

HUNTINGDON, Selina, Countess [of] (1707-1791): English EVANGELICAL leader and patron of John and Charles WESLEY and the Welsh preacher Howell Harris, she founded a CALVINIST branch of METHODISM known as "Countess Huntingdon's Connection."

ḤUSAYN, ibn 'Ali (626-680): grandson of MUḤAMMAD and third IMĀM of the SHI'A. Escaping from the CALIPH Yazīd, the son of Mu'āwiya, he and 200 followers were surrounded near Kufa and brutally murdered on October 10, 680. He is considered a MARTYR by the Shī'ites, who see in his death sacrificial value.

HUSS, John (1372-1415): Czech religious REFORMER influenced by John WYCLIFFE who is known as the "morning star" of the PROTESTANT REFORMATION. He was burnt at the stake for HERESY after being EXCOMMUNICATED by the POPE.

HUSSERL, Edmund Gustav Albrecht (1859-1938): German philosopher and founder of PHENOMENOLOGY whose complex work attempts to go beyond KANT and gain an understanding of the essential structures of human consciousness. His work greatly influenced many modern thinkers, including the CHRISTIAN philosopher Herman DOOYEWEERD. His works include *Logical Investigations* (1900-1901, translated 1970) and *The Crisis of European Sciences and Transcendental Phenomenology* (1936 translated 1970).

HUTTERITES: an ANABAPTIST SECT which emerged in Moravia in 1529 and was reorganized by Jacob Hutter in 1553. Until 1599 they enjoyed considerable success in establishing about a hundred *bruderhofs*, or farm colonies, with a membership of around 25,000. A period of persecution followed, and they fled to Slovakia and Transylvania, where over the next 150 years they produced some remarkable devotional literature. Renewed persecution led them to the Ukraine in 1770, where they remained until 1870. The threat of military conscription then led them to emigrate to the United States of America; some groups emigrated from America to Canada in 1917. Today there are around 10,000 Hutterites. They are distinguished by their communal living, traditional dress and hostility to MODERN CULTURE.

HUXLEY, Aldous Leonard (1894-1963): grandson of T. H. HUXLEY. He was an English MYSTICAL writer, novelist, essayist and poet, who experimented with drug-induced states to achieve spiritual insight.

HUXLEY, Julian Sorell (1887-1975): English biologist and HUMANIST who speculated about the emergence of an evolutionary spirituality. Among his many works is *The Humanist Frame*, which he edited in 1964.

HUXLEY, Thomas Henry (1825-1895): English biologist and AGNOSTIC, who was an advocate of scientific training to remedy the intellectual, social and moral needs of humanity. At Oxford in 1860 he had a memorable debate with BISHOP William WILBERFORCE on EVOLUTION. A fierce critic of Christian ORTHODOXY, he extolled HUME and attacked not only the idea of MIRACLES, but also the very possibility that we can know anything about the actual teachings of JESUS.

HYMN: sacred poetry set to music to be sung or chanted by PRIESTS or DEVOTEES of a RELIGION. Popular hymn singing is found in Indian BHAKTI CULTS and among CHRISTIANS, where since its beginning hymns have been sung in praise of GOD and CHRIST.

HYPOTHESIS: a judgment which the mind entertains to explain an area of REALITY. It consists of a THEORY, or theories, assumed to be true which enables predictions to be made about the behavior of phenomena.

I

I AM MOVEMENT: a North American NEW RELIGIOUS MOVEMENT of THEOSOPHICAL origin founded in the 1930s by Guy BALLARD. Unlike Theosophy and many similar movements, this movement's ascended masters, of whom ST. GERMAIN is the most important, are found not in Egypt or Tibet but in places like Mt. Shasta in California, and the American West generally, giving the movement a NATIONALISTIC character. Belief in the OCCULT significance of color to produce harmony is an important aspect of the teachings of this movement.

I CHING: one of the five Confucian classics (*see* CONFUCIUS), it is known as *The Book of Changes*. The core text dates from about 1000 B.C. The philosophy of the book is based on the notion that the whole UNIVERSE is in a constant state of FLUX. The book itself is a means of divination to assist the individual in making meaningful choices.

I-THOU: the Jewish philosopher Martin BUBER in his poem book *I and Thou* (1937) distinguished between two basic attitudes men assume toward BEINGS and things in the world. These attitudes are openness, receptivity and engagement, or OBJECTIV-ITY and detachment. The two postures are represented SYMBOLICALLY by two primary words, "I-Thou" and "I-It." "I-Thou" implies openness and a personal relationship, while "I-It" suggests a cold objectivity and detachment.

IAMBLICUS (250-330): Syrian NEOPLATONIST philosopher who developed the teachings of PLOTINUS and taught a form of POLYTHEISM. He is the author of *On the Egyptian Mysteries* which surveys various PAGAN beliefs of his time.

'IBĀDAT: ISLAMIC term meaning religious observance and the ordinances of divine WORSHIP.

IBN AL-'ARABĪ (1165-1240): famous Islamic MYSTIC whose DOCTRINES tended to PANTHEISM and whose poetry was criticized for its eroticism.

IBN ḤAZM (993-1064): an influential Spanish convert to ISLAM who insisted on the literal interpretation of the QUR'ĀN and ḤADĪTH and strongly attacked CHRISTIAN and JEWISH SCRIPTURES.

IBN IS'ḤĀQ (704-768): biographer of MUḤAMMAD and noted authority on the events of his life.

IBN MĀJA, Muḥammad (824-886): a collector and compiler of MUSLIM TRADI-

TIONS whose work is recognized by the SUNNĪS as a sixth CANONICAL collection.

IBN MAS'ŪD (d. 652/3): one of the earliest MUSLIM converts. He settled in Kufa where he kept his own version of the QUR'ĀN which contained variant readings and fewer *Sūras* than the official version.

IBN TŪMART, Muhammad (d. 1130): Islamic REFORMER who opposed literalistic interpretations of the QUR'ĀN and all forms of ANTHROPOMORPHISM. He declared himself MAHDĪ in the Maghreb and with 'Abd al-Mu'min led a JIHĀD against infidels and MUSLIMS he considered heretical. The dynasty they established lasted for over a hundred years in Spain and the Maghreb.

ICON [IKON]: flat images of CHRIST, the Virgin MARY or the SAINTS which are used in the WORSHIP of EASTERN ORTHODOX CHURCHES. Their use goes back to the fifth century, and they are believed to be the channel through which divine blessing and HEALING comes to the faithful.

ICONOCLASTIC CONTROVERSY: from 717 to 843 a bitter dispute raged in the Eastern ORTHODOX CHURCH about the use of ICONS. Opponents of icons destroyed them as IDOLATROUS images forbidden in the BIBLE, but eventually the supporters of icons won the day.

IDEAL TYPES: a term used by Max WEBER to denote social arrangements peopled by ideally RATIONAL BEINGS. It is used to describe theoretical models of institutions, social relations and political systems which are "ideal" in the sense of being construed entirely according to theoretical laws and not according to observation of the actual world.

IDEALISM: the speculative PHILOSOPHY which considers the similarities and differences, identities and opposites which make up REALITY, and always looks to the UNIVERSAL, or what is common, behind the apparent diversity. An ANALOGY with slight idealism interprets the universal as FORM or the basic pattern which underlies reality. It looks for the permanent aspect which goes beyond the sensible world. Idealism is based on the supposition that sight and insight, concept and vision, and thought and form are identical, because BEING itself is spiritual. Idealism is one of the basic forms of Western METAPHYSICS.

IDEOLOGY: a set of BELIEFS which consciously or unconsciously shapes a person's outlook. In Marxism (*see* MARX) ideology is viewed as ABSTRACT and false thought, illusion, false consciousness, unreality or upside-down REALITY.

IDOLATRY: the making of images to represent GOD or the gods. Critics of idolatry say that people who use such things believe that they either are gods or are in some way indwelt by gods. Most worshipers of such images argue that they simply represent gods and act as aids to WORSHIP. Although popular in many religions, such as those of ancient Egypt and Greece, HINDUISM and other religions of Indian origin, the making of such images was condemned in the HEBREW BIBLE and subsequently by CHRISTIANITY, ISLAM and RABBINIC JUDAISM. Ancient CHINESE and Japanese religions seem to have been free from the use of images to represent the gods until the introduction of BUDDHISM, when they quickly accepted this new art form.

IGNATIUS (c. 35-c. 107): early CHRISTIAN convert and BISHOP of Antioch who was MARTYRED in Rome. His letters provide important insights into the development of the EARLY CHURCH.

IHSĀN: ISLAMIC term for VIRTUE and morality.

I'JĀZ: the quality of matchless eloquence attributed to the QUR'ĀN by the faithful. The Qur'ān is believed to be a literary MIRACLE, and its poetic form is said to be evidence of its divine origin.

IJMĀ: communal agreement or consensus whereby the MUSLIM community in SUNNĪ Islam identifies authentic developments in Islamic law and practice.

IJTIHĀD: the individual initiative and work of experts whereby valid IJMĀ is created within the community or, as in SHĪ'A, mediated to it.

ILHĀM: inspiration in ISLAM. The way GOD reveals himself to individual men in contrast to *wahy*, or REVELATION, which refers to the work of the PROPHETS and also to the QUR'ĀN.

'ILM AL-KALĀM: the term means THEOLOGY in ISLAM.

IMAGE OF GOD: according to Genesis 1:26 humankind was created in the "image of God." Exactly what this means has been a matter of dispute. In general CHRISTIANS agree that the BIBLE places a high value on the human being. The issue is complicated by the DOCTRINE of the FALL. ROMAN CATHOLICS maintain that the fall caused humans to lose certain SUPERNATURAL endowments and gifts but that the essential human nature remained intact. The PROTESTANT REFORMERS rejected this view and argued that through the fall SIN goes to the root of human existence, distorting all our relationships and even our ability to REASON correctly.

IMĀM: the person who leads WORSHIP in ISLAM. This office must not be confused with that of a PRIEST because anyone of sound mind and good character may lead to worship. Among the SHĪ'A, however, an imām must be a descendant of MUHAMMAD through his daughter FĀTIMA, while in India and Pakistan imāms are expected to be great scholars.

ĪMĀN: the Arabic term for FAITH, in Islam the correlative of *dīn*, or practice.

IMMACULATE CONCEPTION: the ROMAN CATHOLIC DOGMA, declared in 1854, that the mother of JESUS, the Virgin MARY, was conceived without SIN.

IMMANENCE: the nearness, presence or indwelling of GOD in CREATION. When God is regarded as IMMANENT he is believed to be active in sustaining and preserving creation as well as being concerned about the affairs of individuals. The term is usually contrasted with TRANSCENDENCE which means that God's activity and power are apart from the

world. CHRISTIAN THEOLOGY has always asserted both the immanence and transcendence of God, thus rejecting both DEISM and PANTHEISM.

IMMORTALITY: some form of EXISTENCE of the human personality after physical DEATH.

IMPERIALISM: a term which until the nineteenth century meant adherence to an emperor or imperial form of government. The modern usage developed in England after 1870. Today it generally means rule by a foreign and stronger national power and is closely associated with colonialism.

IMPLICIT: involved in or capable of being construed from, as the oak is implicit in the acorn.

INARI: SHINTŌ GOD of rice, food and fertility.

INCA RELIGION: much of what is known of Inca religion comes from Spanish sources and archaeological evidence. The Inca appear to have WORSHIPED a CREATOR GOD who had no name but was given a series of titles. Numerous other DEITIES also existed and were worshiped. Ceremonies were held in large areas in the open air, and TEMPLES were used to store RITUAL paraphernalia. Many PRIESTS and attendants served the religion, which involved large public ceremonies and constant SACRIFICE. Human victims— mainly women and children—appear to have been sacrificed in times of crisis. The Spanish regarded the Inca religion with horror as a bloodthirsty CULT: even allowing for their own lust for gold and conquest, their account seems essentially true and chilling.

INCARNATION: the taking on of human FORM; to make real or to provide with a body. In RELIGION the term refers to the appearance of a DEITY or some other spiritual entity in either the flesh or some other MATERIAL form. CHRISTIANS believe in the INCARNATION OF CHRIST while HINDUS speak about the incarnations of various DEITIES. In ISLAM the QUR'ĀN is often referred to as the incarnation of GOD's Word.

INCARNATION OF CHRIST: one of the key and unique BELIEFS of CHRISTIANITY which teaches that JESUS CHRIST, the SON OF GOD, was both fully God and fully human. This is quite different from other ancient religious MYTHOLOGIES where a god either takes on human form or has human offspring who are partly God and partly human. In Christian THEOLOGY the CREATOR GOD took on human form to become fully human while, at the same time, remaining fully divine. Early Christian CREEDS went to great lengths to explain what this meant, while at the same time distinguishing Christian teaching from similar-sounding PAGAN notions of God-men. The NICENE CREED, for example, says, "I believe . . . in one LORD Jesus Christ, the only-begotten Son of God, Begotten of the Father before all worlds; God of God; Light of Light; Very God of Very God; Begotten, not made . . . who . . . was incarnate by the Holy Ghost of the Virgin Mary, And was made man. . . ." Elaborating on this, the creed attributed to ATHANASIUS says, "He is God, of the Substance of the Father . . . and he is Man, of the Substance of his Mother . . . Perfect God; Perfect Man . . . Who although he be God and Man, yet he is not two, but is one Christ. One altogether; not by conversion of Godhead into flesh, but by taking Manhood into God; One altogether; not by confusion of Substance but by unity of Person. . . ." For Christians this is a crucial DOCTRINE because they believe that it enables Jesus Christ to act as the mediator between God and man (1 Timothy 2:5).

INCENSE: an aromatic substance burnt as an aid to WORSHIP and as a symbol of PRAYER.

INDEMNITY: a central belief in UNIFICATION CHURCH THEOLOGY, with a meaning similar to that of PENANCE in the ROMAN CATHOLIC CHURCH.

INDIVIDUAL: a self-conscious person acting on his or her own volition and for his or her own ends.

INDIVIDUALISM: a term which became popular with the rise of liberal political and economic thought to express a belief that the individual is the basic unit of SOCIETY and that individual rights and freedoms take precedence over GROUP rights.

INDRA: the greatest of the VEDIC GODS to whom over 250 VEDIC HYMNS are addressed. He was the god of war and was depicted as a hard-drinking warrior riding in a chariot. In classical HINDUISM the role of Indra was greatly reduced and in many ways replaced by that of KRISHNA.

INDUCE: to REASON inferentially from the particular, or particulars, to the general.

INDUCTION: that branch of logic which covers all cases of nondemonstrative argument; i.e., arguments not based on DEDUCTION.

INDULGENCES: a practice which emerged in medieval ROMAN CATHOLICISM, based upon the belief that the CHURCH has the power to forgive SIN, whereby PRIESTS had the power to remit the sins of individuals who made appropriate contributions to the church or undertook pilgrimages or other SACRED duties. Martin LUTHER'S protest against the sale of indulgences was part of the PROTESTANT REFORMATION.

INDUS VALLEY CIVILIZATION: an ancient urban civilization which flourished in the Indus valley in what is now Pakistan from the third millennium B.C. to around 1500 B.C., when it suddenly declined. We know very little about the civilization except that it was highly organized and left behind artifacts which appear similar to later HINDU DEITIES. Its most famous remains are those of the ruined city of Moenjodaro in the Sindh. Some archaeologists speculate that it was a society organized by PRIESTS, but this is uncertain.

INEFFABLE: incapable of being expressed in words. A term often used in association with MYSTICAL experiences.

INERRANCY: the belief held by many religious traditions that their sacred books or SCRIPTURES are without error. Certain HINDUS make this claim for the RG VEDA while Moslems claim it for the QUR'ÄN. Traditionally, CHRISTIANS have held that the original manuscripts of the BIBLE are inerrant.

INFALLIBILITY: the belief that because of their SACRED power of HOLINESS a religious individual or writing cannot err. Since 1870 the ROMAN CATHOLIC CHURCH has explicitly held that when the POPE makes an authoritative pronouncement on matters of FAITH or MORALS, either in concert with a general council or officially with the authority of his office (i.e., EX CATHEDRA, "from the chair") his teachings are infallible. Traditionally, PROTESTANTS have reserved the term *infallible* to refer to the Bible as the only true source of FAITH and DOCTRINE.

INFINITE: without limits or external boundaries. In ABRAMIC religions this truly applies to GOD alone.

INGE, William Ralph (1860-1954): ANGLICAN writer and DEAN of St. Paul's Cathedral in England. His sympathies with Platonism (see PLATO) led him to publish a long series of devotional and THEOLOGICAL writings dealing with MYSTICAL subjects. He is best known for his *Christian Mysticism* (1899).

INNER LIGHT: the source of authority in the SOCIETY OF FRIENDS or QUAKERS which says that neither the Bible nor the CHURCH but only the inner working of GOD'S HOLY SPIRIT is to guide CHRISTIANS.

INQUISITION: an organization established by the PAPACY in the thirteenth century to search out and eradicate HERESY.

INSPIRATION: in religious terms, to be inspired means to be under the influence of the HOLY SPIRIT or the Spirit of God or even some other spirit, such as that of an ancestor. In PROTESTANTISM, inspiration came to be identified with the writings of the BIBLE and any other "inspiration" was judged in terms of consistency with SCRIPTURE. In ROMAN CATHOLICISM, it is the CHURCH that judges what is to be considered inspired. Other religious systems have their own ways of determining what is and what is not genuinely inspired in terms of the BELIEFS of the particular FAITH involved. In ISLAM, the ḤADĪTH is considered inspired, but the QUR'ÄN is considered REVELATION.

INSPIRATION OF THE BIBLE: both CHRISTIANS and JEWS believe that the HEBREW BIBLE was written under the influence of the SPIRIT of GOD and possesses AUTHORITY for faith and practice. This concept was extended by Christians to the writings of the NEW TESTAMENT. BIBLICAL CRITICISM practically destroyed belief in verbal inspiration and put an intellectual strain on belief in plenary (full but not word-by-word) inspiration. Nevertheless, verbal and plenary inspiration is maintained by FUNDAMENTALIST and most EVANGELICAL Christians today.

INSTRUMENTALISM: the philosophical view, promoted by John Dewey and his followers, that ideas, theories, laws, etc., are instruments or tools which enable the resolution of the scientific problems and puzzles of life. The truth or falsity of such ideas is irrelevant. What matters is whether they are powerful and useful enough to cause and/or explain change, thus serving human purposes and meeting needs.

INTELLECTUAL: until the middle of the twentieth century intellectuals, intellectualism and intelligentsia had unfavorable connotations in English, implying theorists lacking common sense. This usage has changed somewhat to a more neutral usage describing what people do. Sometimes, however, intellectuals are identified with generalists who tend to identify with causes, as opposed to specialists who know an issue in depth.

INTER-VARSITY CHRISTIAN FELLOWSHIP: an EVANGELICAL CHRISTIAN organization which developed out of the union of four university groups in England in 1873. The first InterVarsity conference was held in England in 1919; the work spread to Canada in 1928 and then to the United States in 1939. Known today as Universities and Colleges Christian Fellowship in the United Kingdom and InterVarsity Christian Fellowship in the U.S. and Canada, the movement can be found worldwide, and the various national member groups are members of the International Fellowship of Evangelical Students.

IPSE DIXIT: literally "he said it to himself." It refers to a DOGMATIC utterance unsupported by evidence.

IQBAL, Muḥammad (1873-1938): Indian MUSLIM thinker and poet who formulated the political theory that led to the founding of Pakistan in 1947. He sought to adapt ISLAM to contemporary society and challenged Western ideas of MODERNIZATION. His chief work was *The Reconstruction of Islamic Thought in Islam* (1934).

IRANIAN RELIGION: the ancient religion of Iran before ZOROASTER can only be deduced from ZOROASTRIAN and Indian sources. It appears to have been POLYTHEISTIC and probably involved the worship of a sky GOD. RITUAL SACRIFICES involving bulls may have taken place and a form of DUALISM upheld.

IRENAEUS (130-200): BISHOP of Lyons and early CHRISTIAN APOLOGIST who strongly opposed GNOSTICISM and insisted on the importance of the INCARNATION OF CHRIST. His two surviving works are *The Demonstration of the Apostolic Preaching* and *Against Heresies*.

IRRATIONAL: contrary to REASON.

IRRATIONALISM: a BELIEF system which sets aside REASON to promote beliefs based on emotion and other SUBJECTIVE criteria.

IRVING, Edward (1792-1834): Scottish PRESBYTERIAN minister whose encouragement of SPEAKING IN TONGUES and CHARISMATIC gifts and arguments against political reform, CATHOLIC emancipation, and the University of London—which he called "the SYNAGOGUE of SATAN"—led to a CHURCH SCHISM. His followers formed

the CATHOLIC APOSTOLIC CHURCH. His writings include *For the Oracles of God* (1832) and *The Orthodox and Catholic Doctrine of Our Lord's Human Nature* (1830).

ISAAC: the son of ABRAHAM and PATRIARCH of ISRAEL in the HEBREW BIBLE.

ISAIAH (8th century B.C.): BIBLICAL PROPHET and traditional author of the highly influential book of Isaiah found in the HEBREW BIBLE.

ISHMAEL: son of ABRAHAM by Hagar and regarded as the progenitor of the Arabs. He is described as a PROPHET in *Sūra* XIX, verse 55, of the QUR'ĀN.

ISHO'DAD OF MERV (9th century): NESTORIAN biblical scholar whose Syriac commentaries on the BIBLE are important in terms of the insight they give into the history of biblical interpretation.

ISIDORE (560-636): Spanish ARCHBISHOP of Seville who fostered education and promoted learning. He edited an encyclopedia and wrote various books summarizing the knowledge of his age.

ISIS: ancient Egyptian GODDESS, the wife of OSIRIS and mother of Horus, who was often depicted as a woman suckling her child. Her CULT was popular throughout the Greco-Roman world and resembles that of the Virgin MARY.

ISLAM: the FAITH, obedience and practice of the followers of MUHAMMAD, believed by them to be the final and perfected RELIGION revealed by GOD. When the word is written "islām" it denotes surrender to God, but when written "Islam" it denotes the religion established by Muḥammad in the seventh century A.D. Fundamentally it means submitting oneself to God and renouncing any other object of WORSHIP. It is sometimes said that the word *islām* means peace, but this does not seem correct linguistically.

The first MIRACLE of Islam is considered to be the poetry of its HOLY book—the QUR'ĀN. The second miracle is the early conquests of Muslim armies. During Muḥammad's lifetime his followers were confined to Arabia. After his death, Syria was quickly conquered, Damascus being taken in 635, and then Jerusalem in 636. Mada'in, the Persian capital, fell in 637. Within a century Muslim armies had reached the borders of China and spread westward to conquer North Africa. In 711 Spain was invaded. But in 732 the Muslims were defeated at Tours, France, and this battle ended Islam's first major thrust into Europe.

Today there are over two hundred million Muslims in the world. Islam is a MONOTHEISTIC religion based on the CREED "There is no God but God and Muḥammad is his PROPHET." ABRAHAM, MOSES, JESUS and other biblical figures are also recognized as prophets, but their REVELATIONS are said to have been distorted by their followers. Muḥammad was the last of the prophets to whom God revealed his holy Word, the Qur'ān. Muslims are expected to observe five basic religious duties: the recitation of the creed; praying five times a day; FASTING during the month of RAMAḌĀN; the payment of religious tax, zakāt; and pilgrimage to MECCA at least once in their lifetime. To these duties JIHĀD—religious war or the defense of Islam by military force—is added. The duties are not inflexible but may be modified according to circumstances and, in theory at least, depend upon the individual's conscience for their performance.

Islam makes no distinction between religious and civil law, the SECULAR and the SACRED, or what Christians term "Church and State." As a result the whole of life is governed by religious law, which is ultimately based upon the Qur'ān. Since the beginning of the twentieth century several formerly Muslim countries, such as Turkey, have experimented with creating a secular state. Such experiments are rejected by orthodox Muslims. The interpretation of law is therefore one of the great concerns of Islam about which scholars argue, and it is also one of the major issues today as Islamic societies face MO-DERNITY and the challenge of SECULARISM. One major point of conflict is that of the role and rights of women. Islamic APOLOGISTS argue that the women in Islam have always been able to own property and have enjoyed a much higher status than women in the West. This claim appears true, in terms of the formal documents, but is highly questionable in terms of actual practice, which tends to make women subordinate to their nearest male relative.

ISMĀ'ĪLĪS: adherents of a dynamic and essentially LIBERAL ISLAMIC SECT. The movement developed from SHI'ISM and teaches that the QUR'ĀN has an internal as well as an external meaning. They claim to derive their teachings from a hidden source which must receive absolute obedience. There are various grades of members and associates who receive teaching only according to their capacity. The lowest grades receive external instruction in keeping with normal Islamic practice, but other grades develop to more ESOTERIC teaching. Their leader claims descent from MUḤAMMAD and is known as the AGA KHAN. In recent times the movement has proved to be highly flexible and able to adapt its beliefs to modern society.

ISNĀD: the evidence and attestation of a genuine TRADITION of MUSLIM thought and interpretation which can be traced back through a chain of reliable authorities to the COMPANIONS OF THE PROPHET. It is what the tradition uses to legitimate its claims, as opposed to what it teaches.

ISRAEL: the name given by GOD to the PATRIARCH JACOB in the HEBREW BIBLE, it was later transferred to the JEWISH people who became known as the People of Israel. In the Bible the term originally applied to the descendants of Jacob's twelve sons, but later it was applied to the ten northern tribes only while the two southern tribes were known as JUDAH. The ancient kingdom of Israel was destroyed by the Assyrians in 721 B.C. and its people taken into SLAVERY and exile. In the New Testament the CHURCH is referred to as having the attributes of Israel to signify that it has been chosen by God as his new people consisting of Jews and Gentiles. In 1948 a new Jewish STATE known as Israel was established in the land of Palestine after a bitter struggle with local Arabs.

ISRAEL ben Eliezer Baal Shem Tov (1700-1760): founder of HASIDISM in Eastern Europe. In the mid-1730s he revealed himself as a healer and subsequently gathered a movement which grew rapidly. Folk tales about his life and teachings show his personal charm, magnetism and ecstatic personality. He advocated devotional joy and contributed greatly to the revitalization of JUDAISM.

ĪŚVAR: SANSKRIT word, meaning LORD, which is used to refer to GOD as the supreme personal BEING and is frequently used in BHAKTI. Usually the lord is identified with VISHNU, Śiva or BRAHMAN, or even all three together. The lord is thought of as the CREATOR of the world and often as its destroyer.

J

JACOB (18th century B.C.?): grandson of ABRAHAM through Isaac, and twin brother of Esau. In the HEBREW BIBLE he appears as a patriarch of Israel, but a very unscrupulous character until he "struggles with GOD" (Genesis 32), after which he takes the name ISRAEL. The Jewish race, the children of Israel, are his descendants. His favorite and most famous son was JOSEPH. His life story is told in Genesis 25:21—50:13.

JAINISM: although this RELIGION probably dates to at least the eighth century B.C., most Western scholars trace its founding to MAHĀVIRA in the sixth century B.C. A highly conservative movement, it stresses ASCETICISM and holds BELIEFS similar to those of its main rivals, BUDDHISM and HINDUISM. The UNIVERSE is conceived of as an everlasting succession of HEAVENS and HELLS to which all BEINGS are bound by KARMA and from which liberation is attainable only through ascetic practice.

JALĀL al-Dīn Rūmī (1207-1273): MUSLIM MYSTIC and the founder of the Māwlawi Order in Islam commonly known as the "Whirling Dervishes." His most famous work is the *Mathnawi* which contains stories interspersed with THEOLOGICAL discussions. His mystical theology sees the world as being created for man as a microcosm which reflects the ATTRIBUTES of GOD. Although men can choose GOOD and EVIL and are responsible for their actions, the religious RITES are obligatory. The aim of life is to love God and through devotion to lose one's individuality by being absorbed into God. His theology has a distinctly PANTHEISTIC tinge, and it also teaches the essential unity of all religions.

JAMES (1st century): the brother of JESUS OF NAZARETH and a leader in the EARLY CHURCH. He is the traditional author of the epistle of James in the NEW TESTAMENT.

JAMES, William (1842-1910): brother of the American novelist Henry James; their father was a Swedenborgian theologian (*see* SWEDENBORG). James was successively professor of psychology (1889-1897) and philosophy (1897-1907) at Harvard University. His book *The Varieties of Religious Experience* (1902) laid the basis for the PSYCHOLOGY of RELIGION while his *Pragmatism* (1907) strongly influenced the development of American thought during the first half of the twentieth century.

JAMMA: the Swahili word for "family" was adopted by Placide Tempels, a FRANCISCAN MISSIONARY, for the highly successful REVITALIZATION movement he founded within the ROMAN CATHOLIC CHURCH in Zaire in the 1940s. Tempels outlined his basic outlook in *Bantu Philosophy* (1959), where he emphasizes human dignity, a sense of community, and the need to take African TRADITION seriously. The movement spread rapidly and took on a life of its own after ill health caused Tempels to leave the Congo in 1962, giving rise to tensions between the membership and the church hierarchy.

JANSEN, Cornelius Otto (1585-1638): ROMAN CATHOLIC theologian and educator who opposed the JESUITS and theologians of the COUNTER-REFORMATION through his educational activities and major work *Augustinus* (1640). His followers became known as the Jansenists and strongly influenced Blaise PASCAL.

JANSENISM: French religious movement within the ROMAN CATHOLIC CHURCH named after Cornelius Otto JANSEN. Jansenists stressed vigorous personal PIETY and PREDESTINATION. They opposed the theology of the JESUITS.

JANUS: the Roman GOD of beginnings. He was represented by two faces looking in opposite directions.

JASPERS, Karl (1883-1973): German EXISTENTIALIST philosopher. He practiced in psychiatry and then moved via psychology to philosophy, finally accepting a professorship at Heidelberg in 1921. He was ousted from his post during the Nazi era, but returned after the war. In *Nietzsche and Christianity* (1946), *The Perennial Scope of Theology* (1948), and *Myth and Christianity* (1954), Jaspers sees religious answers emerging from METAPHYSICAL descriptions of BEING. He rejects THEISM, PANTHEISM, revealed religion (*see* REVELATION) and ATHEISM as mere ciphers or symbols which should not be taken literally, and argues that one should look to PHENOMENOLOGICAL descriptions of the fringes of inward and outer experiences for understanding.

JEANNE D'ARC: *see* JOAN OF ARC.

JEFFERSON, Thomas (1743-1826): American DEIST and author of the *Declaration of Independence* who played an important role in shaping American thought. He became the third president of the United States.

JEHOVAH'S WITNESSES: a highly RATIONALIST, ADVENTIST-type, pacifist SECT founded by Charles Taze RUSSELL in the late nineteenth century. It originally mixed a blend of interpretation of biblical PROPHECY with PYRAMIDOLOGY and other ESOTERIC teaching to foretell the end of the world. Orthodox Christian beliefs such as the TRINITY and INCARNATION of CHRIST were rejected, and a unique DEISTIC theology similar to ARIANISM developed. EVOLUTION is totally rejected, as are, peculiarly, blood transfusions.

JEN: "Humanness" in Confucian philosophy (*see* CONFUCIUS).

JEREMIAH (7th century B.C.): BIBLICAL PROPHET who denounced his people, JUDAH, for trusting in Egyptian military armament rather than GOD against the might of the Babylonians. By tradition he was stoned to death for his unwelcome oracles. His writings reveal the value of a living relationship with God and a prophet sensitive to the plight of his own people. His personal suffering and gloomy view of his nation's future have caused his name to be associated with a pessimistic attitude to life.

JEROME (342-420): biblical scholar who translated the HEBREW BIBLE and NEW TESTAMENT into Latin, the common language of his day. His translation was called the Vulgate and became the official Bible of the ROMAN CATHOLIC CHURCH. Jerome wrote commentaries on virtually all the books of the Bible and through his great scholarship made a tremendous impact on the development of Western CHRISTIANITY.

JERUSALEM: ancient city in Palestine

which is SACRED to CHRISTIANS, JEWS and MUSLIMS.

JESUIT ORDER: the name given in 1540 to the Society of Jesus, a brotherhood founded six years earlier by Ignatius LOYOLA. During the period 1540-1555 it grew rapidly, acquiring an autocratic structure provided by Loyola's military training and discipline, which he promoted in his *Spiritual Exercises* (1548). The Jesuits established MISSIONS, orphanages, houses for reclaiming prostitutes, schools, centers of poor relief and even a system of banking for destitute peasants. Francis XAVIER is perhaps the most famous Jesuit missionary. By the time of Loyola's death in 1556, the Society was one thousand strong, with its influence being felt most strongly among the aristocracy. Through the establishment of colleges in university settings, the Society became a teaching order and a leader in ROMAN CATHOLIC higher education. The Jesuits strongly supported the POPE at the COUNCIL of TRENT; they spearheaded the intellectual attack on the REFORMATION and became the foremost Roman Catholic APOLOGISTS. Today they are still a powerful intellectual and educative force within the Catholic Church and run numerous universities, including the Gregorian University in Rome.

JESUS OF NAZARETH (c. 5 B.C.-c. A.D. 30): the founder of CHRISTIANITY, which is based upon the story of his life, death and resurrection. He was given the title Christ (meaning "anointed one") by his followers to acknowledge their BELIEF that he was the expected MESSIAH (Hebrew for "anointed one") of ISRAEL. Jewish authors reject this claim although some, along with MUSLIMS, accept that he was a PROPHET—or at least performed a prophetic role. Traditionally, however, Jews have regarded him as an impostor and attacked him in such works as the medieval TOLEDOTH YESHU. Most of our evidence about his life comes from Christian sources, although he is mentioned by several Ro-

man and Jewish writers. Although documentary evidence about his life is scant by modern proportions, it is in fact more extensive and reliable than for any other ancient figure. Very little is known of his life before the age of thirty: our only reliable source is the NEW TESTAMENT, particularly the Gospels, which records many of his sayings and tells about his birth and one incident in Jerusalem at the age of twelve. All other stories concern his ministry after the age of thirty. Tales that he visited England or India during the hidden years are pure speculation with no basis in fact.

At about thirty years of age Jesus was baptized by JOHN THE BAPTIST. Conscious of a unique filial intimacy with God which allowed him to address God as "Abba" ("Father") and an authority attributed to the HOLY SPIRIT, he began proclaiming the presence of the KINGDOM OF GOD, calling ISRAEL to REPENTANCE and warning of the coming destruction of Jerusalem and the return of the SON OF MAN, a term by which he characteristically spoke of himself. His ministry was characterized by itinerancy, teaching in varied Palestinian settings, speaking in parables, having table fellowship with "sinners" and other outcasts, performing HEALINGS, EXORCISMS and other MIRACLES, and entering into controversy with Jewish religious authorities regarding matters of Jewish law and observance. His calling of twelve disciples seems to have signified an intention to renew Israel, and the latter part of his ministry seems to have been characterized by a growing consciousness of his coming rejection and death at the hands of the authorities, an event he interpreted as an end-time drawing down of God's wrath upon himself for the sake of the people of God.

After a summary trial of dubious legality by both Jewish and ROMAN authorities, he was executed by crucifixion. His death took place on the eve of the Jewish PASSOVER. After being buried in a rock tomb for three days, his body disappeared, and his disciples claimed that he had risen from the dead. Forty days later he was said to have ascended into heaven to reign with God. In recent years various accounts of his "death" which assume a swoon and slow recovery followed by flight to Kashmir, Tibet or even Japan have circulated. However, like the tales about his life before the age of thirty, such accounts are speculations lacking all historical basis.

JESUS MOVEMENT: a spontaneous RELIGIOUS REVIVAL originating in the late 1960s in California where many young people who had been HIPPIES or members of the drug subculture became CHRISTIANS. The Jesus Movement was identifiable by its relaxed hippie-style dress, use of modern music and rejection of traditional forms of WORSHIP. In time many members of the Jesus Movement joined established DENOMINATIONS or formed new independent CONGREGATIONS. Others, however, joined various HERETICAL NEW RELIGIOUS MOVEMENTS such as the CHILDREN OF GOD.

JESUS PRAYER: the ancient PRAYER used for CHRISTIAN MEDITATION in Eastern ORTHODOX CHURCHES which involves the repetition of "Lord Jesus Christ, Son of God, have mercy upon me a sinner."

JEWISH: relating to the RELIGION of JUDAISM. Ethnically, the word refers to the descendants of JACOB.

JEWISH CHRISTIANITY: that branch of the EARLY CHURCH which had its roots firmly planted in JUDAISM and the teachings of PETER rather than PAUL.

JEWISH CHRISTIANS: sometimes known as Messianic Jews, these are contemporary converts from JUDAISM to CHRISTIANITY who attempt to preserve Jewish TRADITIONS while accepting JESUS OF NAZARETH as the MESSIAH.

JEWS FOR JESUS: a new religious movement founded by Moishe Rosen, a JEWISH convert to CHRISTIANITY, which seeks to convert Jews. It originated in the COUNTERCULTURE of the 1960s as part of the JESUS MOVEMENT.

JIHĀD: a HOLY war or striving with infidels by force or intellectual persuasion to make converts (see CONVERSION). Traditionally ISLAM divides the world into dār al-Islam—the realm of Islam—and dār al-ḥarb—the realm of war: a notion which reflects the idea that war must continue until Islam is the UNIVERSAL RELIGION.

JINN: a class of beneficent or malevolent BEINGS in ISLAMIC cosmology that inhabit the earth and are capable of assuming many forms and exercising SUPERNATURAL powers.

JĪVANMUKTA: an "Enlightened One" in HINDUISM who continues to live in this world following his ENLIGHTENMENT.

JĪVANMUKTI: in HINDUISM, LIBERATION in this life.

JÑĀNA: HINDU term meaning WISDOM, knowledge or comprehension.

JOACHIM OF FIORE (1132-1202): on a PILGRIMAGE to Jerusalem, he experienced a religious CONVERSION and later entered the CISTERCIAN ORDER. After a short spell as ABBOT of Corazzo, he resigned to devote himself to APOCALYPTIC writings which develop an elaborate interpretation of HISTORY involving three great stages based on the persons of the TRINITY. Although he said little about the third phase, or age of the Spirit (see HOLY SPIRIT), except that it would see the rise of new religious orders which would convert the whole world, it became the focus of speculation in the movement known as JOACHIMISM. The Spiritual FRANCISCANS, various PROTESTANT groups and, in recent times, NEW AGE movements have all been influenced by his work.

JOACHIMISM: a medieval APOCALYPTIC movement based on the works of JOACHIM OF FIORE. It developed an eschatology anticipating the coming of the age of the Spirit.

JOAN OF ARC (1412-1431): known as the "Maid of Orleans." She was a peasant girl who as a teenager began to experience visions, heavenly voices and PROPHETIC REVELATIONS from various ROMAN CATHOLIC SAINTS. Believing that her mission was to save France from English rule, she made several prophecies which brought her to the notice of the king of France. A series of successful military campaigns followed. But eventually she was betrayed to the English by the Duke of Burgundy and burnt for HERESY as a witch.

JOB: a BIBLICAL character whose trials and triumphs of faith are depicted in the book of Job.

JŌDŌ: a Japanese school of PURE LAND BUDDHISM founded by HŌNEN which proclaimed AMIDA the BUDDHA of Infinite Light and Great Compassion. It became the most popular form of Buddhism in Japan. Under SHINRAN it developed into Jodō-Shinshū which proclaimed the DOCTRINE of *tariki*, or "other power," which offered salvation by GRACE and FAITH through the recitation of Amida's name. Through trust in the vow of Amida, DEVOTEES were promised REBIRTH in the Western PARADISE, from where they would achieve LIBERATION.

JOHN (1st century A.D.): a disciple of JESUS OF NAZARETH who is traditionally credited with writing the NEW TESTAMENT books known as the Gospel of John, the three epistles of John and the book of Revelation.

JOHN BAPTIST OF LA SALLE (1651-1719): ROMAN CATHOLIC educator who is credited with creating the modern secondary school and teachers' training courses; also known for his PIETY.

JOHN CLIMACUS (570-649): an ASCETIC spiritual writer who became an anchorite and promoted dispassionateness as the ideal of CHRISTIAN PERFECTION.

JOHN OF DAMASCUS (675-749): an Arab CHRISTIAN theologian and the earliest Christian commentator on ISLAM. His work deeply influenced the development of the Greek ORTHODOX CHURCH as well as Western theologians such as Thomas AQUINAS. He was a strong defender of ICONS and the use of images as aids to WORSHIP. His most important theological work was *The Fount of Wisdom;* his *Tractate on Islam* is the first Christian APOLOGETIC against Islam.

JOHN OF SALISBURY (1115-1180): one of the leaders of the twelfth-century RENAISSANCE and the first medieval scholar to be acquainted with the entire works of ARISTOTLE.

JOHN OF THE CROSS (1542-1591): ROMAN CATHOLIC MYSTICAL writer and Spanish CARMELITE reformer best known for his meditation *The Dark Night of the Soul,* which is based on his own experience and shows profound insight into spiritual and psychological states. His work, which was guided by TERESA OF ÁVILA, encountered strong opposition, and he was repeatedly persecuted by CHURCH authorities for his views.

JOHN THE BAPTIST (1st century A.D.): a JEWISH preacher, prophet figure and ASCETIC who, according to the NEW TESTAMENT, was the cousin of JESUS OF NAZARETH and prepared the way for Jesus' ministry. John proclaimed JUDGMENT, and preached REPENTANCE and BAPTISM for the remission of SINS in anticipation of the imminent arrival of the KINGDOM OF GOD. He was executed by HEROD ANTIPAS for denouncing his immorality. John's disciples seem to have formed a distinct community which for a time coexisted with CHRISTIANITY.

JOHN XXIII (1881-1963): Italian POPE who convened the Second VATICAN COUNCIL (1962-1963). His reforms and attempts to modernize the CHURCH had a far-reaching effect on ROMAN CATHOLICISM.

JOHNSON, Samuel (1709-1784): English essayist, man of letters and defender of CHRISTIANITY against DEISM and other forms of criticism.

JŌJITSU: a school of BUDDHISM introduced into Japan by Korean MONKS around 625. It was nihilistic in tone, being based upon a study of COSMOLOGY and

PSYCHOLOGY strongly influenced by HINDU thinkers such as NĀGĀRJUNA and DEVA. It taught that both the ego and all DHARMAS are equally illusory, and it conceived the past and future as nonexistent, while the present vanishes as soon as it occurs.

JONES, Bob (1883-1968): American FUNDAMENTALIST leader known for his separationist policies. He founded Bob Jones University in Greenville, South Carolina.

JONES, Jim (1931-1978): minister of the CHURCH OF CHRIST and founder of the PEOPLE'S TEMPLE. His followers committed mass SUICIDE at JONESTOWN, Guyana, in 1978. A professed Marxist, he was active in numerous left-wing causes and, before his bizarre suicide, widely respected for his social work.

JONES, Sir William (1746-1794): employee of the British East India Company who, during his eleven-year stay in India, developed a keen interest in Indian antiquities. In 1784 he founded the Asiatic Society of Bengal, and during his time in India acquired a good command of SANSKRIT. His translation of Sanskrit dramas influenced GOETHE and HERDER.

JONESTOWN: the small UTOPIAN communal settlement in the jungle of Guyana founded by Jim JONES in 1978. It became the site of a notorious mass murder/ suicide in 1979 which claimed the lives of over 700 people.

JOSEPH [1] (17th century B.C.?): the eleventh son of JACOB and great-grandson of ABRAHAM. His father's gift of a "coat of many colors" led to his brothers selling him into SLAVERY in Egypt. His subsequent imprisonment and then elevation as Pharaoh's chief advisor is recounted in a masterpiece of Hebrew narrative in Genesis 37—50 and sets the stage for the story of MOSES and the EXODUS.

JOSEPH [2] (1st century B.C.?): the husband of the Virgin MARY and, according to the NEW TESTAMENT, the legal but not biological father of JESUS OF NAZARETH.

JOSEPHUS, Flavius (A.D. 37-100): Jewish historian whose writings are our chief source of information about first-century JUDAISM.

JOWETT, Benjamin (1817-1893): master of Balliol College, Oxford, IDEALIST philosopher and translator of Greek classics, who promoted liberal THEOLOGY in England. He contributed a highly controversial essay titled "The Interpretation of Scripture" to the Victorian theological world in Essays and Reviews (1860).

JOY FOR THE WORLD: the earliest known BUDDHIST play and an important document in the history of Buddhism, it was written in the fifth century A.D. to convey the TRUTH of Buddhism to popular audiences. In 1987 it was translated for the first time into English by Professor Michael Hahn of Marburg University.

JUDAH: In the Hebrew BIBLE, JACOB's fourth son, after whom the largest of the ten tribes of ISRAEL was named. After the death of King Solomon around 900 B.C. Judah became an entirely separate kingdom from ISRAEL and remained independent until it was destroyed by the Babylonians in 587 B.C. The nation was restored around 530 B.C. after the overthrow of Babylonian power by the Medes.

JUDAISM, ANCIENT: the religion of the HEBREW BIBLE which proclaims a COVENANT between GOD and the people of ISRAEL. From ABRAHAM the Jewish people developed as a distinct nation who experienced the SALVATION of God at the time of the EXODUS. At Sinai, the covenant was made with the nation, the law given and cultic worship established. Following the wilderness period the Israelites, under the leadership of Joshua, entered the "promised land" of CANAAN. A transition from tribal leadership to kingship came under leadership of Samuel, with a dynasty established in David (c. 1000 B.C.) and his descendants. A centralization of the CULT was achieved under king Solomon, with his building of a temple in Jerusalem. But the unified nation was soon divided into northern and southern kingdoms shortly after Solomon's death (922 B.C.), with the temple and Jerusalem remaining in control of the southern kingdom. In 722 B.C. the northern kingdom was conquered by Assyria and subjected to a policy of exile. In 587 B.C. the southern kingdom was conquered by Babylon, the Jerusalem temple destroyed, and much of the population taken into exile in Babylon. The period surrounding the fall of the northern and southern kingdoms, as well as the period of the Babylonian exile and return, was distinguished by the classic prophets of Israel and their message of impending judgment and future hope. After the Babylonian captivity Judaism underwent major changes. The period of restoration (538 B.C.—), characterized by the reorganization of the community, renewal of the covenant, rehabilitation of Jerusalem, reconstruction of the temple and reinstitution of cultic sacrifice, were initiated by EZRA and Nehemiah.

During the Hellenistic period (300-63 B.C.) Hellenism influenced Jewish thought and the theocratic STATE gave way to a commonwealth. Judaism became radically pluralized, with some groups seeking to be faithful to their visions of traditional covenantal norms and others pursuing accommodation to Hellenistic influences and political realities. The result was a liberalized interpretation of law on the part of some and a radical adherence to the demands of purity on the part of others. The best-known parties, or "Judaisms," of the first century A.D. were the SADDUCEES, PHARISEES, ESSENES and a "fourth philosophy" of resistance to Rome (*see* ZEALOTS). Religion, particularly the concerns of purity, was highly politicized and focused on the Jerusalem temple as the focus of the ideals of purity. An apocalyptic perspective and an accompanying messianism was also shared by a broad spectrum of Jews in this period. This picture of a diverse Judaism was brought to an abrupt end with a revolt against Roman rule and the destruction of JERUSALEM in A.D. 70. That point marks the emergence and ascendancy of RABBINIC JUDAISM.

JUDAISM, MEDIEVAL: during the European Middle Ages Judaism flourished as rabbinic Judaism developed a rich TRADITION of PHILOSOPHY and MYSTICAL experience. Influencing the intellectual development of both CHRISTIANITY and ISLAM, medieval Judaism enriched both Arab and European cultures. The greatest rabbinic scholar of this period is Moses MAIMONIDES (1135-1204).

JUDAISM, MODERN: essentially those branches of Judaism which have developed since the eighteenth century and are in many respects a reaction to the ENLIGHTENMENT and Jewish emancipation in Europe. The most important expressions of modern Judaism are: (1) Reformed Judaism, which originated in nineteenth-century Germany and seeks to accommodate traditional Jewish beliefs to the modern world by adopting a rational liberalism and rejecting messianic expectations; (2) Orthodox Judaism, which also arose in Germany, and seeks a modified accommodation with modernity, stressing ritual practice and tradition; and (3) HASIDISM, which grew up during times of persecution in Poland and Eastern Europe during the eighteenth century and promotes a MYSTICAL relationship to GOD. The collective psyche of modern Judaism was seared by the NAZI HOLOCAUST, which has become a central fact of Jewish life. How could a good God allow the murder of six million Jews? How could a formerly Christian nation, where the Jews were highly assimilated, perpetrate such an atrocity? The horror of this event led to the founding of the STATE of ISRAEL in 1948 and the fact that today the largest Jewish community is to be found in the United States of America.

JUDAISM, RABBINIC: after the loss of JERUSALEM and the destruction of the TEMPLE in A.D. 70, the scattered Jewish community sought a new center. This they found in the growing collection of rabbinic teaching that in the second century A.D. was written down in the Mishnah. A dialectical collection of previously oral tradition which applied principles of TORAH to life (see HALAKHAH)—now organized by topic, Mishnah became a paradigm for rabbinic thought. MIDRASH, on the other hand, was a method of interpretating biblical texts in which, typically, the text became an occasion to invoke rabbinic teaching. Beginning in the third century, the ongoing teaching of the rabbis was brought into textual dialogue with the Mishnah by appending the Tosefta ("additions") to Mishnah. In due course, rabbinic scholarship developed a commentary on Mishnah which became known as TALMUD ("learning"). This is found in two versions: the Jerusalem Talmud (c. 400) and the Babylonian Talmud (6th century), the latter being the more influential. Thus for rabbinic Judaism everything worth knowing was to be found in the *Torah*— and interpreted by the *Talmud*—which evidences concern for the whole of life. The central motive of rabbinic Judaism was henceforth the quest for underlying MEANING and ethical action in Jewish life, and the LAW replaced the temple and SACRIFICE as the center of Jewish WORSHIP.

JUDAIZERS: CHRISTIANS seeking to restore the requirements of Jewish law within the Christian community; a movement among early Christians which sought to reform JUDAISM and make GENTILE converts conform to Judaic practice. After the destruction of the TEMPLE in A.D. 70 and the disappearance of the church at JERUSALEM, the movement seems to have lost its force, although similar groups appear throughout church history.

JUDAS ISCARIOT (1st century A.D.): a disciple of JESUS OF NAZARETH whom he betrayed to the Jewish authorities.

JUDGMENT: this can mean either the logical act of reaching a conclusion or an act of judgment in the afterlife which rewards or punishes acts committed in this life. Many religious systems believe in the judgment of the dead and in a last judgment at the end of time.

JULIAN (332-363): nephew of CONSTANTINE and reforming Roman emperor who did everything possible, short of open persecution, to eradicate CHRISTIANITY through the REVIVAL of the old Roman PAGAN religion, which he encouraged by his own writings and through education. He is generally known as "Julian the Apostate."

JULIAN OF NORWICH (1342-1416?): obscure English MYSTIC and HERMIT, possibly influenced by NEOPLATONISM, who claimed to have received healing from GOD and sixteen REVELATIONS on May 8 and 9, 1373. She wrote about these revelations twenty years later in *The Sixteen Revelations of Divine Love*, which extols divine love as the answer to all problems, especially the PROBLEM OF EVIL.

JUNAYAD, Abū al-Qāsim al- (d. 910): famous ṢŪFĪ leader who was convinced that Ṣūfī FAITH and practice were fully compatible with orthodox SUNNĪ Islam. Although he taught that everything comes from and returns to GOD he rejected PANTHEISM.

JUNG, Carl Gustav (1875-1961): Swiss psychiatrist and early disciple of FREUD who developed his own system of psychology with strong religious and even OCCULT overtones. Drawing upon ALCHEMY, YOGIC RELIGIONS and various ESOTERIC traditions, he developed a theory of ARCHETYPES which verges on PSEUDOSCIENCE. His ideas are generally rejected by modern PSYCHIATRY, although they are very popular with many religious and literary writers. His works include *Psychology and Alchemy* (1953).

JUNO: the Roman GODDESS identified with the Greek goddess Hera, who is closely associated with life and sexuality.

JUPITER: the ancient Roman sky GOD who was associated with the Greek god ZEUS—a god of the state and of war.

JUSTIFICATION: a technical THEOLOGICAL term used in the NEW TESTAMENT writings of PAUL to signify that act by which GOD restores humans to a right relationship with himself. PROTESTANT REFORMERS and ROMAN CATHOLIC theologians disagreed as to how justification was to be interpreted. For the Roman Catholic it meant making the sinner just through the infusion of SUPERNATURAL GRACE that blots out sin and regenerates the SOUL, making it worthy of God. For the Reformer, justification was an act of divine forgiveness brought about by FAITH in the SACRIFICE of CHRIST.

JUSTIN MARTYR (100-165): Christian convert from PAGANISM who was the first Christian thinker to attempt to reconcile FAITH and REASON. He taught that the truths of pagan PHILOSOPHY find their fullest expression in CHRISTIANITY. His *Apologies* and *Dialogue with Trypho* are amongst the earliest Christian APOLOGETIC writings.

JUSTINIAN (483-565): late Roman/early Byzantine emperor who sought to restore the unity of the empire. He is remembered for his legal reforms resulting in the Code of Justinian, which became the basis for much European law. In particular he was the first ruler to formally recognize a clear distinction between religious and SECULAR affairs. To him, the CHURCH and STATE were separate but interdependent entities.

JUWAYNĪ, Abu 'l-Ma'ālī 'Abd al-Malik al- (1028-1085): famous ISLAMIC scholar and teacher of al-GHAZĀLĪ.

K

KA: in ancient Egyptian thought, Ka is the psychic double of the individual which is born with them at their physical birth and protects them during life.

KABBALA: *see* CABBALA

KAʿBA: the building in MECCA toward which all MUSLIMS must face during PRAYER.

KABĪR, Kabir (1440-1518): a forerunner of the Sikhs (*see* SIKHISM), he grew up in a MUSLIM home in Banaras. He became a prominent religious teacher and began to attack the external differences between Muslims and HINDUS. A disciple of RAMA-NANDA, he opposed the WORSHIP of images and the CASTE system. He taught that there was only one GOD, whom he called both Ram and ALLAH to emphasize that God transcends human understandings of him. His disciple NĀNAK was the main founder of Sikhism.

KAGAWA, Toyohiko (1888-1960): Japanese CHRISTIAN convert from BUDDHISM who was a noted pacifist, democrat, social reformer and outstanding CHURCH leader.

KAHN, Herman (1922-1983): leading American futurist who popularized the use of scenarios to create models of the future. His controversial views and opti-mism aroused strong criticism but, unlike those of many other modern PROPHETS, they have stood the test of time. His books include *1979 and Beyond* (1979) and *The Next 200 Years* (1976).

KAIROS: Greek term used in the NEW TESTAMENT to mean a time of decision or moment of truth. It has been used in LIBERATION THEOLOGY to criticize more traditional theologies and the conserva-tism of CHRISTIAN CHURCHES.

KAIROS DOCUMENT: an influential radical critique of South African society produced by a group of black ministers in Soweto which bears the stamp of the white Dominican Albert Nolan. The doc-ument ably identifies the evils of South African society but goes on to critique LIBERALISM and the theology of reconcili-ation. After its publication a number of imitative publications appeared, such as the *Evangelical Witness in South Africa* (1986), which expressed the basic Kairos con-cerns in slightly milder language.

KAKUTARO, Kubo (1890-1944): one of the cofounders, with Kotani KIMI, of REIYŪKAI.

KĀLĪ: HINDU GODDESS of time and de-struction. She is the consort of Śiva and is usually depicted as a ferocious figure wearing a necklace of skulls.

KALI YUGA: the fourth age of the present eon, which in traditional HINDU cosmology started with the MAHĀBHĀRATA war some 5,000 years ago. It is the last age of a series of ages during which RELIGION and social life have been in decline, and will eventually end in social chaos.

KALPA (Sanskrit), KAPPA (Pali): a measure or rule; a period of time, an age, or an eternity lasting millions of years.

KĀMA: an Indian term for pleasure or sensual enjoyment. It is one of the four traditional ends or aims of life in HINDU thought.

KAMI: a comprehensive Japanese word for DEITY meaning "above" or "superior."

KAMIDANA: Japanese term for a family ALTAR.

KANNUSHI: term used to designate PRIESTS in SHINTŌ temples. It comes from a term meaning "Master of the Deities." The Japanese emperor is the highest Kannushi of all.

KANNON: the most revered BODHISAT-TVA in Japanese BUDDHISM, to whom many TEMPLES are dedicated. He is the All Compassionate Lord of Mercy.

KANT, Immanuel (1724-1804): one of the most important philosophers in the Western tradition. Born in Königsberg, East Prussia, he spent most of his life in scholarly study. Awakened from what he called his "dogmatic slumber" by the works of David HUME, he began to seek a philosophical basis for knowledge which avoided complete SKEPTICISM. The first exposition of his work came in *The Critique of Pure Reason* (1781), which was followed by works applying his ideas to METAPHYSICS, ETHICS, AESTHETICS, RELIGION and PHILOSOPHY. He argued that our knowledge of things is conditioned by mental structures or "categories" that order our experience. As a result we cannot know "things-in-themselves," "the noumena," but only the PHENOMENA which result from the interaction between our minds

and what is observed. Kant argued that we can neither prove nor disprove the existence of GOD, with the result that religion must be based on FAITH. In his view religion becomes practical morality.

KAPILAVATTHU: according to tradition, this is the small town in the Himalayas which was the paternal home of GAUTAMA (BUDDHA).

KARAITES: a Jewish SECT founded in Babylon in 750 by 'Anan ben David, whose aim was to reform JUDAISM in terms of SCRIPTURE rather than in terms of tradition as represented by the *Talmud*.

KARMA: one of the central DOCTRINES of YOGIC RELIGION which is probably best described as a BELIEF in a universal cause and effect which embraces all things. The SANSKRIT meaning of the term is "action" or "deeds." It is through the workings of karma that humans and other beings are bound to SAMSĀRA, the WHEEL OF EXISTENCE. Within Yogic religions karma takes many forms, although it is generally seen in terms of a cosmic moral order which is responsible for REBIRTH. Many NEW RELIGIOUS MOVEMENTS incorporate their own versions of karma which range from highly sophisticated PHILOSOPHICAL analyses of existence to crude beliefs in a tar-like substance which clings to the SOUL, thus binding it to this world. See T. Day, *The Conception of Punishment in Early Indian Literature* (1982), and A. G. Hogg, *Karma and Redemption* (1909).

KEBLE, John (1792-1866): English TRACTARIAN leader and author of *The Christian Year*. In 1831 he was elected professor of poetry at Oxford. He became increasingly concerned about what he saw as the dangers threatening the CHURCH OF ENGLAND from the REFORMING and LIBERAL movements. On July 14, 1833, he preached a university sermon entitled "National Apostasy," and from then on he took a leading part in the OXFORD MOVEMENT. In 1870 Keble College, Oxford, was founded in his memory.

KEGON SCHOOL: a branch of BUD-

DHISM introduced into Japan by the Korean monk Jinjo (d. 742) which had a significant influence on the rise of ZEN through its identification of NIRVĀNA and SAMSĀRA.

KEMPE, Margery (1373-1433): English MYSTIC whose work *The Book of Margery Kempe* outlines her mystical experiences.

KEPLER, Johannes (1571-1630): German astronomer who discovered the laws of planetary motion as a result of observation and his belief in MYSTICAL theories.

KERYGMA: Greek for "preaching" or "proclamation"; the term is used to refer to the essential message of CHRISTIANITY.

KESWICK CONVENTION: annual summer gathering of EVANGELICALS at Keswick in the English Lake District. It originated in the MOODY-SANKEY revival of 1873, and the first conference at Keswick was held in 1875. The movement aims to promote "practical HOLINESS." Its motto is "All One in Christ Jesus."

KEYNES, John Maynard (1883-1946): the most influential economist of his time. His revolutionary economic theory led to a break with classical economics and a boom following World War II: this era is often referred to as the "Keynesian Era." His greatest work is *General Theory of Employment, Interest and Money* (1936). Keynes placed great stock in the role of ideas in society and believed that ultimately ideas determine events.

KHADĪJA (d. 619): wealthy widow who at the age of forty married her business manager, MUHAMMAD, who was then twenty-five.

KHĀLID ibn al-Walīd (d. 641/2): famous MUSLIM general who was given the name "Sword of God" by MUHAMMAD. Although at first he was opposed to Islam and actually defeated Muhammad's forces, he later converted and led the Islamic invasions of Persia and Syria.

KHANDHA (Pali); SKANDHA (Sanskrit): a term referring to a "group" or "aggregate" of factors in BUDDHISM. According to Buddhist analysis the individu-

al "PERSON" may be analyzed into five Khandhas, which upon examination, prove the nonexistence of the "person."

KHĀTM AL-NUBUWWA: the seal of PROPHETHOOD in ISLAM.

KHAZARS: a Crimean tribe, possibly of Turkish origin, which converted to JUDAISM around the tenth century.

KHNUM: ancient Egyptian CREATOR GOD.

KHŌJĀS: a MUSLIM community which originated through the CONVERSION of HINDUS, and is now found along the West coast of India and in East Africa. Their allegiance is to the AGA KHAN.

KHOMEINI, Ruhollah al-Musavi (1902-1989): Islamic scholar and jurist known in the West for his role in the IRANIAN ISLAMIC REVOLUTION. He is conceivably the most important religious figure in the twentieth century because of the new confidence he has injected into Islam. Khomeini was a MYSTIC deeply immersed in daily affairs. Exiled by the Shah of Iran for his protests against SECULARIZING policies, Khomeini learned of the brutal murder of his eldest son by the Shah's secret police on November 23, 1977. On February 1, 1979, he returned in triumph to Iran after the Shah had fled. Following his return, he directed the creation of a modern Islamic state based on traditional practices and beliefs. His most important translated work is *Islam and Revolution* (1981).

KHOMYAKOV, Aleksei Stepanovitch (1804-1860): Russian philosopher and theologian who attacked the thought of both ARISTOTLE and HEGEL, arguing instead for a form of Platonism (*see* PLATO) which found expression in the faith of the Eastern ORTHODOX CHURCH.

KHONSU: ancient Egyptian moon GOD.

KHUDDAKA-NIKĀYĀ: a collection of canonical books which form the fifth section of the PALI CANON in BUDDHISM.

KIERKEGAARD, Søren Aabye (1813-1855): Danish Christian philosopher and "father" of Christian EXISTENTIALISM. Reared in the atmosphere of Hegelian DIALECTICS, in works such as *Either-Or*

(1843) he opposed HEGEL's work with his own existential dialectics. His statement "Subjectivity is TRUTH" (see SUBJECTIVISM) powerfully expresses his viewpoint which links truth to the existing subject, not to an object. His works, rediscovered in the twentieth century, have deeply influenced philosophy and theology through the writings of HEIDEGGER, SARTRE, BARTH and BULTMANN.

KIMBANGU, Simon (d. 1951): AFRICAN prophet and CHURCH founder who claimed to have received a VISION of JESUS. After preaching for a few months in 1921, he was arrested by the Belgian authorities and spent the rest of his life in prison. However, people began to report seeing him in dreams, and his church spread until it became one of the largest in Africa. It is now a member of the WORLD COUNCIL OF CHURCHES.

KIMI, Kotani (1901-1971): cofounder with Kubo KAKUTARO of REIYŪKAI.

KINDĪ, Yaʻqūb ibn Isḥāq, al- (813-873): known as "the philosopher of the Arabs," he is the only MUSLIM philosopher of pure Arabic descent. He was deeply influenced by NEOPLATONISM, and even his *Theology of Aristotle* was Neoplatonic.

KING, Martin Luther, Jr. (1929-1968): American BAPTIST minister and Black Civil Rights leader. In 1957 he became the president of the Southern Christian Leadership Conference which created the Civil Rights Movement. He is best remembered for his 1963 speech "I Have a Dream" which reflected the goals and IDEOLOGY of the Civil Rights Movement. In 1968 he was assassinated in Memphis, Tennessee. His works include *Stride Towards Freedom* (1958) and *Why We Can't Wait* (1964).

KINGDOM OF GOD: a symbol that has an extraordinarily rich and varied history. The term means "reign of God." NEW TESTAMENT scholars are divided as to the exact meaning of the term in the preaching of JESUS, who spoke of the kingdom as both present and future. AUGUSTINE identified the kingdom of God with the elect.

His usage easily slipped over into the identification of the kingdom of God with the CHURCH in medieval Europe. Christians today who equate the kingdom of God with God's sovereign rule view it as both a present reality and as the final culmination of world history.

KINGSLEY, Charles (1819-1875): English ANGLICAN theologian, social reformer and novelist who helped promote CHRISTIAN SOCIALISM.

KINTU: legendary king of the Baganda people of Uganda who both founded the nation and, through various exploits, interacted with a sky GOD to bring both BLESSINGS and death to earth.

KLUCKHOHN, Clyde (1905-1960): American anthropologist (see ANTHROPOLOGY) with a particular interest in RELIGION. His famous work *Navaho Witchcraft* (1944) presents a highly romanticized VISION of the function of WITCHCRAFT as a social mechanism for the maintenance of social harmony.

KNIGHT, J. Z. (1946-): highly successful American OCCULTIST, promoter of trans-channeling and founder of the church I Am. She claims to be the MEDIUM through which a SPIRIT entity named Ramtha communicates with humanity. Raised in a Christian FUNDAMENTALIST home, she dabbled in the occult and drifted into SPIRITUALISM before developing her own unique teachings. Shirley MACLAINE is one of her many clients.

KNOX, John (1513-1572): Scottish CALVINIST REFORMER whose famous tract *The First Blast Against the Monstrous Regiment of Women* (1558) was aimed at the three women in power in Scotland, England and France, who were persecuting the Protestants. However when the Protestant ELIZABETH I came to the throne in England she also took offense at Knox's writings.

KO HUNG (c. 283-343): Chinese TAOIST philosopher whose mammoth work *Pao P'u Tzu* (317) popularized ALCHEMY and the magical aspects of Taoism. He taught that humans have two SOULS which survive for a short time after death before entering the Great Unity where personality is finally lost. Anyone wishing to continue a personal existence needed to become a "Hsien" (immortal) through Taoist practice.

KŌAN: a term in ZEN BUDDHISM meaning an exercise given by a Zen Master to a disciple designed to break their intellectual limitations and produce a sudden flash of ENLIGHTENMENT.

KŌBŌ DAISHI (774-835): the posthumous name of Kūkai, a Japanese BUDDHIST SAINT and founder of the SHINGON sect of Buddhism. After studying in China, he introduced TANTRIC practice and pantheistic mystical ideas into Japanese Buddhism. His teachings involved a SYNCRETISTIC mysticism which influenced the development of SHINTŌ.

KOESTLER, Arthur (1905-1983): Hungarian novelist and journalist who developed strong interests in the paranormal. He is the author of *Darkness at Noon* (1940), *The Sleepwalkers* (1959) and *The Lotus and the Robot* (1966).

KONKŌ KYŌ: a SHINTŌ sect founded by Kawate Bunjiro (1814-1883) in 1881 which seeks to revitalize Shintō for contemporary society. The name means "Golden Lustered Teaching." It emphasized belief in one GOD, good health as a result of fellowship with God, and the repudiation of superstition associated with RITUAL practice and MAGICAL charms.

KORAN: *see* QUR'ĀN.

KORE: meaning "maiden." She was an ancient Greek earth GODDESS, also known as Persephone, the daughter of Demeter. In the rites of the ELEUSINIAN MYSTERIES it appears that worshippers reenacted the search for her.

KRÄMER, Hendrik (1888-1955): Dutch CHRISTIAN MISSIONARY educator and theorist who ministered in Indonesia from 1922 to 1937. His most important book is *The Christian Message in a Non-Christian World* (1938) which emphasizes the uniqueness of the biblical message.

KRISHNA (Kṛṣṇa—Sanskrit): the most important incarnation of VISHNU in HINDU MYTHOLOGY. The name literally means "the Black One." The stories of the MAHĀBHĀRATA are about aspects of his earthly existence, the most important spiritual section of which is the BHAGAVAD-GĪTA. Legends about Krishna abound and often contain erotic love stories. Other accounts involve his rescue from a massacre of children and his death from an arrow which struck his heel, the only vulnerable spot. Some scholars see these latter stories as reflecting the influence of stories about CHRIST and Greek LEGENDS about Achilles. Others suggest that the Krishna stories are based on a historical figure who later became a GOD.

KRISHNAMURTI, Jiddu (1895-1986): Indian MYSTIC who, from the age of 12, was reared and educated by C. W. Leadbeater, Annie BESANT, and other Theosophists at Adyar, outside Madras, to prepare him to become the next World Teacher. A fever of excitement built up in the 1920s as the THEOSOPHICAL SOCIETY geared itself for the expected manifestation of the Lord Maitreya through Krishnamurti. But the period of preparation culminated in a series of shattering psychic and physical experiences for Krishnamurti that led him to reject all religions, philosophies and preconceptions about enlightenment. In 1929 he parted company with the Theosophical Society and began teaching a kind of therapeutic DIALECTIC.

KRONOS: the father of ZEUS and chief GOD in preclassical Greek religion. Later he was identified, many would say mistakenly, as the god of time.

KṢATRIYA: the second of the four CASTES in traditional Indian society, the warrior caste which shares power with the BRAHMINS.

KUAN-TI: a popular Chinese DEITY revered as a GOD of war, patron of literature and giver of wealth.

KUBLAI KHAN (1216-1294): the grandson of the Mongol Emperor Genghis Khan who deliberately adopted Chinese CULTURE and founded the Yüan Dynasty. During his reign China was open to foreign influences. Until 1255 he tolerated all RELIGIONS but thereafter sided with the BUDDHISTS and had TAOIST books destroyed. He seems to have favored TIBETAN BUDDHISM but continued to protect CHRISTIANS and MOSLEMS. In 1274 and 1281 he made unsuccessful attempts to invade Japan which failed disastrously but had far-reaching religious impact in Japan through the preaching of NICHIREN.

KUEI: Chinese term for disembodied SPIRITS, DEMONS, ghosts and other incorporeal beings.

KUHN, Thomas Samuel (1922-): very influential philosopher of science whose book *The Structure of Scientific Revolutions* (1962) has had immense impact, especially in THEOLOGY, the social sciences and education, where his ideas have been used to promote RELATIVISM and question the OBJECTIVITY of scientific scholarship. He argues that science advances by a series of unrelated jumps rather than gradual improvements. The key term in his work is PARADIGM, which he uses to express the outlook of a given scientific community. In recent years the historical basis for his arguments has been severely criticized and rejected by most historians of science.

KULTURKAMPF: literally, "the struggle for CIVILIZATION." The term was used to refer to the conflict in 1871-87 between Otto von Bismarck, German Chancellor, and the ROMAN CATHOLIC CHURCH, as the former attempted to subject the latter to STATE controls.

KUMĀRAJĪVA (344-413): although the exact details of his life are uncertain, he appears to have been an Indian BUDDHIST MONK kidnapped by Chinese raiders when he was about forty. He spent the rest of his life in China, where he became an important translator of Buddhist literature and EVANGELIST for Buddhism. It was largely through his efforts that Buddhism

developed in China to the point where it came to be regarded as a PHILOSOPHY equal to TAOISM and Confucianism (*see* CONFUCIUS).

KUNDALINĪ: feminine serpent power in traditional HINDU physiology which plays an important role in TANTRA. It is pictured as coiled around the LINGAM, thus preventing the movement of vital powers toward the head. When awakened by YOGA, tremendous heat is produced, and the YOGI can gain PURIFICATION and power which ultimately results in LIBERATION. Kundalinī is also identified with the coiled serpent power which gave birth to the UNIVERSE.

KÜNG, Hans (1928-): Swiss ROMAN CATHOLIC theologian who studied at the German College in Rome. He gained fame as a progressive but not radical thinker within the Roman Catholic Church and an important figure in the discussions of the Second VATICAN COUNCIL. His early works such as *Justification* (1965) and *Infallible?* (1971) dealt with ECCLESIASTICAL matters. His *On Being a Christian* (1977) became a bestselling APOLOGETIC which was supplemented by *Does God Exist?* (1980). More recently in books like *Christianity and World Religions* (1986) he has moved toward UNIVERSALISM. He sought to create an inter-religious ECUMENICISM and now teaches under a ban from the VATICAN.

KUR: the Sumerian term for underworld or "land of no return" to which the dead go.

KUYPER, Abraham (1837-1920): Dutch CALVINIST theologian, philosopher and statesman. During his first pastorate in the small fishing village of Beesd he converted to Calvinist orthodoxy from the theological LIBERALISM he had espoused at the University of Leyden. As a result of his educational and ecclesiastical concerns, he entered politics in 1869 and quickly became the leader of the Anti-Revolutionary Party founded by GROEN VAN PRINSTERER. Among his many accomplishments are the founding of a daily newspaper, a weekly religious magazine, a labor union, a political party, the Free University of Amsterdam (1880) and a period as prime minister of the Netherlands from 1901 to 1905. A voluminous writer, his translated works include: *Lectures on Calvin-* *ism* (1898), *Principles of Sacred Theology* (1898) and *The Work of the Holy Spirit* (1900).

KYRIE ELEISON: Greek term used in Christian LITURGY meaning "Lord have mercy."

KYRIOS: the Greek term for "LORD," used to speak of both GODS and rulers.

L

LAITY, LAYPERSON: members of a RELIGIOUS TRADITION who are not ORDAINED or set aside to perform the functions of a PRIEST or of the CLERGY. A layperson is an ordinary member of any religious tradition without special recognition or status.

LALITAVISTARA: means *Detailed Narrative of the Sport* (of the Buddha) in SANSKRIT. This is one of the most important texts in MAHĀYĀNA BUDDHISM; it tends toward a form of Buddhist BHAKTI and gives a very different account of the BUDDHA's life which emphasizes the "play" or "sport" of a divine BEING. The date of the text is unknown.

LAṄKĀVATĀRA SŪTRA: one of the nine major texts of MAHĀYĀNA BUDDHISM and an important source for Chinese and Japanese Buddhism. It contains conversations of the BUDDHA which are represented as presenting the orthodox teaching of Buddhism. The text contains a strong critique of HINDU PHILOSOPHY. An early form of the text was translated into Chinese around 420; prior to that nothing is known about its history.

LAO TZU (6th century B.C.): the greatest of the TAOIST masters about whom very little is known, although LEGENDS abound.

He was an older contemporary of CONFUCIUS. Traditionally he is the author of the *Tao Te Ching* or *Book of Lao-Tzu.*

LARES: Roman DEITIES of the cultivated fields, possibly connected with ancestor worship, who came to be associated with crossroads. Later they were worshiped in homes as the center of the family CULT.

LAUD, William (1573-1645): English ARCHBISHOP of CANTERBURY and strong opponent of PURITANISM, who was believed by his enemies to be promoting ROMAN CATHOLICISM in the CHURCH OF ENGLAND. He was executed for corruption and various crimes.

LAW, William (1686-1761): English spiritual writer who was greatly appreciated by John WESLEY, George WHITEFIELD and Henry Venn. Among his writings are *On Christian Perfection* (1726) and *A Serious Call to a Devout and Holy Life* (1728). He was inspired by the teaching of THOMAS À KEMPIS and spiritual writers of the Greek ORTHODOX CHURCH.

LAWRENCE, Brother (1605-1691): French MYSTIC and lay brother of the CARMELITE ORDER known for his holy and prayerful life. *The Practice of the Presence of God* is a modern anthology of his writings.

LAYMAN: *see* LAITY, LAYPERSON.

LEACH, Ronald Edmund (1910-1987): British anthropologist (*see* ANTHROPOLOGY) who popularized STRUCTURALISM and the work of Claude LÉVI-STRAUSS. He wrote extensively on the interpretation of the BIBLE, his best-known work in this area being *Genesis as Myth* (1966). Among his many works *Rethinking Anthropology* best represents his viewpoint (1961).

LEE, Ann (1736-1784): originally a Shaking QUAKER, she withdrew from her husband in 1766 and assumed leadership of the local SHAKERS. Her cardinal DOCTRINES were CONFESSION as the door to the regenerate life, and CELIBACY as its rule and cross. "Mother Ann, the Word," as she was called, and seven followers emigrated from England to New York in 1774, and the movement grew rapidly. She formulated the characteristic beliefs of the Shakers: celibacy, communism, pacifism, MILLENNIALISM, elitism and spiritual manifestations through barking, dancing and shaking.

LEE, Witness (20th century): Chinese follower of Watchman NEE who founded the controversial LOCAL CHURCH, which encourages a form of communal living and various liturgical practices such as "prayer-reading" of the BIBLE.

LEEUW, Gerardus van der (1890-1950): Dutch scholar and professor of the History of Religion at Groningen, whose book *Religion in Essence and Manifestation* (1948) is one of the classic statements of the PHENOMENOLOGY OF RELIGION.

LEGALISM: a term derived from CHRISTIANITY which denotes any religious system which teaches SALVATION through WORKS rather than GRACE. The effect of legalism is that the individual is overwhelmed with rules and regulations rather than encouraged in the development of a relationship with GOD. Martin LUTHER preached strongly against legalism in the ROMAN CATHOLIC CHURCH. In a derivative sense it refers to religion that recognizes the priority of grace in salvation but legislates

behavior by burdensome and rigid codes.

LEGEND: a short prose narrative, often tied in with a particular place or locality, which tells an apparently historical story which has little basis in actual fact. Legends often contain mysterious, MAGICAL and SUPERNATURAL elements.

LEGITIMATION: justification, making legitimate or acceptable. The act of appealing to some TRADITION or other evidence to justify contemporary actions or the existence of a movement. Legitimation often implies an appeal to evidence which appears to justify a group's existence or action when in fact it does not. In this sense legitimation is a term used to signify the false use of evidence or the use of poor evidence in popular PROPAGANDA.

LEIBNIZ, Gottfried Wilhelm, Baron von (1646-1716): German rationalist philosopher (*see* RATIONALISM), mathematician, and inventor of calculus, whose work led to the development of symbolic logic. He is also known for his work on THEODICY. He taught that the UNIVERSE is made up of ultimate entities known as monads. GOD is the supreme monad responsible for the state of the universe. He is eternal and absolute truth who created this world as the best possible world. EVIL is a problem, but it is to be understood as a consequence of freedom, which makes the world a far better place than if humans lacked the ability to choose.

LENIN, Vladimir Ilyich (1870-1924): Russian intellectual heir of MARX and ENGELS and professional REVOLUTIONARY who founded the Soviet Communist Party and eventually led it to power. His works include *Imperialism the Highest Stage of Capitalism* (1916) and *Materialism and Empirico-Criticism* (1908).

LENT: a TRADITIONAL season in the CHRISTIAN year consisting of forty days of FASTING, penitence and spiritual discipline. It immediately precedes and is preparation for the celebration of EASTER.

LESSING, Gotthold Ephraim (1729-1781): German ENLIGHTENMENT philosopher, publicist, playwright, critic and art theorist. He worked for the free and democratic development of the German people and their CULTURE and adopted a highly critical stance concerning the possibility of historical knowledge (see HISTORY), especially knowledge of religious events.

LEVELLERS: an extremist SECT during the PURITAN REVOLUTION and English Civil War which advocated civil and religious equality.

LÉVI-BRUHL, Lucien (1857-1939): French philosopher and armchair anthropologist (see ANTHROPOLOGY) who wrote *Primitive Mentality* (1922), in which he claimed that "primitive" tribal peoples lack the ability to make logical distinctions.

LÉVI-STRAUSS, Claude (1908-): French anthropologist (see ANTHROPOLOGY) and originator of STRUCTURALISM. Although immensely influential in anthropology, he did very little fieldwork and is more a philosopher and armchair anthropologist in the tradition of Sir James FRAZER than he is an empirical scientist. His works include *Totemism* (English ed. 1963), *The Savage Mind* (English ed. 1966) and *Structural Anthropology* (English eds. 1963 and 1976).

LEVIATHAN: a Hebrew word meaning "coiled" or "twisted" which is used to refer to a sea monster in the HEBREW BIBLE. This is the title of Thomas HOBBES's book on political philosophy.

LEVIRATE MARRIAGE: the marriage of a man to his brother's widow, provided no son has been born to the deceased man. This is practiced in many societies and is mandated in the HEBREW BIBLE in Deuteronomy 25:5-10.

LEVITATION: the BELIEF held in many YOGIC RELIGIONS and NEW RELIGIOUS MOVEMENTS that a SPIRITUAL being is able to overcome the force of gravity and levitate themselves through MEDITATION. Claims about the ability to teach levitation are made by adherents to TRANSCENDENTAL MEDITATION.

LEVITES: the descendants of JACOB's son, Levi, who became an order of assistants to the Aaronic PRIESTS in ancient JUDAISM.

LEWIS, Clive Staples (1898-1963): novelist, poet, literary critic, CHRISTIAN APOLOGIST and ANGLICAN LAYMAN who taught at the universities of Oxford and Cambridge. He is best known for his Chronicles of Narnia (1950-1956, 7 vols.), *The Screwtape Letters* (1941) and *Mere Christianity* (1952). The story of his CONVERSION is told in *Surprised by Joy* (1955) and *The Pilgrim's Regress* (1933).

LI: Chinese concept developed in Confucianism (see CONFUCIUS) which denotes the proper procedure whereby rites must be performed.

LI CHI: the *Book of Rites and Ceremonies* which is one of the five classics in Confucianism (see CONFUCIUS).

LIBATIONS: the pouring of liquid offerings, such as water, blood or wine, in religious RITUALS.

LIBERAL: someone who seeks moderation and claims to deplore DOGMA.

LIBERAL PROTESTANTISM: a loose designation for a wide range of religious thought unified more by a temper of mind than specific beliefs. It originated in the nineteenth century and reached its height in America in the decades preceding the Second World War. It was characterized by: (1) an eagerness to discard old ORTHODOXIES when judged IRRATIONAL in the light of modern knowledge or irrelevant to the central core of religious experience; (2) a confidence in the power of human REASON guided by experience; (3) a belief in FREEDOM; (4) a belief in the social nature of human existence; (5) FAITH in the benevolence of GOD and the goodness of creation. Liberal Protestantism enthusiastically endorsed BIBLICAL CRITICISM. The movement is generally traced back to the German theologian Friedrich SCHLEIERMACHER and is seen in the work of Albrecht RITSCHL, who emphasized the need for relevance in THEOLOGY. By the early twentieth century liberal Protestantism was characterized by an emphasis on the fatherhood of God and brotherhood of man.

LIBERATION: in YOGIC RELIGIONS such as HINDUISM and BUDDHISM the goal of the devotee is expressed by many terms, all of which assume the cessation of REBIRTH and freedom from the bonds of KARMA. This aim may generally be termed liberation.

LIBERATION THEOLOGY: a movement which originated among ROMAN CATHOLIC theologians, especially JESUITS, in Latin America in the late 1960s. It sought to apply Marxist analysis to the situation of the poor in an attempt to create a THEOLOGY which would speak to the masses. Using stories from the HE-BREW BIBLE, such as that of the EXODUS, they sought to interpret the NEW TESTA-MENT message of JESUS in terms of polit-ical action and REDEMPTION from oppres-sive social conditions. Although popular in intellectual circles in Europe and North America, the movement seems to have had little local support in Latin America due to internal contradictions, such as the refusal of many advocates of liberation theology to accept birth control. Impor-tant works in the development of the movement are Giulio Girardi's *Marxism and Christianity* (1968), Gustavo Gutierrez's *A Theology of Liberation* (1973), Helder Camara's *Church and Colonialism: The Betray-al of the Third World* (1969) and Camilo Torres's *Revolutionary Priest* (1971). As a movement it inspired BLACK THEOLOGY and provoked strong criticism from writ-ers like Michael Novak in *The Spirit of Democratic Capitalism* (1982).

LIEH-TZU (4th century B.C.): TAOIST philosopher and traditional author of the *Book of Lieh-tzu* which argues that, because life is fleeting and ends in death, it is futile and, therefore, HEDONISM is the only possible response.

LIMBO: according to traditional Roman Catholicism, an intermediary state be-tween HEAVEN and HELL where people go who have not received Christian baptism.

LINGAM: the main emblem of Śiva and an object of WORSHIP in HINDUISM: the lingam is a phallus. The origin of lingam worship may be traced back to pre-ARYAN India and the DRĀVIDIANS of the south.

LINGĀYAT: a HINDU SECT within Śaivism originating with the teachings of Basava (twelfth century) which concentrated on the LINGAM as the one true symbol of di-vinity. In theory the sect rejects CULT images, the CASTE system and many ritual practices found in Hinduism. The THEOL-OGY of the group is a form of qualified NON-DUALISM which sees the world as created by Śiva to whom every SOUL must return. Members of the sect wear a lingam around their neck.

LITURGY: a term used to describe the order or structure of a formal WORSHIP service in CHRISTIANITY.

LIVINGSTONE, David (1813-1873): MIS-SIONARY, explorer and opponent of the slave trade. In 1838, he joined the London Missionary Society and became passion-ately interested in Africa. Reports of his explorations and experiences aroused wide interest in England. His principal work was *Missionary Travels and Researches in South Africa* (1857).

LLOYD-JONES, David Martyn (1899-1981): a distinguished Welsh physician who became a PRESBYTERIAN minister in 1929 and was one of the greatest twen-tieth-century preachers. His popular bib-lical expositions include *Studies in the Sermon on the Mount* (1959-1960) and his multi-volume *Lectures on Romans* (1955-1968). His lectures on PURITAN THEOLOGY helped revitalize British and American EVANGEL-ICALISM by encouraging a revival of evan-gelical scholarship allied to pastoral con-cerns.

LOCAL CHURCH: a highly controversial new religious movement which was founded by Witness LEE, a follower of Watchman NEE. The group is strongly influenced by the theology of the PLY-MOUTH BRETHREN, especially the writings of J. N. DARBY. It has been accused of HER-ESY by various other CHRISTIAN move-ments who question its interpretation of the INCARNATION and the TRINITY. Its devotional practice of "prayer-reading" the Bible, use of meditative prayers sim-ilar to the "JESUS PRAYER" of the Eastern ORTHODOX CHURCH and the communal living of some members have also caused concern among outsiders.

LOCKE, John (1632-1704): philosopher whose *Essay Concerning Human Understanding* (1690) developed a CHRISTIAN EMPIRICISM. He was strongly influenced by CALVINISM, and became the "father" of modern polit-ical LIBERALISM through his advocacy of religious and political TOLERATION evi-denced in his *Letter on Toleration* (1698) and *Two Treatises on Government* (1690). An avid student of the BIBLE, he was working on several biblical commentaries when he died.

LOGICAL POSITIVISM: a form of rad-ical EMPIRICISM developed by the VIENNA CIRCLE which denied meaning to all met-aphysical statements. The movement dominated Anglo-Saxon philosophy dur-ing the 1950s, 1960s and early 1970s.

LOGOS: a term used by HERACLITUS (fourth century B.C.) to speak about the rational law or principle which governs the universe. It was developed in STOICISM and PLATONISM, eventually finding its way into CHRISTIANITY where it is used at the beginning of the Gospel of John. The concept enabled early Christian APOLO-GISTS to accommodate their religion to Greek PHILOSOPHY.

LOHAN: a Korean and Japanese BUD-DHIST term for ARAHANT, or one who has achieved ENLIGHTENMENT.

LOLLARDS: the fourteenth- and fif-teenth-century followers of John WYC-LIFFE, forerunners of the REFORMATION.

LONERGAN, Bernard (1904-1984): Ca-nadian JESUIT PRIEST reckoned among the most important DOGMATIC theologians of this century. Instead of assuming that one or other contemporary philosophy or

WORLDVIEW is correct, Lonergan sets out to determine the structure of the human mind which has given rise to the variety of philosophies and worldviews, on the basis of which each is to be criticized as inadequate. He applies this structure to THEOLOGY through such works as *Insight* (1957), *Method in Theology* (1957) and *The Way to Nicea* (1976).

LORD: in ancient HEBREW RELIGION GOD was described as ADONAY, or "Lord." The New Testament applied this term to JESUS with the implication that he too is God.

LORIAN ASSOCIATION: a Californian organization founded in 1973 by David SPANGLER to promote the NEW AGE MOVE-MENT. It is an offshoot of the FINDHORN COMMUNITY. The association has promot-ed New Age music, publishing and a variety of other activities, including the popularization of TRANSCHANNELING. See Dorothy Maclean, *To Hear Angels Sing* (1980).

LOSSKY, Nikolai (1870-1965): Russian philosopher who argued that all things move toward GOD. His writings include *The Intuitive Basis of Knowledge* (1906) and *History of Russian Philosophy* (1951).

LOSSKY, Vladimir (1903-1958): Russian THEOLOGIAN and son of Nikolai LOSSKY who became the leading exponent of Eastern Orthodoxy (*see* ORTHODOX CHURCH) in the West. His works include *The Mystical Theology of the Eastern Church* (1944) and the posthumous *In the Image and Likeness of God* (1967).

LOTUS SŪTRA: probably the most im-portant text of MAHĀYĀNA BUDDHISM. Its rich MYTHOLOGY and DOCTRINE inspired the development of PURE LAND BUDDHISM and a variety of other Buddhist SECTS in China and Japan. It was translated into Chinese in the second century and stresses the omniscience and eternal pow-er of the BUDDHA, who draws all BEINGS to ENLIGHTENMENT.

LOU, Tseng-Tsiang (1871-1949): Chinese statesman and ROMAN CATHOLIC BENEDIC-TINE MONK who saw CHRISTIANITY as the completion of the Confucian tradition (*see* CONFUCIUS). His major work was *Ways of Confucius and of Christ* (1948).

LOURDES: the site of an alleged VISION of the VIRGIN MARY in 1858 by Bernadette Soubirous, it has become a major center for ROMAN CATHOLIC PILGRIMAGE. Many MIRACULOUS HEALINGS are said to have taken place at the Lourdes SHRINE.

LOVE: "affection" or "taking into the heart"; the supreme VIRTUE in both CHRISTIANITY and Confucianism (*see* CONFUCIUS) where the term is used in a remarkably similar way. *See* AGAPE.

LOVEJOY, Arthur Oncken (1873-1962): American philosopher and historian of ideas who argued in favor of DUALISM. His major works are *Revolt Against Dualism* (1930) and *The Great Chain of Being* (1936).

LOYOLA, Ignatius (1495-1556): Spanish MYSTIC and religious innovator who founded the Society of Jesus, whose members were called JESUITS. After being wounded in battle in 1521, he experienced a religious CONVERSION which led him to abandon his military career to become a "soldier for Christ." For the next thirteen years he devoted himself to study and ASCETIC practices which led to a VISION of CHRIST, followed by the founding of the Society of Jesus in 1540.

LUBAVICH: an Eastern European NEW RELIGIOUS MOVEMENT of JEWISH origin which developed in Russia out of HASIDISM. The movement, which is MYSTICAL in nature, is led by a spiritual master and has its present headquarters in New York.

LUCIFER: the DEVIL or source of evil in CHRISTIANITY.

LUKE (1st century): the author of the Gospel of Luke and The Acts of the Apostles in the NEW TESTAMENT. He appears to have been a converted Roman physician with a keen sense of HISTORY and the value of historical evidence.

LUMBINI: one of the four HOLY places in BUDDHISM, traditionally the birthplace of BUDDHA.

LUTHER, Martin (1483-1546): German THEOLOGIAN and biblical scholar and one of the most important figures in Western CHRISTIANITY. He reluctantly launched the PROTESTANT REFORMATION as a result of his study of the BIBLE where he rediscovered the principle of JUSTIFICATION BY FAITH. The family of LUTHERAN CHURCHES are named after him and follow guidelines he established for ECCLESIASTICAL organizations. Ordained as a ROMAN CATHOLIC PRIEST in 1507, he taught moral PHILOSOPHY at the new University of Wittenberg. In November 1510, Luther went on PILGRIMAGE to ROME where he was shocked by the worldliness of CHURCH leaders. The sale of INDULGENCES provoked him to protest against the practice, leading to his posting of his Ninety-five Theses in October 1517. This act led directly to the REFORMATION. Originally he sought internal REFORM of the ROMAN CATHOLIC CHURCH and taught that SCRIPTURE alone is the source of authority for the Church. Catholic theologians, led by John ECK, rejected his suggestions and began the active persecution of Luther's followers. The Reformation followed. His writings are available in English in *Luther's Works* (56 vols.), ed. J. Pelikan and H. T. Lehmann.

LUTHERANISM: the religious movement and community within PROTESTANTISM which traces its origin to Martin LUTHER and his teachings.

LYELL, Charles (1797-1874): Scottish lawyer and founder of modern geology who was a popular writer and lecturer in Victorian Britain. His major contribution to science was his enunciation of the principle of uniformity, which he termed "ordinary forces," as the basic methodological assumption in geology. On the basis of this principle he argued that observable geological forces, such as erosion, can explain the development of the earth over vast periods of time. This view was outlined in his book *Principles of Geology* (1830-1833, 3 vols.). Lyell's work undermined trust in the biblical account of

CREATION and strongly influenced T. H. HUXLEY, Herbert SPENCER and Charles DARWIN, although Lyell himself was very uneasy about the implications of EVOLUTION and never fully accepted the theory.

M

MACAULAY, Thomas Babington (1800-1859): perhaps the greatest English literary historian of the nineteenth century. He served in the British East India Company in India where he urged educational REFORMS based on the English model. Although he grew up in an EVANGELICAL home, he had a strong aversion to CHRISTIANITY which found expression in his influential *History of England* (1848).

MACAULAY, Zachary (1768-1838): Scottish ANGLICAN LAYMAN who devoted his life to the abolition of SLAVERY. He was the father of the historian Thomas Babington MACAULAY.

MACCABEES, BOOK OF: found in the APOCRYPHA, it tells of the exploits of Judas Maccabeus (d. 160 B.C.) and his family, who freed the Jews from Syrian rule.

MACHEN, John Gresham (1881-1937): American PRESBYTERIAN scholar who taught at Princeton Theological Seminary and championed orthodoxy in the FUNDAMENTALIST-MODERNIST controversy. In 1929, when Princeton was officially reorganized to include liberalism, he and other faculty members left to form Westminster Theological Seminary. In 1935 he was tried and suspended from the Presbyterian ministry over his continued support of the proscribed independent Presbyterian Board of Foreign Missions. Subsequently he helped in establishing a new Presbyterian denomination. His many books include *Christianity and Liberalism* (1923) and *What Is Faith?* (1924).

MACHIAVELLI, Niccolò (1469-1527): Italian political philosopher whose work *The Prince* (1513) marks the beginning of modern political thought devoid of religious influences.

MACKINTOSH, Hugh Ross (1870-1936): Scottish PRESBYTERIAN theologian who popularized German LIBERAL THEOLOGY in Britain. He is best known for his *Types of Modern Theology* (1937) and *The Christian Doctrine of Forgiveness* (1927).

MACLAINE, Shirley (1935-): popular actress and film star turned MYSTIC. In many ways she is the Madame BLAVATSKY of the late twentieth century, using Western ideas to interpret distorted forms of YOGIC RELIGIONS to a mass audience, and has been influential in the promotion of the NEW AGE MOVEMENT. Her religious beliefs are to be found in her bestselling biographies *Out on a Limb* (1983), *Dancing in the Light* (1985) and *It's All in the Playing* (1987).

MADHVA (1197-1276): Indian philosopher and chief exponent of the Dvaita school of VEDĀNTA DUALISM. Stories about his life involving MIRACLES appear to reflect the influence of the CHRISTIAN gospel. His followers regarded him as the true mediator between GOD and man.

MĀDHYAMIKA: a school of MAHĀYĀNA BUDDHISM founded by NĀGĀRJUNA. Its central DOCTRINE is the negation of all EMPIRICAL CONCEPTS. The school greatly influenced the development of various other Mahāyāna schools of PHILOSOPHY, including the YOGĀCĀRA and the religion of Tibet (see TIBETAN BUDDHISM).

MAGI: the Magi appear in the Gospel of Matthew as coming to see the child JESUS. They were apparently members of a group or tribe of Persian PRIESTS and OCCULTISTS who probably embraced ZOROASTRIANISM.

MAGIC: the production of effects in the world by means of invisible or SUPERNATURAL CAUSATION; action based on a BELIEF in the efficacy of SYMBOLIC FORMS when performed in the correct manner. Magical belief holds that if the appropriate RITUAL is performed correctly, then the desired result will automatically and of necessity be attained. In the past magic was seen as separate from religion and as belonging essentially to a more primitive thought form, but recent scholarship has tended to blur the distinction between religion and magic.

MAHĀBHĀRATA: an Indian epic which is important in HINDU mythology. It is the "Great Story" which records the HISTORY of the descendants of Bhārata. The epic is about 100,000 verses long and includes numerous subsections. The main story is clearly older than the historic text which is believed to have been originally compiled sometime between 400 B.C. and A.D. 400, although there are no extant manuscripts before the sixteenth century A.D. There is no scholarly consensus as to whether the epic is based on historical events or purely artistic invention. The central theme develops from the MYTHS of

VISHNU's AVATĀRS. The GODDESS Earth is oppressed by DEMONS and overpopulation, and is in danger of being submerged in the ocean. To relieve her, the GODS take human FORM and descend to earth, headed by Vishnu, who is born as KRISHNA and who declares the THEOLOGY of the epic in the BHAGAVAD-GĪTA. The story then focuses on the HISTORY of the dynasty and its response to crisis over four generations.

MAHĀBODHI SOCIETY: founded in 1891 in Ceylon, modern Sri Lanka, by a Buddhist PRIEST, Angarika Dharmapāla, the society aimed at restoring the Buddhist TEMPLES of India and reviving BUDDHISM in the land of its birth.

MAHĀKĀŚYAPA THERA (6th century B.C.?): a prominent disciple of the BUDDHA. He is referred to in many BUDDHIST canonical writings but little is known about his life.

MAHĀSATIPAṬṬHĀNA SUTTA: often considered the most important SCRIPTURE in the PALI CANON of BUDDHISM, it consists of discourses believed to have been delivered by the BUDDHA to his monks on mindfulness and the FOUR HOLY TRUTHS. Recital of these scriptures at the time of death is believed to be particularly beneficial.

MAHĀVAMSA: a PALI chronicle which outlines the history of BUDDHISM in India, before its introduction into Ceylon, and its growth there until the fourth century.

MAHĀVASTU: an important SANSKRIT biography of the BUDDHA written from the viewpoint of the Lokottaravāda school of BUDDHISM, the meaning of which is "the Great Event." According to the teachings of this SCRIPTURE the Buddhas are "Exalted BEINGS" who are "above the world" and therefore only appear to conform to a worldly EXISTENCE. This teaching is a transitional one in the development of the MAHĀYĀNA. The text is usually dated around the third century.

MAHĀVĪRA (550-420 B.C.?): the founder of historical JAINISM and a reformer of the ancient Jain religious tradition. His name means "the Great Hero." Leaving home around the age of 30, he became an ascetic who attained LIBERATION after thirteen years of austerity. Following his ENLIGHTENMENT, he organized the Jain religion. His death came about through RITUAL SUICIDE involving starvation.

MAHĀYĀNA: the "Great Tradition"; one of the traditional schools of BUDDHISM. The origins of Mahāyāna are difficult to determine, but lie somewhere between the first century B.C. and the first century A.D. As a religious system it has a universalist emphasis which gives a greater role to laymen than its main rival HĪNAYĀNA and, in doing so, the importance of COMPASSION is emphasized alongside that of WISDOM.

MAHDĪ: the "Guided One" or messianic IMĀM in SHI'ISM. The term is used in a general sense within ISLAM to refer to an awaited descendant of MUḤAMMAD who will restore the purity of Islam.

MAHINDA (3rd century B.C.): Buddhist MONK, said to be the son of the Emperor AŚOKA, who evangelized the island of Ceylon (modern Sri Lanka) and converted its people to BUDDHISM.

MAIMONIDES, Moses (1135-1204): the greatest medieval JEWISH philosopher, theologian and exponent of ARISTOTLE. His books, *The Guide for the Perplexed* and *Mishnah Torah*, were first published in Arabic.

MAINLINE CHURCHES: see OLD-LINE CHURCHES.

MALCOLM X (1925-1965): black American radical and leader of the BLACK MUSLIMS whose personal RELIGIOUS PILGRIMAGE moved him from an exclusive black nationalism to ORTHODOX ISLAM. He was assassinated by three members of the NATION OF ISLAM.

MALINOWSKI, Bronislaw Kaspar (1884-1942): Polish-born English anthropologist (*see* ANTHROPOLOGY) who developed a method of field research of a qualitatively new kind. He lived for an extended period among the people he was studying, speaking their language and participating in their activities (but never attempting to alter their ways). He invented what is now called "participant-observation." He wrote *Argonauts of the Western Pacific* (1922).

MALTHUS, Thomas Robert (1766-1834): English economist and curate at Albury, Surrey. In his book *An Essay on the Principle of Population* (1798) he predicted inevitable famine due to overpopulation and aroused considerable controversy.

MANDALA: a symbolic FORM which involves symmetrically arranged circles within larger concentric circles used in RITUAL and MEDITATION by DEVOTEES of TANTRA in HINDUISM and BUDDHISM.

MANI (216-277): Iraqi religious PROPHET who claimed to fulfill BUDDHIST, CHRISTIAN and ZOROASTRIAN teachings. Essentially he taught a form of DUALISM which sharply distinguished between mind and MATTER, advocated ASCETICISM and promoted CELIBACY. His work had a great influence on AUGUSTINE OF HIPPO before his CONVERSION to Christianity.

MANICHAEISM: a RELIGION which thrived during the third century in Persia. It was founded by MANI, who taught that there are two irreconcilable warring principles in the UNIVERSE, GOOD, which is spiritual, and EVIL, which is material. It is a synthetic religious system incorporating elements of BUDDHISM, ZOROASTRIANISM, GNOSTICISM and CHRISTIANITY with an elaborate COSMOLOGY involving light particles in the realm of darkness and their LIBERATION by the Father of Light.

MAÑJUŚRĪ: the BODHISATTVA who personifies WISDOM in MAHĀYĀNA BUDDHISM. He is one of the two most important Bodhisattvas in this tradition, the other being Avalokiteśvara, who personifies COMPASSION. There is no mention of him in the PALI CANON or early SANSKRIT works, but he is the principal figure in the LOTUS SŪTRA, where the Bodhisattva Maitreya is said to seek instruction from him.

He is very important in Chinese, Japanese, Tibetan, Javan and Nepalese Buddhism, where wise rulers are regarded as his INCARNATION.

MANNHEIM, Karl (1893-1947): Hungarian SOCIOLOGIST who sought to relate styles of thought, or WORLDVIEWS, to specific historical times and social groups and to show their social function. He wrote *Ideology and Utopia* (1936).

MANTRA: an "instrument of thought" in HINDU and BUDDHIST MEDITATION which takes the form of a HYMN or sound that, when properly repeated, is believed to have the ability to invoke the presence of a particular divinity or create a religious state.

MANU: the father of the human race in HINDU mythology. He is also said to have given the VEDAS to men and to be the great lawgiver.

MÂRA: the EVIL one in BUDDHIST SCRIPTURES, who sought to distract the BUDDHA and so prevent him from attaining ENLIGHTENMENT. His name means "the killer," or the one who destroys morality and the HOLY life. In the Indian religious tradition this concept of a DEVIL-like figure is unique to BUDDHISM, although it is clearly connected with FOLK RELIGION and ideas about DEMONS.

MARCEL, Gabriel (1889-1973): French philosopher, novelist and convert to ROMAN CATHOLICISM, often described as a theistic existentialist (*see* EXISTENTIALISM). His major works are *Being and Having* (1932) and *The Mystery of Being* (1950-1951, 2 vols.).

MARCION (A.D. 85-160): early CHRISTIAN HERETIC and founder of the Marcionite church. He rejected the HEBREW BIBLE and taught, on the basis of his interpretation of THEOLOGY of PAUL, that only some portions of the NEW TESTAMENT were authentic. He emphasized the importance of LOVE and rejected all LEGALISM. He claimed that the DEMIURGE created humans whom he also cursed through the law, but the GOD of love had sent JESUS to overcome the law and save mankind.

MARCUS AURELIUS (121-180): Roman emperor unique in being a STOIC philosopher; he was famous for his *Meditations*.

MARITAIN, Jacques (1882-1973): French CHRISTIAN philosopher and leading exponent of NEO-THOMISM. After World War II he became the French ambassador to the VATICAN but moved to Princeton University in 1948. He developed his political PHILOSOPHY based on the distinction between the PERSON and an INDIVIDUAL. As an individual the human being exists as part of a greater whole. As a person the human has inherent spiritual VALUE and FREEDOM. MARXISM and fascism, he argued, value the individual, while CHRISTIANITY respects the person. His many works include *True Humanism* (1936).

MARTIN, David (1939-): English SOCIOLOGIST who was one of the first writers to challenge the SECULARIZATION THESIS of the 1960s. His work includes *A Sociology of English Religion* (1967), *The Religious and the Secular* (1969) and *A General Theory of Secularization* (1978).

MARTYR: a term used in CHRISTIANITY to refer to witnesses who died for their FAITH in the RESURRECTION of CHRIST. It has come to be applied to all who suffer and die for their religious BELIEFS.

MARX, Karl (1818-1883): German Jewish philosopher who was BAPTIZED as a child and appears to have been a CHRISTIAN while at boarding school but to have rejected all forms of RELIGION as a university student. He became a newspaper editor and writer who is remembered as the founder of MARXISM and modern Communism. After being expelled from Prussia in 1849 for his revolutionary activities, he settled in England, where he did most of his writing. His early writings are important because they show a continuity in his thought and use of HEGELIAN philosophy which continues into his later works. His most famous but little-read work is *Das Kapital* (1867, 1885 and 1895, 3 vols.). Other voluminous writings include the slim but influential *Communist Manifesto* (1848). To date no complete collection of his works has been published in English.

MARXISM: the UTOPIAN intellectual system of MODERN Communism founded by Karl MARX. Since the 1960s many Western academics have developed PHILOSOPHIES based on Marx's early, and supposedly HUMANIST, writings to provide a means of interpreting REALITY. The Communist regimes of Eastern Europe and China claimed to be Marxist-LENINIST, meaning that they followed the teachings of Marx as developed by his disciple Vladimir LENIN. The breakdown of Communism in Eastern Europe has shown these systems to be far more evil than even the majority of CONSERVATIVE critics had claimed; nevertheless, Western Marxists still cling to their BELIEF system, claiming that they always knew Eastern European Communism was corrupt. Such claims are, however, hard to substantiate when the writings of these people or their mentors in the 1960s and 1970s is examined. In many ways Marxism, as the Amnesty International film *Requiem for Dominique* shows, is the great lie of the twentieth century.

MARY (1st centuries B.C. and A.D.): the mother of JESUS OF NAZARETH. See VIRGIN BIRTH.

MASORETIC TEXT: the received text of the HEBREW BIBLE which took on its final form around A.D. 1000.

MASS: the ROMAN CATHOLIC term for the EUCHARIST, or Lord's Supper, which is a CHRISTIAN RITUAL commemorating the DEATH and RESURRECTION of JESUS OF NAZARETH.

MATERIALISM: the DOCTRINE that MATTER is the ultimate SUBSTANCE of the UNIVERSE; it usually takes the form of an atheistic PHILOSOPHY.

MATHER, Cotton (1663-1728): American PURITAN theologian and member of the illustrious Mather family of New England. He was a prolific writer with a keen interest in the new emerging SCIENCES and an early advocate of smallpox inoculation. He was remarkably tolerant of various religious opinions despite his unfortunate but reasoned involvement in the Salem witchcraft trials.

MATTER: the physical component of the UNIVERSE, as distinguished from mind or spirit.

MATTHEW, GOSPEL OF: traditionally the first CHRISTIAN Gospel, or life of JESUS OF NAZARETH. It is written from a decidedly JEWISH perspective with a strong emphasis on the fulfillment of PROPHECY.

MAURICE, Frederick Denison (1805-1872): English theologian and one of the founders of CHRISTIAN SOCIALISM. The son of a Unitarian minister, Maurice gradually accepted ANGLICANISM and was ordained in 1834. Deeply moved by the social and political ethos of his age, he sought to apply CHRISTIAN principles to social life. His book *The Kingdom of Christ: or Hints to a Quaker Concerning the Principle, Constitution and Ordinances of the Catholic Church* (1838) was one of the most important theological works of the nineteenth century. It influenced many very different people, including Abraham KUYPER and Henry CALLAWAY.

MAWLID AL-NABI: the birthplace or birthday of MUḤAMMAD. In MECCA the site of his birth is an honored sanctuary.

MĀYĀ (6th century B.C.): the mother of the BUDDHA.

MĀYĀ: originally meaning "the creative and transforming power of a GOD," this term has come to be translated "illusion." It plays an important role in HINDUISM, especially VEDĀNTA, in which the world is not seen as truly real.

MEAD, Margaret (1901-1978): highly influential American anthropologist (*see* ANTHROPOLOGY). Her first study was made in 1925-1926 in Samoa, where she investigated the fashionable topic of adolescence and extolled the virtues of premarital sex. In recent years the validity of her early work has been severely challenged by Derek Freeman in his book

Margaret Mead and Samoa (1983). Among her many books are *Coming of Age in Samoa* (1928) and *Blackberry Winter* (1972).

MEAN: an important CONCEPT in Confucianism where the idea of universal harmony is a central concept. The "mean" is the position of balance between two extremes. It is the harmony which underlies our moral NATURE and pervades the UNIVERSE, forming a unity between man and nature. *The Doctrine of the Mean* was one of the four key texts in Chinese education and was traditionally ascribed to the grandson of CONFUCIUS.

MEANING: the connotation, sense or significance of a thing; the result of the mind's evaluation of FACTS. In the PHILOSOPHY of DOOYEWEERD "meaning" takes on a special significance as an alternative to the notion of SUBSTANCE; it is the character of created REALITY which points to GOD. In his sense reality *is* meaning.

MEARS, Henrietta Cornella (1890-1963): American BIBLE teacher, educated in Canada, who moved in 1928 to Los Angeles, where she worked at the Hollywood PRESBYTERIAN CHURCH. She was the co-founder of Gospel Light Publications, the Hollywood Christian Group and various other organizations. Her ministry influenced many prominent people and led to the CONVERSION of Bill BRIGHT.

MECCA: the birthplace of MUḤAMMAD and most HOLY city in ISLAM. All MUSLIMS are supposed to make a PILGRIMAGE to Mecca at least once in their lifetime.

MEDINA: the "city of the PROPHET" where MUḤAMMAD found refuge after being driven out of MECCA in A.D. 622. After he conquered Mecca he retained Medina as his capital. Although not part of a prescribed PILGRIMAGE, it is frequently visited by pilgrims in order to see Muḥammad's tomb. It is the second most HOLY city in ISLAM.

MEDITATION: a religious practice found in the YOGIC and ABRAMIC TRADITIONS which involves many different techniques. The aim is to attain a spiritual state often described as communion with the divine or, in the case of BUDDHISM, the transdivine.

MEDIUM: an individual who claims to possess extraordinary powers enabling them to communicate with the dead and act as a vehicle whereby messages from the dead may be received by the living.

MEEKNESS: a spiritual VIRTUE mentioned by JESUS OF NAZARETH in the SERMON ON THE MOUNT and one of the supreme social virtues in China, Korea and Japan, where submission to AUTHORITY was taught by Confucianism (*see* CONFUCIUS) and TAOISM and adapted by BUDDHISM.

MELANCHTON, Philip (1497-1560): German CHRISTIAN humanist, PROTESTANT REFORMER and close associate of Martin LUTHER.

MENCIUS (371-289 B.C.): Chinese Confucian philosopher regarded as second only to CONFUCIUS himself. He is the author of the Book of Mencius, one of the four texts which became the basis of Chinese education. He was educated by Tzu Ssu, grandson of Confucius, and became a teacher. He argued that government is for the GOOD of the people and praised the ideal king who was a philosopher ruled by morality. He opposed MO-TZU's DOCTRINE of universal LOVE with his own teaching about humanity and righteousness.

MENDELSSOHN, Moses (1729-1786): popular German Jewish philosopher who defended the idea that it is possible to demonstrate both the EXISTENCE of GOD and the IMMORTALITY of the SOUL. He played a leading role in Jewish emancipation and German CULTURE and is often referred to as "the Third Moses."

MENNONITES: essentially CONSERVATIVE CHRISTIANS and often EVANGELICAL, the Mennonites descended from the ANABAPTIST movement of the sixteenth century. In recent years some Mennonites have claimed an ethnic identity apart from religious BELIEFS. The movement owes its name to Menno SIMONS (c.1496-1559) whose followers eventually fled persecution and settled in Russia beginning in 1788. They began to emigrate to North America in the 1870s. Their THEOLOGY stresses community and is strongly pacifist.

MERCURY: the Roman GOD of traders, identified with the Greek God Hermes.

MERCY: one of the greatest VIRTUES in the ABRAMIC RELIGIONS; it is often seen to be in tension with the justice of GOD.

MERIT: the BUDDHIST DOCTRINE that certain ENLIGHTENED beings, out of COMPASSION for all sentient beings, forgo entry into NIRVANA and in so doing accrue merit or the power to break the bonds of KARMA which hold other creatures in perpetual bondage to SAMSĀRA.

MERLEAU-PONTY, Maurice (1908-1961): French philosopher and phenomenologist (see PHENOMENOLOGY) who rejected the DUALISM of Rene DESCARTES in favor of a structural theory of REALITY (see STRUCTURALISM). His books include *The Structure of Behavior* (1942) and *The Primacy of Perception* (1964).

MERTON, Thomas (1915-1968): American ROMAN CATHOLIC Trappist MONK and MYSTIC. His many works include *Ascent to Truth* (1951) and *The Seven Storey Mountain* (1948).

MESSIAH: a HEBREW word meaning "anointed" that is principally applied to priests and kings, particularly kings of the Davidic line, and became associated with the varied hope for a man sent by GOD to restore the fortunes of the people of ISRAEL. CHRISTIANS believe that JESUS OF NAZARETH is the expected Messiah.

METAPHYSICS: the RATIONAL analysis of the necessary and universal aspects of BEING and the characteristics which must be shown by anything which exists. It investigates what "to be" means and the universal or general principles found in anything that is. The name itself means "after physics" and is taken from ARISTOTLE's writings. Traditionally in the West, CHRISTIAN THEOLOGY has promoted the study of metaphysics.

METEMPSYCHOSIS: a Greek term meaning REBIRTH or TRANSMIGRATION of the SOUL from one body to another in a cyclic life pattern. As a religious PHILOSOPHY it appears to have originated in India around 600 B.C. and was taught by Pythagoreans (see PYTHAGORAS) in Greece, where it entered the Orphic Mysteries (see ORPHISM) and both Platonism (see PLATO) and NEOPLATONISM. In India it is found in HINDUISM and JAINISM but not BUDDHISM, where the DOCTRINE of REINCARNATION is similar but in important respects different. Some modern writers have attempted to find the idea in such CHRISTIAN thinkers as CLEMENT OF ALEXANDRIA and ORIGEN, but the supposed discovery rests on very dubious assumptions and questionable readings of their works. The doctrine does, however, emerge in the works of Emanuel SWEDENBORG and Annie BESANT.

METHODISM: a religious movement founded by John and Charles WESLEY and a group of associates in the eighteenth century. It grew to be a major CHRISTIAN REVITALIZATION MOVEMENT that made a significant impact on the nineteenth-century MISSIONARY movement and Christian enterprises throughout the world. The original movement has developed into a family of churches loosely connected to the World Methodist Council and claims a membership of over 18 million and a community of 40 million. In 1739 John Wesley started a society in London to promote EVANGELICAL CHRISTIANITY in England. In 1741 he began the training of lay ministers and in 1769 sent his first missionaries to serve in America. In 1784 Wesley and his followers finally broke away from the CHURCH OF ENGLAND and established their own CHURCH. With a few notable exceptions, such as Welsh Methodism, the movement is ARMINIAN in theology with a strong social concern. In the twentieth century mainline Methodism has tended to encourage LIBERAL

THEOLOGY and has moved away from its revivalist roots.

MEYKANDA (13th century): a Tamil SAINT and devotional writer. His book *The Realization of the Knowledge of Śiva* played a crucial role in the development of ŚAIVISM.

MEYNELL, Hugo Anthony (1936-): Canadian ROMAN CATHOLIC philosopher known for his spirited defense of the COSMOLOGICAL ARGUMENT. His works include *Freud, Marx and Morals* (1981) and *The Intelligible Universe* (1982).

MICHELANGELO (1475-1564): the greatest of the RENAISSANCE artists, famous for his religious sculptures and the painting on the ceiling in the Sistine Chapel in Rome.

MIDRASH: the HEBREW word for commentary which is used to describe JEWISH EXEGESIS and interpretation of the BIBLE. Generally speaking, Midrash applies to all non-CANONICAL early Jewish literature, including the TALMUD.

MILINGO, Emmanuel (1930-): African ROMAN CATHOLIC theologian and former ARCHBISHOP of Lusaka who in 1982 was recalled by his superiors to Rome because of his controversial teachings and practice of divine HEALING. Today he is a Special Delegate to the Pontifical Commission on Migration, Refugees and Tourism. His contribution to the development of the CHARISMATIC MOVEMENT and AFRICAN THEOLOGY is enormous, as can be seen from the collection of his writings published as *The World in Between* (1984).

MILL, John Stuart (1806-1873): British philosopher, essayist and political activist whose work still indirectly influences many academic disciplines, including SOCIOLOGY, political science, economics and the PHILOSOPHY of SCIENCE. His best-known works are probably *On Liberty* (1859), *Utilitarianism* (1863) and *The Subjection of Women* (1871), while his neglected *System of Logic* (1843) has recently received renewed attention. Although he wrote little about RELIGION, his posthumous *Three Essays on Religion* (1874) revealed a cautious but SKEPTICAL interest in the subject.

MILLENARIAN MOVEMENTS: Generally, any religious movement that hopes for a SALVATION that is (a) collective, to be enjoyed by all the faithful as a GROUP; (b) terrestrial, to be realized on this earth; (c) imminent, to come soon and suddenly; (d) total, to transform life on earth completely; (e) miraculous, to be brought about by, or with the help of, supernatural agencies.

MILLENNIALISM: the CHRISTIAN BELIEF in a thousand-year period (millennium) in which the KINGDOM OF GOD is to flourish and prosper (*see* CHILIASM). Millennialists tend to fall into two camps: (1) those who believe that the millennium will follow the PAROUSIA, or "Second Coming," of CHRIST (premillennialism); (2) those who believe that the millennium will precede the parousia of Christ (postmillennialism). A third theological option is amillennialism, which asserts that Christ will return but that the millennium is to be understood in spiritual terms and that we cannot know the exact details surrounding the parousia.

MILLER, William (1782-1849): American religious leader whose work led to the growth of several MILLENARIAN groups, the most important being SEVENTH-DAY ADVENTISM. After a surprising CONVERSION from DEISM his study of the BIBLE led him to concentrate on the prophetic books and eventually declare that CHRIST would return around 1843. When this did not happen the date was rescheduled and further disappointments followed until his death. Miller explained his failures in terms of human error and possible mistranslation of the Bible.

MILLERITES: or Second Adventists, an American PROTESTANT SECT founded by William MILLER, who calculated that the "Second Coming" of CHRIST would take place in 1843.

MILTON, John (1608-1674): English poet and PURITAN writer of questionable ORTHODOXY. His works include the classic poem *Paradise Lost* (1667) and *The Doctrine and Discipline of Divorce* (1643).

MIRACLE: an unusual event which is seen as a significant divine intervention in nature and human affairs. Miracles are believed to confirm the spiritual power and AUTHORITY of a teacher or religious leader. Claims to miraculous powers exist in most religious traditions. The idea of miracles came under strong attack from DEISM and the PHILOSOPHY of the ENLIGHT-ENMENT, in which a miracle was defined as an event which broke "the law of nature" and was, therefore, by definition impossible.

MISSIOLOGY: the academic study of MISSIONS and MISSIONARIES.

MISSION: the task of propagating a RELIGION or PHILOSOPHY in the belief that it has a message which is vital to all people.

MISSIONARY: a person who propagates a RELIGION. The nineteenth century saw a great surge of missionary activity among CHRISTIANS which led to the spread of CHRISTIANITY throughout the world. In recent years there has been a rebirth of missionary ISLAMIC activity and the development of HINDU MISSIONS. In the West missions promoting Hinduism and BUD-DHISM are often seen as CULTS or NEW RELIGIOUS MOVEMENTS.

MITHRA: ancient Iranian GOD (*see* IRAN-IAN RELIGION) whose CULT became popular in the Roman Empire.

MITHRAISM: an ancient IRANIAN RELIG-ION involving the worship of the GOD MITHRA. It became popular as a MYSTERY RELIGION in the Roman Empire, especially among soldiers. The THEOLOGY appears to have been a complex form of DUALISM.

MO-TZU (5th century B.C.): important Chinese philosopher, critic of Confucian-ism (*see* CONFUCIUS) and opponent of MEN-CIUS. He taught RIGHTEOUSNESS and uni-versal LOVE based on the will of the supreme GOD. He was PRAGMATIC and UTILITARIAN in his approach to DOCTRINE and deeply concerned about the welfare

and prosperity of the people. The move-ment he founded declined after his death but was revived in the eighteenth century after the publication in 1783 of PI YÜAN's critical edition of his works with commen-tary.

MODERNIST: proponents of theological MODERNISM who in the nineteenth and early twentieth centuries rejected the THEOLOGY and METAPHYSICS of traditional CHRISTIANITY in favor of a Kantian (*see* KANT) EPISTEMOLOGY, EVOLUTION, BIBLICAL CRITICISM and COMPARATIVE RELIGION. They accommodated their FAITH to the latest theories of SCIENCE and promoted LIBERAL ETHICS based on the brotherhood of man and the FATHERHOOD OF GOD. The inherent goodness of man and the inevi-tability of progress were axiomatic (*see* AXIOM), while the BIBLE was seen as a record of human religious experience.

MODERN, MODERNISM, MODERNI-ZATION AND MODERNITY: various terms conveying essentially the same idea. The most important of these are (1) mod-ern, or what is new or innovative as opposed to what is ancient or TRADITION-AL; (2) modernism, which is an explicit and self-conscious commitment to the modern in intellectual, cultural and theological affairs; (3) modernization, or a program committed to remaking SOCIETY, the polit-ical order and theological beliefs in sup-port of the new; (4) modernity, or the quality and condition of being modern. All religious TRADITIONS have experienced the effects of modernity, although they have been most noticeable in CHRISTIANI-TY, where they have been associated with SECULARIZATION and explicit attacks on traditional beliefs and VALUES in the name of SCIENCE.

MOFFAT, Robert (1795-1883): Scottish MISSIONARY to Africa. In 1825 he settled at Kuruman, Bechuanaland, which be-came the headquarters for all his activities for forty-five years. When he left in 1870, a whole region had been Christianized.

MOLTMANN, Jürgen (1926-): German

REFORMED theologian and professor of systematic THEOLOGY at the University of Tübingen. He conceived the outline of a theological program which looks—in hope—to a GOD who liberates humanity in the future. Moltmann is particularly sensitive to the HOLOCAUST and the meaning of Auschwitz. The crucified God points to the God who identifies with the victims of HISTORY by dying on the cross. His work includes *Theology of Hope* (1967).

MONASTICISM: a religious movement consisting of those called to abandon ordinary life and family responsibilities to live in celibate religious communities. The earliest example of monasticism is the SAṆGHA in BUDDHISM, from which it spread first into HINDUISM and then influenced the development of monasticism in CHRISTIANITY.

MONISM: the metaphysical theory that there is one fundamental REALITY of which all other BEINGS are ATTRIBUTES, or modes, if they are real at all.

MONK: a male member of a monastic order (*see* MONASTICISM).

MONOPHYSITISM: a development of CHRISTOLOGY which taught that in CHRIST there was one divine NATURE, as opposed to the orthodox view that Christ was both human and divine. The teaching was condemned at the COUNCIL OF CHALCEDON but flourished in Coptic, Syrian, Armenian and various other branches of Christianity.

MONOTHEISM: BELIEF in one, and only one, GOD, as opposed to HENOTHEISM and POLYTHEISM.

MONTANISM: a prophetic movement in the second century led by women which preached the imminent return of CHRIST. It seemed to court martyrdom and practiced extreme ASCETICISM. TERTULLIAN is often accused of having forsaken Christian ORTHODOXY to join the Montanists. While it is true that he strongly defended their civil liberties, there is no solid evidence that he actually joined the group.

MOODY, Dwight Lyman (1837-1899): American EVANGELIST who gave up business to devote himself to evangelism. He made two tours in Great Britain (1873-75 and 1881-83). He founded Northfield Seminary for Girls (1879), Mount Hermon School for Boys (1881), and the Chicago Bible Institute (1889), which is now called Moody Bible Institute.

MOON, Sun Myung (1920-): Korean founder and prophetic leader of the UNIFICATION CHURCH. His followers are known as "Moonies." *The Divine Principle* is his major work.

MOORE, George Edward (1873-1958): English philosopher; author of *Principia Ethica* (1903) and advocate of emotivism as an ethical system.

MOORE, Hannah (1745-1833): English religious writer who devoted herself to social and religious REFORM and set up Sunday schools. She shared the EVANGELICAL views of William WILBERFORCE and Zachary MACAULAY. She wrote *An Estimate of the Religion of the Fashionable World* (1790) and, to counteract teachings of Thomas PAINE and the FRENCH REVOLUTION, a tract titled *Village Politics* (1792).

MORAL LAW: the widespread and ancient BELIEF, often equated with conscience, that individuals have an innate sense of right and wrong regardless of upbringing or culture. In CHRISTIANITY a distinction has been made between the moral law which is within an individual and the law of GOD as REVEALED in the Bible.

MORAL MAJORITY: a CONSERVATIVE political movement founded in 1979 by BAPTIST minister Jerry FALWELL to combat what was seen as a decline in American values and political life. The movement was dissolved in 1989 with the claim that it had achieved its immediate and limited aims.

MORAL REARMAMENT: a movement founded by Frank BUCHMAN in 1938 in an attempt to unite CHRISTIANS against FASCISM, COMMUNISM and other anti-Christian forces in the preservation of TRADI-

TIONAL RELIGION and MORAL values.

MORAVIANS: a PROTESTANT denomination that traces its origins to John HUSS (1372-1415). They broke with the ROMAN CATHOLIC Church in 1467 by ordaining their own ministers. Although severely persecuted, the movement flourished. In the eighteenth century a religious revival broke out among the Moravians on the estates of Count von Zinzendorf where they had been given protection. Under his able leadership they became an aggressive and controversial religious movement, building large followings in the Netherlands, Germany, Britain and North America. After 1732 the movement played an important role in developing a MISSIONARY consciousness among Protestants and, through its influence on John WESLEY, made a major impact on eighteenth-century religious life.

MORE, Thomas (1478-1535): English ROMAN CATHOLIC who encouraged REFORM and Christian living but was martyred for opposing, on religious grounds, the DIVORCE of King HENRY VIII. His most famous work is *Utopia* (1516).

MORGAN, Lewis (1818-1881): American ethnologist whose work *Ancient Society* (1877) had a strong influence on MARX and ENGELS.

MORMONS: the name given to members of the Church of Jesus Christ of Latter Day Saints, which was founded by Joseph SMITH in 1830. Mormons claim to represent true CHRISTIANITY which was "restored" on earth through the ministry of Smith (who was called a Prophet) after centuries of APOSTASY. Although increasingly similar to traditional Christianity, the Mormons are characterized by their DOCTRINE of continuous REVELATION, which allows them to add *The Book of Mormon, The Pearl of Great Price* and *Doctrine and Covenants* to the BIBLE, as well as to justify the AUTHORITY of their living Prophet. Among their various doctrines is the BELIEF that GOD has a human body, and the law of ETERNAL PROGRESSION,

which states that believers eventually become gods.

MORRIS, William (1834-1896): English SOCIALIST and writer whose views influenced the growth of ROMANTICISM and anti-industrial sentiments.

MOSCA, Gaetano (1858-1955): Italian SOCIOLOGIST whose analysis of MARXISM led him to foresee Stalinism (*see* STALIN). His best-known work is *The Ruling Class* (1939).

MOSQUE: place of WORSHIP in ISLAM where PRAYER must be offered facing MECCA.

MOSES (15th, 14th or 13th century B.C.): the great lawgiver of the JEWS and the founding figure in the emergence of ISRAEL as a people, and who is traditionally credited with writing the PENTATEUCH. According to the HEBREW BIBLE, he was born of Hebrew parents but adopted by an Egyptian princess and educated as an Egyptian prince. Later he was forced to flee Egypt, and he lived in Midian for a number of years before returning to Egypt to lead the Israelites out of bondage into the wilderness. They remained there for forty years and did not enter the promised land until after the death of Moses. Although some modern scholars doubt the historicity of Moses, it seems clear that if he did not exist, someone of a similar stature would need to be posited to explain the tradition that surrounds his name.

MOTHER TERESA (1910-): the Albanian-born ROMAN CATHOLIC NUN and Nobel Prize winner acclaimed for her work among orphans and the terminally ill in Calcutta.

MOTT, John Raleigh (1865-1955): American MISSIONARY statesman; in 1895 he founded the World Student Christian Federation. He chaired three important missionary conferences, in Edinburgh (1910), Jerusalem (1928) and Madras (1938), which led to the founding of the WORLD COUNCIL OF CHURCHES. His most famous book is *The Evangelization of the*

World in This Generation (1905).

MOURNING: RITUALS which accompany DEATH. Most religious TRADITIONS make some allowance for a period of mourning which helps the bereaved come to terms with the death of a loved one, close friend or relative.

MUHAMMAD (571-632): the founder of ISLAM who claimed to be the last in a long line of PROPHETS. His message was that there is one GOD, ALLAH, and that he was God's PROPHET. Through Muhammad the QUR'ĀN was recited and then written down by his followers. The first message of the Qur'ān emphasizes Muhammad's relationship with God who created all people. After initial rejection and persecution in MECCA, his birthplace, in 622 Muhammad led his followers to MEDINA, where he established a following of loyal tribesmen and built up a powerful army. He returned triumphantly to Mecca in 630.

MUHAMMAD 'ABDUH (1849-1905): Egyptian mystical writer who sought to modernize ISLAM. He opposed the WORSHIP of SAINTS and other "medieval" practices, which he saw as retarding social and economic development. Although he held Islam to be the perfect RELIGION, he respected both CHRISTIANITY and JUDAISM as incomplete versions of Islam.

MÜLLER, Friedrich Maximilian (1823-1900): German philologist and orientalist who became professor at Oxford University. He is one of the founders of the discipline of COMPARATIVE RELIGION. His many activities included translating and editing the *Ṛg Veda* (1849-1874, 6 vols.) and writing many books on religious issues, including his famous *Essay on Comparative Mythology*. He made a considerable impact on the development of oriental studies and almost single-handedly created the SCIENCE of RELIGIONS.

MÜLLER, George (1805-1898): German PASTOR, philanthropist and leader of the PLYMOUTH BRETHREN in Britain. After a dissolute life, he was converted during a PRAYER meeting in 1825. In 1832 he began a ministry in Bristol, England, and in 1835 he opened an orphanage which grew from a rented house to a great complex of buildings. It is this orphanage for which he is chiefly remembered. He was a leading representative of the moderate group known as the Open Brethren, in contrast to J. N. DARBY and the Exclusive Brethren. Müller renounced a regular salary and refused throughout the rest of his life to make any requests for financial support, choosing to put exclusive trust in God to meet his needs. His ideas and example provide the basis for modern "faith" MISSIONS. His works include *A Narrative of the Lord's Dealing with George Müller* (1905).

MÜNTZER, Thomas (1490-1525): German ANABAPTIST leader who claimed INSPIRATION through the HOLY SPIRIT and prophetic gifts. He played a leading role in the PEASANT'S REVOLT and was eventually executed by the SECULAR authorities.

MURRAY, Andrew, Jr. (1828-1917): South African Dutch REFORMED minister and CHURCH leader who opposed theological liberalism and led an evangelical revival in the 1860s. He was an advocate of MISSIONS and EVANGELISM, and an opponent of Afrikaner NATIONALISM and its political stance which led to apartheid. Mystically inclined, he was greatly influenced by William LAW. His books *Abide in Christ* (1882), *With Christ in the School of Prayer* (1885) and *Absolute Surrender* (1895) are classics of devotional PIETY which continue to have a strong influence in EVANGELICAL and CHARISMATIC circles even today.

MUSLIM: a person who submits himself to GOD and belongs to the community of ISLAM.

MYSTERY RELIGIONS: a group of RELIGIONS which flourished in the Greco-Roman world and involved the secret initiation of the believer. Often BAPTISM, sometimes in the blood of cattle, was involved, as well as beliefs about IMMORTALITY and the survival of the SOUL. The most famous mystery religions are the ELEUSINIAN MYSTERIES, ORPHISM, MITHRA-ISM and GNOSTICISM.

MYSTIC: one who claims to know GOD immediately through a FORM of SPIRITUAL inwardness, as against knowing through sensation or ratiocination, i.e., logical processes.

MYSTICISM: the implications of this word are often unclear. In the study of RELIGION it refers to the immediate experience of a divine-human relationship, and in particular to the experiences of oneness with a divine or transdivine BEING or STATE. It is difficult to study and describe because MYSTICS tend to claim that their experience is self-authenticating, and that it cannot be satisfactorily expressed in words.

MYTH: a myth is a type of narrative which seeks to express in imaginative form a belief about man, the world, and/or GOD or gods which cannot adequately be expressed in simple PROPOSITIONS. Since this word is used in both contemporary scientific and theological literature, any DEFINITION of it appears to be arbitrary. In common language the word is used to denote stories that have no basis in FACT. This meaning is too loose for anthropologists and philosophers.

Myths can be contrasted with LEGENDS, fairy tales, etc. This implies no JUDGMENT on the TRUTH of the story; indeed, it is possible to have a true story serve as a myth. Critics of myth argue that it tends to open the door to IRRATIONALISM.

Myth has been held to be a truer or deeper version of REALITY than SECULAR HISTORY, realistic description or scientific explanation. This view ranges from irrationalism and post-CHRISTIAN SUPERNATU-RALISM to more sophisticated accounts in which myths are held to be fundamental expressions of certain properties of the human mind.

In biblical studies the use of the term *myth* has had a long, complex and often crude history, from the nineteenth-century MYTH AND RITUAL SCHOOL of BIBLICAL CRITICISM to the DEMYTHOLOGIZING of scholars like Rudolf BULTMANN.

Myth is both a significant and a difficult word. One very useful definition of myth is a story with culturally formative power that functions to direct the life and thought of INDIVIDUALS and GROUPS or SOCIETIES.

MYTH AND RITUAL SCHOOL: a school of biblical interpretation concentrating on the HEBREW BIBLE. It grew out of the observations made by E. B. TYLOR in his book *Primitive Culture* (1871), where he argued that myths originated in the illogical outlook of primitive peoples. Robertson SMITH developed this theme in *The Religion of the Semites* (1889) where he argues that the MYTHS found in the Hebrew Bible arose out of religious RITUALS. This notion was developed into a school of thought by R. Pettazozoni, E. O. James, and Scandinavian scholars such as G. Widengren. The views of the school are perhaps best expressed in S. H. Hooke's *Myth and Ritual* (1933).

N

NAG HAMMADI: the site in upper Egypt where important manuscript discoveries were made in 1946. The texts are COPTIC translations of Greek Gnostic and HERMETIC texts. They include the *Gospel of Thomas* and are our main source of direct information about GNOSTICISM.

NAGANUMA, Myoko (1899-1957): one of the founders of Risshō Kōsei-Kai with Nikkyo NIWANO. She was an energetic woman who played the role of SHAMAN to this important new religious movement in Japan.

NĀGĀRJUNA (2nd century): Indian Buddhist philosopher who founded the MĀDHYAMIKA school of MAHĀYĀNA BUDDHISM. Tradition says he was a BRAHMIN who converted to Buddhism. Central to his thought was the idea of "voidness," which he used to describe ultimate REALITY.

NAGASENA (?): a BUDDHIST MONK mentioned in the PALI text *The Questions of King Milinda*, where he appears extremely learned. Some modern scholars doubt his historicity.

NAKATOMI: the SHINTŌ priestly class in charge of RITUALS, especially STATE ceremonies.

NĀNAK (1469-1539): first SIKH GURU and chief founder of the community. Born a MUSLIM, he was influenced by ŞŪFISM and the HINDU BHAKTI movement. He became a wandering teacher and began to preach the unity of GOD. He composed many hymns which are now part of Sikh SCRIPTURES and taught the formlessness of God, whom he referred to as Sat Kartar (the True CREATOR) and Sat Nam (the True Name). Rejecting the CASTE system, he sought to reconcile Hinduism and ISLAM while reforming Indian society.

NASĀ'Ī, Abū 'Abd al-Rahman Ahmad ben Shu'aib al- (830-915): the compiler of one of the six CANONICAL books of HADĪTH in SUNNĪ ISLAM. He was a traditionalist who died after provoking the wrath of SHĪ'A in Damascus because of his refusal to acknowledge the superiority of Ali, MUHAMMAD's son-in-law.

NATION: a term used in English since the thirteenth century with the primary meaning of a racial rather than political group. Since the eighteenth century it has acquired an increasingly political meaning. Both usages, however, readily lend themselves to pseudoreligious NATIONALISMS.

NATION OF ISLAM IN THE WEST:

radical black NEW RELIGIOUS MOVEMENT founded in 1930 in Detroit by W. D. FARD. Fard's teachings pointed out the evil of whites who oppress blacks and the existence of black space-people who will eventually restore the glory of the black race. After Fard's mysterious disappearance in 1934, the movement was taken over by Elijah MUHAMMAD who transferred its headquarters to Chicago. After his death in 1975 the group was taken over by his son, who moved it in a more ORTHODOX ISLAMIC direction.

NATIONALISM: a political IDEOLOGY which seeks to glorify the NATION, often using religious terminology and themes to promote crude and even racist political ends. It arose in European thought as a reaction to SECULARIZATION during the ENLIGHTENMENT and still plagues many situations today.

NATIVE AMERICAN RELIGIONS: Like AFRICAN TRADITIONAL RELIGIONS the religious traditions of Native Americans are complex and diverse. Although some common features are to be found in most indigenous religious traditions, many have developed their own unique insights, understanding and practices. Good studies of these TRADITIONS exist in the work of early missionaries; for example, the *Jesuit Relations*, and ANTHROPOLOGISTS, often associated with the Bureau of American Ethnology (1871-1964), including James Mooney on the Ghost Dance, Matilda Coxe Stevenson on the Zuni, Alice C. Fletcher on the Pawnee, John G. Bourke on the Apache, J. O. Dorsey on the Sioux, Franz Boaz on the peoples of the Northwest Coast, A. L. Kroeber on Californian groups and Frank Speck on the Algonquian. Unfortunately the work of JUNG, LÉVI-STRAUSS and Joseph CAMPBELL has encouraged speculation about MYTHOLOGY and RITUAL practices, resulting in an explosion of popular "expositions" of Native American SACRED traditions. Most of these books, which are very popular with the NEW AGE MOVEMENT, are worthless and misleading, many being written by non-Natives claiming either to be Natives or to have undergone sacred INITIATION RITES. Indeed, in 1991 the Canadian Native community in Manitoba asked Winnipeg bookstores to ban the sale of a highly popular American author who claimed to have been initiated into local Native traditions. The Manitoban Natives pointed out that the author was unknown to them and that almost everything said about them in these bestselling books was wrong. Great care must therefore be taken in approaching the complex study of indigenous American religions and respect shown for the views of genuine Native peoples.

NATURAL LAW: a term borrowed from STOIC PHILOSOPHY and used by CHRISTIAN philosophers to argue that a RATIONAL order can be detected underlying the universe, which enables individuals to make informed judgments about RIGHT and WRONG on the basis of REASON. It is regarded as an unchanging law which expresses the divine NATURE. Although some twentieth-century theologians and apologists, such as C. S. LEWIS, have defended natural law, most have followed Karl BARTH in rejecting it along with NATURAL THEOLOGY.

NATURAL REVELATION: the REVELATION of GOD in CREATION apart from his specific revelation in the words and events of the HEBREW BIBLE and NEW TESTAMENT. It is synonymous with general revelation.

NATURAL THEOLOGY: the effort to construct a DOCTRINE of GOD without appeal to FAITH or REVELATION on the basis of REASON and experience alone. Thomas AQUINAS argued that in principle it is possible for philosophers to prove the EXISTENCE of God, although certain truths about his BEING are incapable of discovery by reason alone. LUTHER and CALVIN argued that everyone possesses some sense of DEITY and that innumerable traces of God's glory appear in the created world. Nevertheless, human SIN and stupidity since the FALL make it necessary for God to move our hearts by a special revelation if we are to know him. The idea of natural theology was strongly rejected by Karl BARTH and his followers.

NATURALISM: the view that denies the existence of any REALITY which transcends NATURE. It is opposed to supernaturalism.

NATURE: a complex term with three essential meanings: (1) the quality or character of something, (2) the material world, or (3) the ultimate force which directs human beings or the world or both. Today nature is often deified in a romantic fashion which creates a new RELIGION out of a SECULAR WORLDVIEW.

NATURE-FREEDOM: one of the GROUND MOTIVES of DOOYEWEERD's philosophy which he uses to explain the development of Western PHILOSOPHY. NATURE represents the physical world of SCIENCE and mathematical determinism while FREEDOM expresses the realm of the spirit, individual liberty and a ROMANTIC vision of life.

NATURE-GRACE: the DOOYEWEERDIAN GROUND MOTIVE which expresses the medieval synthesis in Western thought. Here NATURE is contrasted with GRACE, which is the realm of RELIGION and the sphere of the CHURCH.

NAVIGATORS, THE: an EVANGELICAL CHRISTIAN discipleship movement founded in 1933 by Dawson TROTMAN which emphasizes Bible study and the memorization of SCRIPTURE verses. They are active in schools and on campuses throughout the world.

NAZARENE, THE CHURCH OF THE: an international CHRISTIAN denomination growing out of METHODISM. It was organized in 1908 as a protest against worldliness and lack of HOLY living.

NAZI: the National Socialist German Workers' Party, originally founded in 1919 and eventually controlled by Adolf HITLER. Ideologically the party promoted a form of FASCISM but is perhaps more accurately seen as a modern MILLENARIAN movement. Throughout its history the Nazi Party expressed strong religious sentiments, utilizing RITUAL and MYTH to promote its view of a Jewish world conspiracy and the need to destroy JUDAISM (see HOLOCAUST). Cf. James M. Rhodes, *The Hitler Movement* (1980); George L. Mosse, *The Nationalization of the Masses* (2nd. edition 1991).

NAZIRITES: members of an ancient JEWISH SECT which took vows to GOD to live a HOLY and ASCETIC life. A JUDAIZING sect in the EARLY CHURCH also took the name as did a German Pietist sect in the nineteenth century and various AFRICAN INDEPENDENT CHURCHES today.

NEANDER, Johann August Wilhelm (1789-1850): German CHRISTIAN theologian who converted from JUDAISM and wrote a standard work on CHURCH HISTORY.

NECROMANCY: evoking the dead in DIVINATION RITUALS.

NEE, Watchman (1903-1972): Chinese CHRISTIAN writer who greatly influenced contemporary EVANGELICALISM through his highly MYSTICAL writings such as *The Normal Christian Life* (1969). Several groups accused of heresy by other Christians, such as the LOCAL CHURCH, find the source of their teachings in his writings.

NEEDLEMAN, Jacob (1934-): American college professor and author of *The New Religions* (1970). He was one of the earliest commentators and promoters of NEW RELIGIOUS MOVEMENTS.

NEO-CALVINISM: the term used to describe modern CALVINIST movements; it is usually associated with the thought of Abraham KUYPER, although it is sometimes used of that of Karl BARTH.

NEO-ORTHODOXY: a modern theological movement, in Europe sometimes called CRISIS THEOLOGY, which rejects theological MODERNISM. The movement is frequently said to have begun following the publication of Karl BARTH's *Epistle to the Romans* (1918). It attempts to restore the validity of FAITH in a TRANSCENDENT GOD by emphasizing the relation between time and eternity, referred to as the DIALECTIC. It places great emphasis on the idea of God's GRACE and the need for REVELATION. It stresses the infinite qualitative distinction between God and humankind, the reality of SIN and the necessity of God's grace to bridge the gulf between God and humans through his gift of saving faith.

NEOPAGANISM: the collective term used by diverse groups of NEW RELIGIOUS MOVEMENTS, including WICCA and the FINDHORN COMMUNITY, which LEGITIMATE their activities by an appeal to their supposed roots in a pre-CHRISTIAN past. Such groups usually worship nature SPIRITS and some form of a GODDESS.

NEOPLATONISM: a religious and philosophical movement which emerged in Greco-Roman society as a blend of essentially PLATONIC, PYTHAGOREAN, STOIC and ARISTOTELIAN elements: its chief exponent was PLOTINUS. The philosophy had a strong MYSTICAL inclination and was easily adapted to the needs of CHRISTIAN thinkers seeking to reconcile Christian and PAGAN thought.

NEO-REFORMED THEOLOGY: see NEO-ORTHODOXY.

NESTORIANISM: a religious movement in Eastern Orthodoxy (see ORTHODOX CHURCH) led by a zealous monk, NESTORIUS, who opposed the use of the term "mother of God" with reference to the Virgin MARY. Nestorians developed their own understanding of the INCARNATION of CHRIST and stressed that he had two separate PERSONS, the human and the divine. Disagreements with church authorities led to charges of HERESY and the eventual formation of the Nestorian Church which made important contributions to the early EVANGELIZATION of Asia and the retention of Greek scholarship in the ISLAMIC world.

NESTORIUS (d. 451): a Syrian MONK and member of the ANTIOCH school of CHRIS-TIAN THEOLOGY who became BISHOP of Constantinople in 428 where he stood out as strongly orthodox. After a dispute over references to MARY, the mother of JESUS, as "mother of God," his teachings were condemned by the POPE in 430 and he was excommunicated. In 431 he was sent back to his monastery at Antioch, and in 435 his books were condemned to burning and he was exiled to Upper Egypt, where he died. Only fragments of his works survive, and historians are divided about the justice of his cause and his actual teachings.

NEVIUS, John L. (1829-1893): highly successful American PRESBYTERIAN MISSIONARY who worked first in China and then in Korea. He developed the so-called Nevius System which promoted self-sufficient CHURCHES run by local people. His most important writings are *The Planting and Development of Missionary Churches* (1899) and *Demon Possession* (1894).

NEW AGE MOVEMENT: a movement which arose in the 1970s and gained notoriety in the 1980s that promotes a MYSTICAL OCCULTISM based on a synthesis of YOGIC and ABRAMIC RELIGIONS and philosophies. It began as a self-conscious movement with the publication of the *East-West Journal* in 1971 and found its most forceful advocate in the writings of actress Shirley MACLAINE.

NEW CHURCH: the religious organization founded by the followers of Emanuel SWEDENBORG.

NEW HARMONY: the town in Indiana where in 1825 Robert OWEN established a UTOPIAN SOCIALISTIC community.

NEW RELIGIOUS MOVEMENTS: during the late 1960s and 1970s various new religious groups, such as the HARE KRISHNA MOVEMENT, the MOONIES, ECKANKAR and SCIENTOLOGY emerged in Western society. Usually called CULTS by their detractors, academics adopted the name New Religious Movements to avoid prejudging the authenticity and genuine RELIGIOUS motivation of such groups.

NEW TESTAMENT: the THEOLOGICAL and HISTORICAL basis for CHRISTIANITY recorded in a series of twenty-seven books accepted by CHRISTIANS as the continuation of the HEBREW BIBLE as GOD'S REVELATION to humankind. The first four books of the New Testament are known as GOSPELS. They tell the story of the life and DEATH of JESUS CHRIST. The fifth book is The Acts of the Apostles which describes the establishment of the Christian CHURCH after the death of Jesus. Most of the remaining books are epistles, or letters, which were written by Christian leaders, such as PAUL, PETER and JAMES, to local CONGREGATIONS and individuals. The final book is Revelation, an APOCALYPTIC work dealing with the significance of Christ for the end time. Thus the New Testament contains a variety of different types of literature, including biography, history, instruction, correspondence and apocalypse. The earliest fragments of New Testament manuscripts date from the second century A.D. while the first complete manuscript of dates from the mid-fourth century A.D. In addition there are 4,000 partial or whole Greek manuscripts of the New Testament.

NEWMAN, John Henry (1801-1890): one of the most controversial and important English ANGLICAN theologians of the nineteenth century who eventually became a ROMAN CATHOLIC CARDINAL (1879). His *Apologia Pro Vita Sua* (1864) is a spiritual classic, while *The Idea of a University Defined* (1873) is still read by educators. One of the authors of *Tracts for the Times* (1834-1841), he sought to return the CHURCH OF ENGLAND to a medieval theology, but, after the publication of *Tract 90* (1841), he abandoned the OXFORD MOVEMENT for Catholicism.

NEWTON, Isaac (1642-1727): English physicist and philosopher who formulated the law of gravitation and helped create MODERN SCIENCE. His mechanistic model of the UNIVERSE, often referred to as the "Newtonian WORLDVIEW," held sway until the advent of the QUANTUM THEORY. In addition to scientific work, he spent many years in the study of the BIBLE, particularly the PROPHETIC books.

NEWTON, John (1725-1807): English ANGLICAN CLERGYMAN who spent four years in the African slave trade before experiencing an EVANGELICAL CONVERSION which led him to renounce SLAVERY and become an advocate of abolition. A prolific HYMN writer, he is best known for "Amazing Grace" and "Glorious Things of Thee Are Spoken." His works include the popular pastoral *Letters of John Newton* (1810).

NICHIREN, Shōshū (1222-1282): Japanese BUDDHIST PRIEST and founder of NICHIREN BUDDHISM. When he was twelve, his family placed him under the care of Seichoji Temple of the TENDAI sect. Later he journeyed to Mount Hiei near Kyoto where he pursued his studies of the SŪTRAS. Driven out of Mount Hiei because of his radicalism, he moved on to Mount Koya to study the ESOTERIC teachings of SHINGON. He finally came to the conviction that the only TRUE FAITH was taught by Dengyō DAISHI, who had introduced Tendai Buddhism to Japan and taught the ultimate superiority of the LOTUS SŪTRA over all other Sutras.

NICHIREN BUDDHISM: Japanese MAHĀYĀNA BUDDHIST SECT which traces its origin to the thirteenth-century Buddhist PRIEST NICHIREN who sought to restore what he saw as Buddhist ORTHODOXY. Members of this religious family stress that (1) the BUDDHA is eternal; (2) Sakyamuni's personal ENLIGHTENMENT guarantees the enlightenment of all sentient BEINGS; (3) the LOTUS SŪTRA was given by the Buddha to replace all other teachings; (4) Nichiren is the INCARNATION of a BODHISATTVA through whose suffering his followers may attain SALVATION.

NIEBUHR, Helmut Richard (1894-1962): American Protestant theologian and brother of Reinhold NIEBUHR. He was professor of CHRISTIAN ETHICS at Yale University. He wrote *The Meaning of Revelation* (1941), *Christ and Culture* (1951) and *Radical Monotheism and Western Culture* (1961).

NIEBUHR, Reinhold (1892-1971): American Protestant theologian and brother of H. Richard NIEBUHR. He was professor at Union Theological Seminary, New York, and was active in the creation of the NATIONAL COUNCIL OF CHURCHES, the New York Liberal Party, and Americans for Democratic Action. He wrote *Moral Man and Immoral Society* (1932), and *The Nature and Destiny of Man* (1941). He was critical of Karl BARTH for what he called "bibliolatry" and for his aloofness from society. He ran for Congress as a Socialist in 1930. The New Deal and World War II caused him to reject SOCIALISM and pacifism. In 1941 he founded the magazine *Christianity and Crisis* to bring realism into American Christianity's view of world problems.

NIEMÖLLER, Martin (1892-1984): World War I naval hero and LUTHERAN minister who was a leader of the CHRISTIAN opposition to the NAZIS and was imprisoned in Sachsenhausen and Dachau. He was the president of the EVANGELICAL CHURCH in Hessen and Nassau and, from 1961 to 1968, of the WORLD COUNCIL OF CHURCHES. He was the author of many books, including *From the U-Boat to the Pulpit* (1934).

NIETZSCHE, Friedrich Wilhelm (1844-1900): German philosopher who profoundly influenced modern thought by his radical rejection of CHRISTIANITY and the Western intellectual tradition. In *The Gay Science* (1887) he told the parable of the madman, which contains the prophetic phrase "God is dead," to describe the condition of modern life. Rejecting the mob, he advocated a heroic ethic which despised women and looked for the coming of the "superman." A brilliant essayist, his work is a profound critique of MODERNITY and modern ideologies which anticipates many twentieth-century themes.

NIHIL EST INTELLECTU NISI PRIUS FUERIT IN SENSU: the EMPIRICIST maxim that there is nothing in the intellect which is not first in the senses.

NIHONGI: the earliest chronicles of Japan and prime source for our knowledge of the origins of SHINTŌ.

NIKON (1605-1681): Russian MONK and REFORMING PATRIARCH of Moscow. Although his LITURGICAL reforms were accepted, he was unsuccessful in seeking to establish the complete freedom of the CHURCH from STATE control. He is regarded by many as the greatest Russian Orthodox BISHOP.

NIMBĀRKA (14th century?): Indian HINDU religious leader in the Vaisnavite tradition who incorporated the WORSHIP of both Rādhā and KRISHNA into his devotions. Following RĀMĀNUJA, he taught that SOULS are offshoots of GOD and are eventually absorbed back into God, even though they remain distinct from him.

NINIAN (360-432): a MISSIONARY and educator from Cumbria, England, who established missions to Scotland and other parts of the British Isles.

NIRVĀNA: the complex SANSKRIT term which expresses the ideal in BUDDHISM. Its meaning is "blowing out" or "cooling" and is called Nibbāna in PALI. Western writers sometimes describe it as annihilation although Buddhists generally deny this to be the meaning. The problem here is that Nirvāna is correctly described as "the unconditioned," which means that because everything we experience is conditioned, we cannot really know the true nature of Nirvāna, although by MEDITATION we may experience it.

NIWANO, Nikkyo (1906-): joined the REIYUKAI where he was introduced to the LOTUS SŪTRA and to the group counseling practice called HŌZŌ. Eventually he became dissatisfied with the attitude of the leader toward the Lotus Sūtra and, together with Mrs. Myoko NAGANUMA, formed a new organization called Rissho Kōsei-Kai, which has become one of the leading NEW RELIGIONS of Japan.

NOAH: according to Genesis 6—9 in the HEBREW BIBLE, God saved Noah and his family from the judgment of a UNIVERSAL FLOOD by instructing him to build an ark which housed his extended family and two of every creature found on earth. He and his family emerged from the ark to repopulate the earth.

NOMINALISM: the theory of knowledge which teaches that UNIVERSAL CONCEPTS, such as "human," "tree" etc., have no independent separate REALITY but are simply names used to identify things with similar characteristics. The most extreme nominalist was William of OCKHAM, who argued that only individuals exist and that universal concepts are no more than sounds.

NONBEING: the opposite of being. The term and idea is popular in various forms of EXISTENTIALISM, where it is defined as the "nothingness" from which finite BEING emerges and into which being passes.

NONCONFORMISTS: after the English Civil War, the Restoration of the monarchy and the Act of Uniformity of 1662, various EVANGELICAL and PURITAN CHRISTIAN groups, including BAPTISTS and PRESBYTERIANS, refused to conform to the standards and authority of the CHURCH OF ENGLAND. As a result they were called Nonconformists.

NON SEQUITUR: a LOGICAL FALLACY which involves drawing a conclusion which does not follow from the premise.

NORITO: priestly RITUAL PRAYERS in SHINTŌ.

NORM: a criterion, standard or rule for evaluation.

NOYES, John Humphrey (1811-1886): religious and SOCIAL REFORMER who de-veloped PERFECTIONIST and ADVENTIST views contrary to CALVINISM. In 1834 he pronounced himself "sinless." He established two communes—one in Putney, Vermont (1840-1848), and one in ONEIDA, New York (1848-1881)—to practice and propagate his ideas of perfectionism, biblical communism, complex marriage, male continence, population control, mutual criticism and education. In 1876 he emigrated to Niagara Falls, Ontario. He was the author of *History of American Socialism* (1870).

NUMINOUS: a term coined by Rudolf OTTO (in *The Idea of the Holy*, 1917, ET 1923) to evoke the feeling or sense of the HOLY which he viewed as fascinating, fearful and beyond RATIONAL analysis.

NUNS: female religious DEVOTEES living in communities devoted to the service of the CULT or a particular religious service. They are usually CELIBATE. The earliest evidence about the institution comes from BUDDHISM, from where the practice seems to have spread to HINDUISM and eventually appeared in CHRISTIANITY.

NUṢAYR, Muḥammad bin (9th century): SHĪ'ITE religious leader whose followers formed the extremist Nuṣayris sect of ISLAM.

NUT: the Egyptian sky GODDESS who gave birth to ISIS and OSIRIS through incest with her brother.

NYĀYA: one of the six traditional PHILOSOPHICAL schools in HINDUISM, concentrating on questions of logic and the rules of argument. It produced a form of theism based on proofs for the existence of GOD. The main text of the school is the *Nyāyasutra* which was probably written in the second century.

O

OBJECTIVE: that which exists in its own right independent of an evaluating mind; the opposite of SUBJECTIVE.

OBJECTIVISM: the PHILOSOPHY of Ayn RAND which seeks to oppose the SUBJECTIVE direction of modern thought and restore a strongly EMPIRICAL value system (*see* EMPIRICISM).

OBJECTIVITY: the act of undertaking research in an objective manner, free from bias, as opposed to being subjective. Traditionally this was the ideal of academics seeking TRUTH. In recent years the possibility of objectivity has been severely questioned by people like Thomas KUHN. It seems, however, that even though bias may be admitted there is no reason to abandon objectivity as a desired goal.

OBSCURANTISM: the tendency to oppose RATIONAL thought and take refuge in the status quo.

OCCULTISM: a modern term used to describe a wide spectrum of BELIEFS and practices which involve RITUAL MAGIC and the practice of various forms of SPIRITUALISM. In recent years many occult ideas have merged in the so-called NEW AGE MOVEMENT.

OCKHAM, William of (1285-1349): English FRANCISCAN MONK who was the most important scholastic philosopher and interpreter of ARISTOTLE after AQUINAS. He is known for his radical NOMINALISM and agreement with the FRANCISCAN Spirituals (so called because they refused to obey the POPE's order to alter their rule against owning property), for which he was eventually excommunicated after a dispute about TRANSUBSTANTIATION. His maxim known as "Ockham's razor" states, "Entities are not to be multiplied without necessity," or, "It is vain to do with more what can be done with fewer." The meaning of this is that things should be interpreted using the least number of assumptions or hypotheses.

OLD BELIEVERS: Russian Orthodox CHRISTIANS, largely peasants and anti-Western PRIESTS who, in the seventeenth century, opposed LITURGICAL REFORM and were EXCOMMUNICATED in 1667. Persecution followed until 1881, when they were at last recognized by the state.

OLD CATHOLICS: a small group of traditionalist Catholic churches which broke away from ROMAN CATHOLICISM over the question of the INFALLIBILITY of the POPE.

OLD-LINE CHURCHES: sometimes called mainline churches. These are old-established churches with rich endowments, such as the ANGLICANS, PRESBYTERIANS, CONGREGATIONALISTS, METHODISTS and ROMAN CATHOLICS. The name implies a contrast with newer EVANGELICAL and CHARISMATIC churches which today often command more popular support and depend for their finances on regular giving rather than endowment income.

OLD TESTAMENT: a CHRISTIAN term for the HEBREW BIBLE.

OLDHAM, Joseph Houldsworth (1874-1969): English ANGLICAN MISSIONARY statesman and organizing secretary of the World Missionary Conference of 1910, who played an important role in the creating of the WORLD COUNCIL OF CHURCHES. His book *Christianity and the Race Problem* (1924) is an important landmark in the fight against RACISM.

OMNIPOTENCE: the possession of the perfect or complete form of power. This is an ATTRIBUTE traditionally predicated of GOD enabling him to do all that he wills.

OMNIPRESENCE: that ATTRIBUTE of GOD which sees him as everywhere present. Traditionally this has meant that God is not localized in time or space and that his creativity and power are at work in everything.

OMNISCIENCE: literally "the knowing of all things"; an ATTRIBUTE traditionally ascribed to GOD alone.

ONEIDA: a religious community founded by John NOYES in 1848 on the basis of CHRISTIAN communism and a belief in human perfectibility. Believing that SIN was rooted in selfishness, they shared all things, including wives. The community disbanded in 1880 when its profitable manufacturing industries became a joint stock company.

ONTOLOGICAL ARGUMENT: the so-called PROOF FOR THE EXISTENCE OF GOD which is distinguished by its claim to be an A PRIORI argument. It is associated with ANSELM of CANTERBURY who argued that God is the BEING "than which nothing greater can be conceived." Since existence is greater than nonexistence, the greatest conceivable being must of necessity exist. Therefore God exists necessarily. In a second form of the argument, Anselm argues that God cannot be conceived as not existing because existence is logically appropriate to the idea of God as PERFECTION. Therefore either the idea of God is self-contradictory, or it is consistent and God exists necessarily.

ONTOLOGY: the SCIENCE of the essential properties, NATURE and relations of BEING as such; another term for METAPHYSICS.

ORACLES: various devices or deities used or consulted to foretell the future. Sometimes oracles are distinct from DIVINATION; at others they are part of elaborate divination RITUALS.

ORAL TRADITION: the TRADITIONAL wisdom of pre-MODERN societies transmitted by word of mouth rather than written documents. Most religious traditions contain an oral element, and many SCRIPTURES seem to have passed through an oral stage before finally being reduced to writing.

ORDINATION: the RITUAL setting-aside of individuals in the presence of witnesses who devote their lives to the service of a DEITY or religious order.

ORIGEN (185-254): one of the earliest Christian thinkers to attempt to reconcile CHRISTIANITY with Greek PHILOSOPHY. Born to Christian parents, he studied in Alexandria where he developed his theological views. He was aware of problems of BIBLICAL interpretation, which he sought to resolve by the use of ALLEGORY. Origen taught the preexistence of human SOULS but vigorously denied REINCARNATION and related DOCTRINES. Today many NEW AGE groups illegitimately appeal to Origen as a source for their views.

ORIGINAL SIN: the CHRISTIAN BELIEF that as a result of the FALL all humans are born in a state of rebellion against GOD, and that they naturally seek to serve themselves without reference to God's will. This state of ALIENATION from the CREATOR is abolished through FAITH in CHRIST, who died to obtain forgiveness of SIN for all who believe in him.

ORPHEUS: the MYTHICAL founder of the Greek MYSTERY RELIGION associated with the ELEUSIAN MYSTERIES. The CULT originated in the sixth or seventh century B.C.

ORPHISM: a Greek MYSTERY RELIGION, centered on the GOD Orpheus and associated with the ELEUSINIAN MYSTERIES, which featured REBIRTH as one of its central beliefs.

ORR, James (1844-1913): Scottish theologian and professor of APOLOGETICS at the United Free Church College in Glasgow. Promoting a modified CALVINISM adapted to meet the challenges of MODERNITY, he sought to defend CHRISTIANITY against contemporary critics. His works include *The Resurrection of Jesus* (1905) and *A Christian View of God and the World* (1893).

ORTEGA Y GASSET, José (1883-1955): Spanish CONSERVATIVE philosopher who developed his own unique notions of the relationship between ideas and the life of individuals where BELIEFS are acted out. His best-known book is *The Revolt of the Masses* (1929).

ORTHODOX CHURCH: also termed the "Eastern," "Greek" or "Greco-Russian" Church; a family of churches which are situated mainly in Eastern Europe. Each member church is independent in its internal administration but shares the same FAITH in communion with other churches of the same tradition. All Orthodox churches acknowledge the honorary primacy of the PATRIARCH of Constantinople and reject the claims of the POPE. Orthodox churches are distinguished by their rich LITURGICAL TRADITION, a theology founded on the Nicene Creed, a Christology emphasizing the Incarnation, an understanding of salvation that stresses the restoration of humans to the divine life and worship distinguished by

aesthetic features such as ICONS. In recent years they have experienced rapid growth in North America.

ORTHODOXY: a religious system which claims to be the TRUE or right BELIEF. It contrasts itself with HERESY or deviation from the HISTORICAL TRADITION of a particular FAITH.

ORWELL, George (1903-1950): English author best known for his novels *1984* (1949) and *Animal Farm* (1945), both of which are strong critiques of TOTALITARIANISM. What is less well known is that *1984* was meant to criticize *not* a future society but propaganda techniques and trends already present in 1948. It is also not usually recognized that, in addition to criticizing Communism, both works were also intended as an attack on CHRISTIANITY.

OSIRIS: the ancient Egyptian GOD of the dead and ruler of the underworld.

OTHER-DIRECTED: a term coined by David Riesman to signify the social change in SOCIETY which he believed he had identified in America in the late 1940s and early 1950s. It is based on the idea of what he called "Modes of Conformity" and signifies a concern with others and the development of one's self-concept, ethics and other beliefs on the basis of what others think or say.

OTTO, Rudolf (1869-1937): German theologian who pioneered the PHENOMENOLOGY OF RELIGION. His *Idea of the Holy* (1923; rev. ed. 1929) sets out the thesis that RELIGION is essentially the apprehension of the NUMINOUS, which humans grasp through religious insight.

OWEN, John (1616-1683): PURITAN theologian and vice-chancellor of Oxford University during the Commonwealth. A tolerant and fair scholar, he was a prolific writer who is best known for such works as *The Death of Death* and *The Work of the Holy Spirit*.

OWEN, Robert (1771-1858): a Scot who promoted SOCIALISM and communal living. Attacking the "individualist superstition," he believed in progress and the power of education to REFORM individuals and SOCIETY. His *Address to the Inhabitants of New Lanark* (1816) advocated a spirituality of charity unconnected to faith. After various UTOPIAN schemes collapsed, he founded NEW HARMONY in America. Although this project also failed, his work inspired many communal experiments in Europe and America. An authoritarian figure whose ideas about industry and the treatment of workers often appealed to TOTALITARIAN governments, he turned to SPIRITUALISM in later life.

OXFORD MOVEMENT: also known as TRACTARIANISM and ANGLO-CATHOLICISM, it was a nineteenth-century REVITALIZATION MOVEMENT within ANGLICANISM which sought to revive SPIRITUALITY through LITURGICAL renewal and a return to medieval religious practices associated with ROMAN CATHOLICISM.

P

PA KAU: the HEXAGRAMS which were supposedly invented by the Chinese emperor Fu Hsi (3rd millennium B.C.) that became the basis of the I CHING.

PACCEKA-BUDDHA: one who attains ENLIGHTENMENT in isolation and does not proclaim the TRUTH of EXISTENCE to the world.

PAGAN: traditionally, a person in the Greco-Roman world who was not a CHRISTIAN. Later the term came to be applied to all non-Christians, especially to those who are not monotheists.

PAGODA: a sacred, multistoried BUD-DHIST shrine which often contains RELICS of SAINTS or the BUDDHA.

PAHLAVI LITERATURE: medieval Persian texts containing our main source of information about ZOROASTRIANISM.

PAINE, Thomas (1737-1809): born in England of QUAKER parents, he emigrated to America in 1774 where he became a leading propagandist in the American REVOLUTION. His books *Common Sense* (1776) and *The Rights of Man* (1791-1792) stand as passionate appeals for democratic republicanism (*see* DEMOCRACY), while *The Age of Reason* (Part I, 1794, and Part II, 1796), written in a French revolutionary prison, is a devastating attack on religious BELIEF. A much neglected thinker, Paine anticipated modern criticisms of RELIGION, including those of FEUERBACH, MARX and FREUD. His SKEPTICISM influenced a wide variety of people, from Joseph SMITH to METHODIST Sunday-school teachers in England who lost FAITH as a result of reading his books.

PALESTINE: Palestine, the region in which many biblical events took place, is the Near-Eastern coastal strip roughly defined by the boundaries of the Mediterranean Sea on the west and the trans-Jordan highlands on the east, and by Mount Lebanon in the north to the Negev in the south. For Israel this is the traditional land of promise granted by God to ABRAHAM and his descendants through Isaac. It geographically defines the important territorial dimension of Judaism.

PALEY, William (1743-1805): English theologian and UTILITARIAN philosopher who was archdeacon of Carlisle. His book *The Principles of Moral and Political Philosophy* became the ethics text at the University of Cambridge, while his attacks on DEISM in *A View of the Evidences of Christianity* (1794) and *Natural Theology* (1802) were standard works to be read by all undergraduates at both Oxford and Cambridge. Paley's work, which used examples from NATURE to prove the PROVIDENCE and existence of GOD, greatly impressed and influenced Charles DARWIN, whose theory of EVOLUTION secularized Paley's arguments.

PALI: the ancient language of the CANONICAL texts of THERAVĀDA BUDDHISM which was preserved in Ceylon, Burma, Thailand, Laos and Cambodia.

PANENTHEISM: a view which combines the insights of PANTHEISM and DEISM by arguing that the world is included in GOD's BEING or by using the ANALOGY of cells in a larger organism. This view was systematically elaborated philosophically by Alfred North WHITEHEAD and applied to THEOLOGY by Charles Hartshorne (1897-).

PANDORA: the first woman in Greek MYTHOLOGY, she was created by the GODS to punish men for accepting the gift of fire from PROMETHEUS. Insatiably curious, she opened a box which contained all the ills which afflict humanity.

PAN-ISLAM: the modern idea that MUSLIMS should unite to counter Western domination and NATIONALISM.

PANJ PYARES: the original five members of the Khālsā, or Inner Council, of the SIKH brotherhood.

PANNENBERG, Wolfhart (1928-): German LUTHERAN theologian and student of Karl BARTH and Karl JASPERS who was greatly influenced by Günther Bornkamm. His *Basic Questions in Theology* (1970-1973) and *Theology and the Philosophy of Science* (1976) locate theological academic study as "the SCIENCE of GOD" offering knowledge about "the one who determines the whole of reality." Following HEGEL, he argues that REALITY is essentially historical and that God can be fully known only at the end of HISTORY. Therefore he takes the theologically conservative position that the historicity of Jesus' RESURRECTION is crucial for CHRISTIANITY.

PANTA REI: a Greek term meaning "all flows" which is used in connection with the PHILOSOPHY of HERACLITUS.

PANTHEISM: the DOCTRINE that all things and beings are modes, ATTRIBUTES or appearances of one single, unified REALITY or BEING. Hence NATURE and GOD are believed to be identical. Although the term is often incorrectly used to describe HINDUISM and various other YOGIC religions, it appears to describe more accurately many NEW RELIGIOUS MOVEMENTS and the views of most NEW AGE thinkers.

PAPACY: the religious office of the POPE, the Bishop of Rome, head of the ROMAN CATHOLIC CHURCH and based in Rome.

PAPIAS (60-130): early CHRISTIAN theologian and BISHOP who recorded the earliest TRADITIONS of the CHURCH on such issues as the authorship of the Gospels. Although his original works are lost, fragments of them were preserved by other writers, and they are of great importance for understanding the development of CHRISTIANITY.

PAPYRUS: ancient Egyptian writing material made from reeds and formed into a scroll.

PARABLE: a story told to drive home a truth, point of teaching or WISDOM. Parables may be found in the HEBREW BIBLE and in RABBINIC JUDAISM, but they were used to their greatest effect by JESUS OF NAZARETH.

PARACELSUS (1493-1541): a Swiss physician and alchemist who pursued OCCULT and HERMETIC studies and advocated a MYSTICAL form of PANTHEISM.

PARACLETE: a Greek term meaning advocate or helper. It is used in the NEW TESTAMENT to refer to the HOLY SPIRIT.

PARADIGM: a very popular ESOTERIC and confusing term used in many different and undefined ways by Thomas KUHN in his book *The Structure of Scientific Revolutions* (1962) to signify "what members of a scientific community share." It is commonly taken to mean "a coherent system of CONCEPTS which confers order on the whole field of knowledge or a segment of it belonging to a particular scientific discipline." Kuhn's usage legitimates RELATIVISM in many fields, although he denies that his view is relativistic. In many respects Kuhn's use of paradigm is similar to DOOYEWEERD's more carefully defined GROUND MOTIVE.

PARADISE: the realm of HEAVEN where the blessed, or saved, go after DEATH. In ISLAM paradise is vividly depicted as a garden with abundant water, luxurious foliage and beautiful maidens who constantly serve men.

PARETO, Vilfredo (1848-1923): Italian SOCIOLOGIST and economist who, with Max WEBER and Emile DURKHEIM, ranks as a "founding father" of twentieth-century academic SOCIOLOGY. In particular he contributed important ideas to the psychological dimension of sociology. In his *Socialist Systems* (1902), he accepted that class struggles were a reality, but he dissented from the Marxist view that a proletarian victory would bring them to an end.

PARITTA: a chant used in BUDDHISM to give protection.

PARMENIDES (513-448 B.C.): Greek philosopher influenced by PYTHAGORAS who profoundly influenced PLATO through his thought about UNIVERSALS. He founded the ELEATIC SCHOOL of philosophy and taught a highly developed form of MONISM. Only fragments of his work *On Nature* survive.

PAROUSIA: a Greek term used in CHRISTIANITY to refer to the return of Christ, also known as his Second Advent.

PARSĪ: this is the name given to the followers of ZOROASTER who fled Persia in the eighth century to settle in India. Today they number about 200,000.

PARSONS, Talcott (1902-1979): American SOCIOLOGIST and opponent of Marxism who translated and interpreted WEBER to the English-speaking world. He developed a version of structural-FUNCTIONALISM and, unlike most American sociologists, was essentially a theorist who did little EMPIRICAL research. His wide-ranging works include *The Structure of Social Action* (1937) and *The Social System* (1951).

PASCAL, Blaise (1623-1662): French mathematician, author, scientist and lay theologian. A profound MYSTICAL encounter with CHRIST led him to devote his life to defending CHRISTIANITY. He supported JANSENISM and strongly opposed the JESUITS, using satire to attack what he perceived as their moral laxity. A forerunner of KIERKEGAARD, he is often referred to as a "father" of EXISTENTIALISM. His most famous religious work is the *Pensées*, a religious classic.

PASSION: a term used to describe the suffering of JESUS OF NAZARETH before and during his execution by crucifixion.

PASSOVER: the annual Jewish feast commemorating the story of the escape of the ISRAELITES from bondage in Egypt as told in EXODUS 12.

PASTOR: a PROTESTANT minister who performs the duty of caring for the members of a CONGREGATION or CHURCH.

PATAÑJALI (2nd century B.C.): Indian philosopher and author of the first three books of the *Yoga Sūtra*.

PAṬICCA-SAMUPPATION: the BUDDHIST DOCTRINE referred to as the "chain of causation" or "dependent origin" which expresses the idea that all physical things are conditioned by other things or states. The doctrine rejects any permanently existing entity, especially the ego, SOUL or SELF.

PATRIARCH: a term originally applied to the fathers of the people of ISRAEL, such as ABRAHAM, but later applied to certain leaders of the CHRISTIAN CHURCH such as the POPE and the bishops of the Eastern ORTHODOX CHURCH sees of Alexandria, Antioch, Constantinople and Jerusalem.

PATRICK (390-460): born in England and taken into SLAVERY in Ireland at the age of sixteen. While a slave, he underwent a religious CONVERSION, escaped and returned to England. After a short period of religious training, he returned to Ireland to evangelize the Irish and become their patron SAINT.

PATRICK, TED (1930-): an African-American who became the founder and advocate of DEPROGRAMMING, or the forceable kidnapping and detention of members of NEW RELIGIOUS MOVEMENTS, who are held prisoner until they recant their FAITH.

PAUL, THE APOSTLE (1st century): the APOSTLE to the GENTILES who, after JESUS OF NAZARETH, is the most important figure in CHRISTIANITY. According to his own account, recorded in the NEW TESTAMENT, he was a Pharisee and a zealous opponent of the EARLY CHURCH, being a leading figure in the persecution which followed the death of Jesus. In about A.D. 33, on the road to Damascus, he encountered the risen Jesus in a VISION that he understood to be both his conversion and call. This dramatic experience has become the ARCHETYPE for Christian CONVERSION. After a period of about three years in Arabia, probably engaged in preaching, he made his first post-conversion trip to Jerusalem to meet the leaders of the church. The next ten years were spent evangelizing Gentiles in Cilicia and Syria, until A.D. 47 when he started on his first of several missionary journeys. Paul was an itinerant EVANGELIST, supporting his work through his trade as a tentmaker and focusing his efforts on bringing the gospel to the Gentiles. In the course of his career he travelled extensively throughout the Mediterranean world and eventually went to Rome where, according to TRADITION, he was executed for his FAITH. His letters, which are found in the New Testament, are a significant part of the CANON of SCRIPTURE. His theology, with its emphasis on a theology of the cross, justification by faith and a law-free gospel, has had a deep and formative impact on Christianity, particularly on those traditions tracing their roots to the PROTESTANT REFORMATION.

PAVLOV, Ivan Petrovich (1849-1936): Russian physiologist and experimental psychologist famous for his experiments with dogs. He is a "father" of behaviorist PSYCHOLOGY, which essentially denies human FREEDOM and responsibility.

PEALE, Norman Vincent (1928-1986): a popular American writer and preacher whose "POSITIVE THINKING" inspired post-World War II Americans and helped develop a THEOLOGY of success. He published the influential magazine *Guideposts*; his most popular book was *The Power of Positive Thinking* (1952).

PEASANTS' REVOLT: a violent rebellion by peasants, inspired in part by the REFORMATION but condemned by LUTHER and brutally crushed by German princes in 1525.

PEIRCE, Charles Sanders (1839-1914): American PRAGMATIC philosopher credited with inventing the term *pragmatism* in 1878 to describe his theory of TRUTH in terms of the consequences of action which together makes up the MEANING. His writings were edited by Charles Hartshorne and Paul Weiss as *The Collected Papers of C. S. Peirce (1931-1935)* in 1958; a further collection was published by A. Burk.

PELAGIANISM: the teachings of the British MONK PELAGIUS and his school concerning the relationship between divine GRACE and FREE WILL. Pelagius seems to have denied the DOCTRINE of ORIGINAL SIN, arguing that it denied the freedom of the will. AUGUSTINE OF HIPPO attacked Pelagius, saying that he taught humans can save themselves (*see* SALVATION) and, therefore, do not need divine grace.

PELAGIUS (360-420): British MONK and "father" of PELAGIANISM whose works were attacked by AUGUSTINE because he denied ORIGINAL SIN.

PENANCE: from the Latin for "punishment"; the term came into general use from the third century A.D. onward as a CHRISTIAN practice whereby serious SIN was to be expiated by the actions of repentant individuals who, guided by PRIESTS in CONFESSION, took upon themselves acts of self-punishment and charity.

PENN, William (1644-1718): English QUAKER who immigrated to America and founded Pennsylvania. He held unorthodox views about the TRINITY, ATONEMENT and JUSTIFICATION, attacking CALVINISM in his book *Sandy Foundation Shaken* (1668). His most famous book, *No Cross, No Crown* (1669), is considered a spiritual classic.

PENTATEUCH: the name given by Christians to the first five books of the HEBREW BIBLE, the Hebrew Torah. The meaning is "five volumes."

PENTECOST: the JEWISH Feast of Weeks which fell fifty days after the Feast of PASSOVER. In CHRISTIANITY it marks the giving of the HOLY SPIRIT to the CHURCH as recorded in Acts 2.

PENTECOSTAL: a modern CHRISTIAN REVITALIZATION MOVEMENT with roots in the nineteenth-century HOLINESS MOVEMENT. Its inception is usually traced to the Azusa Street revival in 1906. The new movement emphasized the GIFTS of the HOLY SPIRIT, especially HEALING and SPEAKING IN TONGUES. It quickly led to the formation of various new DENOMINATIONS, including the Assemblies of God. In the mid-1960s the ingredients of the movement spread in the form of the CHARISMATIC MOVEMENT to the ROMAN CATHOLIC CHURCH and other OLD-LINE CHURCHES which had previously resisted Pentecostal teachings. An outstanding spokesperson and catalyst for this spread of the Charismatic movement was David du Plessis.

PEOPLE'S TEMPLE: a congregation of the OLD-LINE and theologically LIBERAL PROTESTANT DENOMINATION the DISCIPLES OF CHRIST (*see* CHURCH OF CHRIST) led by the charismatic figure (*see* CHARISMA) Jim JONES. Widely praised for its social action programs and radical political stance, it founded a SOCIALIST settlement at JONESTOWN, Guyana, in 1977. Following a mass SUICIDE at the settlement on November 18, 1978, the group was labeled a CULT by the media and became a key element in the American ANTICULT MOVEMENT.

PERCEPT: an impression received by sense experience, as opposed to a CONCEPT derived by pure thought.

PERFECTIONISM: because JESUS OF NAZARETH said, "Be perfect, therefore, as your heavenly Father is perfect" (Matthew 5:48), various CHRISTIAN groups have claimed that perfection is an obligation and a real possibility in this life. Traditionally the ROMAN CATHOLIC CHURCH held that perfection is defined as perfect LOVE, which is only achieved by SAINTS. The PROTESTANT REFORMERS denied even this, arguing that perfection is a goal which can never be attained in this life. John WESLEY, however, taught that in principle all Christians can become perfect—free from any known sin. Critics of perfectionism argue that the DOCTRINE, besides being unbiblical, inevitably leads to LEGALISM and a depressing preoccupation with self-improvement.

PERICOPE: a passage of SCRIPTURE isolated for interpretation or appointed to be read in a CHRISTIAN CHURCH.

PERSON: in Roman law a person was a legal entity or party to a contract, while in Roman theater a person was the mask worn by an actor to play a specific role. Neither usage identifies a person as a self-conscious being. CHRISTIAN usage developed from these Roman ideas; TERTULLIAN created the formula "three persons in one substance" to describe the TRINITY. He argued that GOD was one with respect to his BEING, NATURE or SUBSTANCE, but three with respect to the exercise of his sovereignty. Jesus Christ was one person having two natures: divine and human. From this theological origin the term came to be applied to individual identity and is often associated with the SOUL. BUDDHISM denies the EXISTENCE both of the individual person and of the soul.

PERSONALISM: the PHILOSOPHY which regards the individual PERSON as the highest form of REALITY. American PROTESTANT LIBERALISM was deeply influenced by a personalism which saw HISTORY as the unfolding of the moral aspect of GOD's will, a view espoused by the METHODIST philosopher and theologian Edgar Sheffield Brightman (1884-1953).

PERSPECTIVISM: the philosophic position that every standpoint is TRUE when seen from its own perspective.

PERSPICUITY OF SCRIPTURE: the EVANGELICAL DOCTRINE that, while the BIBLE may not be entirely clear, those things necessary for SALVATION are sufficiently plain that anyone reading SCRIPTURE can discover them without the assistance of PRIESTS or the CHURCH.

PETER (1st century): leader of the early disciples of JESUS OF NAZARETH, known for his enthusiasm and impulsive behavior. The ROMAN CATHOLIC CHURCH claims that it was founded by Peter, but this cannot be proved historically.

PETER LOMBARD (1100-1160): French ROMAN CATHOLIC philosopher and author of the *Sentences* (1155), which outlined basic CHRISTIAN DOCTRINE and, after initial criticism, became the standard THEOLOGICAL text of the Middle Ages.

PETER THE HERMIT (1050-1115): AUGUSTINIAN MONK who played an important role in encouraging the first CRUSADE.

PETITIO PRINCIPII: a Latin term used in logic which means "begging the question." It describes an argument where the conclusion is also used as one of the premises.

PETTAZZONI, Raffaele (1883-1959): Italian historian of RELIGION who argued, against the views of Father SCHMIDT, that the term MONOTHEISM cannot be applied to primitive religions, although the concept of a HIGH GOD is appropriate. His books include *Essays on the History of Religion* (1954).

PEYOTE CULT: a religious REVITALIZATION MOVEMENT which swept through various North American Indian tribes in the late nineteenth century and survives today as a religious movement which combines TRADITIONAL practices and BELIEFS with others derived from CHRISTIANITY. The central SACRAMENT of the cult is the use of mescaline from the peyote cactus as a hallucinogenic drug.

PHALLUS CULTS: various religious movements which worship the phallus and give strong religious significance to sexuality. The practice is common in HINDUISM and is rationalized as the recognition of creative energies. It is one of the distinctive features of the WORSHIP of Śiva.

PHARISEES: a JEWISH religious group, political party or SECT that flourished at the time of JESUS and is depicted in the NEW TESTAMENT as zealous in observing the Mosaic law (*see* MOSES), particularly regarding issues of ritual purity, and as hostile to Jesus' teachings. They appear to have believed in the RESURRECTION of the dead and in the existence of spiritual beings such as ANGELS, which their main rivals, the SADDUCEES, denied.

PHENOMENOLOGY: a term developed in the PHILOSOPHY of Edmund HUSSERL (1859-1938), who tried to establish the basic structure of consciousness and conditions for all possible experience. His work is highly technical, concentrating on logical and methodological problems in an attempt to create a completely objective, scientific, philosophical method. More recently the term has acquired a general usage designating a method of investigating fundamental human activities such as RELIGION.

PHENOMENOLOGY OF RELIGION: a term first used by the Dutch scholar Chantepie de la Saussaye in 1887, in a way which has affinities with Husserl's PHENOMENOLOGY. Phenomenologists attempt to gain insight into the inner workings of a RELIGION through the calculated and temporary abandonment of their own viewpoint and the careful use of comparisons. They also attempt to place themselves in the position of the believer to understand what a BELIEF means to someone who accepts its TRUTH.

PHENOMENON: the appearance of any conceivable thing, FACT or part of REALITY, as opposed to the thing itself. The term played a key role in the PHILOSOPHY of KANT.

PHI: spirit in Siamese FOLK RELIGION who is the CAUSE of human sickness and EVIL.

PHILIP OF HESSE (1504-1567): the SECULAR protector of Martin LUTHER and the German REFORMATION.

PHILISTINES: known as "the sea people." They appear to have settled in PALESTINE where they established a flourishing culture around the twelfth century B.C. In the HEBREW BIBLE they are depicted as a people hostile to the ISRAELITES.

PHILO (30 B.C.-A.D. 50): the greatest Hellenistic JEWISH philosopher of his age and outstanding member of the School of Alexandria. He argued that MOSES had anticipated the WISDOM of the Greeks, and he promoted the ALLEGORICAL INTERPRETATION of the HEBREW BIBLE. His writings greatly influenced CHRISTIANITY. Some scholars even suggest that the writer of the Gospel of John, who uses the CONCEPT of LOGOS, was familiar with Philo's work.

PHILOKALIA: a classic of the Eastern ORTHODOX CHURCH; its title means "the love of the beautiful." It consists of a collection of MYSTICAL writings dating from the fourth to the fifteenth century and was first published in 1782.

PHILOLOGY: the study of texts, languages and words to determine their meaning, frequently giving special attention to change in language over time and the relationships between cognate languages. The term comes from the Greek words *philein*, "to love," and *logos*, "word." Thus the term literally means a "love of words" or "love of learning." The term came to be applied in the late eighteenth and early nineteenth centuries to the study of languages, especially ancient languages, and religious texts. The discipline of philology has been intimately related to BIBLICAL CRITICISM and the study of other religious texts.

PHILOSOPHY: literally, "love of WISDOM," understood as the study and knowledge of things and their causes. Traditionally it was divided into metaphysics, and moral and natural philosophy. Since the nineteenth century the word SCIENCE has replaced *natural philosophy* in English. In common usage *philosophy* is also a general name for any system of ideas or even a way of life. Today academic philosophy is largely limited to logic and the theory of knowledge.

PHILOSOPHY OF RELIGION: a product of the ENLIGHTENMENT which involves the analysis and evaluation of religious experience and BELIEF.

PHOTIUS (810-895): Eastern ORTHODOX PATRIARCH of Constantinople who opposed Western influences and played an important role in rejecting the FILIOQUE CLAUSE in Western versions of the CREED. His major work, a standard Greek Orthodox THEOLOGICAL text, is *Treatise on the Holy Spirit.*

PI-HSIA YUAN-CHUN: the TAOIST GODDESS who is the protector of women and children.

PIAGET, Jean (1896-1981): French psychologist, biologist and philosopher, whose work on child development has greatly influenced modern education. His book *Structuralism* (1971) sets out his basic philosophical orientation.

PIETISM: any religious movement which promotes PIETY. It is usually applied to a CHRISTIAN religious movement which originated as a reaction to the ENLIGHTENMENT in eighteenth-century Germany and profoundly influenced the English-speaking world through METHODISM and the EVANGELICAL MOVEMENT.

PIETY: personal religious devotion to a GOD or a SAVIOR figure.

PILGRIMAGE: the practice of visiting SACRED sites which have historical or other significance in a given religious TRADITION. In CHRISTIANITY the cities of

ROME and JERUSALEM were traditional centers of pilgrimage, although lesser sites such as GLASTONBURY Abbey in England were also important. In ISLAM the major center of pilgrimage is MECCA, while BANARAS is the holy city of India. Places of pilgrimage often contain RELICS of SAINTS or the founders of the religion.

PILLARS OF ISLAM: there are five fundamental duties of a devout MUSLIM. These are are called the "pillars": (1) confession of the FAITH by reciting the phrase "There is no GOD but ALLAH and MUHAMMAD is his PROPHET"; (2) PRAYER five times a day at dawn, noon, mid-afternoon, evening and night; (3) FASTING during the month of RAMADĀN; (4) zakāt or almsgiving; and (5) the ḤAJJ, a pilgrimage to MECCA to be made at least once in one's lifetime.

PILTDOWN MAN: a skull discovered between 1909 and 1915 at Piltdown Common, England, that seemed to prove the truth of the THEORY of EVOLUTION. It was exposed as a clever forgery in 1953. Some critics suspect that the ROMAN CATHOLIC theologian Pierre TEILHARD DE CHARDIN was linked with the plot.

PIUS IX (1792-1878): reactionary PRIEST who became POPE in 1846. He promulgated the ROMAN CATHOLIC DOCTRINES of the IMMACULATE CONCEPTION and papal INFALLIBILITY. In 1864 he issued the SYLLABUS OF ERRORS condemning LIBERALISM and MODERNISM.

PISACA: ancient Indian spirit or DEMON hostile to humans.

PLAINSONG: also known as GREGORIAN CHANT. This is the traditional music of Western European CHRISTIAN CHURCHES.

PLANCK, Max (1858-1947): German theoretical physicist who helped develop QUANTUM mechanics and is one of the founders of modern physics.

PLANTINGA, Alvin (1938-): American CALVINIST philosopher who has written extensively on both the ONTOLOGICAL ARGUMENT and the PROBLEM OF EVIL. His book *God and Other Minds* (1969) is a mod-ern philosophical defense of THEISM.

PLATO (427?-347 B.C.): Greek philosopher of aristocratic Athenian descent who saw Athens decline politically and commercially as a result of the Peloponnesian War (431-404 B.C.). He founded the Academy (perhaps in 386 B.C.), which became the first endowed university and flourished until it closed in A.D. 529. Plato held that the material and sensible world is merely a temporary copy of permanent unchanging FORMS, the objects of all real knowledge. True ethical values are attained only by those individuals who have the proper perspective of SOUL or mind and who place REASON above the baser elements of their personality. The best government is possible only when philosophers, who are the most rational members of the state, become rulers. His teacher was SOCRATES, and ARISTOTLE was his pupil—together they are the three greatest Greek philosophers.

PLATO'S ACADEMY: the school of PHILOSOPHY founded by PLATO in Athens in about 386 B.C. It closed in A.D. 529.

PLOTINUS (A.D. 205-270): the last great NEOPLATONIST of the Greco-Roman world. His PHILOSOPHY had a great impact on CHRISTIANITY and the development of both THEOLOGY and MYSTICISM. He is the author of *The Enneads*.

PLURALISM: philosophically, any system which emphasizes diversity and rejects MONISM. Many modern societies use the term to refer to social systems where different religious communities live together in one NATION.

PLUTARCH (A.D. 46-120): Greek philosopher who is remembered for his *Lives* of great Greeks and Romans. He was an initiate of the MYSTERY RELIGIONS.

PLYMOUTH BRETHREN: one of the most influential NEW RELIGIOUS MOVEMENTS to emerge in the 1830s and closely associated with John Nelson DARBY (1800-1882). The Brethren split into a number of different groups, including the extremist EXCLUSIVE BRETHREN and moderate

OPEN BRETHREN. Despite their small size, they have had an immense influence on MODERN CHRISTIANITY. Their emphasis on the imminent RETURN OF CHRIST helped popularize both PREMILLENNIALISM and DISPENSATIONALISM, while their rejection of a paid CLERGY has strongly influenced the growth of HOUSE-CHURCH MOVEMENTS and similar anticlerical groups worldwide. They have been particularly influential in the field of MISSIONS, where their idea of FAITH MISSIONS influenced groups as diverse as the CHINA INLAND MISSION and L'Abri (*see* SCHAEFFER).

PNEUMA: the Greek word for "wind" which came to be used to speak of the spirit, human or divine.

POGROM: the organized persecution of a religious group, especially Eastern European Jews or another ethnic minority.

POLANYI, Michael (1891-1976): Hungarian chemist and philosopher whose works, such as *Personal Knowledge* (1958), have played an important role in modern debates about the relationship between RELIGION and SCIENCE.

POLYCARP (1st century): early CHRISTIAN writer and MARTYR who provided a link between the APOSTLES and the EARLY CHURCH.

POLYGAMY: marriage to more than one wife, sometimes called plural marriage. The practice is found in the HEBREW BIBLE but has been traditionally forbidden in CHRISTIANITY although tolerated in most other religions, including ancient and medieval JUDAISM. In ISLAM the number of formal wives is limited to four. During the nineteenth century MORMONISM attempted to reintroduce polygamy into American society, but the attempt was abandoned in the 1890s.

POLYTHEISM: a BELIEF in the EXISTENCE of a plurality of gods, as opposed to MONOTHEISM, which is a belief in the existence of only one GOD.

PONTIUS PILATE (1st century): Roman governor of Judea whom the Gospels depict as sentencing and administering the execution of JESUS OF NAZARETH. Tradition states that his wife became a CHRISTIAN.

POOR CLARES: a ROMAN CATHOLIC order of NUNS founded by FRANCIS OF ASSISI and his disciple Clare between 1212 and 1214 on the FRANCISCAN model.

POPE: the title given to the BISHOP of Rome, the head of the ROMAN CATHOLIC CHURCH.

POPPER, Sir Karl (1902-): Austrian-born British philosopher whose Jewish parents converted to CHRISTIANITY. After a short period as a Marxist, he became disenchanted and associated himself with the VIENNA CIRCLE, which he also found inadequate. His own philosophy is set forth in *The Logic of Scientific Discovery* (1934) and a series of other books, including the powerful *The Open Society and Its Enemies* (1945), which is a sustained attack on both Marxism and FASCISM. He argued that what separates MODERN, or open, SOCIETY from tribal, or closed, SOCIETY, is the scientific method, which he sees as a technique for testing theories through their FALSIFICATION. A controversial figure, his arguments are often avoided by many contemporary scholars, who prefer to ignore them rather than face their full force.

PORPHYRY (A.D. 232-303): Palestinian NEOPLATONIST philosopher and student of PLOTINUS who popularized his master's work. He was a severe critic of CHRISTIANITY and the Christian CHURCH.

POSITIVE THINKING: a distinctly American movement originating in the nineteenth century which believed in PROGRESS and stressed the role of thought in the creation of material well-being. It has influenced many religious groups from CHRISTIAN SCIENCE to the WORD OF FAITH movement. The best-known modern exponents are Norman Vincent PEALE and Robert SCHULLER.

POSITIVISM: a PHILOSOPHIC and religious movement founded in the nineteenth century by the French philosopher Auguste COMTE. It was not only a THEORY of knowledge but was also a scheme of HISTORY and program of SOCIAL REFORM. Today it denotes a more general and widespread position not directly dependent on Comte's views. The modern usage reflects a suspicion of all speculation not controlled by FACTS and sense experience. Positivism accepts only knowledge or theories based on positive (meaning *observable*) evidence. In England positivism became both a freethinking radicalism (*see* FREE THINKERS) and a scientific movement.

POST HOC ERGO PROPTER HOC: literally, "after this, therefore on account of this," it is the logical FALLACY which assumes that because "A" precedes or is the antecedent of "B" it causes "B." For example: someone who eats ice cream and then claims that the ice cream caused their headache has committed this fallacy. The ice cream may or may not have caused the headache, and the observation that it preceded the headache does not prove that it caused it. Further investigation and evidence is needed to discover the true CAUSE.

POSTMODERNISM: there are various contemporary understandings of the meaning of postmodernism, the most popular being a largely literary INTELLECTUAL movement strongly influenced by French PHILOSOPHY, especially the views of DERRIDA and FOUCAULT, which seeks to DECONSTRUCT texts to arrive at new insights into their meaning. A more general use of the term implies a movement which recognizes the limitations of locality and ethnicity implicit in ENLIGHTENMENT and other forms of MODERN thinking such as MARXISM. In the latter sense postmodernism is an attempt to gain a HOLISTIC view of things which goes beyond the limitations of nineteenth-century and earlier forms of twentieth-century IDEOLOGIES.

POSTULATE: a philosophical term indicating a proposition which is to be regarded as the starting point of an argument. Postulates are neither self-evident nor demonstrable but rather are the necessary assumptions made to begin a discussion.

PRABHUPADA, A. C. Bhaktivedanta, Swami (1896-1977): founder and GURU of the HARE KRISHNA MOVEMENT. A successful businessman, Prabhupada left his family to become a MONK when he was fifty-eight years old. After extensive study, in 1965, at the age of seventy, he felt called to spread "Krishna consciousness" in America. For the rest of his life he worked ceaselessly to establish the Hare Krishna movement and to spread HINDU BHAKTI practices in the West.

PRAGMATIC: the rejection of dogmatic or principled views in favor of the practical.

PRAGMATISM: a theory concerning the meaning of words originated by the American philosopher C. S. PEIRCE. The term and basic idea was borrowed and developed by William JAMES and John Dewey (1859-1952) to create a thoroughly MODERN American PHILOSOPHY known as pragmatism, based on the theory that whatever works is true (*see* TRUTH).

PRAKṚTI: a SANSKRIT term used in HINDUISM to refer to the material nature and natural process of the UNIVERSE. The idea is tied up with the urge to reproduce and is also the name of a GODDESS.

PRANAYAMA: breath control in YOGA.

PRATT, Parley P. (1805-1859): early MORMON EVANGELIST and theologian. In his creative speculation about the law of ETERNAL PROGRESSION in his classic *The Key to Theology* (1855), he sought to harmonize MODERN SCIENCE and RELIGION.

PRAYER: addressing a DEITY with spoken or unspoken words. It is the means by which an individual or group attempts to enter into verbal or mental communication with GOD or a god.

PRAYER MAT: a small mat used in PRAYER by MUSLIMS for RITUAL cleanliness and SYMBOLIC separation from the world.

PRAYER MEETING: a gathering of CHRISTIANS for the purpose of intercessory PRAYER. The practice is particularly important in HOLINESS and revival movements (*see* REVIVALISM) and in EVANGELICAL CHRISTIANITY.

PRAYER MOUNTAINS: a practice derived from Korean BUDDHISM whereby mountain areas are set aside for PRAYER and meditation. Many Korean CHARISMATIC CHURCHES acquired prayer mountains and the practice spread to North America in the late 1980s and early 1990s.

PRAYER WHEEL: a device used in TIBETAN BUDDHISM consisting of a cylinder containing written PRAYERS and MANTRAS which is believed to take effect when rotated.

PRAYERS FOR THE DEAD: the practice of praying for deceased people in the belief that such prayers will improve their lot in the afterlife.

PREDESTINATION: a term often confused with GOD's FOREKNOWLEDGE; it means that before the CREATION of the UNIVERSE, God determined and foreordained all that would come to pass. In a narrower sense it refers to God's eternal decree respecting the SALVATION or DAMNATION of individuals. Although ideas about predestination are found in many CHRISTIAN traditions, including ROMAN CATHOLICISM, they are particularly associated with CALVINISM. Predestination also plays an important role in ISLAM.

PRESBYTER: an elder, overseer or BISHOP in the EARLY CHURCH. By the second century A.D. the term had been restricted to a local church leader or minister. The English word PRIEST is derived from the Greek word for presbyter.

PRESBYTERIANISM: one of the three major methods of church government, the other two being CONGREGATIONALISM and EPISCOPALIANISM. The Presbyterian churches arose out of the CALVINIST REFORMATION, first appearing in Scotland in the late sixteenth century. Today there are over 120 independent Presbyterian church groups spread worldwide and loosely united in the World Alliance of Reformed Churches. They are distinguished by their form of church government based on presbyters or ELDERS and an ascending series of church courts. The lowest court is that of the session of elders in a local congregation; above it are presbyteries made up of representatives from congregations within a district, above the presbyteries are the SYNODS of larger regions. Finally there is the General Assembly or National Synod. Each court consists of elders and ministers who appoint new ministers and determine the policy of both local CONGREGATIONS and the church as a whole. Apart from their distinct method of church government, Presbyterian churches traditionally accept the Calvinist CREEDS, the most important of which are the WESTMINSTER CONFESSION, the Helvetic Confession and the HEIDELBERG CATECHISM.

PRESBYTERY: the sanctuary or eastern part of the chancel of a church which lies beyond the choir; a residence for ROMAN CATHOLIC PRIESTS; or the CHURCH administrative body or court in a PRESBYTERIAN system of church government.

PRESUPPOSITION: the basic THEORY or BELIEF system which, although fundamental in the development of an argument, is accepted uncritically and often unconsciously.

PRIDE: one of the SEVEN DEADLY SINS in CHRISTIANITY.

PRIEST: a religious functionary who performs priestly duties including officiating in worship, the administering of SACRAMENTS and offering of SACRIFICES to GOD or the gods. In ROMAN CATHOLICISM the aspect of sacrifice is subsumed under the celebration of the MASS. The idea of priesthood was rejected by the PROTESTANT REFORMERS, who replaced it with that of the PRIESTHOOD OF ALL BELIEVERS.

PRIESTHOOD: an organized group of PRIESTS or the office of being a priest.

PRIESTHOOD OF ALL BELIEVERS: the PROTESTANT belief, based upon the NEW TESTAMENT, that under the new COVE-

NANT GOD no longer requires SACRIFICES offered by a distinct PRIESTHOOD, but that all believers offer themselves to his service and act as PRIESTS through PRAYER and FAITH in JESUS CHRIST.

PRIMAL RELIGIONS: those religious traditions, such as AFRICAN TRADITIONAL RELIGIONS, NATIVE AMERICAN RELIGIONS, etc., which are essentially oral TRADITIONS. Primal religions are also identifiable with REDFIELD'S LITTLE TRADITIONS where CHARISMATIC effects, HEALING, PROPHECY, VISIONS, etc. are the principal concern of DEVOTEES. In primal religions a SHAMAN or a similar RITUAL figure who communicates between this world and the next or with the ANCESTORS plays a key role.

PRIMITIVISM: many RELIGIOUS REVITALIZATION MOVEMENTS seek to return to what is imagined to be a lost ideal or golden age found in the past. In ISLAM the Days of the Prophet, in HINDUISM the time of some particularly important GURU, in BUDDHISM the reign of AŚOKA, the REFORMATION or EARLY CHURCH in CHRISTIANITY all serve as ideals for various RESTORATION movements. Primitivism has been a particularly strong idea in both the development and interpretation of American religious history where many CHURCHES, such as the CHURCH OF CHRIST, have sought to return to create ECUMENICAL fellowship through a return to the purity of the original Christianity as REVEALED in SCRIPTURE. Such movements often claim to be devoid of DOCTRINE because they base their BELIEFS on "the Bible alone."

PROBLEM OF EVIL: the traditional philosophic and practical problem which asks how an all-knowing and all-powerful GOD, who is both the CREATOR of the UNIVERSE and by definition GOOD, can allow SUFFERING and EVIL. It concerns the basic human problem of MEANING and significance in the face of death and suffering. It is often seen as a particularly difficult question for THEISM which attributes both power and goodness to the DEITY, creating the famous dilemma: either God is able to prevent evil and will not, or he is willing to prevent it and cannot. If the former, he is not merciful; if the latter, he is not OMNIPOTENT. It is, however, an equally great problem for all people who think about the meaning of life. Various religions answer it in different ways. In HINDUISM it is answered in terms of KARMA and MĀYĀ with the great dialogue between Arunja and KRISHNA in the BHAGAVAD-GĪTA. BUDDHISM meets the problem by stating that all life is characterized by impermanence which can be escaped through the attainment of NIRVĀNA. JUDAISM and ISLAM find the solution in submission to the will of GOD, while CHRISTIANITY presents a complex answer beginning with the FALL and ending with the ATONEMENT. The biggest difference between the YOGIC and ABRAMIC solutions to this problem is that Yogic religions see it in terms of ONTOLOGY, while the Abramic religions recognize a moral issue.

PROCESS THEOLOGY: a type of EVOLUTIONARY THEOLOGY developed by Charles Hartshorne on the basis of the PHILOSOPHY of Alfred WHITEHEAD. It emphasizes that the world and BEING, including GOD, are in constant process and change, and it accepts a PANENTHEIST view of the UNIVERSE.

PRODHON, Pierre Joseph (1809-1865): French journalist and radical writer who is the "father of ANARCHISM." The title of his famous book *Property Is Theft* (1840) was borrowed as a slogan by Karl MARX even though he strongly attacked Prodhon's political views.

PROGRESS: the belief that HISTORY is moving in a linear fashion toward a goal, and that as it does so life on earth, especially human achievement, is ever improving through the increase of knowledge and scientific discoveries.

PROMETHEUS: the Greek titan (giant) who defied ZEUS by giving the gift of fire to humans.

PROOFS FOR THE EXISTENCE OF

GOD: the most famous A PRIORI argument is the ONTOLOGICAL ARGUMENT associated with ANSELM of CANTERBURY. The classic a posteriori arguments are found in the works of Thomas AQUINAS and include the COSMOLOGICAL, moral and TELEOLOGICAL arguments.

PROPHECY: the act of REVELATION whereby a PROPHET gives an inspired message from GOD. Usually prophecy is associated with foretelling the future, but it can also include messages of inspiration or admonishment which reveal the will of God toward a particular people or individual.

PROPHET: a person, male or female, who prophesies by foretelling the future or delivering inspired, divine messages. Sometimes prophets use divination and special devices to obtain their messages; on other occasions they speak as directly inspired. The HEBREW BIBLE says that prophets should be tested according to the results of their message. Throughout much of CHRISTIAN HISTORY prophets have been discouraged by the CHURCH, but in recent years the office has been revived by the CHARISMATIC·MOVEMENT.

PROPHET, Elizabeth Clare (1940-): SHAMANISTIC leader of a SPIRITUALIST-type NEW RELIGIOUS MOVEMENT originally known as the SUMMIT LIGHTHOUSE and now called the CHURCH UNIVERSAL AND TRIUMPHANT which has its headquarters in Montana.

PROPITIATION: the removal of divine wrath by the offering of SACRIFICES or gifts. In the HEBREW BIBLE the idea of propitiation is linked to RITUAL sacrifices offered by PRIESTS at the TEMPLE in JERUSALEM. In NEW TESTAMENT passages such as Romans 3:24 it is associated with the DEATH of CHRIST. Modern critics often object to the idea on the grounds that it requires a notion of a wrathful GOD, arguing instead that God is LOVE.

PROPOSITION: a formal assertion in LOGIC that sets forth something which is asserted or denied and that is capable of being judged true or false.

PROSELYTE: a convert (see CONVERSION). Originally the term was used of converts to JUDAISM. Today it is often applied to people who switch DENOMINATIONAL allegiances within CHRISTIANITY or join a SECT.

PROSELYTIZE: to seek converts. The term is often used to signify CONVERSION from one closely related religious group to another; e.g., when an ANGLICAN is persuaded to become a BAPTIST.

PROTAGORAS (490-410 B.C.): Greek SOPHIST philosopher remembered for his saying "Man is the measure of all things." Agnostic with respect to the GODS, he was accused by PLATO and ARISTOTLE of promoting moral RELATIVISM.

PROTESTANT: a member of any of the CHRISTIAN DENOMINATIONS that reject papal authority and support the REFORMATION principles of JUSTIFICATION BY FAITH, the PRIESTHOOD OF ALL BELIEVERS and the AUTHORITY of SCRIPTURE.

PROTESTANT PRINCIPLE: a term used by Paul TILLICH to define the essence of Protestantism; it may be expressed as the protest against any ABSOLUTE claim made for a FINITE REALITY such as a CHURCH, PERSON, book, SYMBOL or event.

PROTESTANTISM: the CHRISTIAN REVITALIZATION MOVEMENT springing from the REFORMATION which sought to reform the CHURCH on the basis of the authority of the Bible.

PROVERBS, BOOK OF: part of the WISDOM LITERATURE of the HEBREW BIBLE, traditionally attributed to King Solomon.

PROVIDENCE: the means by which GOD sustains all creatures in their distinctive NATURES and powers and by which God fulfills his purposes through guiding HISTORY. Providence may thus apply to the world as a whole and the affairs of entire groups—such as nations—or to the working of God in the lives of individuals.

PSALMS: the religious poetry of ancient JUDAISM, found primarily in the book of Psalms in the HEBREW BIBLE.

PSEUDEPIGRAPHA: a written work attributed to a famous author as a means of endowing it with religious AUTHORITY when in fact it was written by someone else. Extra-CANONICAL biblical writings, such as the book of Enoch, fall into this category.

PSEUDOSCIENCE: the practice of such things as PYRAMIDOLOGY, trans-channeling and belief in UFOs, ancient astronauts, etc., on the basis of supposed scientific evidence which is in fact nonsensical. Pseudoscience uses scientific-sounding terminology but totally lacks scientific support. It ignores systematic investigation and scientific methodology and is usually openly hostile to MODERN SCIENCE.

PSYCHIATRY: that branch of modern medicine with deals with mental illness and is practiced by a qualified physician.

PSYCHOANALYSIS: a technique developed by Sigmund FREUD for treating neurosis and other mental illness through the analysis of a person's mental life, especially childhood experiences.

PSYCHOLOGY: although used from ancient times to refer to the nonphysical aspect of the human person, it only developed its technical meaning as the study of human consciousness and motivations after 1879, when Wilhelm WUNDT began experimental work. In the twentieth century it was taken up by FREUD, JUNG, ADLER and various others to develop into a university discipline boasting a number of rival theories and techniques.

PSYCHOLOGY OF RELIGION: the academic study of RELIGION from the perspective of PSYCHOLOGY. It was first developed by Wilhelm WUNDT and later by William JAMES, JUNG and others. FREUD was hostile to religious claims and used his influence to discredit RELIGION. Today it is one of the more underdeveloped areas in RELIGIOUS STUDIES, although the unexpected rise of CULTS and new religions led to a revival of studies of CONVERSION in the 1980s.

PTOLEMY (2nd century): Greek Alexandrian philosopher and scientist renowned for his work on astronomy which dominated Western thought until COPERNICUS. He argued that the earth is a globe in the center of the UNIVERSE.

PŪJĀ: the WORSHIP of a GOD in HINDUISM involving offerings of flowers and food. In BUDDHISM Pūjā is offered to the BUDDHA; in JAINISM, to the JINAS.

PUNDIT: a HINDU recognized for his learning.

PURĀṆAS: post-VEDIC literature which belong to the CANON of HINDUISM that may be described as "ancient tales" or "stories from the past." They deal with such themes as CREATION, the action of the GODS, and the lives of kings and heroes. Theologically they tend toward BHAKTI and present BRAHMĀ, VISHNU and ŚIVA as three manifestations of God. There are eighteen principal Purāṇas, all of which date from the Gupta period in the fourth century, although most scholars believe they contain many older elements.

PURDAH: the wearing of the veil by Hindu women. It is called ḥijāb in ISLAM.

PURE LAND: the Western PARADISE of the AMIDA BUDDHA.

PURE LAND BUDDHISM: East Asian MAHĀYĀNA BUDDHIST SECTS which emphasize FAITH in AMIDA BUDDHA expressed through meditation and the recitation of his name as a means of attaining REBIRTH in the Western PARADISE or PURE LAND.

PURGATORY: a ROMAN CATHOLIC DOCTRINE which teaches that after death SOULS must be purified before they can enter HEAVEN. This doctrine was the basis for sale of INDULGENCES and the saying of PRAYERS FOR THE DEAD.

PURIFICATION: the practice found in many RELIGIOUS TRADITIONS whereby DEVOTEES must purify themselves from worldly contact and concerns before WORSHIPING or having other dealings with the DIVINE. Purification RITUALS are often sexual in nature.

PURITANS: a much-maligned dynamic

religious movement which arose in the sixteenth century as a CALVINIST party within the CHURCH OF ENGLAND. They emphasized preaching, pastoral care and the REFORMATION of the church in terms of biblical norms. Popular with the lower and middle classes, they emphasized education and the improvement of daily life through hard work and innovation. They were bitterly persecuted before and after the English Civil War, causing many to flee to America where they played a significant role in shaping the main themes of American RELIGION. Favoring republican forms of government, they contributed to the development of modern DEMOCRACY and are credited by many historians with playing an important role in the rise of MODERN SCIENCE. As a result of aristocratic propaganda, which could not forgive them for the execution of King Charles I, the name "Puritan" came to be falsely identified with dour killjoys.

PYRAMID TEXTS: ancient Egyptian religious texts written in hieroglyphics on the inner walls of PYRAMIDS dealing with funeral rites, RITUALS, MAGICAL spells, PRAYERS and other issues affecting the dead.

PYRAMIDOLOGY: a MODERN PSEUDO-SCIENCE which has featured in the growth of many NEW RELIGIOUS MOVEMENTS, from BRITISH ISRAELISM to the JEHOVAH'S WITNESSES. It uses the measurements of the PYRAMIDS—particularly the Great Pyramid—as a basis for predictions and the interpretation of PROPHECY.

PYRAMIDS: ancient Egyptian monuments erected to bury and honor kings and important individuals.

PYTHAGORAS (6th century B.C.): Greek philosopher, mathematician and founder of geometry. He established a VEGETARIAN community of scholars who shared all things in common and were initiated to membership through religious RITUALS. Emphasizing the importance of mathematics and music in the quest for TRUTH, he taught TRANSMIGRATION and believed that the SOUL is imprisoned in the body. His work greatly influenced PLATO.

Q

Q: the symbol used by NEW TESTAMENT scholars to refer to material common to the Synoptic Gospels Matthew and Luke, and not found in Mark. It stands for the German word *Quelle,* meaning "source." The theory of a "Q" collection of sayings of Jesus, used by Matthew and Luke in addition to the Gospel of Mark, was introduced by nineteenth-century German biblical critics (*see* BIBLICAL CRITICISM). In the English-speaking world it was developed by B. H. Streeter, an Oxford professor. His views and the way they were set forth were strongly criticized by various scholars, including more recently W. R. Farmer, though they remain widely accepted by scholars today.

QUA: Latin term meaning "in so far as" or "in the capacity of."

QUAKERS: a small PROTESTANT group known as the Society of FRIENDS which arose in the seventeenth century as a result of the preaching of George FOX. They emphasized the leading of the HOLY SPIRIT, or "INNER LIGHT," rejected the SAC-RAMENTS, insisted on "plain speech" and simple dress, and repudiated all forms of art, including music. There are two possible origins of the name: the first is that it is derived from Fox's call to Justice Bennet in 1650 that he should "quake" before the Word of God; the second is that it comes from the practice of some members of the group who would "shake" or "quake" during services. Strongly pacifist, the Quakers have been very active in social REFORM and education.

QUANTUM THEORY: classical physics as developed by NEWTON held that it was possible to know both the speed and position of any particle. With HEISENBERG's uncertainty principle, modern physics recognized that we can know either the speed or the position of a particle but not both. Certainty gave way to probability, and an electron had to be considered as both a wave and a particle at the same time. The implication of these findings, which were given expression in the work of Nils Bohr, Max PLANCK and Albert EINSTEIN, is that the older mechanistic and essentially deterministic view of the physical UNI-VERSE no longer holds true. As a result, arguments such as those of David HUME against the possibility of MIRACLES are no longer as sound as they once seemed.

QUIETISM: a form of SPIRITUALITY which emphasizes "waiting on GOD" and the abandonment of SELF to God. More specifically it refers to the practice of MYSTICS like Madame GUYON who alarmed the seventeenth-century ROMAN CATHOLIC CHURCH because their views were thought to lead to PANTHEISM.

QUIMBY, Phineas Parkhurst (1802-1866): Lebanese-born American religious innovator, healer and hypnotist who formulated a "science of happiness." His work gave rise to "New Thought" and inspired Mary Baker EDDY, the founder of CHRISTIAN SCIENCE.

QUINE, Willard van Orman (1908-): American philosopher and logician whose essay "The Two Dogmas of Empiricism" (1951), republished in *From a Logical Point of View* (1953), seriously challenged reductionism and the VERIFICATION PRINCIPLE. His later work concerned the nature of language and has been seen as supporting the view of John Dewey as well as encouraging a radical approach to translation.

QUMRAN: the site of a JEWISH community which flourished between 150 B.C. and A.D. 68, where in 1947 an Arab shepherd boy discovered in nearby caves the first scroll of what proved to be a unique collection of ancient HEBREW and Aramaic manuscripts. These are now known as the DEAD SEA SCROLLS and are thought to have belonged to a Jewish SECT called the ESSENES which occupied the site.

QUO VADIS: according to an ancient CHRISTIAN legend, in A.D. 64 the APOSTLE PETER was fleeing from ROME to escape Nero's persecution. On the road he met CHRIST and asked him, "Quo vadis, domine?" which means, "Where are you going, Lord?" The reply was, "I am returning to Rome to be crucified again." In 1895 Henryk Sienkiewicz wrote a popular novel based on the legend.

QUR'ĀN: the HOLY book of ISLAM which is believed by MUSLIMS to have been revealed by GOD through the ANGEL GABRIEL to MUḤAMMUD, who commissioned various scribes to record it. The name means "that which is read" or "recited." The essential teaching of the Qur'ān is that God is one and that he demands absolute submission from mankind; hence the name of the religion: ISLAM. Muslims believe that the Qur'ān was given by waḥy—REVELATION—which is not to be confused with ILHĀM or INSPIRATION. For Muslims the Qur'ān is the eternal Word of God and as such is a divine ATTRIBUTE. Islamic teaching about the Qur'ān does not correspond to CHRISTIAN views about the BIBLE; while Christians believe that the Bible was inspired by God and is the authentic Word of God they also accept that it was written by men. Muslims, however, reject the idea of any human intervention and believe the Qur'ān descended from heaven; therefore, while it is correct to speak of PAUL as the author of Romans, it is incorrect to say that Muḥammad was the author of the Qur'ān. Nevertheless, originally a number of variant readings of the text did exist; they were destroyed on the orders of ABŪ BAKR to prevent confusion and to create a standardized text. In this sense it is similar to the MASORETIC TEXT of the HEBREW BIBLE, and the elimination of variants avoided the type of problem some people believe Christians face when studying the SYNOPTIC GOSPELS. The fact that only one text of the Qur'ān was allowed to survive contrasts with the situation in New Testament studies where over 5,000 surviving manuscripts contain numerous variant readings. To Muslim scholars the lack of variants is an asset, while Christian scholars regard it as weakening the historical claims of Islam. A further difficulty involves the question of translation. Because the Qur'ān is believed to have been spoken by God its language is SACRED and considered inimitable and, therefore, pious Muslims argue that it cannot be translated and only truly exists in Arabic. Versions in English and other languages must be regarded as renditions rather than translations. Such an approach is taken by Marmaduke Pickthall in his *The Meaning of the Glorious Qur'ān* (1930).

R

RA: the Egyptian sun GOD who was also the god of the state.

RABBI: literally, "master." During the first century this referred to an expert in JEWISH law. Over the centuries it has evolved to a communal office concerned with educational, pastoral and religious matters.

RABBINIC JUDAISM: see JUDAISM, RABBINIC.

RĀBI'AH al-Adawīyya (717-801): female MUSLIM ascetic, MYSTIC and ṢŪFĪ SAINT who taught a DOCTRINE of love for GOD.

RACISM: political and social BELIEFS and actions based on the supposed superiority of one race over another. The practice was rationalized in THEORY by Count GOBINEAU in the nineteenth century and found its clearest expression in the NAZI Party. CHRISTIANITY and all the other WORLD RELIGIONS condemn racism, insisting on the unity of humanity.

RAD, Gerhard von (1901-1971): German OLD TESTAMENT scholar who is noted for his many contributions, including his theories about the development of Israel's religious traditions and Old Testament theology.

RADCLIFFE-BROWN, Alfred Reginald (1881-1955): British anthropologist and first professor of social ANTHROPOLOGY at the University of Oxford. He pioneered the techniques of fieldwork and participant observation. His works include *Structure and Function in Primitive Society* (1952) and *Method in Anthropology* (1958).

RADHA SOAMI MOVEMENT: a HINDU REFORM movement which emerged after the death of Shiv Dayal, who incorporated SIKH beliefs and practices around a form of YOGA. The movement differentiates itself from the Sikhs in that the GURU replaces the SCRIPTURE as the source of religious knowledge and Sikh initiation is rejected.

RADHAKRISHNAN, Sarvepalli (1888-1975): influential BRAHMIN interpreter of HINDUISM and Indian PHILOSOPHY who became the vice-president of India. He expounded a universalistic version of VEDĀNTA which minimized the DOCTRINE of MĀYĀ. His many books include *The Bhagavadgita* (1948), *The Hindu View of Life* (1927), and the two-volume *Indian Philosophy* (1923-1927) and *Eastern Religions in Western Thought* (1939).

RAHIT: the SIKH code of discipline accepted by all members of the Khālsā.

RAHNER, Karl (1904-1984): prominent ROMAN CATHOLIC theologian who sought to revive Thomism (*see* Thomas AQUINAS) and used EXISTENTIALISM to express his understanding of theological issues. His major work is the twenty-volume *Theological Investigations* (1961-1981).

RĀHULABHADRA [Rāhula] (6th century B.C.): the legendary son of the BUDDHA.

RAIKES, Robert (1735-1811): English social and religious REFORMER who developed the SUNDAY SCHOOL to educate children of the poor and impart CHRISTIAN knowledge.

RĀJAGRHA: the ancient Indian city which was the scene of the first BUDDHIST Council. It fell into ruins around the seventh century.

RAJNEESH, Bhagwan Sri (1931-1991): a highly successful YOGIC GURU and founder of perhaps the only NEW RELIGIOUS MOVEMENT to claim to have no roots in previous religions and therefore to be completely new. He was born into a JAIN family and appears to have taught philosophy in an Indian college before becoming a professional guru with particular and openly stated appeal to the rich. Preaching self-fulfillment, sexual indulgence and, some claim, the use of drugs, he developed a large following before eventually attempting to flee America after his associates attempted to murder a local district attorney. He was deported to India where he died of unspecified causes. Rajneesh taught an eclectic philosophy which critics called gibberish and was best known for his attempt to build a UTOPIAN community near the small town of Antelope, Oregon.

RĀMA: next to KRISHNA, the most important HINDU GOD and the seventh AVATĀR of VISHNU. He is the supreme example of patience, faithfulness and justice. The saga the RĀMĀYANA describes his exploits.

RAMADĀN: the ninth month of the lunar year in ISLAM. According to tradition it is the month when MUHAMMAD first began to receive the REVELATION of the QUR'ĀN, and it is a time when all Muslims are supposed to fast between each sunrise and sunset.

RĀMAKRISHNA (1836-1886): one of the principal figures in the nineteenth-century HINDU renaissance. He trained in the classical traditions of Hindu MYSTICISM but went beyond the boundaries of Hindu spiritual practice by experiencing ENLIGHTENMENT in a way which embraced both DUALISM and NONDUALISM. He married but claimed to lead a completely "renounced life" without sexual contact. His wife, Śāradā, was known as the "Holy Mother" and was recognized as a SAINT. He abandoned traditional priestly food and taboos, and spoke of his sense of identification with JESUS OF NAZARETH and ALLAH. His most prominent disciple was VIVEKANANDA.

RAMANA, Maharshi (1879-1951): commonly regarded as one of the greatest HINDU SAINTS of the twentieth century. At the age of twenty he settled on the "hill" of Arunacalam near Madras and remained there until his death. He was an Advaita sage who claimed to have experienced the identity of the ĀTMAN and BRAHMAN.

RAMANANDA (13th century): a BRAHMIN who rejected the CASTE system to become a leading advocate of BHAKTI. He sought to synthesize HINDUISM and ISLAM and drew his closest disciples from all walks of life, including amongst them an outcast and two women. His ideas and the movement he founded influenced the development of SIKHISM and several other sectarian groups which renounced caste and promoted Bhakti.

RĀMĀNUJA (1017-1130?): HINDU philosopher and leading opponent of ŚANKARA, whom he attacked for moral laxity and intellectual confusion. He taught a modified version of MONISM which acknowledged GOD and the separate SPIRITS of men as well as the material world or nonspirit. The spirits of men he regarded as essentially different from God, who is both the CREATOR and the material out of which the world is formed. He taught that periodically human spirits are reabsorbed into God, and he distinguished five ways, or stages, of WORSHIP, each successive stage being higher than the other.

RĀMĀYAṆA: with the MAHĀBHĀRATA, this is one of the two great epics of Indian literature. It tells the story of RĀMA and his wife Sītā who is kidnapped by the demon-king of Ceylon. With the help of the monkey king, Rāma eventually slays the demon and rescues his wife, whose loyalty he then questions. Sītā throws herself on a pyre but the fire GOD, Agni, refuses to accept her SACRIFICE, and Rāma realizes her innocence. After he returns to his kingdom and assumes the throne his people again question Sītā's purity, creating doubts which cause Rāma to send her away. She gives birth to twins and asks the earth to swallow her, which it does, thus finally proving her innocence. Years later Rāma recognizes the twins and give them his kingdom, allowing him to return to HEAVEN as VISHNU. The epic is around 24,000 stanzas long and dates from approximately the first century, although sections of it are definitely much later. It is traditionally ascribed to Vālmīki. A version which is far more overtly religious and emphasizes BHAKTI was produced by Tulasi Das in the Hindi language in the sixteenth century.

RAMTHA: the spirit entity which first appeared in 1977 by speaking through the highly successful spiritualist MEDIUM, or transchanneler, J. Z. KNIGHT. It claims to be a warrior from the "lost continents" of Lemuria and Atlantis, making Knight an important figure in the NEW AGE MOVEMENT.

RAND, Ayn (1903-1981): Russian émigrée and OBJECTIVIST philosopher who popularized her views through novels such as *The Fountainhead* (1943), *We the Living* (1935) and *Atlas Shrugged* (1975). Although neglected by most academic philosophers, her views have had an immense influence, strongly promoting INDIVIDUALISM and libertarian political ideas.

RAPTURE: the belief that in the last days believing CHRISTIANS will be removed from the earth before the final TRIBULATION. This is a modern notion based on an interpretation of 1 Thessalonians 4:17, and associated with PREMILLENNIALISM and DISPENSATIONALISM.

RASTAFARIAN: Jamaican religious SECT which believes in the divinity of Ethiopian emperor Haile Selassie and refuses to accept reports of his death. The movement has political overtones and regards the smoking of marijuana a SACRAMENT. Members of the group are accused of involvement in drug trafficking. Their distinctive hairstyle became popular as a result of their music, known as Reggae.

RATIONAL: has the same primary sense as *reasonable;* being endowed with reason or being characterized by REASON.

RATIONALISM: signifies any theological or philosophical position which values REASON as the ultimate arbiter and judge of all statements and therefore rejects the priority of REVELATION. It is a form of SECULAR HUMANISM.

RATIONALIZATION: rational argument constructed to justify behavior.

RAUSCHENBUSCH, Walter (1861-1918): American theologian and social REFORMER regarded as the "father" of the SOCIAL GOSPEL movement. In 1886 he became pastor of a church located on the Lower East Side of New York in an area called "Hell's Kitchen." The sordid living conditions, exploitation of labor and governmental indifference to the poor led him to develop his religious and political theology which he promoted in *Christianity and the Social Crisis* (1907) and *A Theology for the Social Gospel* (1917). His conception of the KINGDOM OF GOD represented an effort to Christianize Darwinian EVOLUTION.

REACTIONARY: right-wing attitudes and positions. It can mean being opposed to REFORMS, wishing to go back to some previous condition or supporting a particular right-wing version of SOCIETY.

REALISM: the theory that maintains that UNIVERSALS have their own EXISTENCE apart from individual objects. It stands in contrast to NOMINALISM, which held that universals had no REALITY apart from their existence in the thought of an individual. Realism has greatly influenced the development of NATURAL THEOLOGY. In modern science realism is the view that SCIENCE actually discovers truth and is not just a set of THEORIES or equations which enable predictions to be made. In this sense realism is the opposite of INSTRU-MENTALISM.

REALITY: what is real; what exists.

REASON: the capacity to reflect, analyze and think in an orderly and logical manner, as opposed to an IRRATIONAL and emotional manner.

REBIRTH: a general term which can mean REINCARNATION, TRANSMIGRATION or some other form of METEMPSYCHOSIS. The term is also used by CHRISTIANS to speak of the experience of CONVERSION, being BORN AGAIN or REGENERATION.

REDEMPTION: the restoring, saving or getting back of something which is lost. The idea is at the heart of many RELIGIONS and is characteristic of CHRISTIANITY, with its idea of sin as rebellion against the will of the CREATOR and the consequent FALL of humanity.

REDFIELD, Robert (1897-1958): American anthropologist who wrote about RELIGION and the differences between urban and rural SOCIETIES in terms of GREAT and LITTLE TRADITIONS. See his *Peasant Society and Culture: An Anthropological Approach to Civilization* (1956).

REDUCTIO AD ABSURDUM: a Latin phrase meaning "to reduce to absurdity." It is used as a technique in argument to show the logical consequences of an opponent's thought.

REDUCTIONISM: to reduce a complex argument or state of affairs to a single or few simple CONCEPTS in such a way as to distort REALITY. An example of reduction-

ism would be the argument that all religious BELIEFS are merely reflections of psychological needs.

REFORM: to strive for improvement and change without making a radical break with the past.

REFORMATION: a term which has come to mean any religious movement which REFORMS a preexisting TRADITION to restore its primitive purity or ORTHODOXY. More specifically it is associated with the religious movement that began in Germany in 1517 with the protest of Martin LUTHER against the sale of INDULGENCES. It led to the creation of independent CHURCHES which renounced the claims of the PAPACY and sought to return to a thoroughly biblical CHRISTIANITY. The REFORMERS taught that the BIBLE is the only source of FAITH and DOCTRINE, rejected TRANSUBSTANTIATION, the WORSHIP of SAINTS and of MARY, emphasized JUSTIFICATION BY FAITH and proclaimed the PRIESTHOOD OF ALL BELIEVERS. Known as PROTESTANTS because of Luther's protest against widespread corruption in the ROMAN CATHOLIC CHURCH, the Reformation quickly spread throughout Northern Europe. It also made significant inroads into Southern European countries, but there it was eventually defeated by the COUNTER-REFORMATION and the INQUISITION, which ruthlessly persecuted Protestants as HERETICS who were to be burnt at the stake. The movement broke into several branches led by Martin Luther, Ulrich ZWINGLI, John CALVIN and Menno SIMONS.

REFORMED: belonging to a religious group which has undergone a REFORMATION. Today the term is used to speak about one wing of EVANGELICAL CHRISTIANITY which emphasizes the theology of CALVIN and the PURITANS.

REFORMED CHURCH: a member of a family of CHURCHES which trace their roots to that branch of the PROTESTANT REFORMATION associated with the work of John CALVIN. They include PRESBYTERIANS, the DUTCH REFORMED CHURCH, and, to a limited extent, the ANGLICANS.

REFORMED JUDAISM: *see* JUDAISM, MODERN.

REFORMER: someone who seeks REFORM. In RELIGION a reformer is often the person who begins a new religious movement.

REGENERATION: CHRISTIAN term which refers to the belief that believers are reborn spiritually through BAPTISM or a spiritual experience such as CONVERSION.

REID, Thomas (1710-1796): Scottish philosopher whose works *Enquiry into the Human Mind on the Principles of Common-Sense* (1764) and *Essays on the Intellectual Powers of Man* (1785) helped develop Scottish "common sense" philosophy. He opposed HUME for developing a destructive skepticism inherent in the EMPIRICIST notion of ideas, and he offered an alternative EPISTEMOLOGY which sought to defend common sense.

REIFICATION: the act of REIFYING something.

REIFY: to materialize an idea and give it concrete EXISTENCE as though it actually existed, even though it is really no more than a CONCEPT in the mind.

REIMARUS, Herman Samuel (1694-1768): German biblical scholar and "father" of HIGHER CRITICISM who rejected the miraculous elements of the BIBLE and charged biblical writers with outright fraud.

REINCARNATION: a technical term in HINDU and BUDDHIST thought associated with the DOCTRINE of KARMA. It implies the continuation of consciousness after physical DEATH but not necessarily the REBIRTH of a SOUL. In the West, however, it is usually confused with ideas of TRANSMIGRATION of the soul or rebirth through many lifetimes and is promoted by claims that people "remember" their "past lives."

REIYUKAI: a NEW RELIGIOUS MOVEMENT of Japanese origin founded in Tokyo in 1925 by Kubo KAKUTARO and his sister-in-law Kotani KIMI. It promotes a form of BUDDHISM.

RELATIONAL: systems of PHILOSOPHY or THEOLOGY which emphasize the importance of relationships rather than ABSTRACT DOGMA.

RELATIVISM: recognizing the importance of the social environment in determining the content of BELIEFS. Relativism maintains that there are no universal standards of good or bad, right or wrong, truth or error. During the nineteenth century and until the 1960s relativism tended to be reserved for religious and moral issues. But after the publication of KUHN's work it has increasingly been applied to SCIENCE. In popular thought support for relativism is often falsely sought in the theory of RELATIVITY.

RELATIVITY: a theory in physics which refers to space-time curvature. It was proposed by EINSTEIN to explain the NATURE of the UNIVERSE after he had destroyed the notion of absolute space and time: hence the term "relativity." It is often misused by religious writers to imply moral or religious RELATIVISM and the rejection of modern SCIENCE.

RELIC: a RELIGIOUS object, including an object believed to have been associated with a long-dead SAINT or religious leader, or the body or body part of such a person, which is believed to have SUPERNATURAL power and is preserved in a SHRINE which becomes a place of PILGRIMAGE.

RELIGION: hundreds of different definitions of religion exist, each reflecting either a scholarly or a DOGMATIC bias depending in the last resort on the presuppositions of the person making the definition. Religion clearly contains intellectual, RITUAL, SOCIAL and ETHICAL elements, bound together by an explicit or implicit BELIEF in the REALITY of an unseen world, whether this belief be expressed in SUPERNATURALISTIC or IDEALISTIC terms. A number of the more common definitions are:

BERGER, Peter: "the human enterprise

by which a SACRED cosmos is established."

DURKHEIM, Émile: "a unified system of BELIEFS and practices relative to SACRED things."

FRAZER, James: "a propitiation or conciliation of powers superior to man which are believed to direct or control the course of NATURE and human life."

HEGEL, Georg: "the knowledge possessed by the finite mind of its NATURE as ABSOLUTE mind."

JAMES, William: "the BELIEF that there is an unseen order, and that our supreme GOOD lies in harmoniously adjusting ourselves thereto."

KANT, Immanuel: "the recognition of all our duties as divine commands."

MARX, Karl: "the self-conscious and self-feeling of man who has either not found himself or has already lost himself again . . . the general THEORY of the world . . . its logic in a popular form . . . its moral sanction, its solemn completion, its universal ground for consolation and justification. It is the fantastic realization of the human essence."

SCHLEIERMACHER, Friedrich: "a feeling for the infinite" and "a feeling of ABSOLUTE dependence."

STARK, Rodney: "any socially organized pattern of BELIEFS and practices concerning ultimate meaning that assumes the EXISTENCE of the SUPERNATURAL."

WHITEHEAD, Alfred North: "what the individual does with his own solitariness."

WEBER, Max: "to say what it is, is not possible . . . the essence of religion is not even our concern, as we make it our task to study the conditions and effects of a particular type of SOCIAL behavior."

The most useful, however, is that of Ninian SMART: "a set of institutionalized RITUALS with a TRADITION and expressing and/or evoking sacral sentiments directed at a divine or trans-divine focus seen in the context of the human phenomenological environment and at least partially described by MYTHS or by myths and DOCTRINES."

RELIGION, TYPOLOGIES OF: the aim of typologies is to provide scholars with intellectual frameworks for identifying different forms of RELIGION. Although there are many ways in which religions may be classified, the typologies of ABRAMIC RELIGION, YOGIC RELIGION and PRIMAL RELIGION are very useful.

RELIGION AND MODERNITY: several religious reactions to MODERNITY exist. The most important are: the development of a dichotomous view of the world which separates the SACRED from the SECULAR; the VENERATION and support of a historic or authentic TRADITION that is often identified with religious ORTHODOXY; a MILLENARIAN or APOCALYPTIC response which sees the modern age as doomed and looks for SALVATION to the direct intervention of GOD or gods in the affairs of the world; the identification of the modern, or ideas taken to be modern, with religion and the claim that modern values represent the essence of religious values.

RELIGION, TYPOLOGIES OF REACTION TO MODERNITY: in practice religious reactions to MODERNITY often take the form of generating new TRADITIONS or new insights into old traditions; an accommodation to the new which maintains an organic connection to some older tradition; attempts to reject the new and preserve the old or what is seen as ancient traditions; a strident reassertion of old or traditional BELIEFS and practices in a new condensed, "purified" or REDUCTIONIST form; the creation of GROUPS which self-consciously celebrate the modern and denigrate tradition and old ways or beliefs; and, finally, the sponsorship and supervision by the state of CULTS celebrating the state's legitimacy.

RELIGIONSGESCHICHTE: a German term for the HISTORY OF RELIGIONS.

RELIGIOUS STUDIES: because it lacks a

unifying THEORY or accepted METHODS which identify distinct academic disciplines, religious studies is best described as an academic field of study, like African, Asian or black studies, which concentrates on the study of RELIGION in all its aspects. Religious studies grew out of nineteenth-century COMPARATIVE RELIGION which had its roots in CHRISTIAN THEOLOGY and MISSIONARY activity but developed into an almost totally SECULAR field within Western universities.

RENAISSANCE: the "rebirth" of learning which occurred in the late fourteenth and fifteenth centuries in Southern Europe. Although some modern historians question the use of the term, others argue that it faithfully reflects a major change in European values and is a watershed between the medieval and MODERN world.

RENAN, Joseph Ernest (1823-1892): celebrated French intellectual who promoted a new RELIGION of learning and REASON. His *Life of Jesus* (1863) denied the SUPERNATURAL elements in the Gospels and promoted the notion of JESUS OF NAZARETH as a great moral teacher.

REPENTANCE: in CHRISTIAN THEOLOGY the sincere act of repenting for and turning away from SIN and toward GOD, accompanied by a deep-felt anguish and desire to turn to and serve GOD.

REQUIEM: PRAYERS for the dead, often said during a MASS.

RERUM NOVARUM: the famous PAPAL encyclical of May 15, 1891, issued by Pope Leo XII and dealing with social relationships and labor relations.

RESTORATION MOVEMENT: a type of REVITALIZATION MOVEMENT which seeks to revive a RELIGIOUS TRADITION by returning to its pristine state of original purity. The term also refers to an American religious movement arising in the nineteenth century which appealed to CHRISTIAN HOLINESS, a return to NEW TESTAMENT teachings, a belief in Christian unity and a strong commitment to the authority of the Bible as the only guide for CHURCH practice and DOCTRINE. This movement eventually developed into the CHURCHES OF CHRIST and DISCIPLES OF CHRIST. More recently the term has been adopted by various PENTECOSTAL and CHARISMATIC groups who are seeking to both restore vitality to the CHURCH and influence Christians to develop their own distinct society within MODERN PLURALISTIC CULTURES through the development of Christian schools and other institutions.

RESURRECTION: the idea that after DEATH there will be a time when humans are restored to life in such a way that they have a distinct identity and bodily form. This BELIEF is shared by the ABRAMIC RELIGIONS and finds unique expression in the CHRISTIAN claim that JESUS OF NAZARETH rose from the dead after his execution by the Romans.

RESURRECTION OF CHRIST: the cornerstone belief of CHRISTIANITY which maintains that JESUS OF NAZARETH was resurrected from the dead after having been crucified, dead and buried. This finished his work of SALVATION and FORGIVENESS OF SIN for humankind and assures believers that they will be resurrected after death.

RETALIATION: in the QUR'ĀN, *Sūra* XVII.35, the right of vengeance is prescribed. This is similar to the HEBREW BIBLE teaching of "an eye for an eye" (Exodus 21:24), and stands in sharp contrast to CHRISTIAN views about forgiveness expressed by JESUS OF NAZARETH as recorded in Matthew 5:38-48.

REVELATION: the act whereby GOD discloses himself and his will to humankind. In JUDAISM revelation comes through the HEBREW BIBLE, in CHRISTIANITY through the Hebrew Bible and NEW TESTAMENT, while in ISLAM the QUR'ĀN is the only source of revelation. HINDUISM associates revelation with Śruti or "what is heard" and has increasingly seen this in connection with the VEDAS, UPANISHADS and other religious literature. BUDDHISM treats the sayings of the BUDDHA as a form of revelation, although it denies the involvement of God, while JAINISM denies all SUPERNATURAL sources of revelation. In other religious traditions revelation comes from ANCESTORS and gods for specific purposes. Traditionally the ABRAMIC religions have claimed that revelation ended with the CANON of their SCRIPTURES. Claims about continuing revelation have led to REVITALIZATION MOVEMENTS and religious REVIVALISM and often provoked the wrath of the orthodox, who saw such claims as HERESY. Recently such ideas have become popular in certain branches of the Christian CHARISMATIC MOVEMENT where PROPHETS and PROPHECY are increasingly common phenomena.

REVITALIZATION MOVEMENTS: any movement which sets out to revive a religious tradition; attempts on the part of previously acculturated groups to regain and reaffirm early religious traditions which are often SYNCRETISTIC in doctrine and ceremonial.

REVIVALISM: outbreaks of intense, often mass, religious excitement, which seek to revive and restore a religious tradition that is believed to be in decline. Revivalism can often take the form of a REVITALIZATION MOVEMENT.

REVOLUTION: indicating fundamental changes, new developments or a turning around of the SOCIAL order. In recent years the term *revolution* has been used to describe changes in SCIENCE, PHILOSOPHY and, following the work of Thomas KUHN, in terms of PARADIGMS. This usage has been increasingly criticized by other scholars, who see gradual development rather than sudden change as the norm.

ṚG VEDA: the most ancient book of HINDUISM which consists of four collections of VEDIC HYMNS. It is usually said to have been composed before 900 B.C. and preserved in ORAL TRADITION until written down in the sixteenth century, originally by MUSLIMS, and in the eighteenth and nineteenth centuries by British antiquarians and MISSIONARIES. The hymns were used in SACRIFICIAL RITUALS by BRAHMINS and are treated as eternally existent. There are 1,028 hymns which refer to the GODS, the most important of which are INDRA, AGNI, VARUṆA and SOMA. VISHNU and RUDRA are present but as minor DEITIES. Many scholars see a tendency toward MONOTHEISM in the hymns. The *Ṛg Veda* was translated into English by Max MÜLLER and H. Oldenberg in the 1890s from SACRED TEXTS written in a language which predated classical SANSKRIT.

RHETORIC: the art of speech and argument involving the correct understanding and use of such means as METAPHOR and METONYMY. TRADITIONALLY a major subject in universities, rhetoric has been scorned by academics, particularly PHILOSOPHERS, throughout most of the twentieth century. Recently, however, there has been a major revival of interest in rhetoric, such as Brian Vickers, *In Defense of Rhetoric* (1989).

RICCI, Matteo (1552-1610): highly successful JESUIT MISSIONARY to China who assumed the role of a Confucian scholar (*see* CONFUCIUS) and adapted CHRISTIANITY to Chinese customs and CULTURE. His most famous work was *The True Knowledge of God* (1603).

RIG VEDA: *see* ṚG VEDA.

RIGHTEOUSNESS: an important CONCEPT in ABRAMIC RELIGIONS where it is seen as an ATTRIBUTE of GOD wherein he is the absolute standard or is consistent with the requirements of any given relationship. In EVANGELICAL CHRISTIANITY it is a divine gift of right standing before God given to the sinner who repents and has FAITH in CHRIST. It is also important in Chinese and Japanese religions where it is one of the four cardinal VIRTUES and the mark of a superior man.

RINZAI: one of the two most important SECTS in ZEN BUDDHISM; it was founded in China in the ninth century and introduced to Japan during the twelfth century. It is distinguished by the practice of SÔTÔ and use of unorthodox means to attain ENLIGHTENMENT.

RISHI: the Sanskrit term for a seer or a SPIRITUALLY knowledgeable person. The term is used of the composers of the ṚG VEDA.

RITSCHL, Albrecht (1822-1889): major LIBERAL or MODERNIST German PROTESTANT theologian who rejected all forms of NATURAL THEOLOGY, MYSTICISM and METAPHYSICS, arguing that THEOLOGY must concentrate on moral and ethical issues. He interpreted JUSTIFICATION and forgiveness of SINS as something achieved through the CHURCH, the community for which JESUS died, and sin as selfishness or human deeds that are in opposition to the achievement of the KINGDOM OF GOD. CHRIST's death therefore was no longer to be viewed as a PROPITIATION for sin but rather as the sharing of his consciousness of Sonship. In all of this Ritschl rejected traditional views of ORIGINAL SIN, INCARNATION, REVELATION, RESURRECTION and the church. He also created a chasm between the Jesus of HISTORY and the Christ of FAITH. His major works include *The Christian Doctrine of Justification and Reconciliation* (1876-1874) and *The History of Pietism* (1880-1885, 3 vols.).

RITUAL: SACRED custom or any form of repetitive behavior which is fixed by TRADITION. In the study of RELIGION it means "traditional religious behavior or actions." The ritual element in religion cannot easily be separated from FAITH and BELIEF. Religious ritual presupposes the existence of a SUPERNATURAL or divine order, revealed by natural occurrences such as the alternation of life and death, day and night, the movements of heavenly bodies and the progression of the seasons. Rituals are of many types, but common to them all is the conviction that what is being done on earth approximates the divine or supernaturally revealed order. Religious REFORMATIONS or REVITALIZATION MOVEMENTS often interpret their own reactions against the ritual expressions of another group as a total

rejection of ritual, but in reality ritual is not left behind. The PLYMOUTH BRETHREN reject the ROMAN CATHOLIC MASS on theological grounds as "dead ritual," yet, in fact, their own services have many rituals even though the participants usually do not recognize the fact. Each ritual corresponds to, and must be understood in terms of, a body of convictions concerning the divine and humankind, and the relationship between the two.

ROBINSON, John A. T. (1919-1983): controversial ANGLICAN theologian and biblical scholar, and BISHOP of Woolwich whose book *Honest to God* (1963) created a theological sensation by its blunt denial of TRADITIONAL CHRISTIAN BELIEFS and DOCTRINES. Although radical in that work, he eventually reached CONSERVATIVE conclusions with respect to biblical scholarship. This included his *Redating the New Testament* (1976), a work which he began critically but in which, after studying the evidence, he accepted the essential historicity and early date of the NEW TESTAMENT. His last book, published posthumously, was *The Priority of John* (1985).

ROMAN CATHOLICISM: in the past it was fairly easy to describe Catholicism. Recent developments make this a much more complex task. The doctrinal statements of the church may be found in the decrees of the Council of TRENT, the CREED of Pope Pius IV, the decrees of the VATICAN COUNCILS, papal utterances claiming INFALLIBILITY and Roman Catholic CANON LAW. Alongside these the LITURGY and hierarchical organization of the CHURCH shape the nature of Roman Catholicism. In this tradition the SACRAMENTS, administered by the church, are channels of GRACE flowing from God to the believer. There are seven sacraments: BAPTISM, CONFIRMATION, the MASS, holy orders, PENANCE, matrimony and extreme unction. The focal point of Roman Catholic WORSHIP is the mass. It is interpreted as TRANSUBSTANTIATION, a DOGMA first promulgated in 1215, which asserts that the SUBSTANCE of the bread and wine used in the RITUAL become the actual body, blood, SOUL and divinity of CHRIST. Confession, which is made to PRIESTS, has played a central role in Roman Catholicism. In the sixteenth century confession was linked to the doctrine of PURGATORY and led to the sale of INDULGENCES for the forgiveness of SINS. It was this practice and related abuses which led to the REFORMATION. Another prominent feature is the adoration of MARY, which, many scholars argue, possibly stems from the mother GODDESS of the Mediterranean world who bore such titles as "Star of the Sea" and played the role of "Our Lady" of various cities.

ROMANTICISM: a movement in art, literature, PHILOSOPHY and RELIGION, in the latter eighteenth and early nineteenth centuries. It was sentimental, full of expression and idealized melancholy. The movement arose as a reaction to the RATIONALISM of the ENLIGHTENMENT, against which it stressed emotionalism, sensualism, fantasy and imagination over rational order and control. REALITY was to be found through feeling, immediate experience, spiritual illumination, brooding and listening to the inner voices. Romantics had a deep interest in the past, especially in the Middle Ages and non-classical and Nordic worlds, mythology, folklore and PRIMITIVISM. They published medieval historical records and literature. The impact of romanticism on religion and THEOLOGY is immense. In America it stimulated TRANSCENDENTALISM and an interest in Eastern religions; in Britain the Romantics tended to view the CHURCH with indifference or join the OXFORD MOVEMENT; in Germany the majority moved toward a Germanic NATIONALISM.

ROSARY: a device, usually consisting of a string of beads, used in many RELIGIONS as an aid to PRAYER. Its use seems to have originated in HINDUISM, from where it spread to BUDDHISM and ISLAM before finally entering CHRISTIANITY.

ROSICRUCIANS: the Order of the Rosy Cross, which was publicized in two books by a LUTHERAN pastor Johann Valentin Andreae (1586-1654) as an ancient secret society possessing ESOTERIC knowledge. The idea was taken up by various thinkers, including DESCARTES and COMENIUS, but no organization was ever discovered. In the late nineteenth century various OCCULT groups claiming to be Rosicrucians emerged, promoting a hodgepodge of religious ideas, including REINCARNATION. Scholars do not believe that any of these groups can be linked with an ancient society.

ROUSSEAU, Jean-Jacques (1712-1778): radical French philosopher who advocated DEISM and a SOCIALIST vision of SOCIETY. Although he wrote at great length in an influential book, *Émile* (1762), about the education of children, he abandoned his own children to almost certain death in the workhouse. His important political work *The Social Contract* (1762) contains a chapter entitled "CIVIL RELIGION" which has provoked renewed debate in recent years.

ROY, RAM MOHAN (1774-1833): a Bengali BRAHMIN educated in England who showed a rationalistic inclination and accepted MONOTHEISM after studying at a MUSLIM institution in Patna. He admired the NEW TESTAMENT and CHRISTIAN ETHICS but rejected CHRIST's divinity. Convinced that the UPANISHADS taught monotheism and were free from social abuses, he founded the Brāhmo Samāj in 1828 for the propagation of his religious and social views. He died in Bristol, England.

RTA: the COSMIC moral order which, in the VEDAS, sustains the UNIVERSE.

RUDRA: a sinister and warlike GOD found in the ṚG VEDA who is described as "the howler" and depicted in bloodthirsty ways as the god of storms. Many scholars believe Rudra developed into the HINDU god ŚIVA.

RUSHDOONY, Rousas John (1916-): an American of Armenian descent, he was a theological LIBERAL who was converted to orthodox CALVINISM through the writings of the REFORMED theologian and apologist Cornelius Van Til. Ordained a PRESBYTERIAN minister, he is the leader of an increasingly influential group of Christian "reconstructionists" who propose radical measures to restore BIBLICAL law as the basis of SOCIETY. His *Intellectual Schizophrenia: Culture Crisis and Education* (1961) has been influential in promoting Christian schools, while *This Independent Republic* (1964) was his first major work on political issues. More recently his views have been developed in *The Institutes of Biblical Law* (1973, 1978, 2 vols.) and through his newsletter *The Chalcedon Report*.

RUSKIN, John (1819-1900): English ROMANTIC essayist and critic of INDIVIDUALISM and industrialization whose work *Unto This Last* (1862) influenced TOLSTOY and GANDHI. He rejected CHRISTIANITY and espoused a MYSTICAL form of SOCIALISM which glorified the past as an alternative.

RUSSELL, Bertrand Arthur William Earl (1872-1970): British philosopher. Given a strict and puritanical upbringing by his paternal grandmother, at Cambridge he was gradually disillusioned and abandoned his early religious BELIEFS. His many writings include *Principia Mathematica* (1903) and *Why I Am Not a Christian* (1957).

RUSSELL, Charles Taze (1852-1916): founder of JEHOVAH'S WITNESSES, he is also known as "PASTOR Russell." He grew up in a pious CONGREGATIONALIST home but rejected his early beliefs after a SECULAR CONVERSION. He retained his love for the BIBLE, eventually developing his own system which centered on the issue of PROPHECY. He formed his own independent CONGREGATION in 1878. Preaching that the Second Coming of CHRIST had oc-

curred invisibly in 1874, he predicted the end of the world would come in 1914. Eventually his followers became known as Russellites and formed the International Bible Students' Association, which later split into a number of groups, the best known being the JEHOVAH'S WITNESSES.

RUTHERFORD, Joseph Franklin, "Judge" (1869-1941): the successor to Charles Taze RUSSELL as leader of the Watchtower Bible and Tract Society and true founder of the JEHOVAH'S WITNESSES. His numerous books and other publications, plus radio broadcasts and able leadership, made the organization the world community it is today.

RUTHERFORD, Samuel (1600-1661): Scottish COVENANTER and theologian whose *Lex Rex* (1644) has been taken by many religious CONSERVATIVES in America to be the inspiration for the American Constitution. Few modern historians, however, would accept such an interpretation, pointing to his intolerance of ROMAN CATHOLICISM and religious diversity.

RYLE, Gilbert (1900-1976): English philosopher who regarded METAPHYSICS as an example of "CATEGORY MISTAKES." His book *The Concept of Mind* (1949) attacks Cartesian DUALISM and other ideas that might promote a belief in the SOUL.

RYLE, John Charles (1816-1900): English EVANGELICAL leader and BISHOP of Liverpool, England, whose books *Practical Religion* (1878) and *Holiness* (1890) are viewed as SPIRITUAL classics by many evangelicals.

RYOBU-SHINTŌ: a SYNCRETISTIC movement which sought to unify Japanese SHINTŌ with BUDDHISM. It was suppressed during the Meiji period, from 1868 to 1912, although certain forms still prosper today.

S

SABBATARIAN: someone who rigidly keeps the SABBATH. The term is usually applied to CHRISTIANS who argue that Sunday should be observed as a SACRED day.

SABBATH: the SACRED day in JUDAISM (both ancient and modern), requiring a complete cessation from all work. It was observed by GOD in Genesis 2:2-3 and commanded as part of his COVENANT with the people of ISRAEL in Exodus 20 and Deuteronomy 5. In CHRISTIANITY the day of worship became Sunday in order to commemorate the RESURRECTION OF CHRIST.

SABELLIANISM: an early CHRISTIAN HERESY which insisted on the unity of the Godhead by arguing that the persons of the TRINITY were actually different modes or operations of GOD.

SACH-KHAND: the realm of TRUTH and harmony in the SIKH tradition. It is attained after many REBIRTHS through the repetition of the divine name.

SACRAMENT: a rite in which GOD (or the gods) is uniquely active. AUGUSTINE OF HIPPO defined a CHRISTIAN sacrament as "a visible sign of an invisible REALITY." The ANGLICAN BOOK OF COMMON PRAYER speaks of "an outward and visible sign of an inward and invisible GRACE." Examples of sacraments would be BAPTISM and the Eucharist, or MASS.

SACRED: that which is set apart; the HOLY. It refers to that which belongs to GOD, the deity, or the SUPERNATURAL, as opposed to the SECULAR or profane. The sacred person, object or place must always be treated with the greatest care and respect. Often PURIFICATION rites must be performed before that which is sacred can be approached.

SACRED TEXTS: the ABRAMIC RELIGIONS are "religions of the Book," which means that they are all based on a REVELATION which their followers BELIEVE to be DIVINELY INSPIRED. Traditionally, the YOGIC RELIGIONS were based on oral TRADITIONS and not sacred texts. BUDDHISM honored scholarship and the transmission of its DOCTRINES in writing while HINDUS scorned written texts. As a result there are many Buddhist manuscripts from the seventh century A.D. and some even earlier. But the earliest manuscripts of Hindu SCRIPTURES date from the sixteenth century A.D. ISLAM has texts which go back to the seventh century, while both JUDAISM and CHRISTIANITY have a few manuscripts from as early as the second century B.C. (Qumran) and many from the fourth century A.D. onward. In general it is easy to obtain information about extant Abramic (the text-critical scholarship on Hebrew and Greek scriptures is extensive) and Buddhist texts but almost impossible to trace the sources for Hindu texts which were investigated by various nineteenth-century scholars, like Max MÜLLER, but have been largely ignored ever since.

SACRIFICE: the act of dedicating a person, animal or thing to a deity to create a bond of friendship, or influence or propitiate the deity. Sacrifices may take many forms but often involve the spilling of blood and death of the victim. Literal sacrifices persist in HINDUISM and many other religions, such as AFRICAN TRADITIONAL RELIGIONS, but have been abandoned in orthodox forms of CHRISTIANITY and JUDAISM, where the language of sacrifice is now used to refer to prayer or to express the act whereby DEVOTEES dedicate their lives to the service of GOD. In ISLAM animals are sacrificed at an annual festival held in memory of ABRAHAM's willingness to sacrifice his son.

SADDUCEES: originating in the second century B.C., they were a religious and political group that rejected belief in the RESURRECTION, ANGELS and SPIRITS. The sect disappeared after the destruction of Jerusalem in A.D. 70. In the NEW TESTAMENT they are depicted as the opponents of JESUS.

SAINT: the Greek term, *hagios*, which stands behind this English word, is used in the NEW TESTAMENT to refer to a believer in CHRIST. Subsequently it came to mean a HOLY person.

ST. BARTHOLOMEW'S DAY MASSACRE: on August 24, 1572, French Catholics slaughtered HUGUENOT leaders and thousands of their followers.

SAINT-SIMON, Claude-Henri (1760-1828): French SOCIALIST philosopher who sought to promote a new form of RELIGION devoid of the SUPERNATURAL trappings of CHRISTIANITY. He strongly influenced Auguste COMTE, whose works develop Saint-Simon's program. His books include *The Reorganization of European Society* (1814) and *The New Christianity* (1825).

ŚAIVISM: the WORSHIP of Śiva in HINDUISM. The CULT of Śiva appears to have roots in the INDUS VALLEY CIVILIZATION before the ARYAN invasions. In classical Hinduism two very different forms of Śaivism emerged. The first gave it ideological sophistication through the MONISM of ŚANKARA and VEDĀNTA, out of which a TANTRIC TRADITION also developed. The second major tradition of Śaivism was a Tamil version which emphasized BHAKTI and a dualistic type of MONOTHEISM.

ŚAKTI: the HINDU CONCEPT of power or the creative force of GOD which is usually seen as female and represented by KĀLĪ and Śiva.

ŚAKTISM: the CULT of ŚAKTI, in which female DEITIES become the focus of popular PIETY.

ŚĀKYAS: the Indian tribe to which GAUTAMA (BUDDHA) belonged.

SALISBURY, John of (1115-1180): English ecclesiastic, SCHOLASTIC philosopher and political theorist.

SALMĀN (7th century): semi-legendary figure who is seen in ISLAM as an ideal seeker after TRUTH because of his CONVERSION after contact with MUḤAMMAD.

SALVATION: deliverance from disease, EVIL or spiritual bondage. JUDAISM and ISLAM regard it as the result of obedience to the law of GOD as expressed in their respective SCRIPTURES. In CHRISTIANITY salvation is achieved through God's grace to anyone who has FAITH in the saving work of CHRIST in his DEATH upon the cross. It sees salvation as the forgiveness of SIN, reconciliation with God, a total healing of the person, and the gift of a new life in the KINGDOM OF GOD. HINDUISM and BUDDHISM essentially see salvation as release from SAMSĀRA through a breaking of the bonds of KARMA.

SALVATION ARMY: an EVANGELICAL CHRISTIAN movement founded in nineteenth-century Britain by "General" William BOOTH to work among the poor and oppressed. From the beginning, the evangelistic efforts of the Army concentrated on practical steps to improve the lot of the poor as well as on proclaiming the GOSPEL to them. A strong but nonmoralistic stance was taken against alcohol and other forms of drug abuse, homes were provided for the homeless, and other chronic social needs were met. Although a numerically small group, the Army has gained great respect throughout the world.

SAMĀDHI: a BUDDHIST term meaning "concentration" which is used in connection with MEDITATION; it refers to the act of focusing one's attention on a single object.

SAMARITANS: the descendants of the inhabitants of the northern kingdom of ISRAEL, who had intermarried with local colonists after many Jews were deported by their conquerors. Jews from the southern province of Judea viewed them with scorn and enmity because of their lack of racial purity. The Samaritans refused to recognize the TEMPLE in JERUSALEM as the center of WORSHIP, and they built their own temple on Mount Gerizim. They accepted their own version of the PENTA-TEUCH but rejected other parts of the HEBREW BIBLE. Today two small communities of Samaritans survive, one at Nablus and the other near Tel Aviv.

SĀMAVEDA: the second of four collections of VEDIC HYMNS consisting essentially of verses from the RG VEDA arranged in liturgical form (see LITURGY) to be sung during RITUALS of SACRIFICE.

SĀMKHYA: one of the six traditional schools of HINDU PHILOSOPHY. It is dualistic, and it teaches the TRANSMIGRATION of SOULS and a complex cosmology based on periodic cycles of CREATION and destruction.

SAMSĀRA: the wheel of REBIRTH in YOGIC RELIGIONS. It is the passing through successive lives as a consequence of the actions of KARMA. Bondage is implied and LIBERATION seen as release from both the bonds of Karma and Samsāra.

SAMURAI: Japanese warrior class who lived by the Confucian ethic (see CONFUCIUS) and adopted ZEN BUDDHISM.

SAN CH'ING: Chinese name for the three supreme TAOIST DEITIES who rule the UNIVERSE.

SANCTIFICATION: from the Latin word *sanctus* meaning HOLY. Sanctification describes the process believed by CHRISTIANS to begin when new life is imparted to the believer by the HOLY SPIRIT following their BAPTISM or CONVERSION. It implies release from the compulsive power of SIN and guilt and a gaining of the ability to love GOD and one's neighbor.

SANGHA: the order of MONKS in BUDDHISM.

ŚANKARA (788-838): Indian BRAHMIN philosopher and advocate of VEDĀNTA who founded a number of monasteries in India and seems to have regarded ŚIVA and VISHNU as equal manifestations of the universal spirit. He taught the illusory nature of the separate EXISTENCE of the spirit of man from the BRAHMAN and emphasized that MĀYĀ existed from all eternity as the only material or substantial CAUSE of the external world. His views were savagely attacked by RĀMĀNUJA, who accused him of being a crypto-BUDDHIST and claimed that his intellect was warped through sexual perversions.

SANKEY, Ira David (1840-1908): singing American EVANGELIST who worked closely with Dwight L. MOODY. His sentimental HYMNS, or "gospel songs," became the standard music of many EVANGELICAL churches until the 1970s.

SANNYĀSIN: a person who has moved on to the last of the four stages of life in classical HINDUISM to become a wandering HOLY man. The term was adopted by Bhagwan Sri RAJNEESH to refer to initiates of his organization.

SANSKRIT: the classical language of India which became the HOLY language of HINDUISM, although the earliest Hindu SCRIPTURES such as the ṚG VEDA and many later BHAKTI works are not actually written in it. It is also the original language of many early BUDDHIST texts, although most of these have been preserved in translation only.

SANTAYANA, George (1863-1952): Spanish-born American materialist philosopher (*see* MATERIALISM) who believed that, although MATTER is the source of all things, the realm of the spirit exists, and that RELIGION is important because of the order and psychological comfort its RITUAL gives to life. His books include *Realms of Being* (1940).

SAOSHYANTS: the SAVIOR figure in ZOROASTRIANISM.

SARGANT, William (1918-1988): British psychiatrist whose book *The Battle for the Mind* (1957) was a sustained attack on EVANGELICAL CHRISTIAN CONVERSION as a form of BRAINWASHING. His work was a response to the success of the Billy GRAHAM Crusade in England in 1951 and was critiqued by Martyn LLOYD-JONES in his *Conversions, Psychological and Spiritual* (1959).

ŚĀRIPUTRA [Śāriputta] (6th century B.C.): chief disciple of GAUTAMA (BUDDHA).

SARTRE, Jean-Paul (1905-1980): French novelist and radical, nihilistic, EXISTENTIALIST philosopher whose novels, such as *Nausea* (1938), spoke to a generation of Europeans following World War II. He was a student of HEIDEGGER; his major philosophical works were *Being and Nothingness* (1943) and *Critique of Dialectical Reason* (1960).

SĀSANA: a BUDDHIST term for what is usually translated as RELIGION in the West.

SATAN: as used in the book of JOB in the HEBREW BIBLE the meaning is "the adversary." As the term developed it took on the meaning of the DEVIL or the personalized force of EVIL who entices humankind

away from the service and love of GOD.

SATAN, CHURCH OF: an American RELIGIOUS MOVEMENT founded in 1966 by Anton La Vey. Intensely INDIVIDUALISTIC, it teaches indulgence, vengeance, physical gratification and the attainment of personal power.

SATANISM: ESOTERIC religious groups who WORSHIP SATAN. They are often associated with RITUAL SACRIFICE and unconventional sexual practices. Satanic groups include the Church of Satan (*see* SATAN, CHURCH OF) and various organizations emphasizing ritual MAGIC.

SATĪ [Suttee]: a HINDU woman who commits SUICIDE on her husband's funeral pyre. The practice was condemned by the SIKHS, CHRISTIAN MISSIONARIES like William CAREY, who was prominent in the campaign for its abolition, and various Hindu REFORMERS such as Ram Mohan ROY. It was banned by the British in 1829 as a result of agitation by Christian missionaries and is illegal in modern India, although considerable evidence exists that it still continues.

SATORI: the Japanese term for BUDDHIST ENLIGHTENMENT.

SATURN: the Roman GOD of agriculture.

SAUTRĀNTIKA: a HĪNAYĀNA school of BUDDHIST PHILOSOPHY that emerged during the second century. It rejected the Abhidarma and taught that the SŪTRAS alone were authoritative.

SAVONAROLA, Girolamo (1452-1498): Italian REFORMER whose oratorical skill brought him temporary fame before he was burnt as a HERETIC for his criticism of the ROMAN CATHOLIC CHURCH.

SAYYID: the title given to the physical descendants of MUḤAMMAD through his daughter FĀTIMA.

SCAPEGOAT: the RITUAL found in the HEBREW BIBLE (Leviticus 16) whereby on the day of ATONEMENT the high PRIEST transfers the SINS of the people of ISRAEL onto a goat, which is then driven into the desert to die. Analogous practices are found in other cultures. Today the term is applied to any individual or group that takes the blame for the actions or misfortunes of another.

SCARAB: the beetle AMULET of ancient Egypt.

SCENARIO: term popular with futurists to denote a possible future or model of the future based on present trends and historical ANALOGIES.

SCHAEFFER, Francis August (1912-1983): highly successful Christian EVANGELIST in the REFORMED tradition and founder of the L'Abri community. A self-professed FUNDAMENTALIST influenced by Princeton THEOLOGY and the PHILOSOPHY of DOOYEWEERD, he moved from a religious ghetto to embrace the world as a speaker comfortable with heated debate, leading a revival of EVANGELICAL interest in philosophy and the arts. His books, which include *The God Who Is There* (1968), *The Church at the End of the Twentieth Century* (1970) and *True Spirituality* (1971), fail to convey the full impact of his charismatic personality.

SCHELER, Max (1874-1928): German PHENOMENOLOGIST and philosopher who converted to ROMAN CATHOLICISM. His work stressed the spiritual nature of REALITY and strongly influenced both CONZE and STOKER. His major book is *On the Eternal in Man* (1921).

SCHELLING, Friedrich Wilhelm Joseph (1775-1854): German philosopher and spokesman of ROMANTICISM whose PANTHEISM saw NATURE as a self-motivated, vitalistic force. His vague spirituality and interest in MYTH contributed to the development of German NATIONALISM and RACISM. His works include *Ideas for a Philosophy of Nature* (1797), *Philosophy of Religion* (1804) and *Of Human Freedom* (1809).

SCHISM: a term used to describe a division of opinion or religious dispute that leads to the creation of a new religious movement.

SCHLEGEL, Carl Wilhelm Friedrich von (1772-1829): German Romantic poet who converted to ROMAN CATHOLICISM. Coining the term *romantic* in 1778 to describe what had previously been called "interested" literature, he set the tone for an entire generation of writers. He developed an interest in MYTH and PANTHEISM, and in 1803 he went to Paris where he studied SANSKRIT, which he believed was the root language of humankind. During this period he came to believe that European civilization was doomed, and he looked to the East, particularly to India, for cultural salvation. These ideas were expressed in his influential *On the Language and Wisdom of India* (1808). Later, however, through his study of medieval paintings, he returned to CHRISTIANITY. Extolling the Middle Ages as an ideal period of human civilization, he rejected his earlier religious views as "pseudoreligion."

SCHLEIERMACHER, Friedrich Daniel Ernst (1768-1834): the most important German PROTESTANT theologian of the nineteenth century and the founder of modern LIBERAL THEOLOGY. He rose to fame following the publication of his *On Religion: Speeches to Its Cultured Despisers* (1799) where he defines RELIGION as the "feeling" or "sense" of ABSOLUTE dependence and separates the study of religion from SCIENCE and other academic disciplines. His work set the tone for the rejection of NATURAL THEOLOGY and the development of nontraditional theological systems which reinterpreted CHRISTIANITY in terms of the MODERN age, a project he began in *The Christian Faith* (1821-1822).

SCHLINK, Basilea (1904-): German CHARISMATIC writer and cofounder in 1945 of the LUTHERAN Evangelical Sisterhood of Mary in Darmstadt. Her books include *Realities of Faith* (1966) and her autobiography, *I Found the Key to the Heart of God* (1975).

SCHLICK, Moritz (1882-1936): German philosopher and acknowledged leader of the VIENNA CIRCLE.

SCHMIDT, Wilhelm (1868-1954): Austrian historian of RELIGIONS and anthropologist (*see* ANTHROPOLOGY) who for many years edited *Anthropos*. The work of this ROMAN CATHOLIC PRIEST and member of the Society of the Divine Word has been neglected by many secular scholars because they assume his religious convictions must have biased his work. Such a conclusion is unfortunate and by no means certain. A prolific writer who argued that the original religion of mankind was MONOTHEISM, Schmidt is best known for his provocative study *The Origin and Growth of Religion: Facts and Theories* (1931).

SCHOLASTIC: derived from SCHOLASTICISM, following the PROTESTANT REFORMATION it became a term of abuse, implying dead arguments based on logic unrelated to real life.

SCHOLASTICISM: a term applied to medieval CHRISTIAN PHILOSOPHY.

SCHOPENHAUER, Arthur (1788-1860): the first German or modern Western philosopher to draw upon Indian PHILOSOPHY for inspiration. Deeply pessimistic, he embraced the concept of MĀYĀ and rejected all appeals to HISTORY as a basis for philosophy. A scathing critic of HEGEL whom he saw as a pedestrian lackey of the Prussian State, he developed a CONCEPT of the will which influenced such thinkers as NIETZSCHE, FREUD and MERLEAU-PONTY and saw women as the servants of men. His major work is *The World as Will and Idea* (1819 and 1844).

SCHULLER, Robert (1926-): minister in the Reformed Church of America and well-known television evangelist who has promoted a mild form of POSITIVE THINKING based on his understanding of the Bible. His books include *Move Ahead with Possibility Thinking* (1967) and *The New Reformation* (1982).

SCHWEITZER, Albert (1875-1965): Alsatian musical genius, philosopher, theologian and medical doctor who established a MISSIONARY hospital in French Equatorial Africa where he labored most of his life. His major theological work, *The Quest of the Historical Jesus* (1909), demonstrated the failure of the LIBERAL theological enterprise and advocated an understanding of JESUS as a misdirected APOCALYPTIC teacher who proclaimed the imminent arrival of the KINGDOM OF GOD.

SCIENCE: in the English-speaking world science has come to be associated particularly with the physical sciences such as physics and chemistry, but the meaning of the term is much wider, namely the systematic classification of knowledge. Science as knowledge needs to be distinguished from both technology and the SCIENTIFIC METHOD. Science is not scientific knowledge or discoveries, but the method used in acquiring that knowledge and in making discoveries.

SCIENCE FICTION: a futuristic story which explores the possible application of science to human affairs and often involves space travel to other worlds or galaxies. Science fiction has played an important role in encouraging the growth of many NEW RELIGIOUS MOVEMENTS such as SCIENTOLOGY. Popular television series such as "Star Trek" are examples of science fiction which also have religious and moral implications, given the commitment of the series to a form of cultural RELATIVISM and its frequent appeal to SPIRITUAL forces. The two major branches of science fiction are science fiction proper, which concentrates on technology, and science fantasy, which invokes OCCULT explanations and stories about beings like fairies.

SCIENTIFIC METHOD: although there are many different methods used in various academic disciplines, the term *scientific method* refers to that process of systematic inquiry which proceeds in a logical manner and involves the testing of theories against the available evidence. It implies an initial SKEPTICISM and an openness of mind before the facts or relevant evidence. Scientific explanations generate testable observations which may be checked against relevant evidence. A THEORY may be called scientific only if it is possible to specify the observations which would prove it to be false. In the context of academic work, *research* therefore means systematic observation for the purpose of testing a theory or theories.

SCIENTISM: the WORSHIP of SCIENCE, or the claim that only scientific knowledge is VALID or true knowledge.

SCIENTOLOGY: a controversial therapy based on a NEW RELIGIOUS MOVEMENT founded by Ron HUBBARD, who in many respects was a modern SHAMAN. It aims at applying religious PHILOSOPHY to recover spirituality and increase individual ability. Originally called DIANETICS, it maintains that the human mind is capable of resolving any and all problems through humans becoming their own SAVIORS and freeing their inner spiritual being, or "theatan." Scientology uses the language of SCIENCE to promote a Westernized version of YOGIC RELIGION supported by the rich MYTHOLOGY found in Hubbard's SCIENCE FICTION novels. Although many attempts have been made to deny the religious nature of Scientology, it has too many features of actual RELIGIONS to be dismissed as a pious fraud or SECULAR philosophy.

SCOFIELD, Cyrus Ingerson (1843-1921): American lawyer and PASTOR who edited the influential *Scofield Reference Bible*, an annotated version of the King James Bible which he published in 1909 with the financial assistance of prominent businessmen. His BIBLE became the standard text of American FUNDAMENTALISM, where it helped promote DISPENSATIONALISM, and it also strongly influenced the PLYMOUTH BRETHREN movement.

SCOTT, Walter, Sir (1771-1832): Scottish leader of British ROMANTICISM whose poetry, novels and biographies created an idealized view of the Middle Ages which reinforced resistance to industrialization and SCIENCE. His first historical novel, *Waverley* (1814), was followed by *Rob Roy* (1817) and *Ivanhoe* (1819), all of which encouraged NATIONALISM and a rejection of MODERNITY. Religiously his work contributed to the popularity of the OXFORD MOVEMENT and the revival of ROMAN CATHOLICISM in Britain.

SCRIPTURE: writings regarded as SACRED. They form the basis of religious BELIEF and practice and are usually regarded as given by GOD through either INSPIRATION or REVELATION.

SECT: an important term which is often loosely used to mean a religious group that has broken away from an older TRADITION. Confusion is created by the fact that it is sometimes used theologically to refer to groups of questionable ORTHODOXY or outright HERESY. Sociologically the term has been contrasted with CHURCH, DENOMINATION and CULT; Rodney STARK defines a sect as "a religious group which lives in a state of relatively high tension with the surrounding society that has a prior tie with another religious organization and was founded by someone who left that organization."

SECULAR: what is profane; the worldly, civil or nonreligious, as distinguished from RELIGION or the SACRED.

SECULARIZATION: the process by which a SOCIETY becomes increasingly SECULAR.

SECULARIZATION THESIS: a theory promoted in the 1960s by SOCIOLOGISTS such as Rodney STARK who argued that SECULARIZATION is a process linked to industrialization and urban life which leads to the disappearance of RELIGION in modern SOCIETY. Today there seems to be considerable evidence that, rather than causing religion to disappear, secularization leads to the growth of NEW RELIGIOUS MOVEMENTS. This has caused Stark and others to revise their earlier ideas.

SEER: someone credited with the gift of PROPHECY or second-sight. Belief in seers is found in all cultures and may be understood in RELIGIOUS or essentially SECULAR terms.

SELF: the INDIVIDUAL PERSON, or ego; our personal awareness of individuality.

SELF-REALIZATION FELLOWSHIP: an organization to promote YOGIC RELIGION founded by the HINDU GURU Paramahansa YOGANANDA in 1920. Based on his understanding of PATANJALI's YOGA SŪTRAS, the movement promotes practice and SPIRITUAL ENLIGHTENMENT more than THEORETICAL knowledge. It has become a major force in the NEW AGE MOVEMENT due to the large number of New Age leaders who were influenced by its teachings and practices.

SENECA, Lucius Anneus (65-5 B.C.): Roman moralist and STOIC philosopher who was the tutor and advisor of the emperor Nero.

SENSE DATA: what is immediately known by the senses or that which is the given in direct awareness.

SEPTUAGINT: the name given to the Greek translation of the HEBREW BIBLE carried out in the second century B.C. in Alexandria, Egypt. The name derives from the seventy translators, who supposedly produced identical translations. It is frequently abbreviated as LXX.

SERMON: a religious discourse intended to convert nonbelievers or inspire the faithful to a more devout life.

SERMON ON THE MOUNT: the most famous sayings of JESUS OF NAZARETH, found in Matthew 5—7.

SETH: various books written by Jane Roberts Butts (1929-1984), who began to play with Ouija boards in 1963 and eventually became a SPIRITUALIST MEDIUM who "communicated" messages from a "spirit entity" she called Seth. Roberts claimed that Seth was the "dramatization of the unconscious" and published numerous books, including *The Seth Material* (1970) and *Dreams, "Evolution," and Value Fulfilment* (1986). Since her death two further collections of Seth material have been published by other MEDIUMS who had contact with Roberts.

SEVEN DEADLY SINS: in TRADITIONAL CHRISTIANITY these are pride, covetousness, lust, envy, gluttony, anger and sloth.

SEVENTH-DAY ADVENTISM: the name adopted in 1861 by a dynamic REVITALIZATION MOVEMENT which expected the imminent return of CHRIST. It has now become a fast-growing denomination with extensive MISSIONARY programs. Its adherents observe the SABBATH, food laws based on the HEBREW BIBLE and VEGETARIANISM, and they avoid tea, coffee and alcohol. Unlike most MILLENARIAN MOVEMENTS, they emphasize education and have an impressive record of medical work. Although some Christians accuse them of HERESY, they are essentially orthodox in their THEOLOGY.

SEYMOUR, William Joseph (1870-1922): black American PENTECOSTAL leader who played a major role in the AZUSA Street revival of 1906-1909.

SHĀFI'Ī, Muḥammad ibn Idrīs ash- (767-820): influential MUSLIM jurist who held that the QUR'ĀN and the ḤADĪTH were the twin bases of ISLAMIC law.

SHAFTESBURY, Anthony Ashley Cooper, Lord (1801-1885): English social REFORMER and prominent EVANGELICAL LAYMAN who, with William WILBERFORCE, worked hard to improve factory working conditions, oppose SLAVERY, and improve the lot of children.

SHAHRASTĀNĪ, Muḥammad bin 'Abd al-Karim ash- (1076-1153): ISLAMIC scholar and author of *The Book of Religious Sects* which deals with various MUSLIM SECTS as well as other RELIGIONS and PHILOSOPHIES.

SHAKARIAN, Demos (1913-): American CHARISMATIC businessman of Armenian descent who founded in 1951 the FULL GOSPEL BUSINESSMEN'S FELLOWSHIP INTERNATIONAL.

SHAKERS: originating in a QUAKER revival meeting in 1847, they are a group of people distinguished by their physical shaking during WORSHIP. They came under the leadership of "Mother" Ann LEE, who came to be recognized as a female CHRIST. In 1774 she emigrated with her followers to America, where they established several colonies. The Shakers were

a UTOPIAN group, known for their austere, utilitarian architecture and furnish-
ing, who practiced CELIBACY and communal living. Among their many achievements is the invention of the washing
machine.

SHAMAN: a word of Northern Asiatic
origin which means PRIEST or "medicine
man."

SHAMANISM: the indigenous RELIGION
of Northern Eurasia where trance and the
control of SPIRITS by a SHAMAN who nego-
tiates between this world and the spirit
world are central features. Shamanism is
found among hunting peoples and presupposes a BELIEF in a multiplicity of
spirits and the survival of the SOUL after
DEATH. As a coherent religious system it is
practically extinct, although a revival of
interest in Shamanism has occurred in
various NEW RELIGIOUS MOVEMENTS, including the UNIFICATION CHURCH and, in a
certain sense, SCIENTOLOGY.

SHANG-TI: the supreme GOD or primal
ANCESTOR in Chinese RELIGION. The term
was adopted by CHRISTIAN MISSIONARIES
to speak about the GOD of the BIBLE.

SHARĪ'A: CANON LAW in ISLAM, based on
the QUR'ĀN, the ḤADĪTH, the *ijmā'* or "ac-
cord of the faithful," and analogical reasoning from the three basic sources.

SHARĪF: the nobility of ISLAM, who are
the descendants of MUḤAMMAD.

SHAW, George Bernard (1856-1950):
Irish playwright and critic, he was a dominant figure in the influential FABIAN
SOCIETY that aimed to advance democratic
SOCIALISM through gradual REFORM. A
strident critic of established RELIGION, he
promoted his own view of an evolutionary spirituality.

SHEKINAH: a HEBREW word meaning the
glory, indwelling or manifestation of GOD
in the world.

SHEMBE, Amos (1907-): the son of Isaia
SHEMBE and leader of the largest branch of
the Zulu AMA-NAZARITE movement,
which had split into two rival factions
after the death of Johannes Galilee

SHEMBE. Under the leadership of Amos,
the group has moved in a more CHRISTIAN
direction with a greater emphasis on the
BIBLE and person of JESUS.

SHEMBE, Isaia [Isaiah] (1867-1935): Zulu
religious leader, healer and founder of the
AMA-NAZARITES, the largest independent
religious movement among the Zulus.
Regarded as GOD by many of his own
people, Isaia Shembe is usually spoken of
as a PROPHET by Europeans, but this designation was vigorously denied by his son
Amos and grandson Londa. His writings
and sayings have been translated by Londa Shembe as *The Prayers and Writings of the
Servant of Sorrows Thumekile Isaiah Shembe,*
making them the first SCRIPTURES of a
NEW RELIGIOUS MOVEMENT in Africa to
appear in English.

SHEMBE, Johannes Galilee (1904-1975):
the successor of Isaia Shembe, whose able
leadership made the AMA-NAZARITES the
second-largest independent religious
movement in Southern Africa.

**SHEMBE, Londa iNsiKayakho (1944-
1989):** brilliant leader of the smaller and
more progressive branch of the AMA-
NAZARITES. He called himself the "Third
Shembe," thus identifying his work and
personality with that of his grandfather
Isaia SHEMBE. He strongly rejected the idea
that the Ama-Nazarites were simply a
form of Africanized CHRISTIANITY, insisting instead that they were an AFRICAN
RELIGION in their own right. He was brutally assassinated on April 7, 1989.

SHEN: a term for SPIRITS in Chinese
RELIGION.

SHEOL: the place of the dead, often
referred to as the "underworld" in the
HEBREW BIBLE.

SHĪ'ISM: there are two major divisions in
ISLAM: (1) the SUNNĪ, whose adherents are
in the majority and claim to be the orthodox group (*see* ORTHODOXY) and (2) the
Shī'a, whose adherents accept the claims
of MUḤAMMAD's son-in-law 'ALI and believe that the spiritual and temporal leadership of Islam should reside with the

descendants of the PROPHET. The Shī'a are the dominant group in Iran and Iraq.

SHINGON: a highly MYSTICAL and syncretistic Japanese BUDDHIST religious movement founded in 806 by KŌBŌ DAISHI. It incorporates within its MYTHOLOGY gods and even demons from other religious traditions as manifestations of the BUDDHA, whose body is the entire COSMOS. It is distinguished by its use of the MANDALA or diagram representing the vitality and potentiality of the UNIVERSE.

SHINRAN (1173-1262): Japanese BUDDHIST scholar and REFORMER who founded JŌDŌ Shinshū, the "True PURE LAND FAITH." He studied TENDAI BUDDHISM at Mount Hiei before leaving to follow HŌNEN. Shinran developed a radical doctrine which emphasized the importance of FAITH rather than the number of recitations of religious formulas. He advocated the marriage of MONKS and sought to minimize the gulf between CLERGY and LAITY.

SHINSHŪKYŌ: an ESOTERIC SHINTŌ religious movement founded by Yoshimura Masamochi in the late nineteenth century to restore Shinto ORTHODOXY and promote divine HEALING. Its best-known rites are a fire-walking ceremony and bodily PURIFICATION using boiling water.

SHINTAI: a SACRED object representing the DEITY kept in a SHINTŌ TEMPLE.

SHINTŌ: the way of KAMI, or the gods, which is the TRADITIONAL RELIGION of Japan, central to Japanese CULTURE and national identity. It is based on prehistoric religious practices, a PRIESTHOOD and household rites. In modern Shintō, until the end of World War II, both the emperor and the physical lands of Japan were considered divine. The status of the emperor today is uncertain, and scholars question whether the deification of the emperor is an integral part of the religion or a development which took place in recent times.

SHIVA: see ŚIVA.

SHOLOKHOV, Mikhail Aleksandrovich

(1905-1982): Russian novelist, supposed author of *And Quiet Flows the Don* (which gives a profound analysis of the effect of REVOLUTION on Cossack SOCIETY) and a hardline Communist. Rumors persist that he was not the true author of the novel but stole it from a prison camp inmate, thus explaining its anticommunist sentiments.

SHRINE: a HOLY place that usually attracts PILGRIMS.

SHU CHING: one of the five Confucian classics (*see* CONFUCIUS); it is known as the *Book of History* or *Book of Records* and preserves an account of Chinese HISTORY.

SHU'AYB (?): a PROPHET mentioned in the QUR'ĀN popularly identified in MUSLIM tradition with Jethro, father-in-law of MOSES.

SHUSHI SCHOOL: the orthodox school of Japanese Confucianism (*see* CONFUCIUS). It was introduced by ZEN monks in the fourteenth century and adopted by the Tokugawa Shogunate as the official system of Japanese morality.

SIBYLLINE ORACLES: a collection of PROPHECIES, Greek in origin, and supposedly made by a prophetess called Sibyl and having to do with disasters to come upon humankind, they are widely attested in the ancient world. A Roman collection of these oracles was the most famous. They were consulted in times of crisis until the books were lost in a fire in 83 B.C. The Jewish and Christian books by this name are part of the PSEUDEPIGRAPHA and come from the second century B.C. to the seventh century A.D. They are dominated by ESCHATOLOGY.

SIGN: an indicator; anything which stands for or represents something else.

SIKHISM: growing out of various Indian movements which sought unity between the best in ISLAM and HINDUISM. It crystallized in the work of NĀNAK, the first of ten GURUS, who created and led the Sikh community. Nānak preached the unity of GOD and taught the centrality of BHAKTI-type devotion using the repetition of the divine name. The CASTE system was repudiated and images banned from WORSHIP.

SIMON STYLITES (390-459): the first CHRISTIAN HERMIT to live in the desert on top of a pillar, thus setting a style of ASCETIC life which became popular for several centuries. His rigorous discipline and powerful preaching is credited with making many PAGAN converts.

SIMONS, Menno (1496-1561): leader of the pacifist branch of the Dutch ANABAPTISTS whose followers became MENNONITES. He emphasized reflection on the earthly life of CHRIST and taught that the HOLY SPIRIT should be viewed as both Father and Mother of Christ.

SIN: tends to be understood in the West exclusively in the sense of the transgression of divine commandments. In COMPARATIVE RELIGION it has the much wider meaning of any departure from a divinely instituted order. Sin can only be moral if and when the underlying conception of GOD is also moral. In the many early ideas of sin, the element of RITUAL is more prominent than the ethical.

SINAI, Mount: the mountain in the Sinai wilderness between Egypt and Palestine where in Exodus 20 MOSES is said to have been given the TEN COMMANDMENTS.

SINE QUA NON: a Latin phrase meaning an indispensable condition without which a thing cannot exist.

ŚIVA: a terrible and powerful GOD in HINDUISM, where he is often referred to as "the destroyer of worlds." Śiva has many aspects and is one of the most popular Hindu gods whose origin is usually traced back to the god RUDRA in the ṚG VEDA. The earliest distinct stories about Śiva date from the fourth century A.D., although it was not until the twelfth century that Śiva achieved widespread devotion.

SKEPTICISM: the belief that the possibilities of knowledge are severely limited and that TRUTH is very difficult if not impossible to attain. As a result skeptical theories may promote an abandonment of the search for certainty and the adoption of systematic doubt.

SKEPTICS: name given to certain philosophers who doubt the adequacy of the senses and REASON to furnish reliable knowledge about the true NATURE of things. They advocate withholding assent and the suspension of judgment.

SKINNER, Burrhus Frederic (1904-1990): American behavioral psychologist famous for his experiments with rats, using the "Skinner Box." His UTOPIAN novel, *Walden Two* (1940), popularized views he developed in *Beyond Freedom and Dignity* (1971), where he argued that we should abandon the notion of "autonomous man" who is a free agent responsible for his or her actions.

SLAVERY: the practice of owning other human beings who are forced to obey their master's every whim. In many SPIRITUAL TRADITIONS the image of slavery is used to describe the condition of the DEVOTEE or CONVERT before their CONVERSION when they are said to be enslaved or blinded by evil. After receiving the TRUTH they become slaves of GOD.

SMART, Ninian (1927-): Scottish philosopher who introduced RELIGIOUS STUDIES to British universities and pioneered the teaching of world RELIGIONS in English schools. His works include *Reasons and Faiths* (1958), *Doctrine and Argument in Indian Philosophy* (1964) and *The World's Religions* (1989), as well as the popular "Long Search" television series.

SMITH, Adam (1723-1790): Scottish moral philosopher and founder of the discipline of economics through his book *The Wealth of Nations* (1776), which is often seen as the textbook of CAPITALISM. Although he argued for a free market economy, Smith was highly critical of greedy businessmen, the creation of monopolies and government indifference.

SMITH, Joseph (1805-1844): American visionary and founder of MORMONISM. He claimed to have begun receiving spiritual visions in 1820. As a result of the religious confusion created by competing SECTS he published *The Book of Mormon* (1830) which he said was translated with the help of an ANGEL from "Reformed Egyptian hieroglyphics" written on golden plates. On April 6, 1830, he founded the Church of Jesus Christ of Latter-day Saints. Teaching the importance of continuing REVELATION, he subsequently published *Doctrine and Covenants* (1835) and *The Pearl of Great Price* (1851) which, together with *The Book of Mormon*, provide the basis for his church's DOCTRINE and organization. Opposition to the practice of POLYGAMY, which he began openly teaching in 1843, led to his arrest and murder by a mob in 1844.

SMITH, Wilfred Cantwell (1916-): Canadian scholar of ISLAM and the HISTORY of RELIGION who is a prominent figure in the field of RELIGIOUS STUDIES. His works include *Modern Islam in India* (1943) and *Questions of Religious Truth* (1967).

SMITH, William Robertson (1846-1894): Scottish biblical scholar and author of *The Religion of the Semites* (1989), which was an early attempt to introduce concepts from ANTHROPOLOGY and SOCIOLOGY into biblical studies. He was also responsible for translating the work of German BIBLICAL CRITICISM (especially that of WELLHAUSEN) into English.

SMUTS, Jan Christian (1870-1950): South African prime minister, army general, statesman and philosopher. His work *Holism and Evolution* (1926) is credited by many as being an early statement of the PHILOSOPHY of the NEW AGE MOVEMENT.

SNAKE HANDLING: an exotic religious practice which emerged in Tennessee in 1909 in which the text of Mark 16:17-18, which speaks about "taking up serpents," was literally interpreted as a SIGN of BELIEF.

SOCIAL GOSPEL: the name given to the central idea of a widely influential movement within American PROTESTANTISM in the late nineteenth and early twentieth centuries. Its greatest spokesman was RAUSCHENBUSCH, a BAPTIST minister and later a theological professor. His premise was that personal EXISTENCE is basically social and that a relevant CHRISTIANITY would "bring men under REPENTANCE for their collective SINS" and would proclaim a corresponding social SALVATION. He appealed to the demand for justice that was characteristic of the Hebrew PROPHETS and to the centrality of the KINGDOM OF GOD in the teachings of JESUS.

SOCIAL JUSTICE: a modern development of the idea of justice; it gives individuals specific rights, such as the right to education or health, as opposed to older CONCEPTS of justice which simply guaranteed equality before the law.

SOCIALISM: a modern political system based on the idea of EQUALITY which advocates STATE intervention in the economy and SOCIETY to ensure SOCIAL JUSTICE. Socialism is opposed to CAPITALISM and ideas such as the free-market economy, which it sees as giving preference to the rich over the poor. Marxism (*see* Karl MARX) calls itself "Scientific Socialism" and is distinguished from other socialist theories in that socialism is seen as a step toward the ideal communist society and not as an end in itself.

SOCIALIST: someone who advocates SOCIALISM.

SOCIALIZATION: the process by which a child is incorporated into SOCIETY and becomes a member of a GROUP.

SOCIETY: the individuals who together form a SOCIAL GROUP.

SOCINIANISM: a RATIONALISTIC THEOLOGY which regards the BIBLE as REVELATION but argues that it contains nothing contrary to REASON. It rejects the SACRAMENTS of the CHURCH, the TRINITY, the DEITY of CHRIST, ORIGINAL SIN, vicarious ATONEMENT and the RESURRECTION of the body.

SOCIOLOGIST: someone who studies SOCIETY using the methods of SOCIOLOGY.

SOCIOLOGY: the modern, systematic and scientific study of SOCIETY. The term was first used by COMTE in 1830, but as an academic discipline it was first developed by SPENCER in the late nineteenth century. It involves the application of statistical and other techniques to understand the way people act and think as members of social GROUPS. Other figures regarded as the founders of sociology are TOCQUEVILLE, MARX, DURKHEIM and WEBER.

SOCIOLOGY OF RELIGION: the applications of methods and theories derived from SOCIOLOGY to the study of RELIGION. Although today the sociology of religion is a minor field within sociology proper, the "founding fathers" of sociology were all vitally concerned with religious questions.

SOCRATES (470-400 B.C.): Greek philosopher and teacher of PLATO who criticized the vice and folly of government and the weakness of popular THEOLOGY. Convicted of corrupting youth and being unfaithful to the gods and the state, he was condemned to either go into exile or drink hemlock (poison): he chose hemlock. Plato idealizes him as a teacher of DIALECTIC, and ARISTOTLE credits him with being the first philosopher to seek UNIVERSAL principles and precise definition. His method of inquiry involving question and counter-question is known as the SOCRATIC METHOD.

SOCRATIC METHOD: the DIALECTICAL method supposedly used by SOCRATES. It involves patient questioning by a teacher to lead the pupil to recognize the TRUTH.

SODOM AND GOMORRAH: cities mentioned in Genesis 18 and 19 which were destroyed by GOD because of their SIN, which involved sexual perversion and inhospitality.

SŌKA GAKKAI: a Japanese NEW RELIGIOUS MOVEMENT founded in 1930 by Tsunesaburō Makiguchi and Jōsei Toda as a lay association of BUDDHISTS. Active in politics, the leaders were imprisoned during World War II for their pacifist stance. After 1947 the movement grew rapidly, especially in cities, where its adaptation of Buddhism to the modern world appealed to many people.

SOLIPSISM: like the idle fancy that the whole world is merely one's dream, solipsism is an epistemological theory that argues that the individual self of the philosopher is the only reality.

SOLOVIEV, Vladimir (1853-1900): Russian philosopher and theologian who was an intimate of Dostoyevsky, whom he greatly influenced. After strongly opposing the ROMAN CATHOLIC CHURCH, he joined it in 1896 through his desire to see a united Christendom. Strongly influenced by German PHILOSOPHY, especially HEGEL, he sought to combine PANTHEISM with the Christian DOCTRINE of the INCARNATION. After the Russian REVOLUTION the influence of his writings is credited with turning Russian émigré intellectuals away from their earlier nihilism and toward CHRISTIANITY. His works included *The Crisis of Western Philosophy* (1874), *Critique of Abstract Principles* (1880) and *Stories of the Anti-Christ* (1900).

SOLZHENITSYN, Aleksandr Isayevich (1918-): Russian novelist and CHRISTIAN thinker who was imprisoned and sent to a labor camp in Siberia for disrespectful references to STALIN. Released in 1953, he wrote *One Day in the Life of Ivan Denisovich* (1962) followed by *The Gulag Archipelago* (1973), which graphically exposed the horrors of the Soviet system. Rearrested in 1974, he was exiled to the West, where his fame as a writer grew. His autobiography, *The Oak and the Calf* (1979), is a moving testimony to endurance and FAITH.

SOMA: the name of a plant that was regarded as divine. It is mentioned in VEDIC literature as valued for its hallucinogenic powers by BRAHMINS, who used it in RITUALS.

SON OF GOD: the title given to JESUS in the NEW TESTAMENT which in some passages clearly implies a special relationship between Jesus and GOD. In CHRISTIAN THEOLOGY it came to represent the DEITY of CHRIST, in contrast to his humanity.

SON OF MAN: a term found in the HE-

BREW BIBLE, especially in the book of Daniel, meaning "the man." In Daniel the Son of Man is a glorious heavenly figure who bears the features of a man and is clearly linked to the idea of the establishment of the KINGDOM OF GOD. In the NEW TESTAMENT JESUS uses the term as a title for himself. CHRISTIANS have popularly understood the title to be the counterpart of the SON OF GOD and seen it as indicating Christ's humanity. Nevertheless, the *New Testament* clearly implies far more than mere humanity by this title. It implies that the Son of Man is the representative of humanity sent by God to fulfill his plan of SALVATION.

SOPHISTS: wandering teachers of RHETORIC and PHILOSOPHY in the Greco-Roman world. They rejected all RELIGION and gave rationalistic explanations to natural phenomena, holding to ethical and social RELATIVISM.

SOPHOCLES (495-406 B.C.): Athenian poet and writer whose play *Oedipus Rex* gave FREUD the idea for his famous complex.

SORCERY: the exercise of RITUAL MAGIC used with EVIL intent and often involving the use of physical objects, spells, potions and poisons.

SOREL, Georges (1847-1922): French Marxist journalist, philosopher, anarchist and revolutionary syndicalist who rejected RATIONALISM and, through the work of BERGSON, eventually developed a MYSTICAL NATIONALISM. Praising both STALIN and Mussolini, he was adopted by the latter as the philosopher of FASCISM. Sorel was a complex figure, whose views constantly changed over time, an advocate of the general strike and an opponent of LIBERAL DEMOCRACY. His works include *The Decomposition of Marxism* (1908) and his famous *Reflections on Violence* (1916).

SOROKIN, Pitrim Alexandrovitch (1889-1968): Russian-born SOCIOLOGIST of peasant parents who became a leading critic of Marxism and the Russian REVOLUTION. His major work, *Social and Cultural Dynamics* (1937-1941), ranks with that of TOYNBEE and SPENGLER as an attempt to provide a general interpretation of HISTORY.

SOTĀPANNA: a convert to BUDDHISM, who is guaranteed FREEDOM from REBIRTH in the HELLS or as anything other than a human, with the ultimate hope of full ENLIGHTENMENT and LIBERATION.

SOTERIOLOGY: that division of THEOLOGY which deals with the DOCTRINE of SALVATION.

SŌTŌ: one of the major divisions of ZEN BUDDHISM founded in China by Tung-shan in the ninth century. It teaches the unity of the ABSOLUTE and the RELATIVE EXISTENCE of all observable phenomena. It was introduced to Japan in the thirteenth century by Dōgen and is based on the practice of ZAZEN MEDITATION.

SOUL: the immortal element in human beings sometimes regarded as our true SELF. The EXISTENCE of the soul is denied in BUDDHISM and certain forms of HINDUISM. Other Hindu philosophies teach the existence of the soul, which is integral to the notion of TRANSMIGRATION. In early CHRISTIANITY, as seen in the three ECUMENICAL CREEDS, the central concept was the RESURRECTION of the body rather than the IMMORTALITY of the soul, but the latter gradually replaced the earlier emphasis.

SOUTHCOTT, Joanna (1750-1814): English MYSTIC who, at the age of forty-two, claimed to hear the voice of God. She declared herself a PROPHET and the bride referred to in Revelation 19. She proclaimed the end of the world and began to practice automatic writing. In 1800 she published six pamphlets recording her views and prophecies, which led to the formation of a small but influential group of followers. Many of her prophecies have been promoted by OCCULT GROUPS and recently by some members of the NEW AGE MOVEMENT.

SPANGLER, David (1945-): American NEW-AGE OCCULT author and theorist who moved to the FINDHORN COMMUNITY in 1970 where he wrested control of the group from Peter CADDY and went on to direct its future growth. In 1973 he returned to America to found the LORIAN ASSOCIATION and promote TRANSCHANNELING. His major works are: *Revelation: The Birth of a New Age* (1976), *The Rebirth of the Sacred* (1984) and *Channelling in the New Age* (1988).

SPEAKING IN TONGUES: an ecstatic SPIRITUAL state whereby an individual either speaks a human language which is unknown to them or a "heavenly language" which has no known meaning. It is one of the marks of PENTECOSTAL CHRISTIANITY and is popular in the CHARISMATIC MOVEMENT as a form of WORSHIP.

SPENCER, Herbert (1820-1903): English POSITIVIST philosopher, sociologist and LIBERAL who was the dominant intellectual figure in the latter half of the nineteenth century. Applying DARWIN's views to SOCIETY, he developed a PHILOSOPHY of PROGRESS expressed in his *First Principles* (1862) and greatly contributed to the development of ANTHROPOLOGY and SOCIOLOGY. His ambitious *Principles of Sociology* (1876-1896, 3 vols.) can be seen as a forerunner of GENERAL SYSTEMS THEORY because of his insistence on the self-regulating NATURE of SOCIAL SYSTEMS.

SPENGLER, Oswald (1880-1936): German historian and philosopher whose influential work *The Decline of the West* (1914-1922) helped set the tone for modern intellectual pessimism and existentialist philosophy (*see* EXISTENTIALISM).

SPINOZA, Baruch [or Benedict] (1632-1677): Dutch MATERIALIST philosopher who was EXCOMMUNICATED for his free thought by the JEWISH community of Amsterdam. He believed that mastery over NATURE and the perfection of man was the purpose of knowledge, and he considered DEMOCRATIC government the highest form of power. His work stimulated the development of modern ATHEISM and BIBLICAL CRITICISM. His works include *Tractatus Theologicopoliticus* (1670) and *Ethica* (1677).

SPIRIT: many religious traditions teach that in addition to our bodies the human person has a spirit or SOUL which lives within the body, giving it life and everything that is distinctly human. It is this aspect of the person which is believed to relate to GOD and the RELIGIOUS realm. In addition to the human spirit most religions believe in the existence of various spirit beings and some, like CHRISTIANITY, speak about the spirit of God or the HOLY SPIRIT.

SPIRITISM: a mode of thought and behavior based on the belief that the SPIRITS of the dead and other spirits interact and sometimes even communicate with the living. Such intercourse normally takes place through dreams, illness and unusual events which reveal the presence of a spirit. When the spirit disturbs the living, a SHAMAN or similar religious expert is called in to solve the problem and, if appropriate, directly contact the spirit or spirits concerned. Appeasement of the spirit may be necessary, which often involves SACRIFICE and RITUALS.

SPIRITS: disembodied entities which display the characteristics of INDIVIDUAL PERSONS that are sometimes regarded as the SOULS of dead ANCESTORS. In most religions spirits are regarded as potentially dangerous and often as utterly EVIL.

SPIRITUAL: concerning the spirit, or RELIGIOUS things, as opposed to a concern for the world and material things. A spiritual life is one devoted to GOD.

SPIRITUAL EXERCISES: generally any practices intended to increase the spiritual awareness of a practitioner. Specifically they are a system of devotional practices devised by LOYOLA and copied by various other religious leaders to promote MEDITATION.

SPIRITUAL HEALING: the belief that through PRAYER or other SPIRITUAL EXERCISES an individual may be healed physically or psychologically. Such healing often involves the intervention of someone who is regarded as having a gift of healing or who is seen as being a SAINT.

SPIRITUALISM: a modern FORM of SPIRITISM dating from 1848, when two teenage sisters, Margaretta and Katie FOX of Hydesville, New York, reported "rappings" in their home. They interpreted these noises as messages from a peddler who had died in the house. Enthusiasm for spiritualism swept through North America, spreading to Europe and Latin America. The teachings of SWEDENBORG, bitter rivalry between competing CHRISTIAN DENOMINATIONS and a growing awareness of the problems of BIBLICAL CRITICISM, as presented by FREE THINKERS like BRADLAUGH and PAINE, may be seen as contributing factors to the growth of the spiritualist movement. After rapid growth in the 1850s, when by some estimates somewhere near 75 percent of Americans visited spiritualists, enthusiasm declined. Spiritualist ideas have had an influence far greater than the number of committed spiritualists would suggest, making an important contribution to the growth of NEW RELIGIOUS MOVEMENTS. In places like Brazil local forms of spiritualism have developed as a result of SYNCRETISM between ROMAN CATHOLICISM and fragments of TRADITIONAL AFRICAN RELIGIONS imported by slaves, and, to a lesser extent, NATIVE AMERICAN religious TRADITIONS.

SPIRITUALITY: the quality of being SPIRITUAL.

SPURGEON, Charles Haddon (1834-1892): popular English BAPTIST preacher who promoted CALVINISM. His printed SERMONS run to many volumes and are still studied for their content, style and eloquence.

SRI AUROBINDO: *see* AUROBINDO.

STALIN, Joseph (1879-1953): Russian THEOLOGY-student-turned-revolutionary who ruled Russia with an iron fist for almost thirty years and caused untold suffering. He was responsible for the deaths of about 17 million people, including 7 million in the Ukraine who died through enforced famine. As early as 1933 he sought a pact with HITLER, which was formally endorsed in 1939 only to be undone by the German invasion of 1941. His daughter embraced CHRISTIANITY and fled to America in the 1960s; she recently returned to Russia.

STANLEY, Henry Morton, Sir (1841-1904): American journalist who set out on an expedition into central Africa to "find" David LIVINGSTONE. His *Through the Dark Continent* (1878, 2 vols.) aroused public curiosity and stimulated the MISSIONARY movement.

STARK, Rodney (1940-): SOCIOLOGIST of RELIGION and early proponent of the SECULARIZATION THESIS, which he later repudiated. He is best known as the coauthor of the article "Hellfire and Delinquency" which found no correlation between religious belief and delinquent behavior—a position which he now regards as wrong due to inadequate sampling. One of America's most creative sociologists, his many books include the bestselling introductory text *Sociology* (1985) and *The Future of Religion* (1985), which he wrote with William Sims Bainbridge.

STATE: a term first used in its modern form by MACHIAVELLI, it generally signifies the political and legal organization of a society or group of societies under one government.

STIGMATA: a strange phenomenon in which the wounds of CHRIST or blisters and sores appear on the bodies of living people. These marks are not susceptible to normal medical treatment and usually appear at religious festivals such as Lent. The first known case of stigmata was that of FRANCIS OF ASSISI.

STOIC: someone who lives by the PHILOSOPHY of STOICISM or, more generally, who acts in a brave and detached manner.

STOICISM: a school of PHILOSOPHY founded in the fourth century B.C. by Zeno of Citium. He taught a PANTHEISTIC MONISM that identified GOD with the principle of universal REASON and advised everyone to accept their place in the scheme of life by doing their duty, which was to follow the most RATIONAL path possible. The STOIC VIRTUES were knowledge, reason, courage, justice and self-discipline, attained through the study of philosophy. Stoics taught the existence of NATURAL LAW known to all people and the common humanity of mankind. The best-known Stoic is MARCUS AURELIUS, whose works have been popularized more recently by such POSITIVE THINKERS as Dale Carnegie.

STOKER, Hendrik Gerhardus (1899-): South African philosopher and student of SCHELER whose work was highly praised by HEIDEGGER. He attempted to develop a CHRISTIAN PHILOSOPHY based on the idea of CREATION and similar to the philosophy of DOOYEWEERD. Unfortunately his work is marred by the fact that he supported a highly theoretical version of apartheid.

STONEHENGE: a circle of standing stones in Southern England, the purpose of which is unknown although it was probably used in some religious RITUAL. Popular imagination has associated the building of Stonehenge with the Druids, but this cannot be verified historically. Today Stonehenge is a source of inspiration to various NEOPAGAN groups.

STRAUSS, David Friedrich (1808-1874): radical German theologian and one of the founders of BIBLICAL CRITICISM. His book *The Life of Jesus* (1835) caused a storm by its denial of the SUPERNATURAL and his use of MYTH, which he defined as a story contrary to the laws of NATURE, to reinterpret the BIBLE in SECULAR terms.

STRUCTURALISM: an interdisciplinary PHILOSOPHY originating with the publication of Ferdinand de Saussure's (1857-1913) *Cours de linguistique générale* in 1916. It argues that, because of the way human brains are structured, our language reflects universal patterns or structures. Structuralists have shown great interest in MYTHS and folklore because they be-

lieve these narratives provide evidence of fundamental forms of human thought and the "deep structures" governing society. These ideas were popularized by LÉVI-STRAUSS and PIAGET, and focus on the common structures underlying linguistics, myths and social life.

STŪPA: a SANSKRIT word meaning a rounded mound of stones or earth. Stūpas seems to have played a role in Indian FOLK RELIGION and came to be regarded as memorials in BUDDHISM, where they became centers of popular PIETY.

SUBJECTIVE: related to the thinking subject; that which exists only when it is apprehended by an active mind, e.g., a mirage in the desert; that which lacks OBJECTIVE ONTOLOGY.

SUBJECTIVISM: an emphasis on the SUBJECTIVE as a total PHILOSOPHY or way of knowing.

SUBSTANCE: a term originating with Greek PHILOSOPHY and meaning the underlying and unchanging substratum of a thing that remains the same in spite of changes in its appearance. It is that which everything depends on or what is REAL.

ŞŪDRAS: the lowest CASTE in the HINDU system, consisting of people who perform the most menial occupations and live on the margins of SOCIETY.

SUFFERING, THE PROBLEM OF: the EXISTENCE of pain and suffering in the world, whether it is individual misfortune or part of the natural order such as storms and earthquakes, raises the question of whether the UNIVERSE is essentially hostile to human life. This is often seen as a problem for THEISM because it is posed in terms of GOD's goodness, knowledge and power; but even if God does not exist, questions of MEANING and purpose would still remain.

ŞŪFISM: an important MYSTICAL movement within ISLAM whose origins are obscure. The name is derived from the Arabic word for wool and reflects the fact that early Şūfīs wore course woolen clothing in protest against what they saw as the decadence of the CALIPHATE in the seventh and eighth centuries. The movement emphasizes love of GOD and has been traced to CHRISTIAN influences by some scholars, although today most authorities think it reflects a genuine flowering of indigenous spirituality within Islam. By far the most important Ṣūfī scholar known to the West was al-GHAZĀLĪ. During the medieval period Ṣūfīs formed a number of great Ṣūfī orders which imposed a disciplined way of life on their members but did not require celibacy. In time these orders became a major force in Islamic MISSIONARY activity and the REVITALIZATION of Muslim society. Beginning in the twelfth century various NEOPLATONIC ideas began to influence the Ṣūfī movement, the theology of which became increasingly PANTHEISTIC. By the nineteenth century the Ṣūfī orders dominated society in the Islamic world. They suffered a major setback in the twentieth century due to the rise of secular NATIONALISM in Muslim countries, many of which, like Turkey, banned the orders. Today they appear to be flourishing, and are embracing wide segments of Muslim society and adapting to MODERNITY.

SUICIDE: most RELIGIONS discourage people from taking their own lives, and the act is uncompromisingly condemned in the ABRAMIC RELIGIONS. Classical HINDUISM also opposed the practice, but JAINISM and some FORMS of BUDDHISM allow for RITUAL suicide, while the CONFUCIAN ethic in China and Japan encouraged SOCIETY to see suicide as a commendable act in situations of loss of face and failure to perform one's duty. The practice of suicide is widespread in many societies and is used by many SOCIOLOGISTS as an indicator of SOCIAL well-being on the assumption that high suicide rates indicate a dysfunctional society and discontented, maladjusted individuals. Recently some writers, notably A. Droge and J. Tabor in *A Noble Death: Suicide and Martyrdom Among Christians and Jews in Antiquity*

(1992) and G. Lloyd Carr in *The Fierce Goodbye* (1990), have suggested that historically neither Christianity nor Judaism has categorically condemned suicide.

SUMMA: a medieval Latin word for a literary compendium or work of SCHOLASTIC PHILOSOPHY.

SUMMUM BONUM: Latin for the highest or supreme GOOD.

SUNDAR SINGH (1889-1929): Indian EVANGELIST who converted to CHRISTIANITY from the SIKH religion of his family after a VISION of JESUS when he was thirteen years old. He adopted the dress of a HINDU HOLY man and sought to spread the GOSPEL in terms of Indian life and CULTURE.

SUNDAY, William Ashley, "Billy" (1862-1935): American REVIVALIST and popular FUNDAMENTALIST figure who opposed the theory of EVOLUTION and strongly advocated the temperance movement.

SUNDAY-SCHOOL MOVEMENT: first begun in 1780 by an ANGLICAN CLERGYMAN, Robert RAIKES in Gloucester, England, to teach children to read and encourage PIETY. The movement quickly spread throughout the English-speaking world and into continental Europe as the forerunner of universal education.

SUNNA: customary practice in the law of ISLAM. In the QUR'ĀN it is used to speak about established decrees, but the term later became attached to the deeds and attitudes of MUḤAMMAD.

SUNNĪ: the majority party in ISLAM, distinguished by its rejection of the claims of 'ALĪ. The name comes from the practice of finding solutions to problems not discussed in the QUR'ĀN by appealing to the SUNNA of MUḤAMMAD in MEDINA or to the ḤADĪTH, in contrast to the SHĪ'ITES, who believe in the AUTHORITY of inspired IMĀMS.

ŚŪNYATĀ: the BUDDHIST term for emptiness, the ultimate REALITY.

SUPEREROGATION: the ROMAN CATHOLIC teaching that certain acts such as sexual abstinence are to be admired and contribute to the SPIRITUALITY of the individual. These acts of "extra goodness" performed by the SAINTS create spiritual power which can help make up for the inadequacies of lesser humans. In many ways the doctrine is similar to MAHĀYĀNA BUDDHIST teachings about MERIT. It was strongly denied by the PROTESTANT RE-FORMERS who saw it as weakening the doctrines of JUSTIFICATION by FAITH and the PRIESTHOOD OF ALL BELIEVERS.

SUPERNATURAL: beyond NATURE. The idea of a SPIRITUAL realm beyond the visible everyday world of the senses is found in most religions. Supernatural events, or MIRACLES, are those ascribed to a spiritual source or the activity of GOD which occur in and influence this world. The distinction between the natural and supernatural is worked out in the THEOLOGY of Thomas AQUINAS, where it is often referred to under the headings of NATURE and GRACE. Although taken for granted in most religious systems, the supernatural became an issue during the ENLIGHTENMENT when many PHILOSOPHERS denied its existence.

SŪRA: the Arabic name for the 114 sections of the QUR'ĀN.

SŪTRA: a term in SANSKRIT meaning thread; it is used to refer to short, pithy sayings, verses or aphorisms in HINDU texts and the great works of the MAHĀ-YĀNA CANON in BUDDHISM.

SUTTA-PIṬAKA: one of the three major divisions of the BUDDHIST CANON, consisting of dialogues and discourses full of parables and stories which encourage popular PIETY. The two other divisions are the VINAYA-PIṬAKA and the Adhidhamma-Piṭaka.

SUZUKI, Daisetsu Teitaro (1870-1966): Japanese scholar who popularized BUD-DHISM in the West through his writings on ZEN. His first book was a Japanese translation of SWEDENBORG's *Heaven and Hell* (1910), while his later writings, including *Mysticism, Christian and Buddhist* (1957), display a firm grip of Western thought leading him to grapple with the problem of interreligious communication. He traveled widely and in 1921 married an American. Professor of Buddhism at Kyoto University, he began the publication of the magazine *Eastern Buddhist*, which he also edited.

SUZUKI, David (1942-): Canadian geneticist turned popular journalist whose views about NATURE and ecology appear to express a BUDDHIST ethic shaped by Western ROMANTICISM.

ŚVETĀMBARA: one of the two major religious divisions in JAINISM whose PRIESTS insisted on wearing white clothing and rejected the rival Digambara view which insists on RITUAL nudity. The movement originated in the third century B.C. and has its own CANON of SCRIPTURE and distinct style of TEMPLE architecture.

SWAMI: a title of honor and respect in HINDUISM.

SWASTIKA: the ancient HINDU SYMBOL of a broken cross which was believed to be a symbol bringing success. It signifies VISHNU and the EVOLUTION of the COSMOS and was deliberately adopted for its OC-CULT significance by the German National Socialists in 1919 as a SIGN of good luck.

SWEDENBORG, Emanuel (1688-1772): Swedish scientist, philosopher, theologian and MYSTIC whose ideas strongly influenced ROMANTICISM and are in many ways the inspiration for the NEW AGE MOVE-MENT and many similar religious groups, including MORMONISM and the UNIFICA-TION CHURCH. After a brilliant engineering career, he experienced strange dreams and visions leading to a religious crisis between 1743 and 1745. This culminated in a VISION of CHRIST and religious CON-VERSION. Renouncing SCIENCE, he spent the rest of his life propagating his new ideas and founded the NEW CHURCH known as the "New Jerusalem Church" or Swedenborgian Movement.

SWIFT, Jonathan (1667-1745): English ANGLICAN theologian and social satirist famous for his novel *Gulliver's Travels* (1726).

SYLLABUS OF ERRORS: the Papal Encyclical *Quanta Cura* issued by POPE PIUS IX condemning eighty EVILS of the modern world, including PANTHEISM, RATIONALISM, the reading of the BIBLE by the LAITY, and LIBERALISM. At the time it was regarded as an infallible pronouncement but has since been downgraded.

SYLLOGISM: the traditional term used in DEDUCTIVE logic for an argument with a specific structure that includes two PROPOSITIONS and a conclusion. On the basis of its formal structure a syllogism may be judged logically VALID. If the propositions are also true in terms of their correspondence to REALITY, then the syllogism is deemed sound. An example of a valid syllogism would be: All pigs have wings; all winged things fly; therefore pigs fly. This would be logically valid because the conclusion follows from the major and minor premises. But, because the major (and minor) premise is untrue, the syllogism is unsound. A sound syllogism would be one such as the classic example: All men are mortal; Socrates is a man; therefore Socrates is mortal. The major premise is defined as the predicate term in the conclusion, while the minor premise is the subject term in the conclusion.

SYMBOL: a word which like MYTH is almost impossible to define. In general it refers to a picture, word or thing that bears a certain MEANING for a person or group. Thus a flag, a cross, a picture of the BUDDHA and a single word can all be symbols depending on their use and the meaning which is ascribed to them.

SYNAGOGUE: a place of WORSHIP and education in JUDAISM.

SYNCRETISM: the combining of teachings, practices and/or DOCTRINES from different and apparently contradictory religious TRADITIONS to create a new interpretation of an existing tradition or a NEW RELIGIOUS MOVEMENT.

SYNOD: a meeting or council of CHRISTIANS to discuss CHURCH affairs. The term is used in many churches to designate a regional or national governing body and its meetings.

SYNOPTIC GOSPELS: the Gospels of Matthew, Mark and Luke, which are the first three books of the NEW TESTAMENT.

SYNOPTIC PROBLEM: one of the major problems of BIBLICAL CRITICISM has been to devise an explanation for the fact that there is some identical, and a great amount of similar, material contained in the first three Gospels of the NEW TESTAMENT as well as materials peculiar to each. Since the late nineteenth century the "problem" has usually been resolved by arguing for the priority of the Gospel of Mark and the existence of a now lost collection of sayings of Jesus known by the scholarly cipher Q (German *Quelle*, "source"). This accepted scholarly interpretation has been strongly challenged in terms of the SOCIOLOGY OF KNOWLEDGE by W. R. Farmer in *The Synoptic Problem* (1964), and LOGIC by H. Palmer in *The Logic of Gospel Criticism* (1968).

T

TA HSÜEH: one of the four Confucian classics, which gives in succinct form the basic moral teachings of CONFUCIUS. Traditionally the author was said to be Tseng-tzu.

TABERNACLE: the portable, SACRED tent of ancient JUDAISM which came to be associated with the glory of GOD.

TABU (taboo): a Polynesian word referring to people or things which are forbidden because they are dangerous as a result of their SACRED nature or HOLY associations.

TABULA RASA: a Latin term meaning "blank tablet" used by the philosopher LOCKE to express his idea that at birth the mind is devoid of innate ideas.

TAGORE, Rabindranath (1861-1941): Bengali writer and poet whose book *The Religions of Man* (1931) expresses a broad HINDU HUMANISM.

T'AI-CHI: a Chinese term for the FINAL CAUSE of all things.

T'AI-I: the supreme DEITY in TAOIST thought and a term synonymous with the TAO, signifying the attempt to find the basic unity underlying the UNIVERSE.

T'AI SHAN: the most SACRED mountain in China.

TALMUD: the ancient JEWISH commentary on Jewish law. There are two collections of talmudic materials which are found in the Palestinian Talmud (*Yerushalmi*, dating from the fourth century A.D.) and the Babylonian Talmud (*Babli*, which reached its final redaction some centuries later). JUDAISM is based on the interpretation of the Talmud. The earliest complete extant manuscript for the Palestinian Talmud dates from 1523 while there are many earlier texts of the Babylonian Talmud which was first printed in 1521.

TAMMUZ: the Mesopotamian GOD of vegetation who died and journeyed to the underworld. FRAZER argued that Tammuz was an example of a dying and rising god. Modern scholars, working with better textual materials, dispute this claim.

TANTRA: a Hindu term which originally referred to SACRED TEXTS. In both HINDUISM and BUDDHISM it came to be understood as a means of attaining ENLIGHTENMENT through the use of MAGIC and RITUALS of a sexual nature.

TANTRIC BUDDHISM: that branch of BUDDHISM which developed TANTRA as an ESOTERIC system involving MAGIC and sexual practices believed to overcome desire by overindulgence.

TAO: a central CONCEPT for both Confucian (see CONFUCIUS) and TAOIST thought meaning "the way" and signifying the course of action, or road, men ought to follow in life. The meaning of the word *Tao* is "way, word, principle, reason, to speak, to lead." It is the basic principle of the entire UNIVERSE.

TAO TE CHING: the main philosophical text and foundation of TAOISM, which combines philosophical speculation with MYSTICAL reflection. Its meaning is "The Tao: Its Virtue and Power," and it is ascribed to LAO TZU. It was written about 250 B.C. as a polemic against Confucianism (see CONFUCIUS) and realist PHILOSOPHIES, and contains many poems.

TAO TSANG: the CANON of TAOISM which contains over 1,120 books; their date and authorship are generally unknown. They use ESOTERIC language and were first collected together around 745 B.C. for use by initiates.

TAOISM: the indigenous Chinese RELIGION which grew out of earlier SHAMANISM and magical CULTS and combined with MYSTICAL elements in the PHILOSOPHY of LAO TZU and Chuang Tzu. It originally aimed at the realization of perfect happiness and the prolongation of life through unity with the TAO by practicing nonactivity, noninterference and humility, and renouncing force, pride and self-assertion. The techniques used included ALCHEMY, ASCETICISM, health and dietary rules, a Chinese form of YOGA, MAGIC, petitionary PRAYER and the WORSHIP of powerful DEITIES.

TAT TVAM ASI: a MANTRA in HINDUISM and a SANSKRIT phrase meaning "thou art that" which sums up the essential message of the Chāndogya Upanishad that the true ESSENCE of the UNIVERSE and the individual SOUL are identical. "Tat" refers to BRAHMAN, or the ABSOLUTE, while "Tvam" means the ĀTMAN, or the individual, thus indicating the essential unity of the part and the whole.

TATAGATA: a term used by the BUDDHA to refer to himself which literally means "he who has come" or "he who has gone." Although there is no agreement as to its exact MEANING, BUDDHIST commentators give literally hundreds of explanations.

TAWḤĪD: a disputed MUSLIM DOCTRINE which probably means that GOD is without equal. It was used by MYSTICS to refer to the unity of God and the experience of ECSTASY during MEDITATION.

TAYLOR, James Hudson (1832-1905): British PLYMOUTH BRETHREN MISSIONARY to China who adopted local dress and pioneered living with the people. Finding no missionary society willing to back his unconventional methods, he founded the China Inland Mission in 1865 as a FAITH mission. His example inspired many similar missionary movements and new ideals of PIETY based on the faith principle, influencing many in the EVANGELICAL missionary movement.

TAYLOR, Jeremy (1613-1667): English theologian and MYSTIC whose works *The Rule and Exercise of Holy Living* (1650) and *Holy Dying* (1651) did much to maintain the mystical tradition in the CHURCH OF ENGLAND.

TE: the Chinese character signifying virtue.

TE DEUM: an ancient CHRISTIAN HYMN praising GOD.

TEILHARD DE CHARDIN, Pierre (1881-1955): French JESUIT whose writings on RELIGION and EVOLUTION made him a CULT figure in the 1960s. His dubious involvement with the PILTDOWN MAN and pro-FASCIST sympathies, however, cast a dark shadow over his academic achievements.

TELEOLOGY: derived from the Greek words *telos* and *logos*, it means end or goal and is generally used to refer to the adaptation of means to ends, or specifically to that branch of PHILOSOPHY concerned with ends or final CAUSES.

TELEOLOGICAL: related to a purpose or a designated end.

TELEOLOGICAL ARGUMENT: an inductive argument from observations about the presence of purpose and apparent design in the UNIVERSE to a Designer or GOD who created order in the universe. The best-known example of this argument is PALEY's ANALOGY of the watch, which begins by assuming that someone who has never seen a clockwork watch before accidentally discovers one. Paley goes on to say that after careful examination of the design and operation of the watch, any reasonable person would conclude that the watch was man-made, and, therefore, anyone who carefully observes the universe must ultimately reach the conclusion that it displays characteristics indicating the presence of a mind behind its design. Although strongly attacked by David HUME, this form of argument has been revived recently by a number of statisticians and astrophysicists.

TELEPATHY: the BELIEF that it is possible for individuals to communicate directly and over large distances through the power of the MIND, without speech or other forms of oral or visual communication. Acceptance of telepathy plays an important role in many NEW RELIGIOUS MOVEMENTS and SCIENCE FICTION stories, although actual evidence for it is highly disputed.

TEMPLARS: a MONASTIC order of medieval knights founded in 1118 by Hugh de Payens to protect pilgrims visiting PALESTINE. They became very influential and wealthy, and this led to rivalry with other orders, and eventually to charges of immorality and heresy and suppression by King Philip of France and the POPE in 1312.

TEMPLE: a HOLY building used for RITUAL SACRIFICE and WORSHIP.

TEMPLE, William (1881-1944): English theologian and philosopher who became ARCHBISHOP of CANTERBURY and had a passionate interest in SOCIAL JUSTICE. His books include *Nature, Man and God* (1934) and *Christianity and the Social Order* (1942).

TENDAI BUDDHISM: the leading Japanese school of BUDDHISM founded by Dengyō Daishi in 805 on the basis of the LOTUS SŪTRA. It is centered on the monastery at Mount Hiei near Kyoto, and teaches that the historical BUDDHA is a manifestation of the eternal Buddha-nature which is the fundamental ESSENCE of the UNIVERSE. As a result the Buddha becomes an object of FAITH, enabling individuals to realize their own ultimate Buddha-nature and thus attain ENLIGHTENMENT.

TENGALAI: followers of RĀMĀNUJA who emphasized his teachings about divine GRACE, known as the "cat-principle," and adhered to non-VEDIC SCRIPTURES known as the Prambandham or collected poems of the Ālvārs. The greatest SAINT of the SECT is Varavara Muni, who is regarded as an AVATĀR of Rāmānuja.

TEN COMMANDMENTS: the essential commandments of the law given by God to MOSES and recorded in the Bible in Exodus 20 and Deuteronomy 5. It is the basis for JEWISH law and accepted as MORAL commands for living by most CHRISTIANS.

TENRI-KYŌ: a modern branch of SHINTŌ which emphasizes educational, MISSIONARY and social work. It was founded by two female SHAMANS, a peasant named Kino and a housewife named Nakayama Miki. Both women appear to have had vivid religious experiences which transformed their lives and led to the formation of this Shintō REVITALIZATION MOVEMENT. The teachings of the group show CHRISTIAN and BUDDHIST influences and in many ways resemble CHRISTIAN SCIENCE. Human SOULS are part of GOD, with the implication that we create our own GOOD and EVIL. Evil is overcome by turning it into good through a process of SALVATION. This enables communication with God to be established by means of PURIFICATION and religious RITUALS.

TERESA OF ÁVILA (1515-1582): Italian ROMAN CATHOLIC Carmelite NUN, religious reformer and MYSTIC whose works *The Way of Perfection, Book of Foundations, The Interior Castle* and autobiographical *Life* are considered among the great classics of mystical writings.

TERMINUS A QUO: Latin term for a starting point from which measurement begins.

TERMINUS AD QUEM: Latin term for an end point where measurement ends.

TERTIUM QUID: Latin term for a mediating alternative between the beginning and end points which is sometimes chosen when people are presented with a dilemma. It is a "mediating alternative," or a "third possibility."

TERTULLIAN, Quintus Septimius Florens (160-225): one of the founders of African CHRISTIANITY, apologist and theologian. It is often claimed that he became a MONTANIST but no contemporary evidence, from his own writings or other sources, exists to substantiate this, except for his attempts to defend the Montanists from persecution. His Greek works have not survived, but thirty-one Latin works remain, making his writings the first significant corpus of Latin Christian literature.

THALES OF MILETUS (640-546 B.C.): the "father" of Greek PHILOSOPHY who achieved fame when he predicted the solar eclipse of 586 B.C. He argued that water is the origin of everything and the basic substance of the UNIVERSE.

THEISM: BELIEF in a personal GOD who is the sole CREATOR and ruler of the UNIVERSE and everything that exists. It is a system of thought that assumes the EXISTENCE of one unified and perfect BEING who, although distinguished from the COSMOS (unlike PANTHEISM), is its source and the power which continues to be active in it, sustaining and providentially guiding it (unlike DEISM).

THEODICY: a word coined by the philosopher LEIBNIZ from two Greek words meaning "GOD" and "justice." It refers to attempts to justify the goodness of God in the face of the manifold EVIL in the world.

THEOLOGY: from the Greek words *theos*, meaning GOD, and *logos*, or discourse; it means the study of GOD, the SACRED or divine, and it covers the entire range of issues concerning the relationship of humans to God. Traditionally it refers to the CHRISTIAN enterprise of presenting a systematic, RATIONAL explanation and justification of FAITH through the use of CONCEPTS derived from PHILOSOPHY and logic.

THEOPHANY: the temporal and spatial manifestation of GOD or the divine in some visible form.

THEORY: derived from the Greek word *theōria*, which means a way of "viewing," or "looking at." A theory is a way of viewing things in their ideal, universal relationships to each other. It is an expression of a general principle or abstraction which gives a systematic account of a particular subject. Theories are found within larger bodies of knowledge which relate together to form a scientific discipline and are used to explain EMPIRICAL phenomena.

THEOSOPHICAL SOCIETY: founded in New York City in 1875 by a Russian SPIRITUALIST, Helena Petrovna BLAVATSKY, and Henry Olcott (1832-1907). The Theosophical Society promotes MAGIC, ESOTERIC MYSTICISM and the study of COMPARATIVE RELIGION. In 1878 the founders moved to India where they established the international headquarters of the movement. After their death their British convert, the former FREE THINKER Annie BESANT, became the movement's leader and promoted her protégé KRISHNAMURTI as the new ĀVATAR. When he rejected this role and repudiated THEOSOPHY the movement suffered a blow from which it has scarcely recovered. Nevertheless it remains important today because of its influence on the growth of Indian NATIONALISM, individuals like GANDHI, the COUNTERCULTURE of the 1960s and the NEW AGE MOVEMENT.

THEOSOPHY: a MYSTICAL tradition propagated by the THEOSOPHICAL SOCIETY. Theosophy is a form of MONISM which teaches spiritual EVOLUTION and seeks REALITY through mystical experience based on finding ESOTERIC meanings in the SACRED writings of the world.

THERAVĀDA BUDDHISM: known as the "Lesser Vehicle" because of its strict interpretation of the BUDDHIST CANON and emphasis upon the MONASTIC order of the SAŃGHA. It is the main rival to MAHĀYĀNA BUDDHISM and is dominant in Sri Lanka, Myanmar (Burma), Thailand and Cambodia. Arising as a result of controversy over the role of the LAITY in the fourth century B.C., it claims to preserve the authentic teachings of the BUD-DHA and to be the oldest and purest form of Buddhism. The Theravādin tradition began to take shape with the second Buddhist COUNCIL in 250 B.C. but took its classical form between the fifth and tenth centuries. When Buddhism was first encountered by the West in the nineteenth century it was this tradition which at first gained recognition because of its apparent RATIONALITY and rejection of the SUPER-NATURAL.

THOMAS à KEMPIS (1380-1471): medieval Dutch MYSTIC whose work *The Imitation of Christ* continues to inspire many CHRISTIANS to PIETY and devotion.

THOMAS, GOSPEL OF: an APOCRYPHAL COPTIC text found at NAG HAMMADI which claims to contain 114 "sayings" of JESUS. The document dates from the fifth century and is generally regarded as a late GNOSTIC manuscript, although an earlier edition of the text may go back to the second century.

THOMAS, M. M. (20th century): Indian CHRISTIAN theologian, SOCIOLOGIST and philosopher whose provocative books *The Acknowledged Christ of the Indian Renaissance* (1969) and *The Christian Response to the Asian Revolution* (1966) saw GOD acting in SECU-LAR HISTORY and made a big impact on MISSIONARY thinking.

THOMPSON, Francis (1859-1907): minor English poet remembered for his poem "The Hound of Heaven" (1893).

THOREAU, Henry David (1817-1862): American TRANSCENDENTALIST philosopher whose reflections on FAITH and self-sufficiency in his book *Walden* (1854) have greatly influenced POSITIVE THINKING and the WORD OF FAITH movement.

THUCYDIDES (450-400? B.C.): Athenian general known as the founder of written HISTORY; he is the author of *The Peloponnesian War* and *A History of the War Between Athens and Sparta.*

TIBETAN BUDDHISM: after the failure of BUDDHISM in India during the twelfth century, Tibetan MONKS became the main inheritors of the Indian Buddhist tradition, preserving many ancient documents and practices which were rejected by THERAVĀDIN Buddhists in the South. From Tibet, Buddhism spread to China, Korea and Japan where the MAHĀYĀNA TRADITION became strong and produced PURE LAND, ZEN and a host of other schools. In Tibet itself a theocratic government was established and TANTRA flourished. Tibetan Buddhism, which is sometimes called "Lamaism," spread to the West in the 1950s following the Chinese Communist invasion of Tibet.

T'IEN-T'AI: an influential branch of Chinese BUDDHISM founded in the sixth century by CHIH-I which based its teachings on the LOTUS SŪTRA and the teachings of NĀGĀRJUNA, who emphasized the totality of BEING, thus identifying the parts with the whole. It declined as a result of persecution in the ninth century but not before it spread its message to Korea and Japan.

TILLICH, Paul (1886-1965): German-American philosopher and theologian who was involved in the German religious-socialist movement before opposition to Hitler and NAZISM led to his dismissal from the University of Frankfurt in 1933. In the United States, where he taught at Union Theological Seminary, New York, Tillich's work combined Platonism (*see*

PLATO), medieval MYSTICISM, German IDEALISM and EXISTENTIALISM. His best-known books are *Systematic Theology* (1963), *The Courage to Be* (1952) and *Theology of Culture* (1959).

TIPIṬAKA [TRIPIṬAKA—Sanskrit]: the PALI CANON of BUDDHIST SCRIPTURE. The name means "Three Baskets" and refers to the threefold division of texts into the VINAYA-PIṬAKA or narratives; the SUTTA-PIṬAKA or dialogues and discourses; and the Adhidhamma-Piṭaka or popular APOLOGETIC and doctrinal works.

TĪRTHAṄKARA: literally, "the ford maker," one who shows the way to LIBERATION. This is the title of the 24 great teachers of JAINISM.

TOCQUEVILLE, Alexis de (1805-1859): French historian and statesman whose book *Democracy in America* (1835) questions the relationship between RELIGION and politics in America and qualifies him as one of the founders of SOCIOLOGY.

TOLAND, John (1670-1722): Irish writer whose book *Christianity Not Mysterious* (1696) is generally regarded as the classic statement of DEISM. He coined the term PANTHEISM to describe SPINOZA's view that GOD can be identified with NATURE.

TOLEDOTH YESHU: a medieval JEWISH document whose Hebrew title means "The History of Jesus." It claims that JESUS was the illegitimate son of MARY by a Roman soldier and that his MIRACLES were the result of black MAGIC.

TOLERATION: the acceptance of the right of individuals to indulge in practices and thoughts which are generally unacceptable to the majority of members of a STATE or SOCIETY. The fight for RELIGIOUS TOLERANCE is one of the major themes in MODERN Western HISTORY and the basis for many political rights which are taken for granted in contemporary democracies.

TOLSTOY, Leo (1828-1910): Russian count, social REFORMER and author best known for his classic novels *War and Peace* (1864-1869) and *Anna Karenina* (1873-1877). A MYSTIC who sought GOD but

rejected such traditional CHRISTIAN doctrines as the INCARNATION and RESURRECTION, he wrote religious works such as *What I Believe* (1882) and *What Then Must We Do?* (1886) which have exercised a profound influence on many modern thinkers, including GANDHI.

TORAH: a term derived from the HEBREW word for "instruction" or "guidance" which the JEWS apply to the first five books of the HEBREW BIBLE, also known as the PENTATEUCH. In the TALMUD this Law is codified into 613 distinct commands which must be observed by all ORTHODOX Jews.

TORII: the distinguishing feature of SHINTŌ TEMPLES consisting of a gate frame representing bird perches that are a SYMBOL of birds invoking the return of the sun GODDESS.

TORQUEMADA, Tomás de (1420-1498): the Spanish Grand Inquisitor (*see* INQUISITION) responsible for the death of about 2,000 Spanish MUSLIMS and JEWS and the suffering of many more people whom he expelled from Spain.

TOTAL DEPRAVITY: a commonly misunderstood CHRISTIAN DOCTRINE taught by LUTHER and CALVIN but first formulated as a doctrine at the Synod of DORT. It states that human beings are affected by SIN in every part of their being. This does not mean that humans are as bad as they possibly can be but, rather, that the infection of sin is total. Thus humans are unable by their own efforts to please GOD and therefore must rely entirely on his GRACE for SALVATION. It is based upon the teachings of PAUL in the NEW TESTAMENT and is seen as an essential premise to the doctrine of JUSTIFICATION by FAITH.

TOTALITARIAN: the organization of a STATE or SOCIETY which allows no autonomous or independent institutions and denies the freedom of association to its members.

TOTEMISM: a name given by Native American Ojibwa people to their ideas and RITUAL practices linking humans and animals in a COSMOLOGICAL drama. It was applied by nineteenth-century scholars to religious systems which teach that humanity and the natural world are linked by psychic forces.

TOYNBEE, Arnold Joseph (1889-1975): English philosopher of HISTORY and author of the multivolume *A Study of History* (1934-1961), which sets out to find a pattern in historical events. In real life his loyalties swung from Marxism to FASCISM to ROMAN CATHOLICISM, throwing doubt on his ability to stand apart from historical events to see a greater whole.

TRACTARIANISM: the name given to the OXFORD MOVEMENT as a result of the publication of TRACTS FOR THE TIMES.

TRACTS FOR THE TIMES: a series of pamphlets published in the 1830s intended to restore medieval PIETY and a form of ROMAN CATHOLICISM, without the POPE, to the CHURCH OF ENGLAND: associated with NEWMAN and PUSEY. The tracts came to a sudden end in 1841 with the storm produced by Newman's *Tract 90*, which was too overtly Roman Catholic.

TRADITION: that which is handed over or passed on from the past, as distinct from modern ideas and theories. It denotes a class of actions motivated by specific perceptions, thoughts and BELIEFS held together by some principle of development. Nevertheless, the reasons for such behavior are to be found in the perceptions of the importance of the act and not in a THEORY justifying it. Traditions are shared by social GROUPS which, in turn, are shaped by them as they create a climate of shared expectations.

TRADITION DIRECTION: David Riesman's term identifying people socialized in TRADITIONAL SOCIETIES outside of Western Europe and North America. For this type of person, Riesman argues, tradition motivates and guides action, with the result that shame rather than guilt controls their ethical behavior and outlook.

TRADITIONAL: following in a TRADITION.

TRADITIONAL RELIGION: those reli-gions, usually of relatively small and isolated SOCIAL GROUPS, which rely upon ORAL TRADITIONS and follow a pattern established over generations without major or conscious input from the great world religions of the ABRAMIC and YOGIC TRADITIONS. The term applies to most African religions, as well as North American Native religions and the religions of Polynesia.

TRADITIONALIST: someone who rigidly follows a TRADITION.

TRADITIONS, GREAT AND LITTLE: terms coined by the American ANTHRO-POLOGIST Robert REDFIELD in his book *Peasant Society and Culture: An Anthropological Approach to Civilization* (1956) to express the difference between the consciously cultivated and deliberately transmitted, usually literate, philosophical and self-reflective tradition of a small, educated, national or cosmopolitan elite, and the popular beliefs and practices of the uneducated masses living in local communities. In RELIGIOUS terms the great tradition is expressed in the literate WORLD RELIGIONS of scholars, which are based upon written SCRIPTURES, and the little tradition in the CHARISMATIC and FOLK RELIGIONS of the masses.

TRANCE: an altered state of consciousness which sometimes occurs spontaneously but is usually induced by RITUAL acts which either evoke a MYSTICAL experience or enable an individual to become a SPIR-ITUALIST MEDIUM or SHAMAN.

TRANSCENDENCE: from the Latin meaning "to surpass" or "go beyond." In general the term is used in three ways: to designate any ideal, thing or BEING that "stands over against" the knowing subject; to signify that which stands "over against" all FINITE being, such as GOD; and to designate certain CATEGORIES that necessarily characterize any conceivable or possible being.

TRANSCENDENT: existing prior to, independent of, and exalted over the UNIVERSE of space and time.

TRANSCENDENTAL MEDITATION

(TM): the first really successful NEW RELIGIOUS MOVEMENT of the 1960s; it emerged from HINDUISM as a group providing therapy and offering psychological well-being. The founder, Maharishi Mahesh Yogi, denied that TM was a RELIGION, thus enabling his movement to appeal to a wide spectrum of people who might otherwise have ignored his teachings, and to apply for American government funding and other forms of assistance. Taken to court in 1978, TM was found to be a religion under the terms of American law. It teaches a simplified form of YOGA and practices initiation with OCCULT overtones, using MANTRAS in SANSKRIT which appear to invoke various Hindu DEITIES.

TRANSCENDENTALISM: growing out of UNITARIANISM in the 1830s, it became one of the most influential religious movements of nineteenth-century America. Associated with EMERSON and THOREAU, and with intellectual roots in German ROMANTICISM and writers like GOETHE, COLERIDGE and CARLYLE, it preached extreme INDIVIDUALISM, LIBERALISM and a PANTHEISTIC view of GOD. Promoting MYSTICISM and an interest in YOGIC religions, transcendentalism contributed to the rise of many modern NEW RELIGIOUS MOVEMENTS.

TRANSCHANNELER: a term invented by OCCULTISTS in the 1980s to facilitate widespread acceptance of SPIRITUALISM. The use of this new term, popularized by J. Z. KNIGHT and Shirley MACLAINE, gives a pseudo-scientific air to ideas which would otherwise be dismissed as discredited superstitions. The name connotes radio and television channels, suggesting that the MEDIUM, or transchanneler, is communicating with the "cosmic realm" or "another reality" often associated with UFOs and similar supposedly "scientific" phenomenon.

TRANSMIGRATION: a form of METEMPSYCHOSIS or REBIRTH which teaches that at DEATH the SOUL leaves the body to be reborn in another body as a baby. It is closely associated with, and often confused with, REINCARNATION.

TRANSUBSTANTIATION: the ROMAN CATHOLIC DOGMA teaching that during the MASS the SUBSTANCE of the elements of bread and wine are transformed into the substance of the body and blood of CHRIST by the words of the priestly consecration, even though their appearance (ACCIDENTS) remains the same.

TRENT, COUNCIL OF: the great ROMAN CATHOLIC church COUNCIL, held intermittently between 1545 and 1563, which provided the definitive definition of Catholicism in reaction to the PROTESTANT REFORMATION. The council affirmed the equal validity of TRADITION and SCRIPTURE as sources of religious TRUTH, the sole AUTHORITY of the church to interpret the BIBLE, and the institution of the seven SACRAMENTS, and it denied the Protestant understanding of JUSTIFICATION by FAITH. Efforts were initiated to REFORM the church, and Protestant DOCTRINES were condemned as heretical.

TRIBULATION: a popular DOCTRINE in FUNDAMENTALIST and EVANGELICAL CHRISTIANITY which teaches that before the LAST JUDGMENT the world and its people will enter a period of extreme suffering during which the full wrath of SATAN is exposed. There is considerable disagreement about whether CHRISTIANS will have to endure this Great Tribulation or whether they will be rescued by CHRIST and taken up into HEAVEN prior to its onset. This idea, known as the "rapture" and based on an interpretation of 1 Thessalonians 4:17, is not part of the historic Christian TRADITION. It became popular through the efforts of John Nelson DARBY and DISPENSATIONALISM.

TRIRATNA: the "Three Jewels" of BUDDHISM, which are the BUDDHA, the DHARMA and the SAṄGHA. In popular PIETY they form a chant: "To the Buddha for refuge I go; to the Dharma for refuge I go; to the Saṅgha for refuge I go."

TRINITY: a Christian DOCTRINE formulated in the fourth century with roots in the NEW TESTAMENT and EARLY CHURCH. Defining ORTHODOXY and HERESY, it is based upon what the BIBLE teaches about the relationship between the CREATOR GOD, referred to as God the Father, the person of JESUS OF NAZARETH, or the CHRIST, and the HOLY SPIRIT. Teaching that there is but one God who exists from ETERNITY, it seeks to explain biblical references to the Father, Son and Holy Spirit as divine BEINGS. The classic Western formula is "three PERSONS in one SUBSTANCE," while Eastern Christians say, "three *hypostases* in one BEING." Ultimately the Trinity is a mystery that is accepted by Christians as the only way to harmonize various biblical teachings. Many attempts have been made to explain it in terms of ANALOGIES involving clover leaves; the appearance of water as ice, liquid and steam; and the mind-body relationship.

TROELTSCH, Ernst (1865-1923): LIBERAL German theologian who devoted his energies to the problems raised for RELIGION by the scientific method applied to HISTORY and the question of CHRISTIANITY and CULTURE. He denied that dogmatic THEOLOGY has access to ABSOLUTE TRUTH and was intensely concerned with social and political questions. His most famous work is *The Social Teaching of the Christian Church* (1912).

TROTMAN, Dawson (1906-1956): American EVANGELIST and founder of the NAVIGATORS who developed the "follow-up" program for Billy GRAHAM's Crusades.

TROTSKYITE: followers of Leon Trotsky (1879-1940) and radical Marxism.

TRUTH: that which is true; the quality of being correct or in some way confirmed by REALITY. The EXISTENCE of truth and/or the possibility of our knowing it has been denied by a variety of thinkers, from ancient SOPHISTS to modern RELATIVISTS. Two major theories of truth have dominated Western philosophy: the COHERENCE THEORY which states that truth is known by its coherence within a system of ideas, and the CORRESPONDENCE THEORY which sees truth as corresponding to an external reality. Other theories of truth include PRAGMATISM, the view that that which works is true; various SCIENTIFIC theories involving experimentation and VERIFICATION; and POPPER's ideas which are based on FALSIFICATION rather than verification.

TURNER, Witter Victor (1920-1986): leading British social anthropologist (*see* ANTHROPOLOGY) and convert to ROMAN CATHOLICISM who wrote extensively on religious themes. His *The Forest of Symbols* (1967) and *The Ritual Process* (1969) are important contributions to the interpretation of symbolism and RITUAL.

TWICE BORN: the three upper CASTES in HINDUISM who undergo full initiation into the community and receive the SACRED "thread." The term is also used in CHRISTIANITY to make the distinction between nonbelievers, who are once born, and believers, who are "twice born," or BORN AGAIN. The psychologist William JAMES used the term in the latter sense.

TYCHE: the Greek CONCEPT of CHANCE personified as a GODDESS.

TYLOR, Edward Burnett, Sir (1832-1917): English "armchair anthropologist" who coined the term ANIMISM in his book *Primitive Culture* (1871) to describe the RELIGION of many nonliterate peoples. He became the first professor of ANTHROPOLOGY at the University of Oxford in 1884, making him one of the founders of the academic discipline.

TYNDALE, William (1494-1536): English BIBLE translator who was burned at the stake after torture for his attempts to give the Bible to ordinary people in their own language.

TYRRELL, George (1861-1909): Irish ROMAN CATHOLIC theologian and MODERNIST whose book *Christianity at the Cross Roads* (1909) suggested that CHRISTIANITY might be a stepping stone toward the establishment of a new global RELIGION.

U

UGARIT: the name of an ancient city discovered in 1928 at Ras Shamra on the Syrian coast where hundreds of religious literary texts were found. The name is applied to the language used in many of these texts which is based on an alphabet and had been previously unknown. The texts are an important source for information about CANAANITE RELIGION and the background of ancient JUDAISM.

'ULAMĀ': a learned man in ISLAM who is able to give FATWĀ, or guidance on the basis of orthodox Islamic belief and practice.

ULTRAMONTANISM: a movement within the ROMAN CATHOLIC CHURCH originating in France during the seventeenth century and favoring direct, centralized control from Rome. The JESUITS were strong supporters of this position, and it came to dominate the church in the nineteenth century.

UMAYYADS: the MUSLIM CALIPHATE established by Mu'āwiyah ibn Abī Sufyān and based in Damascus; it held power for over 600 years.

UNCONSCIOUS: a psychological theory popularized by FREUD and JUNG which argues that below the conscious, RA-TIONAL aspect of the mind there lies a realm which has the ability to affect our dreams, thoughts and actions without our being consciously aware of the source exerting the influence on us. Many other scholars see this as an unproved assumption which is part of modern IRRATIONAL-ISM.

UNDERHILL, Evelyn (1875-1941): English ANGLICAN who wrote extensively on MYSTICISM and SPIRITUALITY. Her best-known book is *Mysticism* (1911).

UNIFICATION CHURCH: a highly controversial Korean NEW RELIGIOUS MOVE-MENT which gained much publicity in the 1970s. The full name of the movement is The Holy Spirit Association for the Unification of World Christianity, and it was founded in 1954 by an engineer, Sun Myung MOON. The principal document is *The Divine Principle*, which lays out its fundamental teachings. The THEOLOGY of the SECT is one of the most comprehensive found in any of the NEW RELIGIOUS MOVEMENTS. It consists of a systematic attempt to interpret the BIBLE from the perspective of Korean thought based on Confucian (*see* CONFUCIUS) and BUDDHIST PHILOSOPHY with insights gained from

Korean SHAMANISM. The result is one of the most ambitious efforts yet to produce an intellectually defensible non-Western theological system based on the Bible. Many ideas generated by this theology are likely to influence similar non-Western theologies in the future, including that of INDEMNITY.

UNITARIANISM: a modern religious movement characterized by its rejection of the DOCTRINES of the TRINITY and the DEITY of CHRIST. It first appeared in Poland and Hungary among ANABAPTISTS during the PROTESTANT REFORMATION, but remained dormant until 1785 and the birth of the first American Unitarian congregation in Boston. The THEOLOGY quickly spread among CONGREGATIONAL churches in Eastern Massachusetts and found support at Harvard Divinity School, which became its center. Unitarianism is a creedless RATIONALIST movement which rejects orthodox views about the AUTHORITY of the BIBLE, stressing instead many forms of divine REVELATION and the inherent goodness of man.

UNITED REFORMED CHURCH: an English denomination formed in 1972 from the union of CONGREGATIONALISTS and PRESBYTERIANS.

UNIVERSAL (noun): something belonging to all the members of a GROUP which therefore identifies the specific NATURE of that group and distinguishes it from other things or particulars. Philosophically the question of universals and particulars, or the "one and the many," has been important since the time of the Greeks, and many answers have been offered to the basic questions raised. For example: What is it that leads us to call poodles and fox terriers dogs and not cats? The quality of "dogginess" is the universal.

UNIVERSALISM: a theological view within CHRISTIANITY, usually deemed HERESY, which teaches that all people will eventually be saved, as opposed to the orthodox position which maintains that only people who show REPENTANCE and

FAITH in CHRIST obtain SALVATION. The term is also used to denote the belief developed in the HEBREW BIBLE that GOD is the God of the whole world, not just of ISRAEL.

UNIVERSALITY: a quality of TRUTH. To be true something must be so under all conditions regardless of the contingencies of time and space.

UNIVERSE: a Latin term meaning "the whole" referring to the COSMOS and all that exists in space and time. For CHRISTIANS the term implies everything which originates in the actions and will of the CREATOR God.

UNIVOCAL: having only one MEANING.

UNMOVED MOVER: the term used by ARISTOTLE to refer to the CREATOR and sustainer of the UNIVERSE. It was taken by CHRISTIANS to apply to GOD.

UNTOUCHABLES: the lowest CASTE in HINDU SOCIETY who are considered ritually unclean and are therefore excluded from both religious and civil society. Although the constitution of India outlaws the practice of untouchability, abuses continue, and many untouchables report being unable to vote in elections.

UPANISHAD: literally "to sit near" or "near sitting." The term can mean "secret"; a MYSTICAL doctrine or teaching; or, most commonly, a collection of texts which since the eighth century B.C. have been known as "the last of the VEDAS." The content and doctrine of the Upanishads vary considerably, from treaties which promote ATHEISM to devotional THEISM. They thus represent a wide spectrum of philosophical schools and outlooks. Indian tradition teaches that the thirteen classical Upanishads were composed between the eighth and fourth centuries B.C., but many later works also use the name, some of which are dated as late as the fifteenth century. The earliest extant manuscripts, or SACRED TEXTS, for any of the Upanishads date from sometime later than the fifteenth century A.D.

URBAN II (1042-1099): reforming POPE

who initiated the First CRUSADE to help defend Eastern European nations against MUSLIM attacks and to obtain free access to JERUSALEM for pilgrims.

URIM AND THUMMIM: a mode of DIVINATION mentioned in the HEBREW BIBLE which Joseph SMITH claimed to use to translate the *Book of Mormon*.

URSULINE ORDER: a ROMAN CATHOLIC order of NUNS originally founded in 1535 by Angela Merici as a society for unmarried women dedicated to teaching. It developed into a religious order in the seventeenth century and began to follow the rule of SAINT AUGUSTINE.

USSHER, James (1581-1656): Irish PROTESTANT BISHOP and scholar who added dates to biblical HISTORY and proposed the date of creation to be 4004 B.C.

USURY: the lending of money at any rate of interest, often restricted to meaning exorbitant interest. The practice was banned by the CHRISTIAN CHURCH and by ISLAM, which still bans all forms of interest on the basis of ARISTOTLE's theory of money. Following the PROTESTANT REFORMATION most Protestant churches distinguished between usury as extortion and interest as legitimate reward for venturing capital. The ROMAN CATHOLIC Church also adopted this position in the late nineteenth century.

UTILITARIANISM: a philosophical movement, often identified with ETHICS, developed by BENTHAM and popularized by MILL in the nineteenth century. It is based on the belief that what is important is whether something is of use to people or not. In ethics the utilitarian principle was developed in terms of promoting "the greatest happiness for the greatest number." Thus the goodness of any act is to be judged by its consequences in terms of the principle of utility. The movement had a great impact on nineteenth-century thought, promoting social and political REFORM, and continues to exert considerable practical influence even today.

UTOPIA: a term signifying an ideal SOCIETY; it was first coined by Thomas MORE, who used it to describe an imaginary island where justice, peace and happiness prevailed. The name literally means "no place" or "nowhere."

UTOPIANISM: a form of SOCIALISM criticized by MARX which postulates an ideal without investigating whether existing social conditions make it possible to achieve. Marxism is held to be SCIENTIFIC because it develops out of THEORIES based on what exists. Utopianism in a more general sense refers to political theories lacking in realism.

V

VAḌAGALAI: followers of RĀMĀNUJA, who emphasized that human effort is the condition of divine GRACE. Their view became known as the "monkey principle" from the fact that a young monkey clings to its mother as she moves about. Thus it is through striving for SALVATION and by fulfillment of VEDIC religious duties that one attains LIBERATION.

VAIŚEṢIKA: one of the six schools of HINDU thought, this PHILOSOPHY expounded an atomistic interpretation of the UNIVERSE. Around the tenth century it merged with the NYĀYA school to promote a form of THEISM based on METAPHYSICS, and it taught that GOD is the BEING who combines and separates the atoms of the universe.

VAIṢṆAVISM: the CULT of VISHNU which emphasizes BHAKTI and the WORSHIP of GODS such as KRISHNA. It is credited with producing the BHAGAVAD-GĪTA and an extensive devotional literature rich in MYTH and SYMBOLISM. Its chief rival in the HINDU tradition is ŚAIVISM which arose around the same period of time—300 B.C. to A.D. 300.

VAIŚYA: the lowest of the three TWICE BORN within the CASTE system of HINDU-ISM. They are the acceptable workers, traders and merchants, by whose labors the members of the other castes live.

VAJRAYĀNA: the final phase in the development of Indian MAHĀYĀNA BUDDHISM which aimed at attaining success and power in this world rather than NIRVĀNA in the far distant future. As a result it concentrated on MAGIC, MIRACLES and OCCULT knowledge. It was eventually carried to Tibet where it became the dominant form of Buddhism (*see* TIBETAN BUDDHISM).

VALENTINE (3rd century): a legendary CHRISTIAN MARTYR after whom Valentine's Day is named.

VALENTINUS (2nd century): Gnostic philosopher who taught that the masculine principle of the UNIVERSE unites with the feminine to produce mind, thus creating a DIALECTICAL process which created everything.

VALHALLA: the ancient Scandinavian realm of dead heroes.

VALID: a term in logic signifying an argument in which the conclusion necessarily follows from the premises. In more general terms, valid can mean true or correct.

VALLABHA (1480-1535?): a BRAHMIN who helped to found the Vallabhācārya branch of HINDUISM. He promoted his own version of NONDUALISM, arguing that MĀYĀ is God's creative activity and not a pure illusion as ŚAṄKARA had suggested. His theology was PANENTHEISTIC with an emphasis on God's GRACE and BHAKTI as means of attaining LIBERATION. He promoted the worship of KRISHNA and his consort Rādhā, arguing that the union of lovers reflects the MYSTICAL union of the SOUL with God.

VALUE: the quality of a thing which makes it an object of desire; something which is esteemed and worth having. Many theories of value exist which seek to explain why certain things, BELIEFS and actions have value.

VĀRĀṆSĪ: one of the seven SACRED cities in India revered by both HINDUS and BUDDHISTS.

VARṆAS: the four traditional CASTES, or classes, in Indian society. The word literally means "color," indicating the racial origin of the caste system.

VARUṆA: a GOD in HINDUISM who appears in the early VEDAS as a sky god but later becomes the all-seeing DEITY.

VASUBANDHU (4th century): a HĪNĀYĀNA BUDDHIST scholar and writer who was said to have converted to the MAHĀYĀNA tradition through the arguments of his brother. Modern scholars believe that this traditional story is probably propaganda.

VATICAN: the residence of the POPE in Rome, which has the status of an independent city-state.

VATICAN COUNCILS: the First Vatican Council, which was highly CONSERVATIVE and emphasized differences between ROMAN CATHOLICISM and PROTESTANTISM, was held in Rome during 1869 and 1870 as the twentieth Ecumenical Council. It ended abruptly with the outbreak of war and the occupation of the city. The Second Vatican Council, lasting from 1962 to 1965, was also held in Rome. It met at the bidding of POPE John XXIII, who attributed the idea to the inspiration of the HOLY SPIRIT. He defined its task as renewing the religious life of the Roman Catholic Church and modernizing its teaching, discipline and organization as a step toward unifying all CHRISTIANS. The far-reaching decisions of the council completely revolutionized the Roman Catholic Church, encouraging both the ministry of the LAITY and, inadvertently, the CHARISMATIC MOVEMENT.

VĀTSĪPUTRĪYA: an unorthodox school of BUDDHISM which emerged in the third century B.C. led by Vātsīputra. It is distinguished by an affirmation of the REALITY of the human person, or SOUL, and by a belief in TRANSMIGRATION.

VĀYU: the HINDU GOD of the wind.

VEDA: literally "knowledge," signifying the SACRED knowledge or REVELATION which has been "heard," according to the HINDU religious tradition. It began as ORAL TRADITION, becoming a written tradition much later. The Vedas are ancient revelations found in a series of HYMNS, RITUAL texts and speculations composed over a period of a millennium beginning 1400 B.C. The earliest documents are probably from around the fifteenth century and were recorded by MUSLIM authors.

VEDĀNTA: one of the six classical schools of HINDU PHILOSOPHY and that which is best known in the West. The name literally means "the end of the VEDA." It is based on the UPANISHADS and interprets the RITUAL practices of the Vedas in terms of symbolic meanings. There are three main schools of Vedānta: that of Advaita which promotes MONISM; Viśiṣṭādvaita or qualified NONDUALISM; and Dvaita, which is a form of DUALISM. All three are similar to Platonism (*see* PLATO) in aiming to go beyond the limits of EMPIRICAL observation to explore the nature of BRAHMAN. Both ŚAṄKARA and RĀMĀNUJA taught forms of Vedānta, even though they presented sharply differing interpretations of the tradition. In the late nineteenth century various thinkers sought to create a synthesis between the different aspects of Vedānta and Western forms of IDEALISM, while VIVEKANANDA, RADHAKRISHNAN and Sri AUROBINDO adapted Vedānta to the theory of EVOLUTION and Western SCIENCE.

VEDI: a sacrificial center in early HINDU-ISM.

VEDIC HYMNS: see ṚG VEDA.

VEDIC RELIGION: the religion of the ancient ARYAN invaders of India which is found in the ṚG VEDA and other early Indian literature. It is similar to ancient Greek religion, being rich in MYTH and RITUAL and involving GODS, SACRIFICE and heroic deeds. It was life-affirming and worldly, and very different from later HINDUISM. Later Vedic religion tends toward MONOTHEISM, and it eventually developed through a series of textual reinterpretations in such works as the UPANISHADS into classical Hinduism, which ignores and even reverses many earlier concerns.

VEGAN: an extreme vegetarian who refuses to eat or use any animal products, including milk and eggs.

VEGETARIANISM: the refusal to eat meat. This is often justified on religious grounds derived from YOGIC RELIGION.

VENERATION: to hold a being or object in great respect or awe akin to WORSHIP; to prostrate oneself before a being or object by kneeling or kissing, and the performance of other acts of respect or reverence. In many RELIGIOUS TRADITIONS certain individuals, HOLY men or SAINTS, and their RELICS are venerated.

VERIFICATION: the process of determining the TRUTH of something, that is, its conformity to FACTS or REALITY.

VERIFICATION PRINCIPLE: the position taken by the VIENNA CIRCLE and promoted by LOGICAL POSITIVISM that holds a statement is meaningful if and only if it can be verified EMPIRICALLY. A modified version of this states that a statement is meaningful if and only if it is *in principle* verifiable empirically. It was popularized

in the English-speaking world by A. J. AYER in his book *Language, Truth and Logic* (1936, second revised edition 1946).

VIA MEDIA: the middle way. This was the position promoted by seventeenth-century ANGLICANS, who saw Anglicanism as a moderate compromise between the extremes of ROMAN CATHOLICISM and PURITANISM.

VIA NEGATIVA: the way of negation. A philosophic position which argues that, because of the limitations of human language, we cannot really say anything positive about GOD. Any statement about the divine BEING can at best only say what God is not, as a way of approximating the REALITY of the DEITY.

VICAR: a title for a pastor or minister in the CHURCH OF ENGLAND. "Vicar of Christ" is a title for the POPE.

VICIOUS CIRCLE: the logical FALLACY which involves supporting an argument by circular reasoning in which the conclusion has already been used to support a premise upon which the conclusion is based. Generally it means using a statement to support a second statement which is then taken without further evidence as proof of a third statement that says essentially the same thing as the first statement. For example: one might argue that the Beatles were better musicians than Bach because people who know about music prefer the Beatles. When asked who these people are who know about music, one is told it is people who listen to the Beatles. Usually such arguments are more complicated and confusing, but the principle is the same.

VICO, Giovanni Battista (1668-1744): Italian ROMAN CATHOLIC philosopher and critic of Descartes who developed the first modern PHILOSOPHY of HISTORY in his *Principles of a New Science* (1725). He gave close attention to language and MYTH and insisted that historical periods must be seen as coherent wholes in which the various aspects of SOCIETY affect each other. His work deeply influenced

HERDER, HEGEL, MARX, CROCE and COLLING-WOOD.

VIENNA CIRCLE: a philosophical movement centered at the University of Vienna in the 1920s which sought to REFORM PHILOSOPHY in terms of the empirical methodology (*see* EMPIRICISM) of modern SCIENCE. It promoted POSITIVISM and the VERIFICATION PRINCIPLE as ways of knowing the TRUTH, and eventually developed into the broader philosophical movement known as LOGICAL POSITIVISM. It is associated with the work of many philosophers and was influenced by both RUSSELL and WITTGENSTEIN. In the English-speaking world it was promoted by AYER.

VIGIL: a religious service often lasting through the night and involving PRAYER and FASTING.

VIHĀRA: a BUDDHIST monastery (*see* MONASTICISM).

VINAYA-PIṬAKA: the first of the three SACRED books of BUDDHIST SCRIPTURES; it is principally concerned with questions of DISCIPLINE and the rules of MONASTIC life.

VIRGIL (70-19 B.C.): Roman poet and scholar whose history of Rome, the *Aeneid*, was adopted as a basic text in education throughout the Roman Empire. His work exercised great influence over early CHRISTIAN thinkers, who appreciated his high moral standards and PHILOSOPHY of HISTORY, and he is the classical author most quoted in the EARLY CHURCH.

VIRGIN BIRTH: the traditional belief that JESUS CHRIST was born of the Virgin MARY. Although the founders of many religions are often depicted as having a miraculous birth, the CHRISTIAN belief does seem unique in its particulars and is important for an orthodox view (*see* ORTHODOXY) of the INCARNATION.

VIRTUE: an idea derived from Greek PHILOSOPHY, especially STOICISM, which expresses the quality of knowing and doing the good. In Greek there were four cardinal virtues: wisdom, courage, justice and moderation. CHRISTIANITY has TRADITIONALLY taught the three cardinal virtues of FAITH, hope and charity or LOVE. See Jonathan EDWARDS, *The Nature of True Virtue* (1755).

VISHNU (Viṣṇu—Sanskrit): HINDU term meaning chief DEITY or supreme LORD; the second member of the trinity which includes Brahmā and Śiva.

VISION: the MIRACULOUS appearance of a DEITY or HOLY personage. Visions often lead to a CONVERSION experience or the formation of a NEW RELIGIOUS MOVEMENT or REVITALIZATION MOVEMENT.

VISUDDIMAGGA: the "path of PURIFICATION," an exposition of the BUDDHIST EIGHTFOLD PATH written in PALI by BUDDHAGHOSA (fifth century A.D.) and one of the most important works in THERAVĀDAN BUDDHISM.

VIVEKANANDA, Swami (1863-1902): Indian RELIGIOUS leader who after studying Western PHILOSOPHY became a SKEPTIC before being CONVERTED to HINDUISM by RAMAKRISHNA in 1881. He believed that Indian civilization could be regenerated through a new interpretation of VEDĀNTA which unified SCIENCE and RELIGION and brought about REFORMS in the social order such as the emancipation of women and abolition of the CASTE system. Following his attendance at the WORLD PARLIAMENT OF RELIGIONS in Chicago in 1893 he founded the RAMAKRISHNA MISSION in 1897. See *The Complete Works of Swami Vivekananda* (1924-1932).

VLADIMIR I (956-1015): Grand Prince of Kiev, Russia, he was a PAGAN who converted to CHRISTIANITY and enforced his new RELIGION on all his subjects.

VOLTAIRE, François Marie-Arouet (1694-1778): French writer with a malicious wit who was exiled to London from 1726 to 1729. There he came into contact with the English ENLIGHTENMENT and developed a lifelong admiration of the English. His books are filled with hatred for orthodox CHRISTIANITY and a deep pessimism created by the EVIL he observed in human affairs. He accepted the TELEOLOGICAL argument and strongly supported DEISM.

VOODOO: an Afro-American RELIGION with West African roots that incorporates elements of ROMAN CATHOLICISM. It is SPIRITIST in nature, involving SACRIFICES and RITUAL fire dances by PRIESTS or PRIESTESSES who are POSSESSED by various gods to become Spiritualist MEDIUMS. Its major base is in Haiti, although it has spread to Cuba, Brazil and North America.

W

WAHHĀBĪYA: an eighteenth-century ISLAMIC REVITALIZATION MOVEMENT owing its origin to Muḥammad ʿAbd al-Wahhāb, who denounced idolatry, including visiting the tombs of SAINTS, invoking PROPHETS, saints and angels and seeking their intercession, and making vows to anyone but GOD. The movement stressed PREDESTINATION and denounced ALLEGORICAL INTERPRETATION of the QURʾĀN. Demanding that FAITH should be proved by works, it made attendance at public PRAYER obligatory, the ROSARY was forbidden and MOSQUES were stripped of ornaments. In 1902 Ibn Saʿūd captured Ryad and the HOLY cities of MECCA and MEDINA, and in 1925 he established a Wahhābi dynasty in Arabia. Although puritanical, the movement is modernizing and has no hesitation about using the results of Western SCIENCE.

WALDENSES: a twelfth-century French REFORM movement in the ROMAN CATHOLIC CHURCH named for its founder, Peter Waldo, that was persecuted but survived until the PROTESTANT REFORMATION, which its members supported. Although still a very small minority in Italy, the movement has managed to survive until today and operates a theological college in Rome.

WANG YANG-MING (1472-1529): Chinese neo-Confucian (*see* CONFUCIUS) scholar whose book *Enquiry on the Great Learning* promoted IDEALISM and had a profound effect on Chinese and Japanese thought.

WARFIELD, Benjamin Breckinridge (1851-1921): American PRESBYTERIAN scholar and professor of THEOLOGY at Princeton Theological Seminary. A committed CALVINIST, he is best remembered for his impact on both EVANGELICAL and FUNDAMENTALIST movements through his arguments about the INERRANCY of SCRIPTURE found in *Revelation and Inspiration of the Bible* (1927). Another influential work is his case against the biblical authenticity of the CHARISMATIC and PENTECOSTAL movements in *Counterfeit Miracles* (1918), which argues that charismatic gifts ceased with the death of the APOSTLES.

WATTS, Isaac (1674-1748): famous English HYMN writer whose works include "When I Survey the Wondrous Cross."

WEBER, Max (1864-1920): German SOCIOLOGIST whose influential works, including *The Protestant Ethic and the Spirit of Capitalism* (1920), did much to promote the SOCIOLOGY OF RELIGION. His important contributions include the use of IDEAL TYPES, discussions of CHARISMA, and his famous Protestant work ethic thesis, which is often referred to as the "Weber Thesis."

WEIL, Simone (1909-1943): French JEWISH MYSTIC and philosopher. She was a convert to a form of Platonic (*see* PLATO) CHRISTIANITY who declined BAPTISM and maintained a distance from the CHURCH. Her books include *The Need for Roots* (1949) and *On Science, Necessity and the Love of God* (1968).

WELLHAUSEN, Julius (1844-1918): one of the most important German biblical critics of the nineteenth century. He further developed the already existing documentary theory of the origin of the PENTATEUCH in which "J," "E" and "P" signify strata which he believed represented the work of various editors who combined earlier literary TRADITIONS. His work sought to relate these sources to Israel's history and did much to win acceptance for HIGHER CRITICISM and the documentary HYPOTHESIS in explaining the origins of the HEBREW BIBLE.

WELTANSCHAUUNG: a German term meaning WORLDVIEW. It refers to an overarching PHILOSOPHY or perspective which molds the outlook of a person or GROUP.

WEN SHU: the Chinese name for the BODHISATTVA MAÑJUŚRĪ who is the personification of thought and knowledge.

WESLEY, Charles (1707-1788): the younger brother of John WESLEY. He was called a "METHODIST" by fellow students because of his methodical habits of study, fanatical zeal for regularity of living, and strict observance of the weekly SACRAMENT of communion. Experiencing an EVANGELICAL CONVERSION in 1738, he became an itinerant preacher and organizer of the Methodist movement. He is best remembered as the author of over 5500 HYMNS, including "Jesus, Lover of My Soul," "Love Divine, All Loves Excelling" and the CHRISTMAS carol "Hark! the Herald Angels Sing."

WESLEY, John (1703-1791): English founder of METHODISM who was influenced by German MORAVIAN PIETY and Count ZINZENDORF. He experienced a dramatic CONVERSION at a PRAYER MEETING in 1738 at Aldersgate Street, London, which led him to commence controversial forms of ministry, including preaching to miners and the poor in fields at Bristol the following year. A compulsive traveler, he made hundreds of journeys on horseback, preaching, making converts and organizing Methodist societies throughout England, Ireland and Scotland. In 1791 the Methodist Church was created. Wesley was a strong opponent of SLAVERY, the author of educational treatises and biblical commentaries, and the compiler of twenty-three collections of HYMNS. His *Journal* (1735-90) is both a spiritual classic and a vivid account of life in eighteenth-century Britain.

WESTCOTT, Brooke Foss (1825-1901): one of the most important British biblical scholars of the nineteenth century who was responsible, with F. J. A. Hort, for publishing a critical edition of the GREEK text of the NEW TESTAMENT in 1881.

WESTMINSTER CONFESSION: the definitive statement of PRESBYTERIAN DOCTRINE published in 1646 after twenty-seven months of deliberation by the Westminster Assembly, a gathering of THEOLOGIANS appointed by the English Long Parliament under Oliver CROMWELL. It is widely regarded as the clearest and most influential systematic statement of CALVINIST teachings to be produced following the REFORMATION. It is the official standard of the Church of Scotland.

WESTPHALIA, THE PEACE OF: the treaty ending the Thirty Years' War in 1648; it marked the beginning of European domination of the world and the birth of the modern world system, which was to hold sway until the independence of India in 1948.

WHEEL OF EXISTENCE: see SAṂSĀRA.

WHIG: originally a LIBERAL-minded group

in the British Parliament. It came to refer to a liberal outlook and in particular to the liberal interpretation of HISTORY in terms of the idea of PROGRESS.

WHITE FATHERS: members of a ROMAN CATHOLIC MISSIONARY order, named after their white robes. The order was founded in 1868 in Algiers to evangelize Africa through teaching agriculture, trades and the advancement of education. It has made a significant impact on many African SOCIETIES.

WHITEHEAD, Alfred North (1861-1947): English philosopher, mathematician, coauthor of *Principia Mathematica* (1910-1913) with Bertrand RUSSELL and exponent of the theory of RELATIVITY. He developed his own METAPHYSICS in *Process and Reality* (1929). This developed his version of PROCESS THEOLOGY in which, although GOD exists from ETERNITY, he is such that everything that happens in the UNIVERSE becomes part of his BEING.

WHITEFIELD, George (1714-1770): English CALVINIST and one of the most powerful preachers ever. After an EVANGELICAL CONVERSION he was ordained, but his first SERMON led to a complaint to his BISHOP that he had driven fifteen people mad. Whitefield was an itinerant mass evangelist who pioneered in extemporaneous preaching, typically in outdoor settings. He played a major role in the Great Awakening in the American colonies, a movement of revival which peaked in the years 1740-1743. He was closely associated with John and Charles WESLEY in the early years, but they eventually disagreed on theological issues.

WHITSUN: the CHRISTIAN feast of PENTECOST which is held fifty days after EASTER. The name comes from the white clothing worn by candidates for BAPTISM.

WICCA: the name applied by INITIATES to certain forms of modern NEOPAGANISM, SPIRITUALISM or WITCHCRAFT in the TRADITION of Gerald GARDNER. It often finds historical LEGITIMATION in the works of Margaret MURRAY. Although Wicca is a generic term that applies to a wide range of neopagan groups in recent years, it has been increasingly used by gender feminists who are frequently lesbian.

WILBERFORCE, William (1759-1833): English philanthropist and leader of the CLAPHAM SECT. His EVANGELICAL CONVERSION in 1785 led him to become a staunch opponent of SLAVERY and committed social REFORMER. His views on religion are set out in *A Practical View of the Prevailing Religious System of Professed Christians Contrasted with Real Christianity* (1779).

WILL TO BELIEVE: a term used by William JAMES to signify the desire to exercise FAITH even when the evidence to support such faith is lacking or very weak.

WILL TO POWER: the term used by NIETZSCHE to express his view that ultimately all human actions are based on a desire for power and control over others.

WILLIAMS, Charles Walter Stansby (1886-1945): English CHRISTIAN poet, novelist and friend of C. S. LEWIS. His books include *War in Heaven* (1931) and *The Descent of the Dove* (1939).

WISDOM: in HEBREW thought, wisdom refers to knowledge based on experience of the order of life and creation under God rather than THEORY; it is practical insight and good judgment that leads to prudent action.

WISDOM LITERATURE: a term used for ancient literature which tells people how to act in a wise way. In the HEBREW BIBLE it refers to the books of JOB, Ecclesiastes and PROVERBS.

WITCHCRAFT: a widespread system of BELIEFS and practices involving SUPERNATURAL power and agencies thought to influence human affairs. It is generally distinguished from SORCERY and takes various FORMS in different CULTURES. Sometimes the conscious action of individuals is involved, on other occasions it operates without conscious effort as a result of reputed inherited powers or alien forces. Since the ENLIGHTENMENT it has been usual to regard witchcraft as an

IRRATIONAL system of beliefs belonging to a primitive past. But anthropologists, beginning with EVANS-PRITCHARD, have shown that witchcraft involves a system of thought which once accepted follows a logical pattern. In the West popular belief in witchcraft died out during the seventeenth and eighteenth centuries to be revived in the late nineteenth century by GARDNER and other OCCULTISTS as a form of RITUAL MAGIC. It continues today with groups like WICCA. In other parts of the world witchcraft has never died out, although its manifestation is very different due to distinct SOCIAL settings from modern witchcraft in the West.

WITTGENSTEIN, Ludwig (1889-1951): Austrian philosopher whose book *Tractatus Logico-Philosophicus* and later works had a profound effect on Anglo-Saxon PHILOSOPHY in the 1960s. He became professor of philosophy at Cambridge in 1939 and exercised a strong influence over a whole generation of British philosophers. A key slogan in his philosophy is "the MEANING of a word is its use in language," from which his ideas about "language games" and "forms of life" developed. In RELIGIOUS STUDIES his work has had a significant and controversial impact.

WOLFF, Christian (1679-1754): German RATIONALIST philosopher who bitterly attacked PIETISM. His clarification and organization of PHILOSOPHY gave us such terms as MONISM, DUALISM, TELEOLOGY and COSMOLOGY. His works include *Rational Philosophy or Logic* (1728) and *Natural Theology* (1736-1737, 2 vols.).

WORD OF FAITH: a development of PENTECOSTAL and CHARISMATIC CHRISTIANITY which began with the teachings of Kenneth HAGIN, emphasizing that GOD's will is for his people to prosper. In its cruder forms it can degenerate into a "name it and claim it" form of magical religion which preaches prosperity and a doctrine of wealth. More sophisticated versions interpret prosperity as the well-being spoken of in JESUS' message about the KINGDOM OF GOD.

WORDSWORTH, Christopher (1807-1885): English ANGLICAN BISHOP and nephew of William WORDSWORTH who promoted the study of the CHURCH FATHERS.

WORDSWORTH, William (1770-1850): English ROMANTIC poet who produced a PANTHEISTIC SPIRITUALITY although he remained a devout ANGLICAN.

WORLD COUNCIL OF CHURCHES: an ECUMENICAL organization of Protestant, Orthodox and Anglican churches founded at a meeting in Amsterdam in 1948. Over the years the movement has become increasingly bureaucratic and radical in its politics, with the result that many members have become disenchanted and alienated. Since its formation the organization has held a series of international assemblies which have been significant events in the history of the ECUMENICAL MOVEMENT.

WORLD RELIGIONS: a term usually reserved for the major RELIGIOUS TRADITIONS of the world which have spread to all continents.

WORLDVIEW: see WELTANSCHAUUNG.

WORLDWIDE CHURCH OF GOD: a NEW RELIGIOUS MOVEMENT founded by Herbert W. ARMSTRONG in 1933. It preaches a form of BRITISH ISRAELITISM supported by an ARIAN CHRISTOLOGY and a denial of such traditional Christian doctrines as the TRINITY. The success of the movement began with Armstrong's innovative radio program "The World Tomorrow" which was later adapted to television and is supported by the free distribution of its magazine *The Plain Truth*. The church experienced a major split in the 1970s; it is based in Pasadena, California, where it operates Ambassador College.

WORSHIP: religious RITUALS which salute, revere or praise the DEITY.

WU-HSING: the Chinese name for the five elements of wood, fire, earth, metal and water, which were traditionally believed to combine in producing the UNIVERSE.

WU-WEI: a TAOIST term meaning "non-activity" which was thought to be the ESSENCE of the TAO and the ideal for human action.

WUNDT, William (1832-1900): German philosopher and physiologist who initiated the study of PSYCHOLOGY as an academic discipline. Arguing that the mental or psychic have primacy over the physical, he opposed RATIONALISM and sought to develop a METAPHYSICS which saw GOD as the source of EVOLUTION. His works include *The Influence of Philosophy on the Empirical Sciences* (1876) and *Elements of Folk Psychology* (1916), which influenced the development of COMPARATIVE RELIGION.

WYCLIFFE, John (1330-1384): English precursor to the PROTESTANT REFORMATION who was master of Balliol College, Oxford. His writings defended civil government from religious interference and attacked the PAPACY and the doctrine of TRANSUBSTANTIATION. He promoted a return to biblical CHRISTIANITY and encouraged the first translation of the BIBLE into English. His thought inspired the LOLLARD movement. His works were destroyed on the orders of the ROMAN CATHOLIC CHURCH and only survived in Czechoslovakia (then Bohemia) where they influenced John HUSS. It is also possible that his writings had an indirect influence on LUTHER.

X

XENOPHANES OF COLOPHON (570-470 B.C.): Greek SKEPTICAL philosopher who noted the ANTHROPOMORPHIC character of many RELIGIONS, pointing out that the Egyptians pictured their GODS like Egyptians while the Greeks saw them in the image of Greeks.

XENOPHON (430-355 B.C.): Greek historian who makes SOCRATES his hero in his *Symposium* and defends him against the charge of ATHEISM in his *Memorabilia*.

Y

YAHWEH: the personal name of GOD in the HEBREW BIBLE which is sometimes transliterated Jehovah. It comes from the consonants YHWH, the vowels being unknown since it was so SACRED that it could not be pronounced. The vowels were replaced in the text by those for the Hebrew word for LORD, which was the word to be read aloud. The vowels supplied in the spelling *Yahweh* are based on scholarly speculation.

YAHWIST: a term used in BIBLICAL CRITICISM to designate one of the literary sources of the PENTATEUCH. It is said to be distinguished by, among other things, the use of the name YAHWEH for GOD.

YAJURVEDA: the third of four collections of the VEDAS consisting of sacrificial formulas. It was composed some time after the ṚG VEDA and was intended for use in RITUAL.

YAKKHA: a class of semidivine SPIRITS mentioned in the BUDDHIST PALI CANON.

YAMA: the BUDDHIST LORD of DEATH.

YAZĪDIS: an ancient Kurdish religion whose followers believe in TRANSMIGRATION and one GOD. They have two SACRED books, the *Kitab al-jilwa* and *Mashaf Rash*, which are written in Arabic. Their other beliefs and practices are believed to reflect CHRISTIAN, ISLAMIC and ZOROASTRIAN influences.

YEN WANG: the Chinese LORD of DEATH who was originally one of the ten kings of HELL.

YIMA: a semidivine Iranian BEING who lives in an underground PARADISE awaiting the last days, when he will emerge to repopulate the earth.

YIN-YANG: the Chinese philosophical theory that everything originates from, and depends on, the interaction of two opposite and complementary principles which proceeded from the "great ultimate." Yin is Earth—negative, passive, dark, female and destructive—while Yang is HEAVEN—light, positive, male and constructive. Through their perpetual interplay all things exist and are continually transformed.

YOGA: a SANSKRIT term meaning "to yoke." It is used to describe a process of spiritual discipline or harnessing of physical and mental powers to attain self-control and ultimate ENLIGHTENMENT. Generally it means a system of MEDITATION which is essentially common to BUDDHISM, HINDUISM and JAINISM and which shares many assumptions concerning KARMA, DHARMA and METEMPSYCHOSIS. The term also refers to one of the six schools of Hindu PHILOSOPHY which teaches and utilizes the practice of yoga to attain LIBERATION, which is conceived as a state of perfect isolation.

YOGĀCĀRAS: a school of MAHĀYĀNA BUDDHISM that subscribed to the idea that consciousness alone is real while objects of consciousness are not, thus making MEDITATION rather than intellectual analysis the central concern of the movement.

YOGANANDA, Paramahnsa (1893-1952): HINDU GURU who stayed on in America to promote YOGIC RELIGION after attending the 1920 Boston International Congress of Religious Liberals.

YOGI: a practitioner of YOGA.

YOGIC RELIGION: those religions, ultimately of Indian origin, that have at their core one or another form of the practice of YOGA. The major Yogic religions are BUDDHISM, HINDUISM and JAINISM.

YOM KIPPUR: the most HOLY day in JUDAISM, known as the Day of ATONEMENT.

YŌMEI SCHOOL: a Japanese school of Confucianism (*see* CONFUCIUS) based on the teachings of WANG YANG-MING and pioneered in Japan by Nakae-Tōju. It promoted devotion to the COSMIC SOUL, of which man, through spiritual training, is a microcosm.

YOUNG, Brigham (1801-1877): the "Saint Paul" of MORMONISM who, after the death of Joseph SMITH, assumed the leadership of those Mormons who accepted POLYGAMY. A brilliant and gifted leader, he created the Utah branch of the Church of Jesus Christ of Latter-day Saints. He taught many DOCTRINES now repudiated by his followers, including "Blood-ATONEMENT" and the "ADAM-GOD" theory, which has proved troublesome for Mormon intellectuals today.

YÜ HUANG: the Jade Emperor, who is the most important GOD in the TAOIST pantheon and the source of all justice. Popular belief in Yü Huang was incorporated into BUDDHISM, in which he was recognized as the ruler of gods and SPIRITS, but subordinate to the BUDDHA.

Z

ZAKAT: the obligatory giving of alms to the poor as an act of FAITH and WORSHIP, it is one of the FIVE PILLARS OF ISLAM. The name comes from an Arabic word meaning "purity."

ZAYDISM: a branch of SHI'ISM which shares many features of the SUNNI tradition, such as accepting the legitimacy of ABŪ BAKR and 'Umar, and rejects many Shī'ite beliefs about 'ALI and the nature of the IMĀM.

ZAZEN: a form of MEDITATION in ZEN BUDDHISM involving sitting in the lotus position and regulating breathing to free the mind from all attachments.

ZEALOTS: a JEWISH resistance movement that was particularly active in the Jewish revolt against the Romans during the period A.D. 66-70. The movement found precedence in an earlier revolt (A.D. 6) led by Judas of Galilee, who had resisted the Roman annexation of Judea.

ZEN BUDDHISM: a development of Japanese BUDDHISM which denies the REALITY of the external world and advocates mental and physical self-control as a path to ENLIGHTENMENT. Zen Buddhism is known for its use of the KŌAN and vivid stories about the sudden enlightenment of particularly HOLY men.

ZEUS: the chief of the GODS in Greek mythology.

ZINZENDORF, Nikolaus Ludwig Graf von (1700-1760): founder of the reorganized MORAVIAN church and an important influence on John WESLEY.

ZION CHRISTIAN CHURCH: commonly known as the ZCC, this AFRICAN INDEPENDENT CHURCH is the largest denomination in Southern Africa, twice the size of any other, with well over three million members. It was founded in 1924 by Ignatius Lekganyane, who had been influenced by the work of John Alexander Dowie. Essentially orthodox in THEOLOGY, the church is CHARISMATIC with a strong emphasis on HEALING and prophecy expressed in terms of TRADITIONAL black cultural SYMBOLS, enabling it to act as an important modernizing force among upwardly mobile and recently urbanized people.

ZIONISM: a MODERN JEWISH political movement with religious overtones which began in the nineteenth century as a nationalist revival that sought a Jewish homeland in PALESTINE. The Zionist movement led to the creation of the STATE of Israel and has strong SOCIALIST and UTOPIAN tendencies.

ZOROASTER (sixth century B.C.): Iranian PROPHET and religious leader who founded ZOROASTRIANISM. He is known through his utterances found in the SCRIPTURES (*Gāthās*) of his RELIGION.

ZOROASTRIANISM: the ancient religion of Iran preached by ZOROASTER. Its tenets remain somewhat obscure, but it was clearly DUALISTIC, involving mankind in a choice between GOOD and EVIL.

ZURVAN: the ancient Iranian GOD of time.

ZWINGLI, Ulrich (1485-1531): Swiss preacher who led the PROTESTANT REFORMATION in Zurich. He admired LUTHER and taught JUSTIFICATION by FAITH but rejected Luther's view of the SACRAMENTS, arguing that they are simply memorials without SUPERNATURAL influence. His willingness to cede power to SECULAR magistrates led GREBEL and others to develop their own ANABAPTISM.

A Reading List for Religious Studies

Introduction. Healthy academic disciplines are characterized by vigorous debate. Look up any reader in anthropology, history, psychology, sociology, or even zoology, and you will find conflicting theories and dissenting views. What is clear to one scholar is rubbish to another, and in academic journals people do not hesitate to criticize the folly of others. Indeed in some fields, such as history, entire libraries of books are devoted to such issues as problems in European civilization, where the student is presented with a series of conflicting views that are expected to expose them to important academic debates with which any educated member of the profession ought to be familiar.

When one turns to religious studies, however, a very different picture emerges. With few exceptions the writers of monographs and textbooks in religious studies are very nice people who want to give every possible viewpoint a fair hearing. Such liberality is commendable in situations of religious intolerance and dogmatism and was justified twenty-five years ago when few Europeans or North Americans were familiar with religious traditions other than Christianity. At the time, against a background of a monopolistic Christianity, the need to develop sympathetic insight was essential. But things are very different today.

Today we face a different situation. Many students know more about Buddhism than Christianity and are certainly far more sympathetic to Eastern religions than they are to their own Western tradition. Therefore, the old liberal approach is an anachronism. As a result this bibliography aims at presenting controversial books which students might otherwise overlook. It is provided in the hope that it will provoke a stimulating academic debate.

Bibliography and Research Guides. The following bibliographic sources are suggested to anyone writing essays, term papers or theses in religious studies.

Dell, D. J., et al. *Guide to Hindu Religion*. Boston: G. K. Hall, 1981.
An invaluable annotated source for works on Hinduism.

Karpinski, L. M. *Religious Studies Without Tears*. Vancouver, B.C.: Reference Publications, University of British Columbia, 1970-1976.
An excellent set of annotated bibliographies in five parts produced by the University of British Columbia library.

Miller, D. E., and B. J. Seltser. *Writing and Research in Religious Studies*. Englewood Cliffs, N.J.: Prentice-Hall, 1991.
A useful introductory text for students which covers very basic issues in research and essay writing.

Reynolds, F. E., et al. *Guide to Buddhist Religion*. Boston: G. K. Hall, 1981.
A companion volume to Dell on Hinduism which is equally helpful.

Reference Works. The following are some standard dictionaries and encyclopedias on religion.

Cavendish, R., ed. *Man, Myth and Magic.* London: Purnell, 1970.

Crim, K., ed. *Abingdon Dictionary of Living Religions.* Nashville: Abingdon, 1981.

Eliade, M., ed. *The Encyclopedia of Religion.* 16 vols. New York: Macmillan, 1987.

Gibb, H. A. R. *Encyclopedia of Islam.* Leiden: E. J. Brill, 1954.

Hastings, J., ed. *The Encyclopedia of Religion and Ethics.* 13 vols. Edinburgh: T. & T. Clarke, 1908-1927.

McDonald, W. J., ed. *New Catholic Encyclopedia.* 17 vols. New York: McGraw-Hill, 1967.

Malalasekara, G. P. *Encyclopedia of Buddhism.* Colombo, Ceylon: Government Press, 1961.

Roth, C., and G. Wigoder, eds. *Encyclopaedia Judaica.* 16 vols. New York: Macmillan, 1972.

Walker, G. B. *Hindu World: An Encylopedic Survey of Hinduism.* New York: Praeger, 1968.

Zaehner, R. C., ed. *The Concise Encyclopedia of Living Faiths.* London: Hutchinson, 1959.

Scholarly Journals. When writing essays one way the serious student gains command of their field is through using scholarly journals in addition to recommended books. In journals one finds the latest thinking in an area and many ideas which can take years to find their ways into books. The following journals will provide a basic introduction to this field.

Faith and Philosophy
An excellent Christian publication which often carries articles related to religious studies.

History of Religions
A good American journal with an emphasis on history and comparative studies.

The Journal of Religion
Probably the best American religious studies journal.

Journal of Religion in Africa
The major journal in this little-developed but important field.

The Journal of Religious Ethics
A useful comparative journal concentrating on ethical systems.

Journal of the American Academy of Religion
An important journal published by the leading American academic society in this field.

Man
This anthropological journal often has articles of a religious nature and is well worth looking at on a regular basis.

Missionalia
A unique publication from the University of South Africa which, although intended for people interested in Christian missions, abstracts a large number of journal articles in religious studies and related fields. Very useful.

Neumen
The journal of the International Association for the History of Religions. Very important.

Philosophy East and West
Important as a source for philosophical articles of a comparative nature.

Religion
The best British and probably the best all-around journal in religious studies.

Religious Studies Review
This excellent quarterly journal reviews current books in religious studies and related fields. Any serious student of religion ought to refer to it regularly.

The Skeptical Inquirer
Not strictly a religious studies journal but rather, as the name suggests, a publication intended to debunk irrationalism. It is especially useful with regard to the apologetic claims of new religious movements and the New Age movement.

Studies in Religion
An excellent Canadian journal which presents a broad perspective in religious studies.

Basic Texts. The following texts should be read by any student who wishes to master the field of religious studies. The list provided here is an introductory one which is intended to introduce the reader to the field.

Basham, A. L. *The Wonder That Was India.* London: Collins, 1954.
An essential and highly informative introduction to Indian religions and civilization.

Conze, E. *Buddhism: Its Essence and Development.* Oxford: Bruno Cassirer, 1951.
No other work approaches Conze's genius for conveying the feel of Buddhism as well as the facts about the Buddhist tradition.

———. *Buddhist Thought in India.* London: George Allen & Unwin, 1962.
A much neglected work which Conze viewed as his greatest contribution to Buddhist studies.

Cragg, K. *The Event of the Qur'an: Islam in Its*

Scripture. London: Allen and Unwin, 1971.
A useful study which sets Islam firmly within its own scriptural tradition.

——. *The House of Islam.* Belmont, Calif.: Dickinson, 1969.
A good popular introduction to Islam.

Earhart, H. B. *Japanese Religions: Unity and Diversity.* Belmont, Calif.: Dickinson, 1969.
A good general survey.

Eliade, M. *The Sacred and Profane: The Nature of Religion.* New York: Harcourt, Brace & World, 1959.
Although a considerable improvement over Joseph Campbell this book, like Eliade's many other works on mythology, does not show his vast scholarship at its best. Nevertheless, it ought to be read because your professors will want you to know about the great man's ideas on the subject of myth.

——. *Yoga, Immortality and Freedom.* London: Routledge & Kegan Paul, 1958.
This is the classic introduction to Yoga. Critics may find fault and some of the material may be outdated, but it is a must for anyone approaching the religions of India.

Gibb, H. A. R., and J. H. Kramers. *Shorter Encyclopedia of Islam.* Leiden: E. J. Brill, 1953.
An invaluable text for understanding Arabic concepts that shape Islamic theology. This is particularly important for anyone studying Islam, a religion that claims to be based on a sacred and untranslatable scripture.

Hopkins, T. *The Hindu Religious Tradition.* Encino, Calif.: Dickinson, 1971.
A good, general introductory text.

Moore, C. A., and A. V. Morris, eds. *The Japanese Mind: Essentials of Japanese Philosophy and Culture.* Honolulu: East-West Center, 1967.
A stimulating work which emphasizes the diversity of Japanese thought.

Nakamura, H. *Ways of Thinking of Eastern Peoples: India, China, Tibet and Japan.* Honolulu: East-West Center, 1964.
A valuable introduction to non-Western ways of thought and action which provides an essential background to understanding religious behavior.

Smart, N. *Doctrine and Argument in Indian Philosophy.* London: George Allen and Unwin, 1964.

——. *Reasons and Faiths.* London: Routledge & Kegan Paul, 1958.
An excellent philosophical introduction to interreligious dialogue and understanding.

——. *The World's Religions.* Englewood Cliffs,

N.J.: Prentice-Hall, 1989.
This is by far the best introductory text currently available in religious studies.

Smith, D. H. *Chinese Religions.* London: Weidenfeld and Nicolson, 1968.
This book is regarded by many as the best survey of Chinese religions available.

Welbourn, F. B. *Atoms and Ancestors.* London: A. J. Arnold, 1969.
The style of this short book easily misleads the uninitiated. Nevertheless, this is by far the best introduction to African religions. A revised edition is being prepared by Irving Hexham.

——. *East African Rebels.* London: SCM, 1961.
Essential reading for anyone who wants to understand interreligious contact, religious change and the impact of missionaries on traditional religions.

Zaehner, R. C., ed. *The Concise Encyclopedia of Living Faiths.* London: Hutchinson, 1959.
An invaluable reference work with essays by leading scholars in all fields. Although first published in 1959, the book has gone through many editions and is still in print.

——. *Hinduism.* London: Oxford University Press, 1968.
An excellent, if philosophical, introduction to the religion we know as Hinduism.

Contrary Works. The following books present alternative points of view, and in one way or another should provoke thought and debate.

Davis, W. *Dojo: Magic and Exorcism in Modern Japan.* Stanford, Calif.: Stanford University, 1980.
A classic study of a new religion in Japan. Raises many problems of interpretation and questions about overreliance on written texts.

Farmer, W. R. *The Synoptic Problem.* London: Collier-Macmillan, 1964.
Equally as telling as Palmer's logical analysis is Farmer's introductory essay in this thought-provoking book which deals with the social construction of the Synoptic problem. A must for all students of the New Testament and anyone interested in the sociology of knowledge.

Kakar, S. *Shamans, Mystics and Doctors.* Boston: Beacon, 1982.
Essential reading for anyone wanting to understand the social dynamics of Indian religion. A challenging and provocative book.

Kaufmann, W. *Critique of Religion and Philosophy.*

London: Faber and Faber, 1958.

A must for anyone interested in the philosophy of religion or biblical criticism. Kaufmann takes an uncomplimentary look at contemporary theological fads and makes some devastating criticisms.

——. *Religion in Four Dimensions: Existential, Aesthetic, Historical and Comparative.* New York: Reader's Digest, 1976.

Princeton philosopher Walter Kaufmann is a figure whose work ought to be known by every religious studies student and read alongside other introductory texts. An iconoclast, of Jewish descent, he is a delight to anyone seeking a different perspective on religious issues. This book is no exception. Instead of presenting the usual clone of other religious studies texts, Kaufmann has written a hard-hitting book which is highly critical of many religious traditions. Christian readers may have difficulty with some of his conclusions about Christianity, but, to be fair, he spares no one.

Koestler, A. *The Lotus and the Robot.* London: Hutchinson & Co., 1966.

Don't mention this one to your Hinduism professor. Perhaps it's not the most reliable book on Indian religions. Nevertheless, it provokes thought and is worth reading for a view that is usually dismissed by academics.

Palmer, H. *The Logic of Gospel Criticism.* London: Macmillan, 1968.

This book presents the reader with a logician's examination of the arguments used by biblical critics. The conclusions are devastating. No wonder it is ignored by biblical scholars, including many evangelicals.

Naipaul, V. S. *Among the Believers: An Islamic Journey.* Harmondsworth, U.K.: Penguin, 1981.

A disquieting look at the Islamic world.

——. *India: A Wounded Civilization.* Harmondsworth, U.K.: Penguin, 1979.

Like Koestler's work this book is hated by many teachers of religious studies. Nevertheless, it presents a perspective which must be taken seriously.

Sankrityayan, R., et al. *Buddhism: The Marxist Approach.* New Delhi: People's Publishing House, 1970.

A very different approach to Buddhism which provokes thought.

Some Christian Responses. The following books offer a variety of Christian perspectives on religion and religions.

Bavinck, H. *The Philosophy of Revelation.* Grand Rapids: Baker, 1979.

Another theological work with important implications for the study of religion and written in 1909 by Kuyper's colleague Herman Bavinck. Although dated it is still a valuable resource for the Christian student.

Bavinck, J. H. *The Church Between Temple and Mosque.* Grand Rapids: Eerdmans, n.d.

A stimulating and orthodox Christian attempt to interpret the reality of religious pluralism.

Berkouwer, G. C. *General Revelation.* Grand Rapids: Eerdmans, 1955.

This should be read alongside Berkouwer's book on theological anthropology (1962). It deals with biblical approaches to revelation outside the Bible.

——. *Man: The Image of God.* Grand Rapids: Eerdmans, 1962.

Essential background thinking for a Christian interpretation of other religious traditions.

Callaway, T. *Zen Way-Jesus Way.* Tokyo and Rutland, Vt.: Charles E. Tuttle, 1976.

A remarkable book by a Southern Baptist missionary.

Cragg, K. *Christ and the Faiths.* Philadelphia: Westminster, 1986.

A modern Christian approach to other religious traditions.

Dawson, C. *Religion and World History.* Edited by J. Oliver and C. Scott. New York: Image Books, Doubleday, 1973.

An excellent introduction to religious history by an insightful Roman Catholic historian. This book is well worth reading.

Freedman, D. H., and D. Freedman. *A Philosophical Study of Religion.* Nutley, N.J.: Craig, 1964.

Written from a Reformed Christian viewpoint, this work raises many issues normally overlooked by more liberal scholars. As such it is a good complement to Kaufmann's.

Holmes, A. F. *Contours of a World View.* Grand Rapids: Eerdmans, 1983.

Apart from knowing about other religious traditions it is important for Christians to have a broad vision of their own religion. This text provides such a vision and helps the reader find other sources for information on Christianity.

Kraemer, H. *Religion and the Christian Faith.*

London: Lutterworth, 1956.
An excellent survey of Christian approaches to non-Christian religions by an outstanding Dutch scholar.

_____ . *World Cultures and World Religions.* London: Lutterworth, 1960.
A valuable work which places the study of religion within its social context.

Kuyper, A. *Lectures on Calvinism.* Grand Rapids: Eerdmans, 1968.
Originally the text of a series of lectures delivered at Princeton University, these essays provide a framework within which Christian students can begin to tackle the immense problems of religious diversity and cultural pluralism.

_____ . *Principles of Sacred Theology.* Grand Rapids: Eerdmans, 1968.
Although it is a theology text, many parts of this work apply to issues in religious studies, especially Kuyper's stimulating discussion about the meaning of "faith."

Lecerf, A. *An Introduction to Reformed Dogmatics.* Grand Rapids: Baker, 1981.
A French Calvinist's approach to the study of religion and theology which has stimulating discussions of Durkheim and various other figures whose work affects our thinking about the nature of religion.

Orr, J. *The Christian View of God and the World.* Grand Rapids: Eerdmans, 1948.
Although somewhat dated (1891), many of the discussions, particularly those found in the extended footnotes, apply directly to issues in religious studies.

Sharpe, E. J. *Faith Meets Faith: Some Christian Attitudes to Hinduism in the Nineteenth and Twentieth Centuries.* London: SCM, 1977.
A very useful survey which sets interreligious discussion in its historical context.

_____ . *Not to Destroy but to Fulfil: The Contribution of J. N. Farquhar to Protestant Missionary Thought in India Before 1914.* Uppsala: Swedish Institute of Missionary Research, 1965.
A valuable, in-depth study of one missionary's interaction with Hinduism.

Verkuyl, J. *Contemporary Missiology.* Grand Rapids: Eerdmans, 1978.
The value of this book lies in the wide range of topics it covers and its excellent bibliographies.